CW01638429

C# Programming for Windows and Android

Dr John Allwork

an Elektor Publication

LEARN | DESIGN | SHARE

This is an Elektor Publication. Elektor is the media brand of
Elektor International Media B.V.
78 York Street
London W1H 1DP, UK
Phone: (+44) (0)20 7692 8344

First published in the United Kingdom 2015

159011-1/EN

British Library Cataloguing in Publication Data
Catalogue record for this book is available from the British Library

ISBN 978-1-907920-43-1

Prepress production: DMC ¦ daverid.com
Printed in the Netherlands by Wilco

About the Author

John Allwork was born in 1950 in Kent, England and became interested in electronics and engineering at school. He went to Sheffield University on their BEng Electrical and Electronic Engineering course. There he developed an interest in computers and continued his education on an MSc course in Digital Electronics and Communication at UMIST. After two years working for ICL as a design, commissioning and test Engineer he returned to UMIST where he graduated with a PhD in 'Design and Development of Microprocessor Systems'

He worked for several years in technical support and as manager in electronics distribution, working closely with Intel Application Engineers and followed this with design work using the Inmos Transputer systems.

Having taught at Manchester Metropolitan University he retired in 2011, but has kept up his interest in electronics and programming as well as his other occupation of walking, geocaching and spending time on his allotment or on his narrow boat.

Table of Contents

Introduction

This book is aimed at anyone who wants to learn about C# programming and how to write programs for Windows and Android smart phone or tablet applications.

It covers programming concepts from the basics to object oriented programming, displaying graphs, threading and databases. Chapters also cover internet communications, using charts and DirectX for sound card for analogue I/O and for capturing video. Chapters had been added on writing C# Android applications using Xamarin which ships with VS2015. This is in favour of chapters in an earlier book which dealt with hardware interfacing to a PC and using the USB port. These chapters should be available through the publisher's web site however.

Although it assumes a little knowledge of programming it does start from the basics and covers the Visual Studio development environment, the .NET framework and C# programming language from data types and program flow to more advanced concepts.

It is complete with many program examples, self assessment exercises and links to supporting videos. Full program examples are available.

The book has been updated for Visual Studio 2015 and more relevant videos have been sourced or (are being!) produced to accompany the book.

I do not pretend to know all there is about C# and the .NET framework. I have a background in hardware and software design. I am sure that there are areas where some programmers may be offended by my code and that there may be better ways to write it, but I have written and tried all the examples and know they work. I hope the examples will spur you on to find solutions to your own problems. Should you need more information then please try the on-line help and the Microsoft forums. There are plenty of programmers out there willing to help solve your problems, often extremely quickly.

I wish to thank my friends for encouraging me and checking the manuscript, especially Dr Hugh Frost, Dr George South (sadly no longer with us) and Brian Hall; Xamarin and Microsoft support staff; readers of my previous books; my students who unwittingly helped me clarify and enhance the book; and the many anonymous people on the internet, forums, blogs and websites who have answered many questions, not just my own – keep up the good work. Not least of all I would like to thank my wife Penny, for supporting me throughout.

And of course you for buying the book!

Conventions used in this book

A few conventions used in the book, used mainly to distinguish normal text from C# code and program output.

Normal Text	Verdana Pro - Used for plain text
Program code snippets	Arial C# source code and snippets of code. Used where code is explained or the reader expected to enter code

`Complete code`	`private void button1_Click(object sender, EventArgs e)`
	`{`
	`    textBox1.Text = "hello there";`
	`}`
	
	`// Used where complete code is displayed`

`Program output`	`Courier New - program output in console window`
Hypertext links	Underlined and italic e.g. *https://msdn.microsoft.com/*

I have also used the 'greater than' symbol to indicate that the reader should follow a sequence of commands, such as File > New Project > Windows application.

Chapter 1 • The Visual Studio 2015 Environment

1.1 • Introduction

C# is now an established programming language and the Visual Studio environment lets you write graphical user interface programs for Windows. The .NET framework provides extensive interface libraries. Programs written in C# can be used alongside programs written in other languages such as VB.NET and F# and J#. The programs are compiled to an intermediate language, or common language runtime CLR, which is then run on the specific computer, see Figure 1-1. This makes your C# programs platform independent. This book will cover writing programs for not only Windows but also Android smart phones.

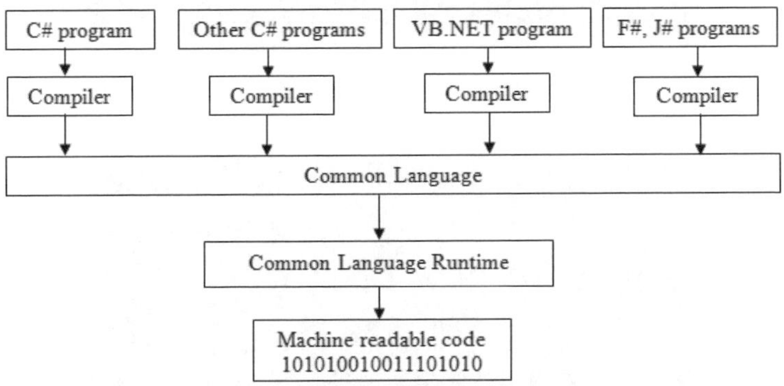

Figure 1-1 .NET common language operation

This design means that C# programs run slower than truly compiled programs such as C++, but the benefits outweigh the disadvantages. C# is known as managed code. This means that security, access and memory allocation and storage are controlled by the CLR. The .NET framework also provides access to programs that execute outside the framework, including access to input and output devices. The current version of the .NET framework is version 4.5.2, but a preview version 6 is available which should be loaded with the C# V6.0 software.

1.1.1 • What's new in VS2015?

Most of what's new is beyond the scope of this book, but of course VS2015 makes it easy to develop apps across multiple platforms including PC desktops, tablets and smart phones. There are a few enhancements that make the Development Environment (IDE) less cluttered and the debugger has been enhanced with an intelligent trace facility. Programming changes make it easier to write multitasking applications.

For more information, refer to '**Visual Studio 2015 Preview**' at:

www.visualstudio.com/en-us/news/vs2015-preview-vs.aspx

Microsoft has an article on C# 6.0 at

https://msdn.microsoft.com/en-us/magazine/dn802602.aspx

There is a short video presentation and discussion of C# 6.0 changes at:

http://channel9.msdn.com/Events/Visual-Studio/Connect-event-2014/116 and http://www.codeproject.com/Articles/808732/Briefly-exploring-Csharp-new-features

But most of the changes are irrelevant to this book.

1.2 • Obtaining the Visual Studio software

At the time of writing, Visual Studio 2015 is a time-limited free offer available from:

https://www.visualstudio.com/en-us/downloads/visual-studio-2015-downloads-vs.

Microsoft say a free version will be available later in 2015. You can use the free Visual Studio Community 2013, see Figure 1-2 which is to be found at:

http://www.visualstudio.com/en-us/products/free-developer-offers-vs

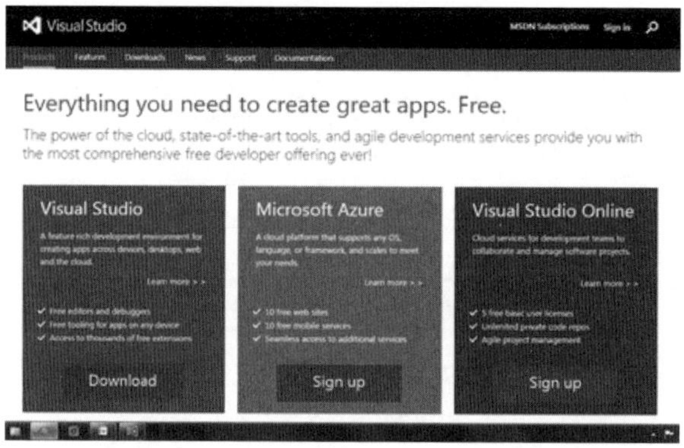

Figure 1-2 Visual Studio download

Click the purple Visual Studio area to downloads vs_community.exe and then run it to install VS. It takes quite a long time

Full details on installing the software are in Appendix A on page 303. Microsoft's 'Get started' guide covers it all. You can find it at:

http://www.visualstudio.com/get-started/overview-of-get-started-tasks-vs

If you want to find out more about what's new in VS 2015, read the MSDN Visual Studio blog at:

http://bit.ly/1OFZmmY

The Microsoft forums are a good place to go for help and if you get stuck there's help at the Visual Studio forums:

https://social.msdn.microsoft.com/Forums/vstudio/en-US/home?forum=TFService

1.3 • The Visual Studio development environment

The development environment enables you to create, run and debug your program. When you run Visual Studio (Start > All programs > Visual Studio 2015) it starts with an introductory page, see Figure 1-3 on page 21. If you are really new to the environment, have a look at the **'New to Visual Studio?'** link. From this page you can start a new project, or see recent ones.

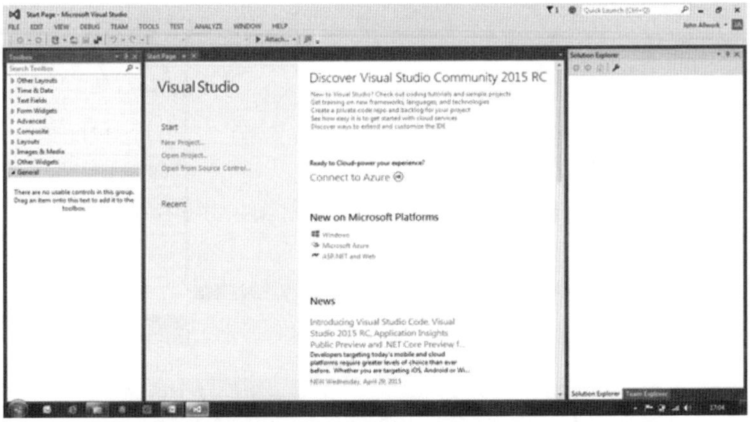

Figure 1-3 Visual Studio introductory page

Start a new project by clicking on the New Project option or choose File > New Project. You can then choose from a selection of options as shown in Figure 1-4. We shall be using 'Windows Forms Application', but note that you can also create a Console, WPF or other applications. We will mention WPF later.

Note also the Windows 8 option and **Windows Universal** which allows development for **Windows 10** and a wide range of devices including mobile, desktop, Surface Hub and Xbox.

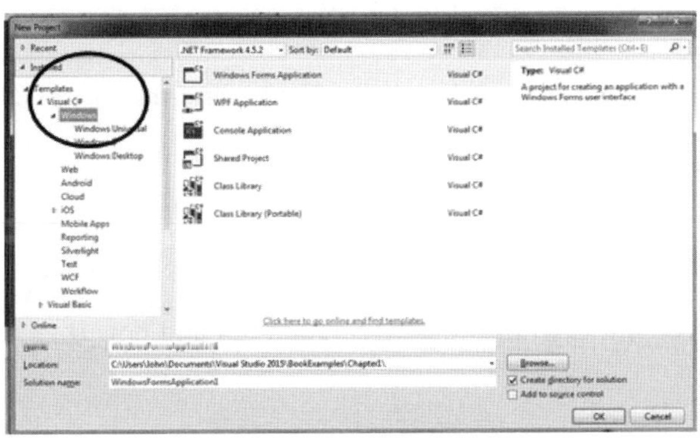

Figure 1-4 C# project applications

Hint: Make sure the language is set to Visual C# and not Visual Basic or C++.

Type a name for your project in the Name box, e.g. 'HelloWorld' and select the location where the files will be saved. Click OK to display the development environment, see Figure 1-5 on page 22. They won't all be there initially and some of the windows may be minimized, we'll see how to display the windows soon.

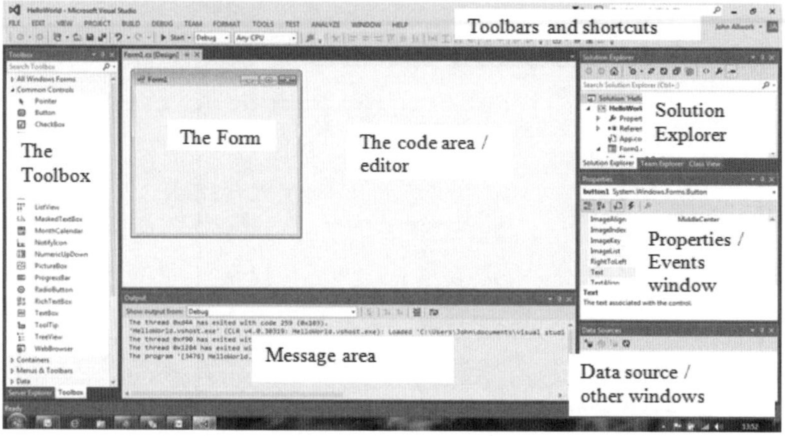

Figure 1-5 The development environment

In the centre is the form where the design is created. On this you place controls such as buttons, labels, text boxes etc. Behind this is the code editing area. The Toolbox that contains the controls is on the left. The short-cut icons are at the top; the Solution Explorer, Properties/Events and Data Sources Windows are on the right and the error/ output window at the bottom. The toolbox expands to show the controls when you click it. To display it permanently click the icon that looks like a drawing pin. If the toolbox or any of the other windows aren't displayed, select View> Toolbox or Other Windows. The tabs above the form can be selected to switch between the design, the code and other development windows. You can drag the windows around to create your own preferred layout.

Note also the tabs in the bottom left hand corner showing the hidden Server Explorer window.

1.3.1 • The Form

This is the most important part of the user interface design, see Figure 1-6. In development it is where the controls (buttons, labels, text boxes etc.) are placed. When the program runs, it is what the user finally sees and how they interact with your program.

Figure 1-6 The form

We shall see how we can change the title and the icon later.

1.3.2 • The Code Editor

The code editor is displayed by double-clicking the form or a control placed on the form. A new tab appears called **Form1.cs** and this is where you will type your code, see Figure 1-7. The tab can also be clicked to display the code editor.

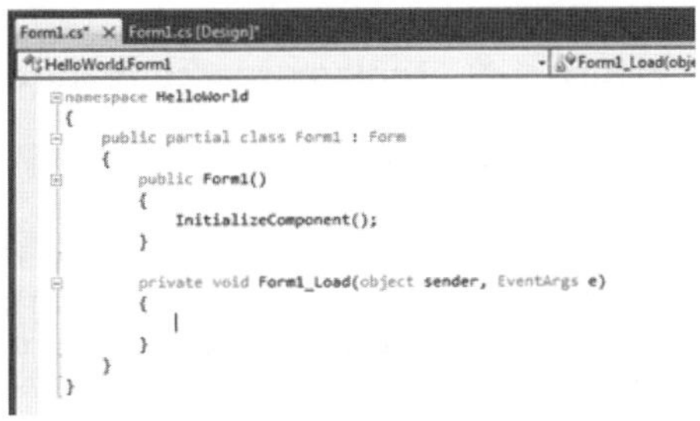

Figure 1-7 The code editor

Notice that some code is already inserted for you, but you will still have to write the important parts!

Warning: Do not delete code that you have not typed as this will cause an error when you compile your code.

To return to the design, click on the Form1.cs[Design] tab: 

1.3.3 • The Toolbox

The toolbox contains the controls we will use in our user interface, see Figure 1-8.

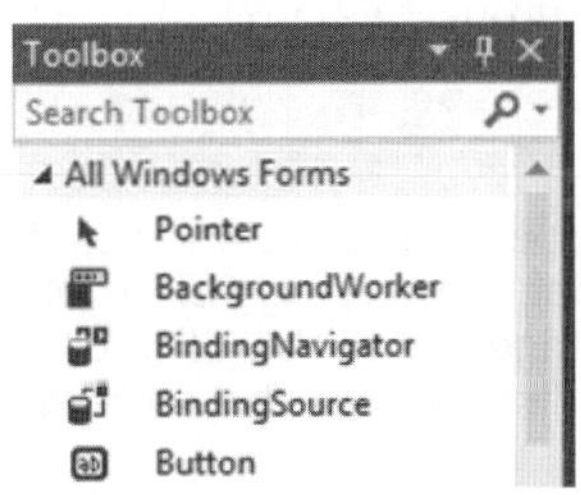

Figure 1-8 The Toolbox

You can choose to auto-hide the toolbox or display it permanently by clicking the drawing pin icon. If it is hidden, to display it just click over the Toolbox side-bar tab (seen in figure 1.9). In order to place a control on the form, simply click the control and drag it to the form. Remember if you can't see the toolbox, it's displayed using View > Toolbox.

The controls are grouped by similar functions; Common controls (buttons, labels, text boxes), Containers (tabbed forms, panels), Menus & Toolbars, etc. We shall introduce the controls as we need them. Note that you can only select controls from the toolbox when the design tab is selected.

Note the 'Search Toolbox' feature, new since VS2012. Typing in the box displays the available controls, see Figure 1-9 on page 24.

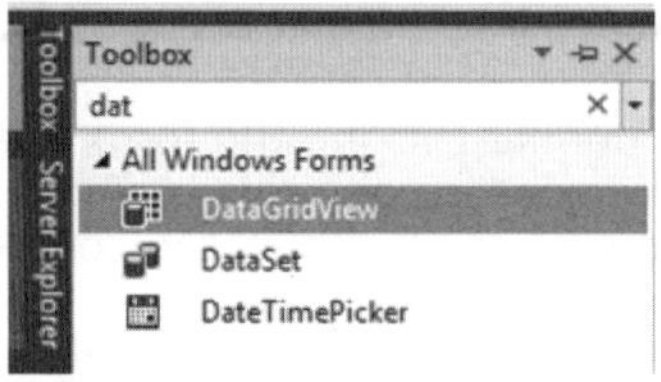

Figure 1-9 Toolbox search feature

1.3.4 • The properties and events box

All controls have their own properties. For example a button will have a certain position on the form (Top and Left properties), a size (Height and Width), Text and Font etc. They are all listed in the Properties box. Figure 1-10 shows that the properties are selected (ringed) and the Text property is set to 'button 1'; this is the text that will be displayed on the button.

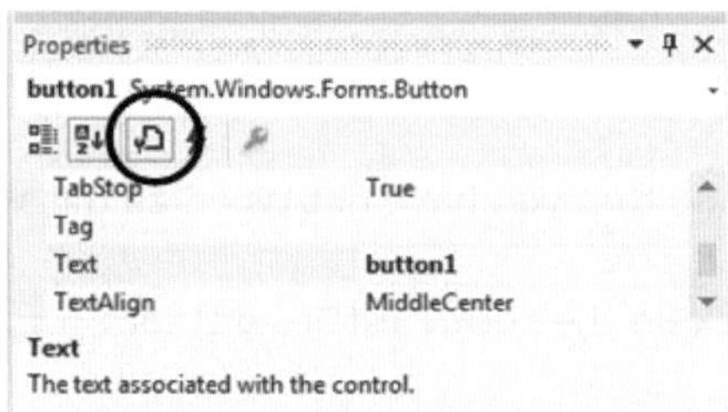

Figure 1-10 Button properties

The order of the properties can be changed between alphabetical and categorized by clicking the first two icons in the properties box:

The third icon (list) orders by property and clicking the lightning bolt icon will change the display to show the events for that control, e.g. Click, MouseHover or Move. Figure 1.11 shows the event icon selected (ringed) and the Click event for the button selected. A short description of the event is displayed at the bottom of the properties window.

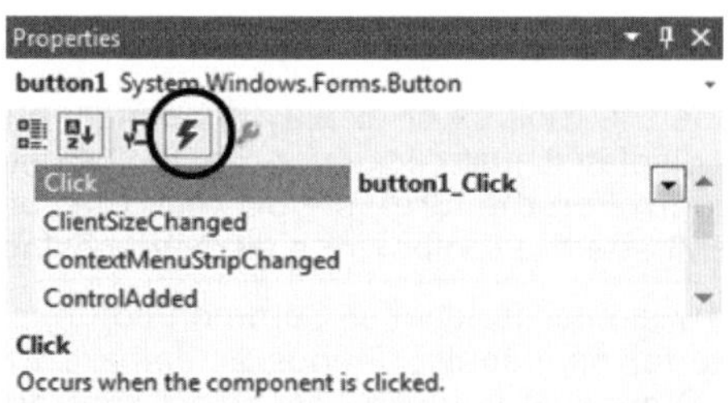

Figure 1-11 Button control click event display

Clicking the list icon to the left of the event icon will redisplay the properties list.

Note that the Properties/Events box and Toolbox will be hidden when the Code window is selected.

C# programs are event driven and these can be generated by the user, your program or the operating system. The program responds to these events. Different controls have different events, for example an event can be generated when text is typed into a textbox but that can't happen with a button. We will look at events later, but common events are:

- Clicking a button (a Click event),
- Typing a key on the keyboard (KeyDown or KeyUp events, or combined make a KeyPress event)
- Mouse events (MouseMove, MouseDown, MouseUp, MouseMove, MouseClick)
- Drag events (DragDrop, DragEnter, DragLeave, DragOver)

Event driven programs can be difficult to debug and we shall see how to debug our programs later.

As you write your programs, the editor's 'IntelliSense' will prompt you for possible entries. The dot notation is used to access the methods, properties and events, e.g. button1. Height. We shall cover methods and events later. Figure 1-12 shows some of the entries that can follow the full stop after 'button1.He' has been typed.

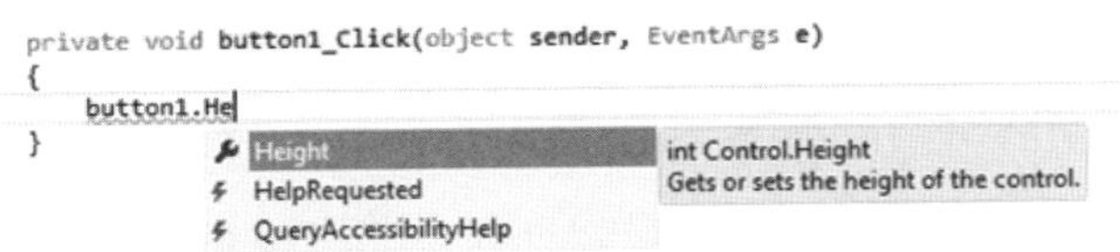

Figure 1-12 IntelliSense prompt

To help you, different icons are used for a method, a property and an event, see Figure 1-13. DrawToBitmap (a method), Enabled (a property) and EnabledChange (an event) respectively.

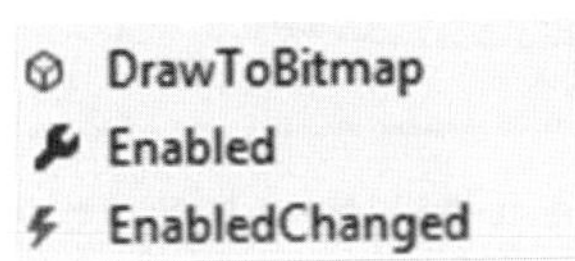

Figure 1-13 Method, Property and Event icons

As you can see in Figure 1-14 the IntelliSense editor underlines code that it doesn't understand so you can immediately see your errors.

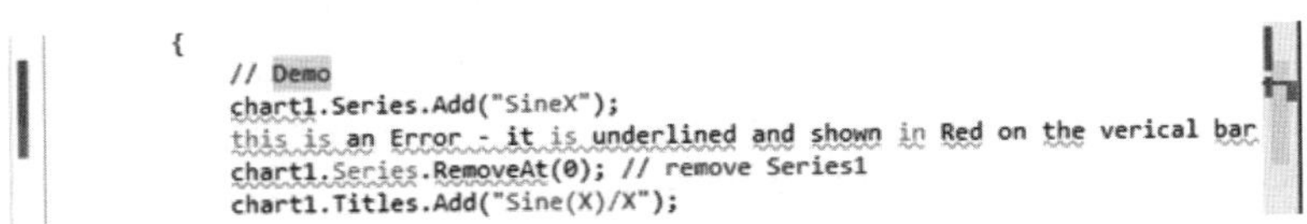

Figure 1-14 Visual Studio coloured messages

The vertical bars around the editing window also show some useful information. They are call line revision marks. You will see a blue line and red, green and yellow bars, see Figure 1-14.

The blue line indicates the currently selected line. The bars indicate errors, or changes that have been made or saved:

Green – line of code changed but saved since opening.

Yellow – line of code changed since last save.

Red – shows an error line in your code.

1.4 • Your First C# Program

1.4.1 • Hello World

To introduce you to the simplest and most common controls, let's write a Windows program to display 'Hello World' on the screen when a button is clicked. (The 'Hello World' is a common program used to introduce users to a new programming language)

Start VS2015 (Start > All Programs > Visual Studio 2015)

Permission will be requested to run your program. Visual Studio is launched which may take a while the first time. You should see a screen similar to that in Figure 1.3.

Note that if you have an account, you can also open your account page *(https://youraccount.visualstudio.com)*, give your project a name and choose a version control, then click 'Open in Visual Studio'.

Under '**Start**' click '**New Project**' (or choose File > New > Project or Ctrl+Shift+N). You should see something similar to Figure 1-15.

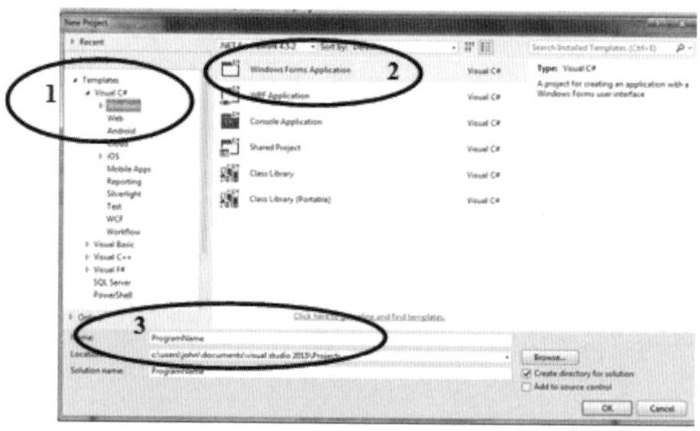

Figure 1-15 New Project window

Make sure that Visual C# Windows is selected (1), choose Windows Form Application (2) and give the project a name (3). Browse for the folder where you want your program to be saved and click OK.

Note that an Android option is available – we'll see that in Chapter 20.

1. Before continuing, get used to saving your project. Select File > Save All. Each project is saved in its own folder.
2. Display the form. If it's not displayed, click the Form1.cs[Design] tab, or use View > Designer.

   Your screen should look like Figure 1-16 on page 27.

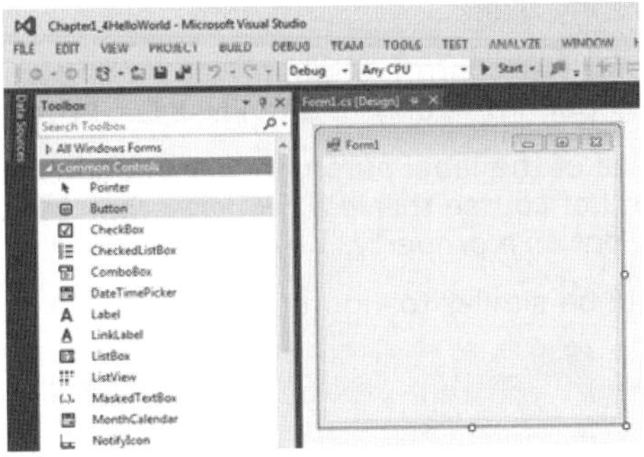

Figure 1-16 Design window

You can choose how you want your design layout but dragging windows around the screen.

Display the Toolbox (use View > Toolbox if it's not displayed) and select a Button control from the Toolbox>Common Controls and place it on the form (either click and drag the control, or click the control and then click the form), see Figure 1-17.

If the Toolbox is on top of the design page, you can click the pin to fix it in place.

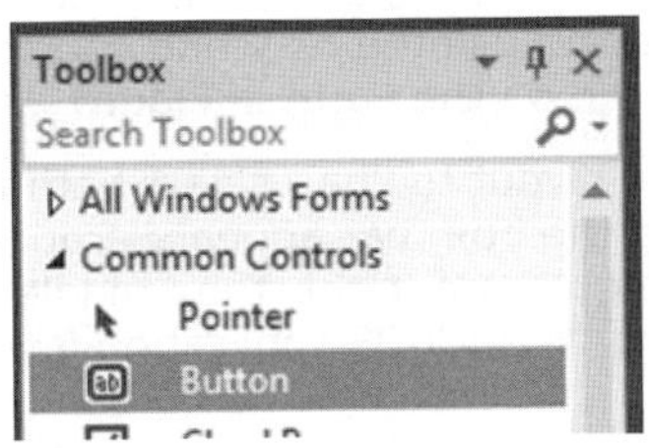

Figure 1-17 Button control

This will place a button named 'button1' on the form. Use the sizing handles to make it a sensible size.

3. Let's change the text displayed on the button. Display the **properties** window (View> Properties Window), scroll to the **Text** property and select it, now type '**Hello world**', see figure 1.18. Select the properties list icon (see Figure 1-10 on page 24) if necessary to display properties rather than events.

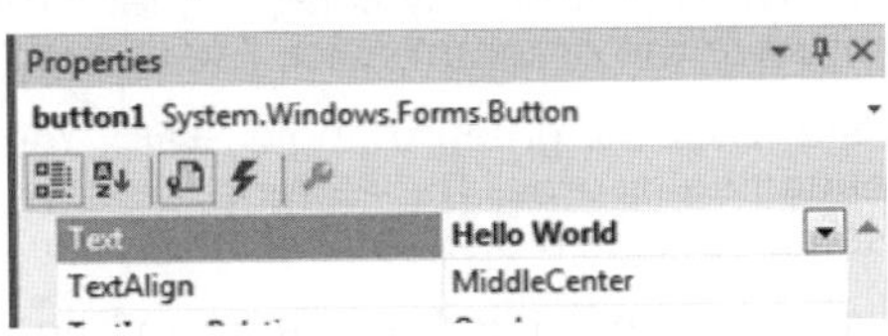

Figure 1-18 The Properties window

4. A TextBox control is used to enter and display data. This is where we will display the message 'Hello world' when our button is clicked. Select a **TextBox** control from the Toolbox (it's in Common Controls) and place it on the form. Note that as you move it around the form alignment lines appear so you can align the controls. Place the controls side by side. Notice that the height of the text box is determined by its Font property, not by a Height property. The text

property is currently blank.

5. Finally add one further control, a **label**. Place it on the form above the others, and change its caption property to '**My First C# Program**'.

   Note how the size of the label automatically changes to fit the text. You may not want this and of course this is a property that can be changed. If you want to, change the Font size property.

6. Your form should be similar to Figure 1-19.

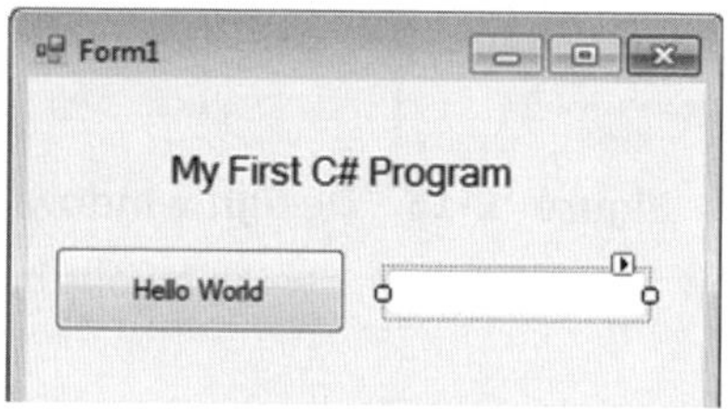

Figure 1-19 Hello World User Interface

   Hint: You can delete any control by clicking it to select the control and pressing the 'delete' key.

7. Familiarise yourself with moving controls around the form. Click and hold the mouse button and move the mouse to move controls around, or single click to select the controls and use the re-sizing controls - the squares around the object - they are shown on the Form in Figure 1-16 on page 27.

8. If you want to try the layout toolbar, select both the button and text box by clicking and dragging the box that appears around them. You can then align the controls to the left, centre, right, top, middle or bottom, change their size or spacing, see Figure 1-20. WPF application layout is different, we'll see that later.

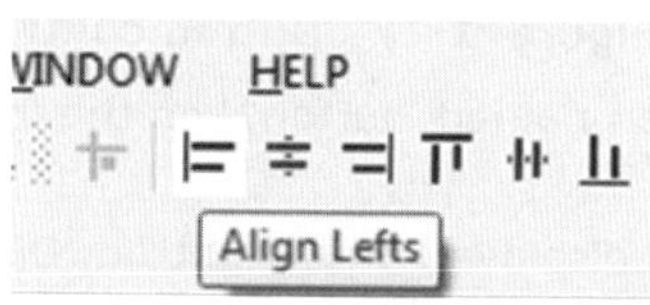

Figure 1-20 The layout toolbar

9. Even thought we haven't written any code yet, let's run the program. Before doing so however, save the program; click File>Save All.

   To run the program, click the green triangle **Start**. You can also use Debug>Start Debugging or press the F5 function key. There are often different ways to do the same operation and you will find your own preferred shortcuts.

   Your 'program' will be compiled and run. You can't do much yet. You can click the button and enter text in the text box, even though you haven't written any code yet.

Stopping your program

You can close your program in the usual way by clicking the close button on Form1, see Figure 1-21.

Figure 1-21 Stopping your program

Alternatively you can click the square red box, choose Debug > Stop Debugging or press shift-F5.

10. The button click event

    The most commonly used event is the button click. To write the code to display a message when the button is clicked, double-click the 'Hello world' button. Event code is added by the editor and you enter the code you want to execute between the curly brackets { }, see Figure 1-22.

```
private void button1_Click(object sender, EventArgs e)
{
    |
}
```

Figure 1-22 Code entry

Enter the following code between the curly brackets:

```
textBox1.Text="Hello World";
```

So that it becomes:

```
private void button1_Click(object sender, EventArgs e)
{
    textBox1.Text = "Hello World";
}
```

This line of code changes the text in the textbox to 'Hello World' when the button is clicked. Note that C# is case sensitive and as we have seen the editor provides hints and code completion as you type. It also highlights in different colours code meanings such as keywords and strings.

Remember some of this has been written for you, don't worry about what that does for now. You only need to enter the code between the curly brackets.

You may also have some empty code for the Form1_Load event:

```
private void Form1_Load(object sender, EventArgs e)
{
}
```

You can ignore this, and certainly don't delete it. You will get errors if you do so.

Remember: It is most important not to delete code that you haven't typed. This is one of the most common errors.

11. Save the project and run it (press F5). When the button is clicked, it should display 'Hello World' in the text box.

    Congratulations, you have just written and executed your first C# program!

The code is shown in Figure 1-23. Remember you have only typed one line of this. We'll explain the other lines of code when we need them.

```
using System;
using System.Collections.Generic;
using System.ComponentModel;
using System.Data;
using System.Drawing;
using System.Linq;
using System.Text;
using System.Threading.Tasks;
using System.Windows.Forms;

namespace Chapter1_4HelloWorld
{
    public partial class Form1 : Form
    {
        public Form1()
        {
            InitializeComponent();
        }

        private void button1_Click(object sender, EventArgs e)
        {
            textBox1.Text = "Hello World";
        }
    }
}
```

Figure 1-23 The 'Hello World' code

Your code may be slightly different; you may have some textBox1_TextChanged code for instance (if at some point you clicked the textbox), or as mentioned some Form1_Load code. Don't worry about that if your code runs – and certainly don't delete any!

Save and close your solution (File > Close Solution).

Reload it and run it again (use File > Recent Projects or File > Open Project and select the Solution file in the Hello World folder.

You can run the program under Windows by finding the HelloWorld.exe application file in the folder containing your files. It will be in the HelloWorld > bin > Debug folder.

The '**using**' statements at the top of your code are links to libraries (called namespaces) that Visual Studio thinks you might need. VS2015 highlights those being used (**System** and **System.Windows.Forms** in Figure 1-23). Unused Namespaces can be removed by right-clicking the code area and selecting Organize Usings > Remove Unused Usings.

1.4.2 • Copying the project

To transfer projects between computers, copy the whole folder and its files. For instance my program resides in the folder: "Visual Studio 2015 > Projects > Hello world"

The 'Hello world' folder contains the Visual Studio solution file (**.sln**) and a second 'Hello world' folder. The solution file can be clicked to open Visual Studio and your program. The 'Hello world' folder contains the executable in the bin > Debug folder, Figure 1-24 on page 31. You can create a Release version when you are happy with your code.

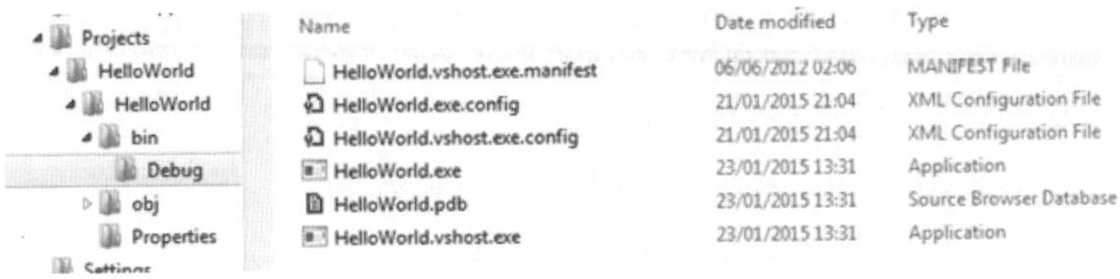

Figure 1-24 Folders and files

To copy the program to another computer, just copy the top-level 'HelloWorld' folder.

You can try it now if you want to. Copy the folder to the desktop, use File > Open Project/ Solution, browse for and select HelloWorld.sln to open it, then click Start to run the program. If the code or design forms aren't displayed, just select them from the Solution Explorer (Hello World > Form1.cs) – see Figure 1-25 on page 33.

1.4.3 • Common errors

I can't display the form

If you can't find the Form Design tab, Try View > Designer or click Shift > F7.

Select Form1.cs from the Solution Explorer (View > Solution Explorer if that's not displayed).

I get an error

Read the error message. You may not understand it, but clicking the message will take you to the line in error. Have you typed everything correctly? Did you delete something you hadn't typed in?

At this stage, it's most probably best to start again. Later, let's hope that later on we can understand the error messages!

How do I stop my program?

Use Debug > Stop Debugging, press shift+F5 or the red square in the Menu.

It says parts of my program are missing

Did you copy it from another PC? Did you copy all the files in the folder? Did you save the project and the .CS file before closing it last time? Have you deleted any code (especially anything you didn't type)? Have a look at the previous section.

1.4.4 • Properties exercises

Now that you understand how to change the control's properties, try changing them from within your program on the button click event:

1. Change the label's text, try: `label1.Text = "new caption";`

   You can let the editor prompt you for the available properties. The text is a string and goes within double quotes. The semicolon is needed at the end of the statement.

2. Change the position of the button, label or textbox using 'Left' and 'Top' properties, say add 5 to each when the button is clicked and see how the textbox moves, e.g.

   ```
   button1.Left = button1.Left + 5;
   ```

3. Change the Width and colour of the textbox (using System.Drawing.Color.Red), the button's caption, or other properties, e.g.

   ```
   textBox1.Width = textBox1.Width + 45;
   textBox1.BackColor = System.Drawing.Color.Red;
   ```

   Can you change the height of the textbox?

4. More button properties:

   The Font property is used to change button's text. You can change the font, style, size, colour and effects. The BackColor and ForeColor properties change the colours and you can choose from System (Windows), Web or Custom colours. You can also choose an image to display on your button and hence could have any design on your button.

5. Exit program

   You can add a button to close your program. There are two ways to do this in code. You can just exit from the application, or you can close the form. If your application has more than one form it will exit when you close the main form.

   Add two buttons to your form and before adding any code change their **Name** properties to **'btnClose'** and **'btnExit'**. This will give you some idea what they are and what they do when you look at your code. This is more helpful than being called button1 and button2. We shall look at naming conventions later. Also change the buttons Text property to suit (e.g. txtDisplay).

   Add the following code for the buttons respectively:

   ```
   Close( ) ;            // for the Close button
   ```

   and

   ```
   Application.Exit( );  // for the Exit button
   ```

   You will now be able to close your program by clicking either button.

As an aside, you can type this.Close(); If you do this, VS2015 will prompt you for the simpler code of just Close(); We shall explain what is meant by 'this' later, but here it means the form.

1.5 • The Solution Explorer

Your code and form design are combined into a project. The Solution Explorer shows how these are combined. In our first program we only have one form and its code, but there could be multiple forms and code segments.

My Solution Explorer looks like Figure 1-25 on page 33:

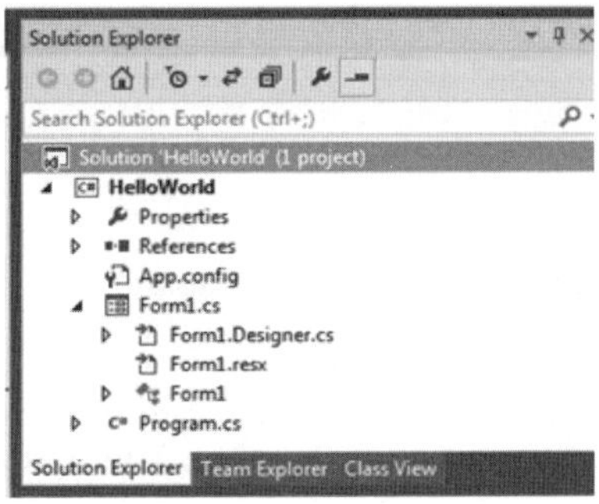

Figure 1-25 Solution Explorer

Hint: If the development environment isn't displaying what you need, try clicking within the Solution Explorer or clicking its icons.

Note that since VS2012, a search function has been added. The keyboard short-cut is Ctrl+; (semicolon). If you want to try this, try searching for 'Main' - this is the starting point for your code.

As stated some code has been written for you if you look for the Form1.Designer.cs code in the Solution Explorer, you will see the code that specifies the layout of your design.

```
//
// button1
//
this.button1.Location = new System.Drawing.Point(12, 96);
this.button1.Name = "button1";
this.button1.Size = new System.Drawing.Size(112, 38);
this.button1.TabIndex = 1;
this.button1.Text = "Hello World";
this.button1.UseVisualStyleBackColor = true;
this.button1.Click += new System.EventHandler(this.button1_Click);
```

We will see that this is different in a WPF application.

1.6 • Program execution

If you look in your folder, you will see that the program application EXE file size is about 9 KB. This is not the whole program. Your program will only run on another computer if it has the .NET framework installed. As we have mentioned, the C# compiler only compiles to intermediate code, which then runs under the .NET framework.

1.7 • Number conversion

The text in a text box is held as a 'string' data type (a series of characters). If you want to input or display numbers, you have to convert from a number to a string and vice versa. We will see this in more detail later but if you want to try it now, a number is converted to a string using .ToString( ). Typical examples are:

```
// this is a comment - declare and initialise an integer number
int integerNumber = 42;
// convert the integer to string and display
```

```
textBox1.Text = integerNumber.ToString( ) ;


// declare and initialise a real number
double realNumber = 3.14159;
// convert the real number to a string and display
textBox1.Text = realNumber.ToString( ) ;
```

The above code declares an integer (42) converts it to a string and displays it in a text box. It is then repeated for a floating-point number. The double-slash is a comment line.

We may need to convert numbers which have been typed into a textBox (i.e. a string) to an integer or floating point number. The **Parse** command is used to do this, for example Int32.Parse( ) or float.Parse( ), as follows:

```
// program to read a string and convert it to an integer
// declare an integer, i
int i;
// read textBox, convert to integer
i = Int32.Parse(textBox1.Text);
// square the number and write back
textBox1.Text = (i * i).ToString();
// read a string and convert it to a floating point number
// declare a realNumber
double realNumber;
// read text box and convert to floating point number
realNumber = float.Parse(textBox1.Text);
// square number and write back
textBox1.Text = (realNumber * realNumber).ToString();
```

Try adding the first part of the code above (the integer code) to a button click event. It should read a number typed into the text box. Repeat for the real number code.

If you try converting a string containing blanks, letters or to the wrong format (e.g. floating point string to an integer) you will get an error but it's worth trying to see what sort of error you get. We shall see how to deal with errors later.

You can also use Convert.ToInt32( ) or Convert.ToDouble( ) which check for a null value and returns a value of 0 if so. For example:

```
int intNumber = Convert.ToInt32(textBox1.Text);
```

and Convert.ToString( ) can be used, e.g.:

```
string strNumber = Convert.ToString(42);
textBox1.Text = strNumber;
```

Note: expressions like Convert.ToInt32( ) that use the brackets ( ) are known as **methods**. The items in the brackets are known as **arguments**. We shall discuss these later on.

1.8 • Exercise: Simple calculator

We shall demonstrate the number and string conversions using a simple calculator. It will have two text boxes for the numbers and one for the result. We shall provide the basic mathematical functions.

Start a new application (remember use File>New Project > Windows application, give it a suitable name).

Firstly, change the title property of Form1 to 'Simple Calculator'. Then place three text boxes on the form, one for each of the two numbers to be calculated and one for the result. In this example we will use the default names for the controls.

Add four buttons, change the Text on each to '+', '-', '*', and '/'. Change the font size (in properties) so the text looks good. Finally add an 'equals' label.

Your form should look like the example in Figure 1-26 on page 35.

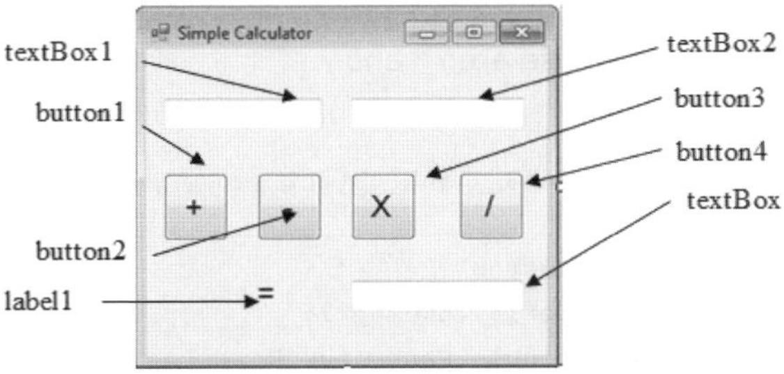

Figure 1-26 Calculator User Interface

The diagram has been labelled so you know which control is which. Later on we will discuss naming conventions and suggest sensible names so that a control's function is obvious. We touched on this earlier, but you might like to think about suitable names for the controls now (e.g. btnAdd) and use them.

Double-click the 'add' button and change the code for the button click event to the following:

```
private void button1_Click(object sender, EventArgs e)
{
   textBox3.Text = (double.Parse(textBox1.Text) +
     double.Parse(textBox2.Text)).ToString();
}
```

The full code is shown here, but remember you only have to add the code between the curly brackets.

In this example the calculation is all in one line of code so we don't have to declare any variables. The text box values are read and converted to floating point double precision numbers, added together, converted back to a string and placed in textBox3.

Save your project and run the program. Enter some numbers in the text boxes and see if it adds the numbers correctly.

Does it work for negative numbers?

We can declare and use variables if we want to. We've done a bit of this already and will look at declaring variables in detail later, but you can try the following code for the subtract button. Double click the button and add the following code between the brackets:

```
private void button2_Click(object sender, EventArgs e)
{
    double fpNumber1, fpNumber2;
    fpNumber1 = double.Parse(textBox1.Text);
    fpNumber2 = double.Parse(textBox2.Text);
    textBox3.Text = (fpNumber1 - fpNumber2).ToString();
}
```

Two double precision variables called fpNumber1 and fpNumber2 have been declared here and the values in the text boxes converted and placed in them.

See if you can add the code for the mutiply and divide buttons before looking at my solution below. The operators to use are: * and /.

My solution:

```
private void button3_Click(object sender, EventArgs e)
{
    // Multiply button
    double fpNumber1, fpNumber2;
    fpNumber1 = double.Parse(textBox1.Text);
    fpNumber2 = double.Parse(textBox2.Text);
    textBox3.Text = (fpNumber1 * fpNumber2).ToString();
}
private void button4_Click(object sender, EventArgs e)
{
    // Divide button
    double fpNumber1, fpNumber2;
    fpNumber1 = double.Parse(textBox1.Text);
    fpNumber2 = double.Parse(textBox2.Text);
    textBox3.Text = (fpNumber1 / fpNumber2).ToString();
}
```

The full code is avaiable via the Elektor web site.

If a text box is empty or doesn't hold a number, a run-time error occurs. We can also get a divide by zero error. You can try putting garbage into a text box and see what happens. We shall see how to deal with errors and use controls the ensure the user only enters correct values later.

1.9 • A Console Application

Not all programs require a Windows Form (WinForms) interface. You can see in Figure 1-15 on page 26 that you have the option of a simple Console Application. Many code examples use this, so we will write a simple 'Hello World' application now. Console applications don't have the full support of the controls we have seen, so to write to the screen we will use the Console.Write() command.

Start a new project, (File > New > Project) but this time choose a Visual C# > **Console Application**. Choose a folder and a name for your program.

Notice the code that appears is different from previously. Don't delete any of it however.

Change the code to the following:

```
static void Main(string[] args)
{
    Console.WriteLine("Please enter your name;");
    string myName = Console.ReadLine();
    Console.Write("Hello, "+ myName);
    Console.ReadLine();
}
```

Save and run the code. Enter your name and press return when prompted, see Figure 1-27 on page 37.

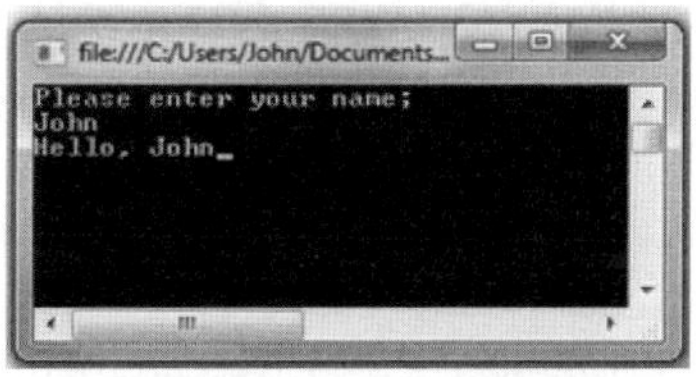

Figure 1-27 Console Application

The final line of code waits for further input so you can see the program's output. Press return to close the program. Try running the program without the last line of code and see what happens.

The **Console.WriteLine** instruction writes the text in the brackets to the window with a return, whereas **Console.Write** leaves the cursor on the same line.

Console.ReadLine reads a line of text entered (and in our case stores it in the string myName. **Console.Read** would just read a single character. You can try that too.

Run the program again and see where the cursor stops. The Virtual Academy videos mentioned in the Self Assessment exercises use Console Applications.

You'll understand later what the *static void Main(string[] args)* line of code means.

1.10 • Windows Presentation Foundation (WPF) applications

WPF is Microsoft's newest User Interface design method. However, for a beginner more work is involved and one of the reasons we use WinForms in this book. The examples on Microsoft's web site also use WinForms. WPF components provide a more flexible design for example, with WPF it's easy to design a button with an image and text on it but this is not an available control with WinForms. WPF uses XAML (eXtensible Application Markup Language) which separates the design (in XAML) from the coding, and may benefit the overall design process. We will see in Android development that WPF has been used. If you want to use WPF in you design of course you can do so, the C# coding is the same, but some of the control properties are different.

We will do a simple Hello World example to introduce WPF here.

Start a new project. This time select a C#, WPF Application.

This time there is a slightly different design. You will that the Toolbox is there, but the design window (MainWindow.xaml) is different and in the Solution Explorer there is also an **App.xaml** file.

Figure 1-28 WPF design window

The MainWindow.xaml is the one displayed by default when the application starts. My XAML code looks like this:

```
<Window x:Class="Chapter1_9WPFApplication.MainWindow"
        xmlns="http://schemas.microsoft.com/winfx/2006/xaml/presentation"
        xmlns:x="http://schemas.microsoft.com/winfx/2006/xaml"
        xmlns:d="http://schemas.microsoft.com/expression/blend/2008"
        xmlns:mc="http://schemas.openxmlformats.orgmarkup-compatibility/2006"
        xmlns:local="clr-namespace:Chapter1_9WPFApplication"
        mc:Ignorable="d"
        Title="MainWindow" Height="350" Width="525">
    <Grid>
    </Grid>
</Window>
```

Already, with WPF design we have to learn about XAML.

Of course, you can run the code at this point to see an empty window displayed.

If you drag a button onto the form, you will that you have more design options. You can skew the button for instance. Any changes you make are reflected in the XAML code.

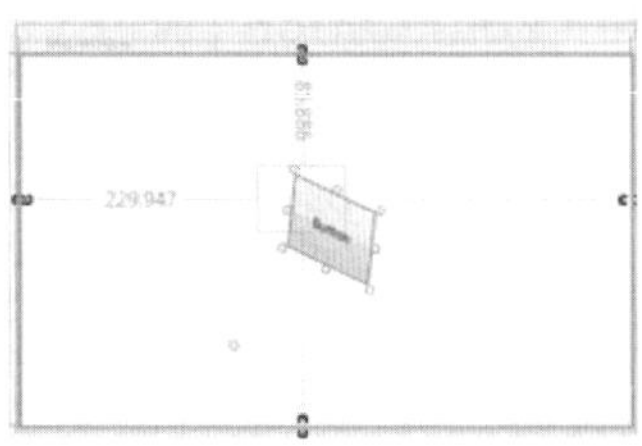

Figure 1-29 A WPF button

You can also make changes to the XAML code and the design will change to suit.

You may have noticed that the Properties and Events window is slightly different.

Change the **Content** property to 'Click me!'

Drag a label to the form and change its design to suit you.

The <*grid*> in my XAML design looked like this:

```
<Grid>
    <Button x:Name="button" Content="Click me!" HorizontalAlignment="Left"
    Margin="184,149,0,0" VerticalAlignment="Top" Width="75"
    enderTransformOrigin="-0.536,2.674" Height="58">
          <Button.RenderTransform>
              <TransformGroup>
                  <ScaleTransform/>
                  <SkewTransform AngleX="20.462"/>
                  <RotateTransform Angle="26.112"/>
                  <TranslateTransform X="19.774"/>
              </TransformGroup>
          </Button.RenderTransform>
      </Button>
      <Label x:Name="myLabel" Content="Label" HorizontalAlignment="Left"
    Margin="133,64,0,0" VerticalAlignment="Top" Width="192"/>
 </Grid>
```

We now have to add the Button Click code. Double-click the button to add the button click code. Change the code to:

```
private void button_Click(object sender, RoutedEventArgs e)
{
    myLabel.Content = "Hello World!";
}
```

Run the program and click the button. The label's Content (its text) should change to 'Hello World'.

Notice that the name for the label's text is Content and not Text as used by WinForms. This is because, as well as text, the Label can contain any other control within it, e.g. an image. You could replace the Label's XAML code to add the image source:

```
<Label x:Name="myLabel"  HorizontalAlignment="Left" Margin="154,73,0,0"
      VerticalAlignment="Top" Width="207" Height="43">
<Image Source="C:\Flag.png" />
</Label>
```

Assuming the png file can be found, an image will appear instead of text.

We saw in Section 1.5 on page 32 how WinForms specifies the layout and the button click event code in the C# code:

```
this.button1.Click += new System.EventHandler(this.button1_Click);
```

Here both the layout and the event is in the XAML code. You will have something like

```
<Button .. Click="button_Click"> .. </Button>
```

So you can see that WPF may be more flexible but there is more to understand, especially for a beginner. See the Self Assessment Exercises for a link to a WPF tutorial.

1.11 • Self Assessment Exercises

1. Microsoft has produced a lot of videos for beginners and beyond at the Microsoft Virtual Academy at:

   http://www.microsoftvirtualacademy.com/training-courses/c-fundamentals-for-absolute-beginners

   The first two are an introductory video and installation for Visual Studio.

   The third and fourth are about creating and dissecting your first program – look at those later.

   The fifth video is a 'Quick Overview of the Visual C# Express IDE'.

   I think it's best to watch the first two and the fifth of these. I suggest you look at the third and fourth when you've read chapter 2.

2. Watch my introductory video at: *https://youtu.be/scof-JlYz1Q*
3. If you haven't done so, expand the Calculator program for the multiply and divide buttons yourself and check your calculator works. We will look at Mathematics functions later.
4. There is a good tutorial on WPF at:

   http://www.wpf-tutorial.com/wpf-application/introduction/

5. Take a look at the various ways of getting help:
   - Select a control and press the F1 function key
   - Click Help > Search and type in a search item
   - Click Help > How do I? and look at the options
   - Visit the Microsoft Developer Network Library and look at the Visual Studio and C# reference links at: *https://msdn.microsoft.com/en-gb/library/ms123401.aspx*

1.12 • Summary

This chapter has introduced the Visual Studio development environment and C# design interface. The development environment windows have been seen: the form where the user interface design is created, the code window, the solution explorer, the properties and events windows and the toolbox. We have used common controls such as buttons, labels and the textbox. Some of the properties and events of these common controls have been used.

It has also introduced .NET framework which provides the libraries that we will use from our C# program.

We have written a simple program to display a message. We have seen how numbers are converted to strings and we have written a basic calculator program.

We have also seen a WPF application and some of the differences and pros and cons of this and WinForms.

In the next chapter we will look at some more useful controls.

Chapter 2 • Common controls, properties and events

2.1 • Introduction

In the first chapter we saw the most commonly used controls; the button and textbox and their properties and events. In this chapter we shall look at these controls in more detail and then look at more of the other common controls.

2.2 • The Button

We have seen that the when a button is clicked, an event occurs (a button click) and the code that has been written for that event runs.

The button's main properties are its **appearance** – Color, Image and Text; its **behaviour** – Enabled or Visible and its **design** - Name, Location and Size. Note the American spelling is used and remember **C# is case sensitive** and the properties **begin with a capital letter**.

The button's main event is (button) Click, but it also has Mouse events such as MouseEnter, MouseHover, MouseMove and MouseLeave. It also has events such as DragDrop and DragEnter to allow dragging and dropping of items, and surprisingly it also has keyboard events such as KeyDown and KeyPress.

One useful property is the Tag property. This is free for you to use and can contain any type of information. All controls have a Tag property but if you want to use it you need to set the data type you want before you use it. We shall see how to use this later.

2.3 • The TextBox

The TextBox enables the user to enter and display text. By looking at this control, we will see how we deal with text generally.

The main properties are similar to the button (appearance, behaviour and design), but it also has text control properties.

The text box property "Text" (e.g. textBox1.Text) contains all the text in the text box. We have used it as a single line, but a textbox can have single or multiple lines which is set by the MultiLine property. In this case, as there can be many lines of text, each line is treated as a string array (an array is a group of similar items) known as the Lines property; we'll see how to access that in the next section.

The text can be ReadOnly and there are also other properties including WordWrap and AutoComplete.

Example properties are shown in Figure 2-1 on page 42.

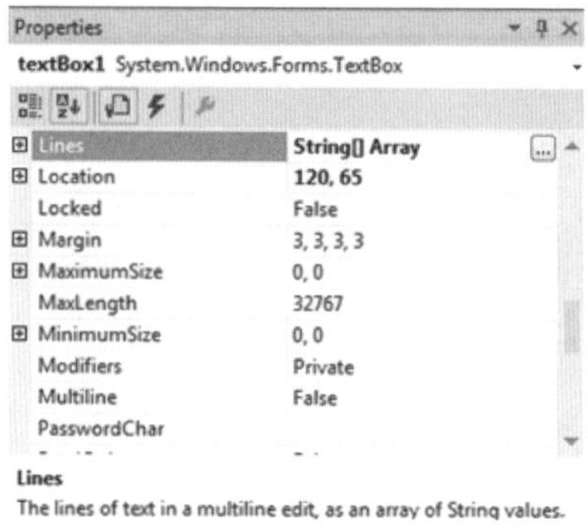

Figure 2-1 TextBox properties

The default event is the **TextChanged** event which appears if you double-click the text box.

The keyboard events are the most relevant events for this control. They are TextChanged, KeyDown, KeyUp and KeyPress (a KeyDown followed by KeyUp). The events will occur when text is changed, or a key is pressed,

As keys are typed, their code can be determined using the **Keys** codes (e.g. Keys.Enter), so you can check for the Return key or specific characters. See the Self Assessment exercises for more details.

2.3.1 • Dealing with text in a TextBox

The individual lines of text are held in the **Lines** property. To see this and add some text, place a textbox on the form and scroll to the Lines property in the Properties window, see Figure 2-2. Remember, if this window isn't displayed, use View > Property Window to display it.

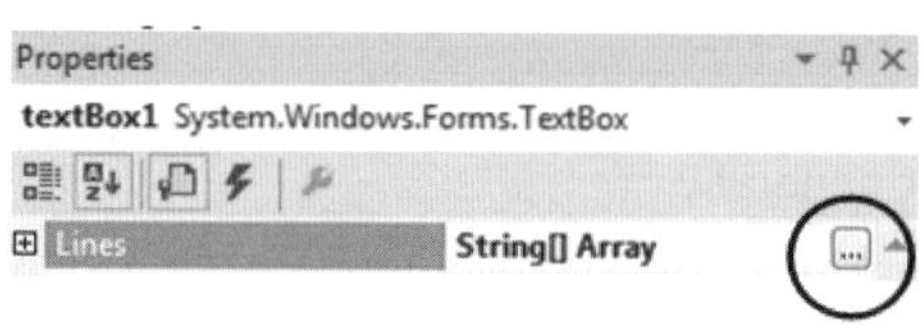

Figure 2-2 The TextBox lines property

The **Lines** property is a String array (a collection of strings), but you don't have to understand what this means yet; we shall cover arrays later on.

Click the box with the three dots (circled above). This displays a dialog box where the text required in each of the lines of the textbox can be added, see Figure 2-3.

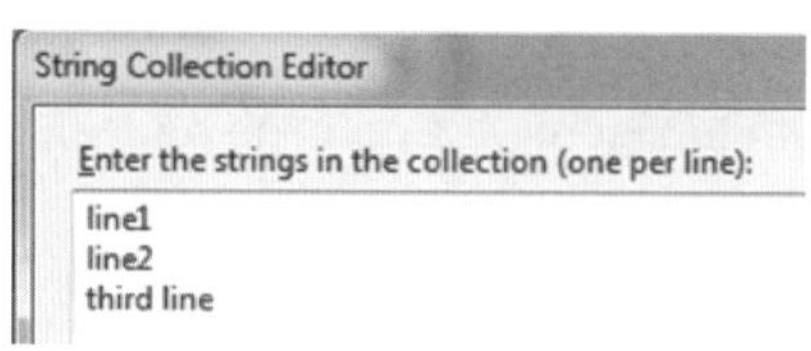

Figure 2-3 Entering text into a TextBox

The Text property will now contain all the text entered. It will be similar to Figure 2-4 on page 43.

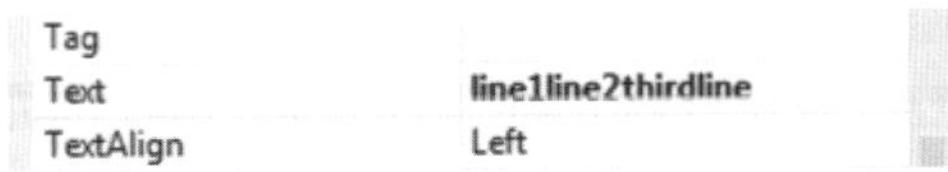

Figure 2-4 Text property showing multiple lines of text

In the property box, the **Lines** property can now be expanded by clicking the plus sign (see Figure 2-2 on page 42). This will show the text for each Line.

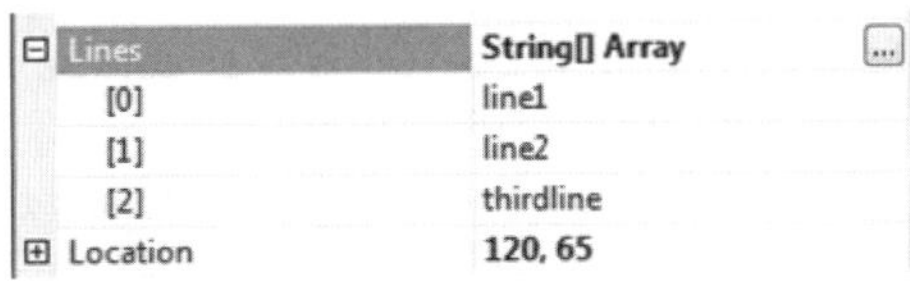

When the program runs, the text is displayed all on one line as shown in Figure 2-5.

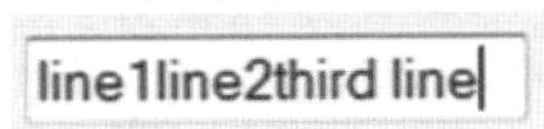

Figure 2-5 TextBox with single line text

The default is for a single line of text. If you want multiple lines of text, set the MultiLine property true (see Figure 2-1 on page 42) and expand the size of the textbox. The text will appear on individual lines as shown in Figure 2-6.

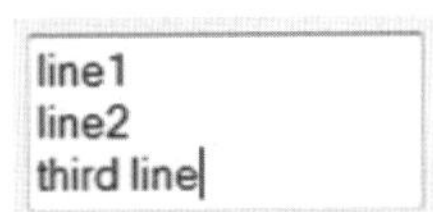

Figure 2-6 Multiline TextBox with several lines of text

If the number of lines becomes too big for the textbox, horizontal and vertical scrollbars can also be displayed by selecting from the properties.

The Text property (textBox1.Text) holds all the lines of text. Individual lines of text the **Lines** property are read as follows:

```
textBox1.Lines[0]
```

Note that Lines[0] is the first line and that it is **read-only.**

To add lines to a text box, the instruction 'AppendText( )' is used. This is called a **method.** Controls like buttons and textboxes are **objects** and have **properties**, **events** and **methods**. We have seen properties and events; a method is code that we call to do some work for us - in this case add text into the textbox. We've seen this in the calculator example with Convert.ToInt32( ). We shall see more of methods soon and write our own.

To add text to a text box, use AppendText:

```
textBox1.AppendText("new text");
```

This just appends text onto the last line and does not create a new line. To add text on to a new line, add the escape characters \r and \n - backslash 'r' and backslash 'n', which mean return and new line (or line feed). For example:

```
textBox1.AppendText("\r\nnew last line");
```

The total number of lines in the TextBox can be found with the **Length** property:

```
textBox1.Lines.Length;
```

Consequently, the last line can be found using the code:

```
textBox1.Lines[textBox1.Lines.Length-1];
```

Remember, data in a textbox is held as a string and you may have to convert it on reading into a form you need.

2.4 • The ListBox control

The ListBox control contains a scrollable list of items that can be selected but not altered by the user (i.e. only changed from within the program).

Items are added at design time in the same way as we did with the text box, but this time using **Items > Collection** in the properties box. Items can also can be added and removed by your program.

If you want to allow your user to select more than one item choose MultiSimple or MultiExtended from the SelectionMode property. The first allows multiple selections but the second also allows use of control and shift to select multiple items.

Like the text box, individual lines are addressed using an array: listBox.Items[x], where Items[0] is the first line. Items are added to the List box using the Add method as follows:

```
listBox1.Items.Add("string");
```

String conversion is done automatically, so you can add strings, integers, floating point numbers etc. For example:

```
private void button1_Click(object sender, EventArgs e)
{
    listBox1.Items.Add("Here's my list:");
    listBox1.Items.Add(34);          // add a number 34
    listBox1.Items.Add("234");       // add a string 234
    double f = 3.1415;               // declare a floating point value
    listBox1.Items.Add(f);           // add the floating point
}
```

Try this now. Place a ListBox and a button on your form and change button click code to that above. Run the program and confirm that the items are added to the ListBox every time the button is clicked.

You can insert items at a specific position using the Insert method:

```
listBox1.Items.Insert (lineNumber, "insertMe");
```

- don't forget to declare the lineNumber first though!

Individual items can be removed using the Remove method:

```
listBox1.Remove("string");          // remove the first occurrence of "string"
```

Or you can remove items at a specific line number using the RemoveAt method:

```
listBox1.RemoveAt(lineNo);
```

You can also clear the list box:

```
listBox1.Clear();
```

Eventually the item added is at the bottom of the list box and scroll bars appear. However the item just added isn't displayed – the user has to scroll to see it. If you want to display the last item added you can use the following code:

```
listBox1.SelectedIndex = listBox1.Items.Count-1;
```

If you want the scroll bars to be permanent, set the **ScrollBarsAlwaysVisible** property to true.

And finally, to identify the selected item use SelectedItem, e.g:

```
textBox1.Text = listBox1.SelectedItem.ToString( );
```

As you can see the ListBox has many commands. We'll see more about **collections** such as these in section 5.8 on page 83.

2.5 • The CheckedListBox

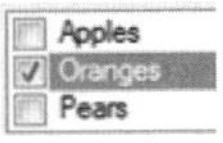

The Checked List Box performs a similar operation to the list box, but with a check box beside each item. Even though it shows up as a SelectionMode option, multiple selections can't be made.

The default event for both the list box and checked list box is SelectedIndexChanged which occurs when the user selects an item.

2.6 • The CheckBox

The CheckBox is used to select an item. The main property of course is **Checked**. It can be set or reset in code using the following:

```
CheckBox1.Checked = True;

CheckBox1.Checked = False;
```

Its main event occurs when its state is changed, CheckedChanged.

It's logical to group checkboxes together. To do this they are placed within a **container** such as a Panel, GroupBox or TabControl. We will see these containers later.

2.7 • The RadioButton

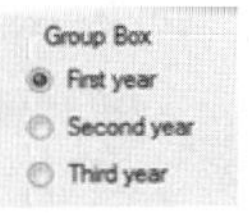

RadioButtons are used when only one item from a list needs to be selected, e.g. First year, Second year or Third year. You can place them anywhere on the Form and selecting one will automatically switch the others off.

Should you need to have more than one group, for instance to select a student's course as well as their year, you need to put the radio buttons in separate containers such as a Panel or a GroupBox (see above).

The text beside a radio button is set by its **Text** property and it has a **Checked** property (true or false) which can be set or read by the program.

Double-clicking the radio button will take you to the **CheckedChanged** event. You can check the radio button's checked state using the 'if' code:

```
if (radioButton1.Checked)
{
        // do something
}
```

2.8 • The NumericUpDown control

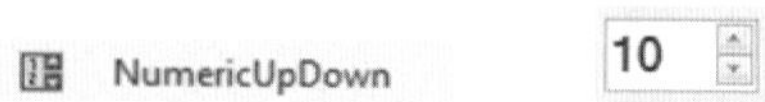

If you want a user to enter a number you can use a text box, but then you will have to check that the user has entered a properly formatted number and request correct input if the input is wrong. The NumericUpDown control ensures your user can only enter numbers within a certain range. It displays a number with up and down buttons to change the number. The user can also enter in the required number in the box. If it is out of range the control will limit the number.

The minimum and maximum values the control will display are set by the **Minimum** and **Maximum** properties, and the current value is in the **Value** property. These can be set at design time or changed from within the program.

The default event for the NumericUpDown is **ValueChanged**. This event is triggered every time the value is incremented or decremented (which may not be what you want).

2.9 • Displaying Images – the PictureBox control

The PictureBox control is used to display an image. To choose the picture for the image select the **image** property, click the three dots [...] (called the ellipsis button) and browse for the image you want displayed. You can choose from a wide range of file formats including gif, jpg, bmp, or png. You can also display animated gifs.

The **PictureBox Tasks** can be displayed by clicking the arrow icon at the top right hand corner of the picture, see Figure 2-7. The picture can be shown in Normal, StretchImage, AutoSize, CenterImage and Zoom modes.

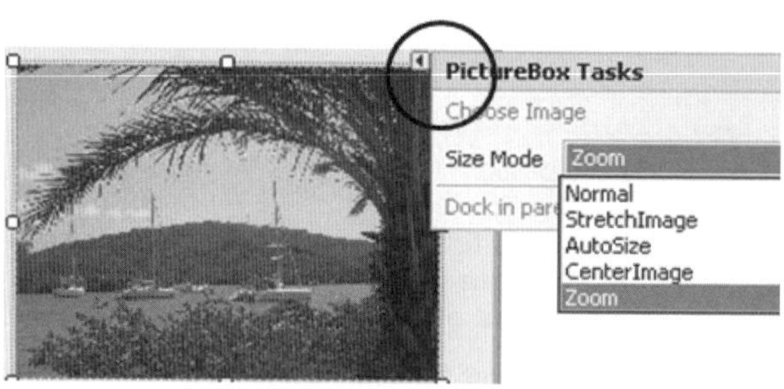

Figure 2-7 PictureBox Tasks.

If you want to select the picture to be displayed from a file, set the **Image** property using the Image.FromFile( ) method as follows:

```
pictureBox1.Image = Image.FromFile("filename");
```

The image file can be selected using an OpenFileDialog control, which we will see later.

2.10 • Focus and TabIndex

This is good place to mention **focus**. When a user clicks on a control it becomes the active control and is said to 'gain focus'. An **Enter** event also occurs. When a user clicks away from a control, it loses focus and a **Leave** event occurs. Of course you don't have to write any code for these events if you don't want to. The order in which the controls gain focus when the user uses the tab key to move around the form's items is controlled by the **TabIndex** property. This is important if you want to guide your users around your interface sensibly and can make the difference between a usable or unusable interface!

2.11 • Even more controls

Some other controls you might like to look at are listed here. We will encounter some of these later. You will have used most of these in your windows applications, they are:

- Combo Box – a drop down list of selectable items
- DateTimePicker – to select a date and time
- MonthCalendar - to select a month
- ProgressBar – to indicate an operation's progress
- WebBrowser
- Print controls

2.12 • The Web browser control

Even at this early stage, we can see how powerful the controls are by creating a web browser.

Start a new project and drag the WebBrowser control to the form. By default it will fill the form. The **Dock** property controls this. Find this and set it to '**None**'. Resize the web browser so that there is enough room for a text box below it and add a text box. Enter a URL (Uniform Resource Locator) for the web browser (e.g. http://www.elektor.com). Now you can run the program, but note that some web sites require JavaScript and you may get JS script error messages. You might have to use the debug break to stop.

We will now add some code for the text box so that when a URL is entered, that web site will be displayed. A **Uri** is used by the browser and we have to convert the text into this.

Find the text box's **Leave** event and change it so that it becomes:

```
private void textBox1_Leave(object sender, EventArgs e)
{
    webBrowser1.Url = new Uri(textBox1.Text);
}
```

Run the program, type a valid URL into the text box and click the web browser (this will 'leave' the text box and run the code). The web browser should show the web site. If it doesn't work, check for any errors displayed in the Output window.

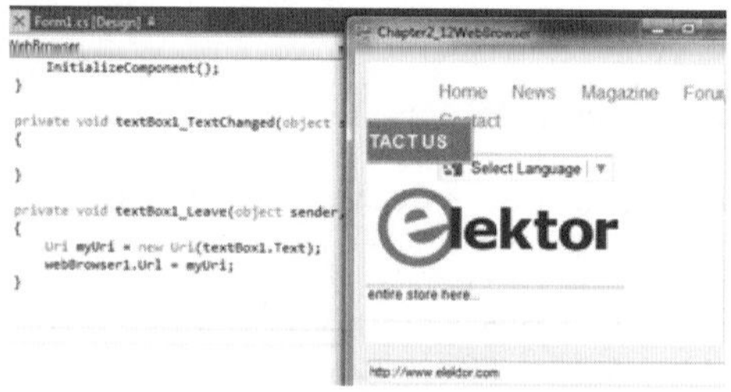

Figure 2-8 A web browser

In one line of code, you have created a simple web browser!

2.13 • The Containers controls

Containers controls are used to group items together on a form. The most common ones (apart from the Form) are the Panel and the GroupBox. The Panel is a simplified version of the Group Box (it doesn't have border or a caption for instance). Containers can hold other containers. The container controls are shown in Figure 2-9:

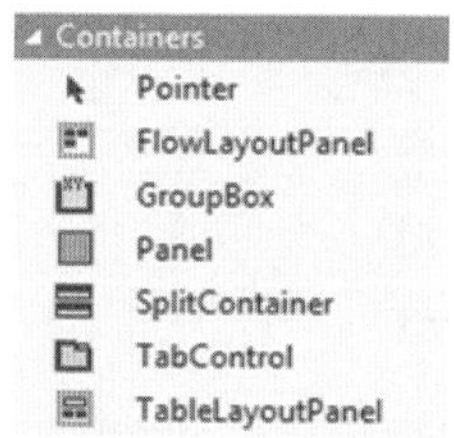

Figure 2-9 The Containers

To see this working, place a GroupBox on the form, then select a Checkbox and drag it over the Group Box. Now try moving the Group Box and notice that the Checkbox moves with it. We will use various containers in the design exercise in the next section.

Notice that a Form is not one of the available containers. You can't place a Form on a Form. Later we will see how to create new forms should you need to do so.

2.14 • Listing controls

Every control you place on a form is recorded in the Form's **Controls** property. The first object is Controls[0], the second Controls[1], etc. The total number of objects on the form is given by Controls.Count.

Every control has a .ToString( ) method, which returns a string of information about the control. There is an example in the Self Assessment exercises which displays all the names of the controls on a form.

2.15 • Exercise: Dating registration form

Let's create a registration form which might be used by a dating agency. We will just consider the design and controls, we won't write any code for this.

The form will have a tab control to select different pages for name, address and details of the person they would like to meet (WLTM).

On the Name tab, there will be TextBoxes for First name and Last Name, radio buttons to select gender (M or F) and a NumericUpDown control to select your age.

The Address tab will have TextBoxes for address and a scrollable list box to select a country (UK, Europe, USA, other).

The WLTM Details tab will have the following controls:

A panel control containing:

- A check box to select common interests (sports, pub, walking, dining out).
- Radio buttons to select age range of the person you would like to meet (range 18-25, 26-39, 40-59, 60+).

Start a new project, choose Windows Forms Application and call it DatingForm.

When the Form appears change its Text to 'Dating Form'. Rather than displaying 'Form1' it will now have a more sensible heading.

Add the Tab Control

From the Containers Toolbox menu, select a TabControl and place it on the form. Resize it so that it takes up most of the form.

Now we'll change the headings. Click **TabPages** in the properties window; a small box with three dots appears [...] (this is called ellipsis button); click this to display the **TabPage Collection Editor**, see Figure 2-10. Here you can select the tab pages and change their Text and the TabPage name. They are currently called tabPage1 and tabPage2. Change their Text properties to 'Name' and 'Address'; you can leave their Name property as tabPage1 and 2 (this is how they would be called by any code). Click the Add button to add a third tab page and change its Text to WLTM. Close the collection editor.

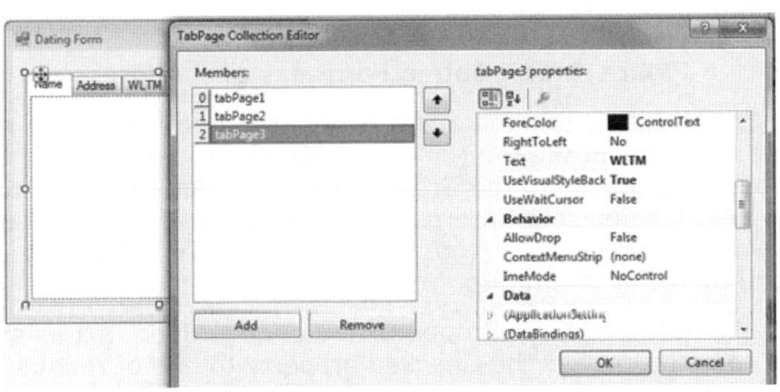

Figure 2-10 The Tab Control and Editor

Add the details

Now select the Name tab and add three labels and change their Text properties to suit (First Name, Last Name and Age). Don't forget you can use the guidelines to that appear to line everything up. Add two textboxes for the name. Add a NumericUpDown control and change the **minimum** property to 18. The first tab should be similar to Figure 2-11 on page 50.

Figure 2-11 Dating Form design - Name

Select the Address tab and add labels and text boxes for the address and post/zip code. You can use copy and paste to duplicate controls. Add a list box and add the countries using **Items collection** properties. The design should be similar to Figure 2-12.

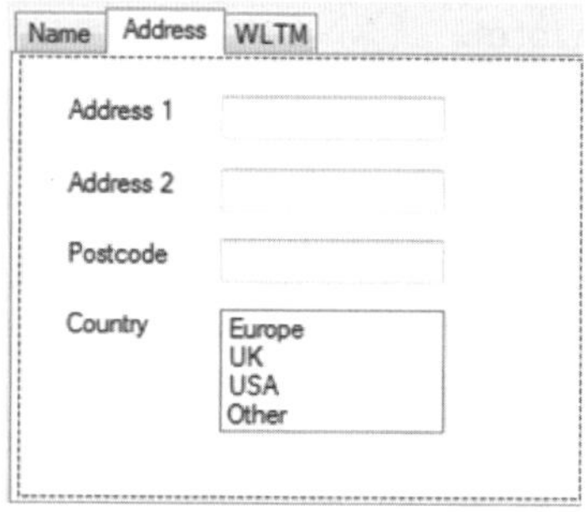

Figure 2-12 Dating Form design - Address

Finally select the WLTM Details tab and add a GroupBox container to the tab. Expand it so that it fills the left hand side of the tab (or use the **Dock** property) and change its Text to 'Interests'. Add four CheckBoxes to the GroupBox and change their Text to those shown in Figure 2.13 or make up your own interests. You can change the Checked property to 'True' to display a default preference. Note that as they are all grouped together, you can move them around the form as a group.

Finally add four radio buttons to the GroupBox and change their Text as shown in Figure 2-13. You can also change the Checked property to one of them as 'True'. As they are in the same GroupBox, only one will be able to be selected by the user.

The WLTM design should be similar to Figure 2-13.

Figure 2-13 Dating Form design – WLTM

Save the project and run the program.

2.16 • Self Assessment Exercises

1. Watch the third video in the Virtual Academy 'Creating Your First C# Program' at:

   http://www.microsoftvirtualacademy.com/training-courses/c-fundamentals-for-absolute-beginners

   It uses a console application which is worth knowing about anyway.

2. Watch the fourth video 'Dissecting the First C# Program You Created' episode at the same link.

   This describes in detail how a (Console application) program runs and introduces some concepts we have mentioned and will use later (e.g. methods and classes). But don't worry if you don't understand all of this.

   After about 14 minutes, the video mentions the other windows used by the Visual Studio IDE, and the file structure, which are worth watching. It also mentions the difference between debug and release versions of your code.

   Taking the assessment tests will show how well you understand it all.

3. The controls mentioned are all displayed in the example code provided at Elektor's web site. Download the code and look at the examples.

4. Experiment with the other controls. Place them on a form and change their properties. If they have a collection of items (e.g. the combo box), add some items to the list and observe its operation.

5. Experiment with the Containers controls. For now place them on a form, add some controls to them and see how they display.

6. Try the Tooltip control. The tooltip control provides a hint for your controls. Add a button and a toolTip control to the form (it will display in the status bar). A property 'Tooltip on Tooltip1' is now added for the button, the form and any other controls you have. Select the button and type a message for this property (e.g. 'Press me'). Run the program and hold the mouse cursor over the button to see the message appear briefly. These techniques make your program more useful and 'user friendly'.

7. Keyboard entry. Add a textbox to a form. Find the KeyDown event (click the lightning bolt in the Properties box, scroll down to and double-click KeyDown).

   Change the KeyDown event code so that it's as follows:

```
private void textBox1_KeyDown(object sender, KeyEventArgs e)
{
    if (e.KeyCode == Keys.Enter)
    {
        MessageBox.Show("You pressed enter");
        textBox1.Clear();
    }
}
```

   Run the program and notice that the message box appears when the Enter key is pressed.

8. Find a list of the escape (backslash) characters such as \r and \n and what they do. Try: *http://en.wikipedia.org/wiki/Escape_sequences_in_C*

9. Events. Try writing some code that executes on different events. For example try writing code for a MouseEnter and MouseLeave events for a control. They could display simple MessageBox.Show messages such as 'Entered' and 'Left'
10. Find out how to use some other controls in the other tabs, such as the ToolStrip and StatusStrip in the Menus & Toolbars tab.
11. Listing controls. The following exercise displays all the names of the controls.

    Place a button and a selection of controls on a form and add the following code for the button click:

```
for (int i = 0; i<this.Controls.Count; i++)
{
    MessageBox.Show("Control number "+i.ToString( ) + " is called " +
        this.Controls[i].Name);
}
```

This is the first time we have encountered a 'for' loop. Don't worry about it for now – we're just using it to loop through and display our controls.

This uses a MessageBox to display the information as shown in Figure 2-14.

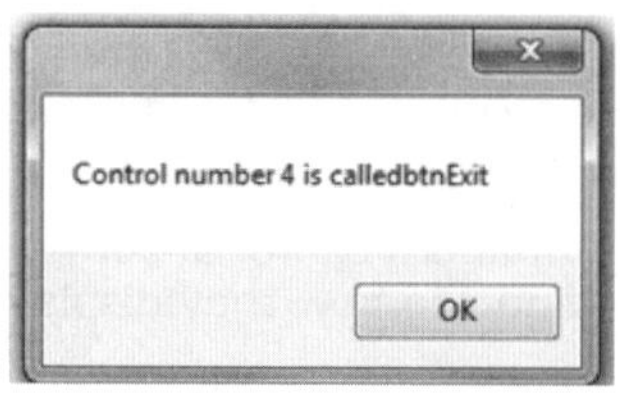

Figure 2-14 Example of the Controls property

We shall see the MessageBox in more detail in the next chapter.

Remember the keyword 'this' refers to the current object, in this case the Form. We will see this later.

2.17 • Summary

In this chapter we have looked at some of the common controls in more detail, including the button, textbox, list box, check box, radio button and their main properties and events. We have seen some of the other events such as Mouse and Keyboard events. Properties, events and methods are the basis of object oriented programming, which is covered later. We have seen that the controls can be grouped together using containers and used these in a design exercise.

Chapter 3 • Dialogs and forms

3.1 • Introduction

In the first chapters we saw that controls such as buttons, labels and text boxes are selected from the toolbox and placed on the form to design the user interface. We also saw that these controls had **properties** (e.g. height, position on the form), **events** (e.g. button click) and **methods** (e.g. Add, Insert and Remove). Now we will look at displaying messages and inputting values using dialogs and forms.

3.2 • User messages – The Message Box Dialog

It's easy to display messages to your users. You will have seen messages boxes and prompts in Windows applications. We shall see how to add them to our programs.

Dialogs are used to display information and if needed accept some input or response. They are not controls you place on your form but appear when the program runs. You can use standard dialogs or create your own using forms.

The simplest way to display a message is to use a MessageBox dialog, see Figure 3-1. We saw this in the previous Self Assessment exercises. The code is simply MessageBox. Show followed by the string to be displayed in brackets, e.g.:

```
MessageBox.Show("Displayed using MessageBox.Show( );");
```

The message box displays as:

Figure 3-1 MessageBox.Show display

To try this, place a button on a form and insert the above code for the button click event. The complete code is:

```
private void button1_Click(object sender, EventArgs e)
{
  MessageBox.Show("Displayed using MessageBox.Show( );");
}
```

Run the program and click the button to display the message.

Note there is no caption on the message box form. You can display a caption by adding a second string to the MessageBox.Show( ) method as follows:

```
MessageBox.Show("text","caption");
```

The Show( ) method can be extended further to add common response buttons such as Yes/No/Cancel, OK/Cancel, Abort/Retry/Ignore. You can also add an icon such as an exclamation mark from a selection of icons. To do this you add the message buttons and icon after the text and caption messages, for example:

```
MessageBox.Show("This will format your disk!", "Format caption",
        MessageBoxButtons.OKCancel, MessageBoxIcon.Exclamation);
```

Figure 3-2 shows how it is displayed.

Figure 3-2 MessageBox with response buttons

You can find out the button groups and icons by letting the C# IntelliSense prompt you with the options, see Figure 3-3.

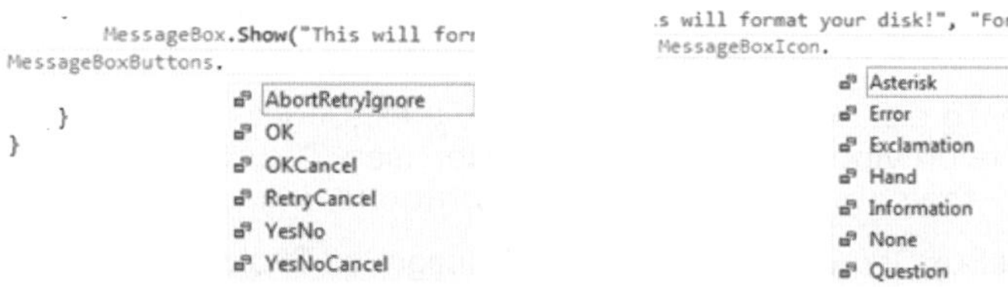

Figure 3-3 MessageBox Buttons and Icons

As we have seen before in this case, numbers are converted to strings automatically, you can type:

```
MessageBox.Show("You are "+25);
```

In this case the + sign adds (concatenates) one string to another.

To display multiple lines use the escape characters \r and \n. For example:

```
MessageBox.Show("You are \r\n"+25);
```

In this case you don't need both the escape characters, but it is good practice.

You have no control over where the message box is placed. We shall see how we can design our own message box using a new form to do this later.

You can see that the brackets are used to pass information to the method and consequently why they are used, even though nothing is passed. It's a common error to forget to put these in.

3.2.1 • Message Reply

Of course we want to know which button is selected and we have to write code to deal with the button press.

The MessageBox.Show method returns a value called a DialogResult that indicates which button was pressed. This can then be used to determine the program's operation. The DialogResult values are Abort, Cancel, Ignore, No, None, OK, Retry and Yes. For example: DialogResult.Yes.

Exercise: Dealing with responses

Enter this for the button click code and see what happens:

```
if (MessageBox.Show("This will format your disk!", "Formatting disk",
 MessageBoxButtons.OKCancel) == DialogResult.OK)
 {
  MessageBox.Show("Formatting disk");
 }
  else
 {
  MessageBox.Show("Did not format disk");
 }
```

Don't worry – it won't really format your disk!

This code uses the **if** statement to compare the user's response (using the '= =' operation) for the OK button. If this button is pressed the Dialog result is DialogResult. OK and the message: 'Formatting disk' is displayed. If the Cancel key is pressed (the only other option here) the **else** statement is executed and it displays the message: 'Did not format disk'.

We will look at the if .. else statements in more detail later.

Note what we have been doing with the simple MessageBox.Show( ) method. Initially we used it to display a message, but then <u>the same method</u> was extended to add a caption, buttons and icons. There are in fact 21 different ways of using the Show method. The IntelliSense knows about all of them and lists them as you type, see Figure 3-4.

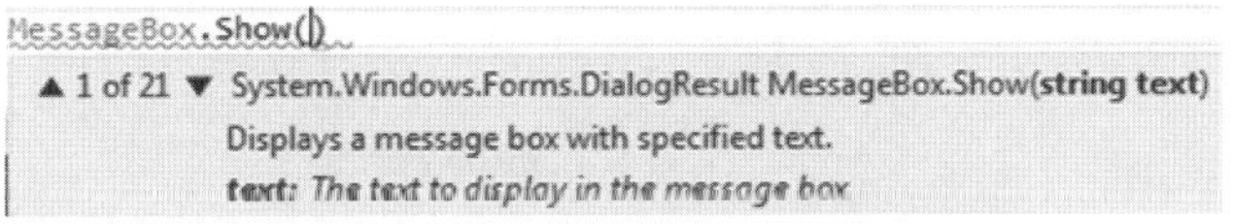

Figure 3-4 IntelliSense Prompt

3.3 • Creating your own dialogs - Prompting for input

The MessageBox.Show( ) is very versatile, but there is no C# method to accept input from the user. To do this you have to create your own message box using forms. We shall do this now as an exercise. (See SAE #1 for a Visual Basic InputBox version).

3.3.1 • User input - Adding forms exercise

Start a new Windows application project and save it. Add a button to form1. Change the button's Name property to '**btnShowForm**' and change the Text property to '**Show my dialog**'.

Now we are going to create our custom dialog form. Add a new form to the project using **Project> Add Windows Form** and select Windows form. For now use the default name of the form, Form2, and click Add - see Figure 3-5 on page 56. The new form appears.

You might like to take this opportunity of seeing what else you can add, for example the standard Help> About Box can be added.

Figure 3-5 Adding a new form

The Form2.cs[Design] tab appears. Controls can now be added to our second form just as we did with our original form. Change the Text property of the new form to 'Custom dialog box'.

Add a text box to the new form and change its properties as follows:

Name:	txtCustomMessage – let's give it a sensible name,
MultiLine:	True – let's allow many lines of text. Doing this gives you sizing handles, so make it almost fill the form.

Add some lines of text to the text box. Click the Text property and add some lines of text. Just click elsewhere or Control-Enter to finish adding text.

Finally add buttons for the response, give them suitable names. Add one with the text 'Cancel', and one with the text 'OK'. We want them to provide a response, so change their DialogResult property to 'Cancel' and 'OK' respectively. Select these from the drop down box in the DialogResult property, see Figure 3-6.

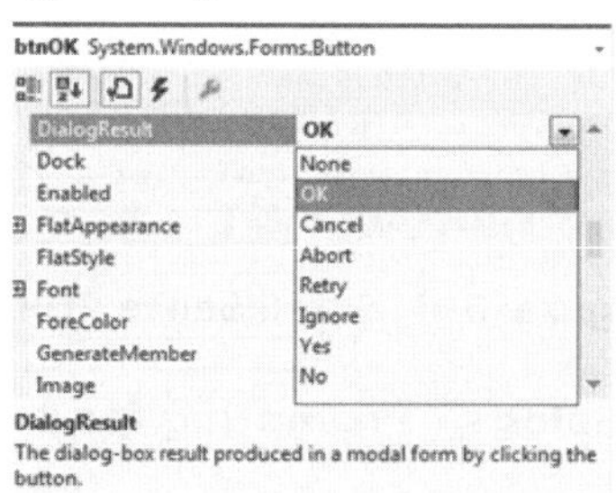

Figure 3-6 Dialog Result options

Your design should be similar to Figure 3-7 on page 57.

If we use the Show( ) method to display this form (as we did with MessageBox), the user can choose to ignore the form by closing it. This may not be desirable, for example for a password dialog. We will ensure the user must click one of the buttons to continue, so the ShowDialog( ) method will be used to display the form. This is known as a **modal** form.

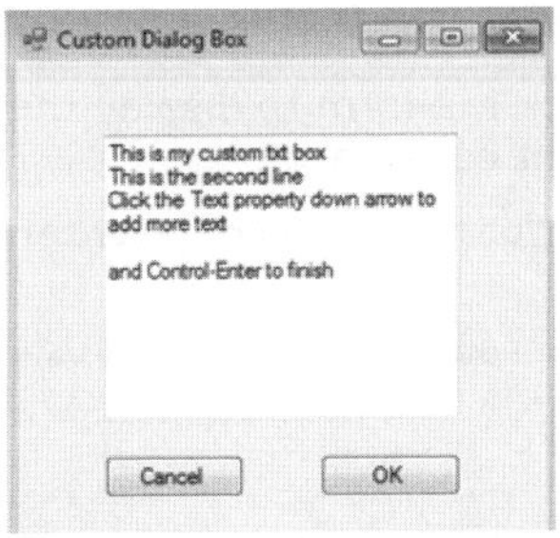

Figure 3-7 Custom Dialog Box

Note that you don't have to write code to close the form, clicking the button will close it automatically and also pass back a DialogResult that can be checked by the program.

Now we need to write the code to display our dialog box. Display form1 (double-click Form1.cs in the solution explorer if it isn't displayed) and double-click the 'Show my dialog' button you added. Change the button click as follows:

```
private void btnShowForm_Click(object sender, EventArgs e)
{
  Form2 dialogForm = new Form2();
  if (dialogForm.ShowDialog() == DialogResult.OK)
  {
   MessageBox.Show("You clicked OK");
  }
  else
   {
     MessageBox.Show("You clicked Cancel");
   } // end if .. else
}
```

Note how we define and use Form2, we declare it in the first line giving it a name new name dialogForm. This is known as creating an **instance** of Form2. We then use this name later in the code, displaying the form using ShowDialog( ).

Run the program. Clicking the button should display our custom dialog box (form2). You can now click OK or Cancel. If you are having problems, check the DialogResult properties have been set correctly.

Actually, the if..then code can be replaced by one line:

```
MessageBox.Show("You clicked " + dialogForm.ShowDialog( ));
```

Can you work out how this works?

At this stage we have managed to show a second form, but haven't yet passed values between the forms (say the text in the text box). Before we do that, let's look at the timer component and 'splash' forms.

3.4 • Splash forms and the Timer control

Now we know how to display a second form, we can display a 'splash' or introduction form that will show for a short time before the main application starts. We will use the timer control to close the form automatically.

Exercise: A splash form

Create a new project. Double-click the form to display the default event, Form1_Load. Change the code so that the event code becomes:

```
private void Form1_Load(object sender, EventArgs e)
{
  Form2 form2Show = new Form2();  // create a new form 2
  form2Show.Show();               // and show it
}
```

Form2 hasn't been created yet, and so will show as an error by the IntelliSense. When form1 is loaded it will show form2 (when we've added it).

Now add a second form (Project > Add Windows Form > Windows Form). Use the default name, Form2. Add a label to form2 and change its caption property to 'Hello'.

Now add a timer control to form2. This is found in the toolbox Components group:

The timer icon will be displayed in the IDE's status bar. It won't be seen at run-time (this is sometimes called a non-visual component). Its most used properties are:

Name:	The usual meaning,
Enabled:	True or False,
Interval:	Time in milliseconds - default 100,
Tag:	Free for use by your application.

Change the timer's **Enabled** property to **True** and the **Interval** to **2000** (2 seconds)

The timer only has one event which is called **Tick**. The code written in the timer_Tick event runs every 'Interval' milliseconds when the timer is enabled. Double-click the timer icon and add the following code so the timer tick event becomes:

```
private void timer1_Tick(object sender, EventArgs e)
{
  this.Close();
}
```

Run the program and observe its operation. You may find that form2 is displayed behind form1. In this case, change Form2's **TopMost** property to True and run the program again.

Form1 is the main form - it displays Form2 when it is loaded. Form2 closes itself on the timer event.

Look again at the timer code: this.Close( ); Remember the keyword 'this' refers to the current object, in this case the form with the timer code. VS2015 will suggest using just Close( ); - it knows which object you mean.

Form events

A form is only loaded once, but activated every time it is displayed. You can see this in action if you move the form load code to the form activated event. Display form1's events in the properties box and scroll to the Activated event. Click this to display the framework code for the **Form1_Activated** event and type in the form load code we used earlier. Run the program again. There will be lots of form2 boxes appearing. Be prepared to stop the program using Shift-F5!

3.5 • Accessing controls on other forms

This is a bit complicated so early on in the book, so feel free to ignore for now and return to it later.

Now that we know how to create and display a second form, let's see how to access controls on the second form.

Remember when we add a form to our project, that's all we do. To display it we have to create an **instance** of it and show it. (That's what the form load code did in the last section). Any controls on a form are private to that form, so to access them from another form we either have to change how they are 'seen' by the rest of the program - declare them public, or preferably create and call a **public method** (you may know this as a procedure or subroutine) which accesses the object.

We'll see much more of this in the chapter on methods. If you feel uncomfortable, please skip this part and return later. I know how daunting this can be!

Let's suppose we have a form1 with a button, which when clicked will change the text in a textbox on form2.

The code for the button on Form1 is:

```
Form2 form2Show = new Form2( );          // define Form2 as form2Show
form2Show.setTextBox1("Hello");          // call the setTextBox method
                                         // in form2 to change the text
form2Show.Show( );                       // and show the form
```

Now we will create a public method on form2 which is called to change the textbox (which is private to form1):

```
public void setTextBox1(string temp)
{
  this.textBox1.Text = temp;
}
```

Let's modify our splash program to see this working.

Exercise – Accessing controls on other forms

- Add the following 'form2Show.setTextBox1("Hello");' code to the Form1_Load event code, so that it becomes:

```
private void Form1_Load(object sender, EventArgs e)
{
  Form2 form2Show = new Form2();      // create a new form 2
  form2Show.Show();                   // and show it
  form2Show.setTextBox1("Hello");     // change textbox text
}
```

- Add a textbox to Form2 and add the setTextBox method code after the closing bracket for the timer tick code as follows:

```
private void timer1_Tick(object sender, EventArgs e)
{
  this.Close();
}
```

```
public void setTextBox1(string temp)
{
  this.textBox1.Text = temp;
}
```

- Run the program. The textbox should display 'Hello'.

To do the opposite and access a control on Form1 (say a label) from the second form, you have to add a method to access the text as above in the Form1 code, but also provide a link for Form2 to Form1.

In a new project add a new form (Form2) and place a button on it. Don't add a timer. Place a label on Form1. We'll write a **method** to change the label's text in Form1's code as follows (see below for the full code and where to put it).

```
public void SetLabel(string strText)
{
  label1.Text = strText;
}
```

To pass the reference for Form2 from Form1, the keyword '**this**' is used. This is done when Form2 is created. Add the following to Form1_Load:

Modify the code we had before to:

```
Form2 form2Show = new Form2(this);
```

As we are now passing some information to Form2 when it is created we need change the code at the top of form2 to:

```
public partial class Form2 : Form
{
  Form1 parent;
  public Form2(Form1 p)
          // form1 is passed as 'this' and is referenced by 'p' - parent
  {
  InitializeComponent();
  parent = p;
  }
```

For form2's button click, change the code to the following:

```
private void button1_Click(object sender, EventArgs e)
{
  parent.SetTextBox("hello there");
  // this will call the SetLabel method on the parent form – form1
}
```

Click the button on Form2 and Form1's label's text should change.

For completeness, the form1 code is:

```
public partial class Form1 : Form
{
  public Form1()
  {
    InitializeComponent();
  }
  private void Form1_Load(object sender, EventArgs e)
  {
    // create a new Form2 and pass reference to Form1
    Form2 form2Show = new Form2(this);
    form2Show.Show(); // and show it
  }
  public void SetLabel(string strText)
  {
    label1.Text = strText;
  }
}
```

And form2 code is:

```
public partial class Form2 : Form
{
    Form1 parent;
    public Form2(Form1 p)
    // form1 is passed as 'this' and is referenced by 'p' - parent
    {
      InitializeComponent();
      parent = p;
    }
    private void button1_Click(object sender, EventArgs e)
    {
      parent.SetLabel("Well done");
      // this will call the SetLabel method on the creating form - form1
    }
}
```

That was a bit complicated for this early on, so well done.

3.6 • Self Assessment Exercises

1. If you have used Visual Basic, you may have used a form that provides an input dialog called the InputBox. You can use this in your C# program, but you have
    a. Add the Visual Basic libraries to your C# project. Click Project > Add Reference, scroll down and click the box to the left of the Microsoft. VisualBasic line in the Reference Manager window that appears (Microsoft. Visual.CSharp is already selected). And click OK
    b. Now you add the following code to a button click:

```
int XPos = 10;
int YPos = 10;
Microsoft.VisualBasic.Interaction.InputBox
 ("Prompt", "Title", "Default Response", XPos, YPos);
```

Run the code. You should see something like this appear:

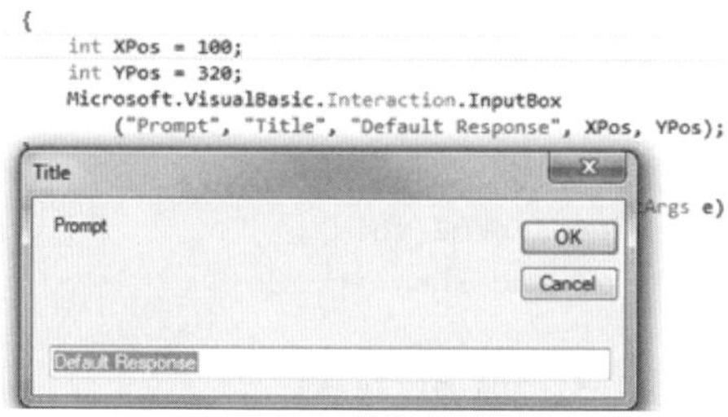

This input box can be placed anywhere on the screen, and shows how other languages can be incorporated in your C# code. If you want to experiment further with this, look at the Microsoft definition at:

https://msdn.microsoft.com/en-us/library/6z0ak68w%28v=vs.90%29.aspx

To read the response, use the code:

```
string response = Microsoft.VisualBasic.Interaction.InputBox
    ("message", "Title", "Default Response");
MessageBox.Show(response);
```

2. Snap game using Timers and the Random class

   This exercise uses timers, picture boxes and introduces random numbers. The game displays different colours in a picture box randomly and a message if the colours are the same.

   Start a new project and:

   - Place a Timer from the component palette on the form. This will not show at run-time. We will write code so that when the timer code runs it will check for a snap and generate new colours.

     Make sure its properties are:

     Enabled = True and

     Interval = 500

   - Add two Pictureboxes to the form. Change their BackColor property to Web>Red. Our program will change their colour and display a message box when they compare.

   Now we'll add a random number. A Random number in C# is an **object** which we have to instantiate using the keyword '**new**'.

   Find the C# code:

   ```
   public partial class Form1 : Form
   ```

   After the open curly bracket { and before the code: 'public Form1( )', add the following to declare a Random object and an integer identifier to hold the number:

```
Random rndColour = new Random( );          // declare a random object
int randomNumber;                          // integer to hold a random number
```

To generate a random number rndColour.Next( ); is used. To generate a range of number (starting at 0) a number is passed. We will generate a number between 0 and 2 using:

```
randomNumber = rndColour.Next(3);          // random number 0 to 2
```

Double-click the timer component and enter the following code between the curly brackets as below.

Your code should be:

```
public partial class Form1 : Form
{
    Random rndColour = new Random(); // declare a random object
    int randomNumber; // integer to hold a random number
    public Form1()
    {
        InitializeComponent();
    }
    private void timer1_Tick(object sender, EventArgs e)
    {
        if (pictureBox1.BackColor == pictureBox2.BackColor)
        {
            // if colours are the same stop the timer
            timer1.Enabled = false;
            MessageBox.Show("Snap!"); // and display message
            timer1.Enabled = true;    // start timer when message is OKed
        }
        // Generate new colours
        randomNumber = rndColour.Next(3);  // random number 0 to 2
                                           // change pictureBox1 colour
        if (randomNumber == 0) pictureBox1.BackColor = Color.Blue;
        if (randomNumber == 1) pictureBox1.BackColor = Color.Green;
        if (randomNumber == 2) pictureBox1.BackColor = Color.Red;

        randomNumber = rndColour.Next(3); // random number 0 to 2

        // change pictureBox2 colour
        if (randomNumber == 0) pictureBox2.BackColor = Color.Blue;
        if (randomNumber == 1) pictureBox2.BackColor = Color.Green;
        if (randomNumber == 2) pictureBox2.BackColor = Color.Red;
        }
}
```

Run the program and see how it works. We will look at the 'if' statement soon. Note how the random object has to be instantiated and then a number generated and saved.

3. Extend the program to:

    a. Add a second timer with a different Interval to control the second picture box.

    b. Add a button and a text box for the user to play Snap. The user is to click the button when they see a snap. The text box will contain the score.

    c. Increment a counter if the player guesses correctly and decrement it if it is incorrect or a Snap is missed. The counter could be a value in a text box; you will have to convert its text from a string to an integer to increment the number.

    d. Add a stop/stop button to control the program. If its caption is 'Start', change it from 'Start' to 'Stop and enable the timer, otherwise (else) change its caption (from Stop) to Start and disable the timer. You will have to use an 'if .. then .. else' statement:

```
if (StartStopButton.Text == "Start")
{
    // change caption to Stop and enable timer
}
else
{
    // change caption to Start and disable timer
}
```

    e. Fully debug and test the program. E.g. can the user guess more than once for a match?

    f. Take a look at some readymade controls at *http://www.microsoft.com/download/en/details.aspx?displaylang=en&id=14422*)

    g. Find out how to write your own controls (a bit early yet!) at: *http://www.codeproject.com/Articles/20146/Write-Your-Own-Bar-Chart-Winforms-User-Control*

    h. You can find out how to use controls in WPF designs at: *http://bit.ly/1FYPRFp*

3.7 • Summary

This chapter has covered using the MessageBox dialog to display simple messages and dealing with the button click response. Some of the many MessageBox possibilities were seen.

We saw how to design and display our own forms. This was taken further to design a splash form which introduced the non-visual timer control. We also covered how to use methods to access objects on one form from another.

In the Self Assessment Exercises, by designing a snap game, random numbers were introduced.

Chapter 4 • The C# Language – the basics

4.1 • Introduction

As well as designing our user interface we have to write some code. We will start by looking at the basic data types, assignments and comparisons. In the next chapter we will look at decision making with control and program flow.

4.2 • Declarations - Variables and data type identifiers

All variables used in our programs must have a data type and a name or identifier. Before we can use a variable or constant its data type (e.g. integer, floating point, string) and its name must be declared. This is done at any time before or when the variable is used.

A variable is declared by stating its data type followed by its name. It can optionally be given an initial value. We saw the following declaration in Chapter 2 on page 41:

```
string strMessage = "Cancel";
```

This declares a **string** data type called strMessage with the initial value "Cancel".

Constants are defined by adding the reserved word const, for example:

```
const float GOLDENRATIO = 1.61803399F;
```

You must declare an initial value for a constant.

C# supports nine integral data types, two floating point types, a type suitable for financial calculations, types for characters and strings and a type for Boolean logical variables (true and false). The data types and example declarations are shown in Table 4-1.

Table 4-1 C# data types

Data type	Example declaration	Description
byte	`byte eightBits = 128;`	0 to 255
sbyte	`sbyte signedByte = -128;`	-128 to +127
short	`short signedWord = 32767;`	-32768 to 32767
int	`int bigNumber = 1234567;`	-2147483648 to +2147483647
long	`long evenBiggerNumber = 12345678;`	Large integer
float	`float floatingPoint = 0.23F;`	Approx. -3.4E38 to +3.4E38
double	`double doubleFloatingPoint = 2.345D;`	Approx -1.79E208 to +1.79E208
decimal	`decimal money = 3.33M;`	Used for currency
bool	`bool trueOrFalse = true;`	TRUE or FALSE
char	`char characterA = 'A';`	Letters of the alphabet : 'A' or '*'
string	`string aString = "this is a string";`	Contained in double quotes
uint	`uint unsignedLarge = 543210;`	Unsigned, 0 to 4,294,967,295
ushort	`ushort unsignedMedium = 43210;`	Unsigned, 0 to 65535
ulong	`ulong unsignedLong = 0;`	Unsigned, 0 to 1020

The keyword var can also be used leaving the compiler to determine the data type. The following two declarations are equivalent:

```
int     i = 10;     // explicitly declared as an int
var     i = 10;     // implicitly declared (up to the compiler)
```

However, variables declared using var must be initialized otherwise the compiler doesn't know the data type, e.g.:

```
var var1 = "This is a string";     // var1 is a string
var var3 = 3.1415926;              // var3 is floating point
```

4.2.1 • Naming convention

As we have said it is a good idea to adopt a convention when naming your variables, constants, methods and class names (when we come to them). I have already suggested you use three letters to indicate the type of control placed on a form, e.g. btn, lbl, txt etc. but that is not preferred see:

*https://msdn.microsoft.com/en-us/library/ms229045%28v=vs.110%29.aspx*l.

You can of course use your own rules, but by convention variables start with a lowercase letter separating each word with a capital letter, e.g. loopCount, moneyOwing. Classes will begin with a capital letter, e.g. CalculateSine, SquareNumber. It's common to use all capital letters for constants.

Preferred naming, layout and other conventions can be found by searching for 'C# naming conventions' on the MSDN site at http://msdn.microsoft.com. I'm afraid I don't always stick to them!

4.2.2 • Some declaration examples:

Here are some examples of declaring variables and constants:

```
const double MYCONSTANT = 2.14159;               // a fixed value
const int MAXSIZE = 10, MINSIZE = 1;             // more than one in a line
const ushort HEXNUMBER = 0xFFFF;                 // 0x used for hexadecimal
int integerNumber;                               // not initialized
double temperature = 98.6; freezing = 0.0;       // two at once
char letterA;                                    // a character
bool lightSwitch = true;                         // a Boolean – true or false
```

4.3 • Assignments and operators

Assignments are made with the equals symbols '**=**' and statement always end with a semicolon, for example

```
sum = one + two;
```

The usual mathematical operators are used: add +, subtract -, multiply *, divide / and remainder %, as is the order of their operation (precedence): Unary (e.g. 'not'), brackets, division and multiplication, add and subtract.

4.3.1 • Shortcuts

Variables can be incremented and decremented by one, using the shortcuts '++' and '--'.

These operators can be put both before and after the variable to be changed. You can have x++ or ++x. In most cases it doesn't make any difference, but if you are assigning the value to another variable, it will. For example the following code displays the value 0.

```
int x;
int y = 0;
x = y++;                              // assign to x then increment y
MessageBox.Show(x.ToString( ));       // shows 0
```

Whereas this code displays the value 1:

```
int x;
int y = 0;
x = ++y;                              // increment y, then assign y to x
MessageBox.Show(x.ToString( ));       // shows 1
```

In both cases, y ends up with the value 1.

Assignments such as x = x+y; can be shortened as well. In this case to x += y;

This is very useful for objects with long names. Note that it's not shortened to x = +y.

The shortened versions are:

```
add = add + 3;                  becomes      add += 3;
div = div / 4;                  becomes      div /= 4;
mult = mult * 5;                becomes      mult *= 5;
sub = sub - 2;                  becomes      sub -= 2;
remainder = remainder%4;        becomes      rem %= 4;
```

4.4 • Comments

We have seen the double slash used for a single line comment.

A forward slash followed by an asterisk is used for multi line comments:

```
/*
Slash-star is a multi-line comment - it is ended with a star-slash
*/
// Or you can use a double slash which ignores the rest of the line
```

You can comment (or uncomment) sections of selected code using the following toolbar icons:

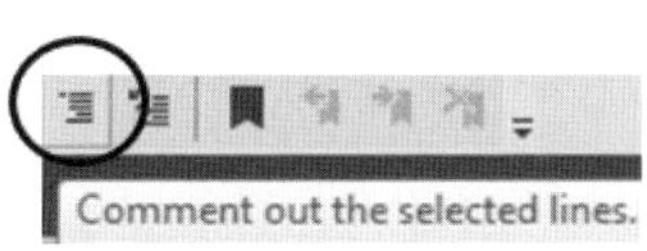

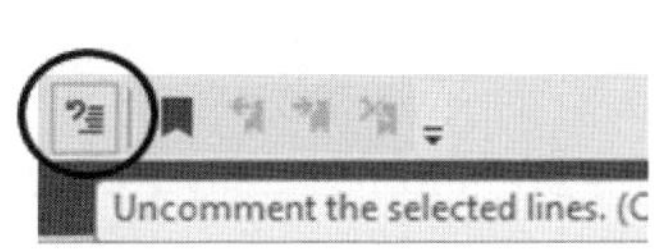

Older versions of Visual Studio used these icons:

4.5 • Converting (casting) data types

You may find that you have to convert from one data type to another to perform an operation. We have already seen conversions from numbers to strings using the .ToString( ) method.

Conversions can be implicit or explicit. Implicit conversions are done automatically and guarantee that no data is lost in the conversion. For instance you can convert a single precision 'float' data type to 'double' without a problem because the double has more precision than the float. However if you try to convert a double precision variable to single precision some data may be lost and you have to explicitly tell the compiler that it's OK (that you know what you are doing!). Consider the following code:

```
double doubleNumber =1.234;        // declare a double precision number
float singleNumber =1.234F;        // declare a single precision number
doubleNumber = singleNumber;       // is OK you can convert float to double
singleNumber = doubleNumber;       // this errors – it requires an explicit cast
```

The 'double' data type has more precision than 'float', so an error occurs for the line of code singleNumber = doubleNumber; as follows:

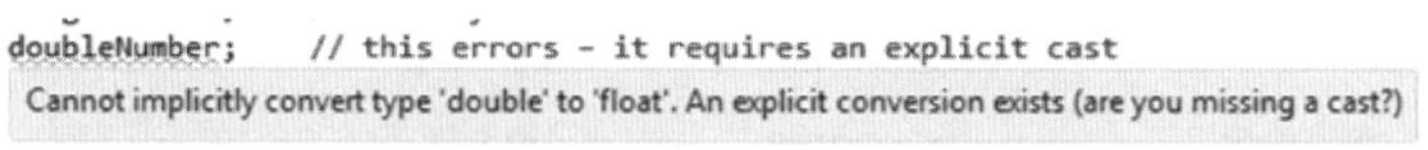

A squigly blue line will appear under the code indicating an error.

If this is what you want to do, then you must explicitly say the change is OK by placing (float) in front of 'doubleNumber', as follows:

```
singleNumber = (float) doubleNumber;        // the (float) means it's OK
```

Table 4-2 shows a list of safe conversions.

Table 4-2 Safe data type conversions

Data type	Can be converted to
byte	char, short, int, long, float, double, decimal
short	int, long, float, double, decimal
int	long, float, double, decimal
long	float, double, decimal
float	double, decimal
double	decimal

Integer divides are automatically truncated, e.g:

```
integerNumber = 124 / 3;
MessageBox.Show(integerNumber.ToString( ));        // displays 41
integerNumber = integerNumber % 3;                 // remainder
MessageBox.Show(integerNumber.ToString( ));        // remainder = 1
```

4.6 • Characters and strings

Characters are declared by using a single quote around the character and strings defined using double quotes around the string. As we have seen in section 1.7, strings that represent a number (e.g. a number typed into a text box) can be converted using the **Parse** method such as float.Parse(string) or int.Parse(string). Examples are:

```
char capitalA = 'A';
string welcome = "Hello there!";
string aZString = "Z";                  // a one character string!
string aNumberString = "1.234";
float floatingPointNumber =  float.Parse(aNumberString);
int integerNumber = int.Parse("123");
```

To incorporate the double-quote character in a string, it is preceded with a backslash character: **\"**. We have already seen the escape sequences in section 2.3.1 on page 42, where we used \r and \n to represent the non-printing characters 'return' and 'line feed'.

You can also use the @ symbol, which will treat the string literally (it means you don't need a double backslash), e.g.: @"C:\temp".

You may want to convert from an ASCII or Unicode value to a character and vice versa. You can do this by casting or using Convert:

```
char capitalA = (char)65;
char lowercaseA = Convert.ToChar(0x61);
```

Of course we can convert a char to a string using the .ToString( ) method!

```
char exclamation = '!';
string strExclamation = exclamation.ToString( );
```

4.7 • Escape sequences

Some of the more common escape sequences are shown in Table 4-3 on page 70:

Table 4-3 Common escape sequences

Character	ACII respresentation	ASCII value	Escape sequence
Line feed	LF	10 or 0x0A	\n
Carriage return	CR	13 or 0x0D	\r
Backslash	\	92 or 0x5C	\\
Apostrophe	'	39 or 0x27	\'
Quotation mark	"	34 or 0x22	\"

4.8 • Logical operations – Boolean data type

The Boolean data type (bool) is used in cases where only true or false conditions exist. Logic operations can be performed on Boolean and other data types. The logic operations are 'NOT', 'AND', 'OR' and 'XOR' (exclusive or). They are performed with the symbols: !, &, |, and ^. The logic operations and results are shown in Table 4-4.

Table 4-4 Logic Operations

A	B	!A	A & B	A | B	A ^ B
		NOT	AND	OR	EXOR
0	0	1	0	0	0
0	1	1	0	1	1
1	0	0	0	1	1
1	1	0	1	1	0

Example:

```
bool A = false;
bool B = true;
bool AExclusiveOrB;
B = !A;     // NOT A
A = A & B; // A AND B
B = A | B; // A OR B
AExclusiveOrB = (!A & B) | (A & !B);
// or
AExclusiveOrB = A ^ B;
```

4.9 • Mathematical Functions

C# provides the mathematical functions with a Math class. Some of the more common Math tasks are shown below.

Name	**Description**
Abs	Returns the absolute value of a number, greater than a minimum and less than a maximum.
Example:	`decimal absA = Math.Abs(-3.141M);    // absA is 3.141`
Acos, Asin, Atan	Returns the angle in radians for the (cos, sin or tan) of the number.

```
double x = 0.707;    // -1< x <1
double theta = Math.Acos(x);         // theta = 0.7855491..
```

Sin, Cos, Tan Returns the sine, cosine, tangent of an angle measured in radians.

```
double theta = 0.7855491;
double sine = Math.sin(theta);      // sine = 0.70721..
```

Cosh, Sinh, Tanh Returns the hyperbolic (cosine, sine or tangent) of an angle.

```
double theta = 0.707;
double tanh = Math.Tanh(theta);     // tanh = 0.608792..
```

Exp Returns e raised to the specified power.

```
double power = 0.5;
double eToPower = Math.Exp(power); // e^0.5, power = 1.648..
```

IEEERemainder Returns the remainder from the division of two numbers.

```
double rem = Math.IEEERemainder(22.3, 7.0); // 1.300..
```

Log Returns the natural logarithm of a specified number.

```
double ln2 = Math.Log(2.0);          // 0.6931..
```

Log10 Returns the base 10 logarithm of a specified number.

```
double log2 = Math.Log10(2.0);              // 0.3010..
```

Max Returns the larger of two specified numbers.

```
double max = Math.Max(2.0, 3.0);            // 3.0
```

Min Returns the smaller of two numbers.

```
double min = Math.Min(2.0, 3.0);            // 2.0
```

Pow Returns a number raised to a specified power.

```
double eight = Math.Pow(2.0, 3.0);          // 8.0
```

Round Rounds a value to the nearest integer or number of decimal places.

```
double round = Math.Round(12.501);          // 13
```

Sqrt Returns the square root of a specified number.

```
double sqrt = Math.Sqrt(3.0);               // 1.732..
```

Truncate Calculates the integral part of a number.

```
double trunc = Math.Truncate(12.501);  // 12
```

There are many variations of these. For more details and examples, refer to the Microsoft library at: *http://msdn.microsoft.com/en-us/library/4zfefwz9(v=VS.100).aspx*

4.10 • Date and Time

The DateTime is a **structure** and split into a **date** part and a **time** part. A structure (struct) is used to group related variables; we shall see these later.

The date part holds a date, month and year and the time part holds hours, minutes, seconds and milliseconds. The smallest interval between two DateTime values is one hundred nanoseconds and is called a **tick**.

Like everything else, a DateTime has to be declared it before it can be used:

```
DateTime theTime = new DateTime();      // can now use theTime
// or you can set your own date using
DateTime xmas2015 = new DateTime(2015, 12, 25);
// will also contain time - Midnight is default
```

You can also set the hours and minutes using the following:

```
DateTime newDate = new DateTime(2001, 2, 3, 4, 5, 6, 7);
// Sets 3 Feb 2001 04:05:06.0007
```

The current date and time can be found by using the property Now. A difference (a time span) is calculated using **TimeSpan**:

We can find out how many days since Christmas 2014 by declaring that date and finding out today's day and using a TimeSpan subtract the two:

```
// declare Christmas 2014
DateTime xmas2014 = new DateTime(2014, 12, 25);
DateTime theTime = new DateTime();
theTime = DateTime.Now;                     // get time now
MessageBox.Show(theTime.ToString());        // display
TimeSpan tspan = theTime - xmas2014;        // difference
int daysToXmas = tspan.Days;
// can also have .Hours, .Minutes, .Seconds
// and display
MessageBox.Show
("Time since Christmas 2014 =  " + tspan.ToString());
MessageBox.Show
("Days since Christmas 2014 =  " + tspan.Days.ToString());
```

You might also want to change the value of a DateTime variable in your code. For instance, you might want to read a DateTime value from a string entered by your user. (But it might be better to use a DateTimePicker control).

Here's one way to do this is:

```
string strDateString = "7/2/2015 10:45:59 AM";
DateTime myDate = DateTime.Parse(strDateString);
```

4.10.1 • DateTime properties and methods

You might want to extract the date or time from a DateTime object. Some of the DateTime properties are:

Month	xmas2014.Month	// returns 12
Day	xmas2014.Day	// returns 25
DayOfWeek	xmas2014.DayOfWeek	// a Thursday

Other properties include: Hour, Minute, Second, Millisecond.

The DateTime structure also contains methods such as:

Add	adds a timespan		
AddDays	Adds a number of days	xmas2014.AddDays(7);	// new year
AddYears	Adds a number of years	xmas2014.AddYears(1);	// xmas2015

There are also AddMilliseconds, AddSeconds, AddMonths and others.

For more information on the DateTime structure see:

https://msdn.microsoft.com/en-us/library/System.DateTime(v=vs.110).aspx

and for the TimeSpan structure, look at:

https://msdn.microsoft.com/en-us/library/system.timespan(v=vs.110).aspx

4.11 • Nullable data type declaration – '?'

We might need to declare a variable as **null**. For example, we might want to know if a datetime has been set or a number entered. We could intialise the variables to **null** and then test to see if they have been set. But we can also use a question mark in the declaration to do this, for example:

```
DateTime? today = null;
int? nullInt = null;
Point? lastPosition = null;
```

In our code we can use the **HasValue** property to test if it is null (or not) and display its value:

```
if (today.HasValue) { MessageBox.Show("Today!"); }
```

The value can be read using today.Value:

```
MessageBox.Show(today.Value.ToString());
```

4.12 • Scope

At this point it may be useful to mention how variables are accessed and where they are valid. We have been very specific about where we place our declarations. In the snap game in the Self Assessment exercises 3.6 on page 61, we declared the Random object outside of the timer tick code:

```
public partial class Form1 : Form
{
    Random randomColour = new Random(); // declare a random object
    int randomNumber;      // integer to hold a random number
    private void timer1_Tick(object sender, EventArgs e)
```

This meant that when we added the second timer tick code, the Random object could be accessed by both timer1_Tick and timer2_Tick code.

If you didn't do the exercise, perhaps you'd like to try it now. If you did it, try moving the Random declaration into the timer1_Tick code and see what happens. If the Random object is declared inside timer1's code, it can't be accessed by timer2's code.

The **scope** of an identifier (such as a variable or method) refers to the region of code where it is valid and can be accessed. Generally, classes have **public scope** (can be accessed by everything) and methods and variables have **private scope** (only accessible within that class). The public and private keywords allow you to override these defaults.

4.12.1 • Block scope

When an identifier is declared within a block of code or method, i.e. within curly brackets, it is given block scope. It is then accessible within the block but not outside it. For instance:

```
if (true)
{
  int blockVariable=0;                    // blockVariable only exists here.
}
// blockVariable not accessible here
```

4.12.2 • Procedure scope

If a variable is declared within a method such a button click, but outside any curly brackets, it is known as **procedure scope**. The variable only 'exists' whilst the procedure runs.

4.12.3 • Class scope

If a variable or object is declared outside of a method, it can be accessed by all the code in the class and exists until the program ends. This is what we did in the Snap game.

The class code starts after the open curly bracket after the class statement, e.g.:

```
public class Form1 : Form
 {
                    // class code and scope starts here.
```

Identifiers declared at this level are accessible by all the code within the class.

The following code may help explain the scope of some variables.

```
public class Form1 : Form
// class Form1 is public and accessible to other classes.
{
  int ClassVariable;                    // accessible within this class
  private void button1_Click(object sender, EventArgs e)
  {
    int MethodVariable1;                // accessible only in this button click
    ClassVariable = 3;                  // is OK
    {                                           // new block of code
      int BlockVariable;                // only exists in this block
      MethodVariable1 = 0;              // is OK
      BlockVariable = 1;                // is OK
    }
```

```
        BlockVariable = 2;              // is an error – not declared at this level
    }
    private void button2_Click(object sender, EventArgs e)
    {
        int MethodVariable2;            // accessible only in this method
        ClassVariable = 4;              // is OK
        MethodVariable2 = 1;            // is OK
        MethodVariable1 = 5;            // is an error
    }
}
```

You should use private scope where possible, otherwise variables can be accessed by different methods and it makes programs more difficult to understand and debug.

We shall see more on scope and in particular, declaration of methods, when we look at the chapters on methods and objects.

For more examples on scope see the self assessment exercises.

4.13 • Self Assessment Exercises

1. If you didn't try the Snap exercise, do it now and try moving the Random declaration around your code and notice any errors.
2. Watch the sixth video 'Declaring variables and assigning values' in the Virtual Academy at:

   http://www.microsoftvirtualacademy.com/training-courses/c-fundamentals-for-absolute-beginners
3. Watch the videos #7 (Branching with the if statement and conditional operators and #8 'Operators, Expressions and Statements' at the same link.
4. Variables.

   Declare variables with different data types. Try to assign them to each other and see the error messages. Where possible try to cast from one data type to another.
5. Declare some variables in one button click code and see if they can be accessed by separate button click code.
6. Scope.

   Watch the Virtual Academy video #19 'Understanding Scope' and read the Microsoft library on scope:

   https://msdn.microsoft.com/en-us/library/ms973875.aspx

   Investigate scope. Place two buttons on a form and change their button click code as follows. Note the regions of code where the string variables exist.

```
public partial class Form1 : Form
{
    string strClassString = "ClassString";
```

```
private void button1_Click(object sender, EventArgs e)
{
    string strMethodString = "MethodString";
    MessageBox.Show(strMyClassString);    // is OK
    MessageBox.Show(strMethodString);     // is OK
}
private void button2_Click(object sender, EventArgs e)
{
    MessageBox.Show(strClassString);    // is OK
    MessageBox.Show(strMethodString);  // will error
}
```

Move the string declarations around and notice any errors.

Declare a second strClassString on the first line of the button2_Click code as follows, and see what happens.

```
string strClassString = "newString";
```

This is a different strClassString from the first one declared.

7. DateTime exercise.

   Watch the Virtual Academy video #14 'Working with DateTime'. Then write a program that works out how many days there are until your birthday. You could extend this to ask a user for their date of birth.

4.14 • Summary

This chapter has covered the basic C# language constructs of data types, assignment and casting or converting data types. Characters and strings have been seen as well as mathematical and logic operations. Structures, such as DateTime have been seen and the scope of variables has been introduced.

Chapter 5 • The C# Language – arrays, structures and strings

5.1 • Introduction

In this chapter we will cover arrays, structures and strings. Arrays enable us to hold many items of the same data type. Structures are arrays that contain different types of data (for example DateTime). Strings are really an array of characters. We shall see how to declare arrays and strings and see some of the methods associated with them. We shall also see how to declare and use variable size or dynamic, arrays.

5.2 • Arrays

Arrays are used to hold a number of items of the same type of data, we've seen this with the Lines property of the textbox, further examples may be a list of peoples' names, ages, birth dates or salary (but as we shall see, we might combine all of those into a structure and later a database).

To declare an array square brackets '[ ]' are placed after the data type and then its size is set when it is instantiated, as follows:

```
int[] intArray;          // an integer array called intArray.
intArray = new int[20]; // create array with 20 items - from 0 to 19
```

This can be done in one line of code:

```
int[] intArray = new int[20];
```

You can also declare and fill the array with data as follows. The size of the array is calculated from the number of items.

```
int[] intArrayOfFive = { 1, 2, 3, 4, 5 };
double[] dblArrayOfThree = { 1.0, -2.0, 3.0 };
string[] arrayOfNames = { "Peter", "Paul", "Mary" };
```

Individual items in an array are accessed by using a number in the square brackets. The item within the square brackets is known as the **index** and can be an expression. The index **starts at zero**; hence the last index is the size of the array minus one. Using the array declared above, for example:

```
intArray[0] = 5;                       // sets the first element to 5
intArray[1] = intArray[6 * 3 + 1];     // copy the last element [19]
                                       // to the second element
```

If your program accesses an index outside the array a run-time error message will occur. If you don't know how large your array needs to be, you can either create one that you know will be large enough or use a dynamic array type which automatically changes its size to suit. We shall see how to do this later.

Arrays have **properties**, the most useful of which is 'Length' which, as it suggests, provides the length of the array. Hence the last item's index is always Length-1. For example:

```
intArray[intArray.Length - 1] = 25;  // set the last element
```

Arrays also have **methods**. But some of these may not work as you think they might. Some examples are:

- Average – computes the average of the array

  Example: `double dblAverage = intArray.Average();`

- Contains – returns true or false if value is in array or not

  Example:

```
if (intArray.Contains(3)) MessageBox.Show("Array contains '3'");
```

- Copy – copies an array, or part of an array starting at an index

  Example:

```
int[] intArray = { 1, 2, 3, 4, 5 };
int[] intArrayCopy = { -1, -1, -1, -1 };
// copy from intArrayCopy to intArray, starting at index 1
intArrayCopy.CopyTo(intArray, 1);
// intArray now contains 1, -1,-1,-1,-1
```

- BinarySearch – This uses a binary search to find an object in an array. This means the array must be sorted. If the item is not found a negative value is returned, otherwise the index of the item is returned.

  Example:

```
double[] dblArray = { 1.0, 2.1, 3.2, 4.3, 5.4 };
double lookingFor = 2.1;
int indexIs = Array.BinarySearch(dblArray, (object)lookingFor);
if (indexIs > 0) MessageBox.Show("Index is = " + indexIs);
// finds 2.1 at index 1
// but if array is reversed, e.g. 5.4, 4.3, 3.2, 2.1, 1.0
// value 2.1 is NOT found
```

- Reverse – Reverses the elements in the array or portion of the array.

  Example:

```
double[] dblArray = { 1.0, 2.1, 3.2, 4.3, 5.4 };
Array.Reverse(dblArray);
// dblArray now contains:  5.4, 4.3, 3.2, 2.1, 1.0
```

  Note that '`Array.Reverse(dblArray)`' is used, not '`dblArray.Reverse`'.

- Sort – Sorts the elements in an array. This does not sort how you might expect. Whilst an integer array sorts as expected, in the following example of a string array, the result of the sort is 1, 111, 12, 2. It is not 1, 2, 12, 111.

  Example:

```
string[] strArray = { "1", "12", "2", "111" };
Array.Sort(strArray);
// strArray now contains 1, 111, 12, 2
```

  More details on array methods can be found at:

  http://msdn.microsoft.com/en-us/library/system.array_methods(v=VS.71).aspx

5.3 • Multidimensional arrays

Multidimensional arrays, i.e. ones with more than one index can be also be defined. They are defined using a comma between the square brackets: **[,]**. For example a two dimensional array of students' scores would be defined by:

```
int[,] score;      // declare 2D array of integer data type
score = new int[3, 2];  // set size 3 rows by 2 columns
```

This creates an array of three indexes (three students) each with two items, as follows:

	Exam 1	Exam 2
Student 1	score[0,0]	score[0,1]
Student 2	score[1,0]	score[1,1]
Student 3	score[2,0]	score[2,1]

To set the array values use the code:

```
score[0, 1] = 68; // Set's student 1's exam 2 mark
```

Two dimensional arrays can also be defined and initialised in one go, as follows:

```
double[,] twoDArray = { { 0.1, 1.1 }, { 2.1, 3.1 }, { 4.1, 5 } };
// is the same as
double[,] twoDArray = new double[3, 2]
{ { 0.1, 1.1 }, { 2.1, 3.1 }, { 4.1, 5 } };
```

This can be extended to three and more dimensions as follows:

```
int[,,] my3Darray;
my3Darray = new int[2, 3, 4];
my3Darray[1, 2, 3] = 2;
int[,,,] my4Darray;
my4Darray = new int[2, 3, 4, 5];
my4Darray[1, 2, 3, 4] = 6;
```

You can also define multidimensional arrays with irregular sizes. These are known as jagged arrays. The following code shows how an array with 2, 4 and 6 elements may be created:

```
int[][] jagArray = new int[3][];  // create multidimensional array
jagArray[0] = new int[2];         // first array has 2 elements
jagArray[1] = new int[4];         // second array has 4 elements
jagArray[2] = new int[6];         // third array has 6 elements
jagArray[0][1] = 9;               // last in array [0]
jagArray[1][3] = 10;              // last in array [1]
jagArray[2][5] = 11;              // last in array [2]
```

Each jagArray[ ] holds a reference to a single-dimensional integer array.

5.4 • Structures

You might want to create a simple array that contains different data types. For instance, you might want a list of employees which contains their name, age and gender, salary etc. This is called a **structure** but sometimes referred to as a record.

The individual data types in the structure are declared along with a way of accessing and changing their values. We will see this in more detail when we cover **classes**, but for now let's look at an example.

A structure is defined using the keyword 'struct'. The data types are declared then followed by a way of accessing them. The keyword 'this' is used to access the data. In your program you can create (or instantiate) as many versions of the structure as you want and 'this' refers to each individual version instantiated. An example personnel record structure might be as follows:

```
struct personnelRecord
{               // declare the data types
    public string name;
    public int age;
    public double salary;
    public char gender;

    // Provide access to the data.
    // Note the same name (personnelRecord) is used
    // The 'public' declaration allows it to be accessed by your code

    public personnelRecord(string name, int age,
    double salary, char gender)
    {
        this.name = name;
        this.age = age;
        this.salary = salary;
        this.gender = gender;
    }
} // end declaration of struct
```

This has only declared the structure. It still needs to be instantiated in our program using the 'new' keyword, as we did with arrays. This way we can declare many different copies of it should we need to do so (e.g. copies for academic staff, technical staff, under-graduate and post-graduate students).

Remember what we said about scope. To provide access to the entire program, the structure must be declared at the top of the class, e.g. after the line of code: public class Form1 : Form {

A personnel list array of type personnelRecord is instantiated and its elements accessed as follows:

```
// one structure called myEmployees
personnelRecord myEmployees = new personnelRecord();
myEmployees.age = 21;
```

```
myEmployees.gender = 'M';
// another called myStudents
personnelRecord myStudents = new personnelRecord();
// Or more usefully a personnelList of 10:
personnelRecord[] personnelList = new personnelRecord[10];
personnelList[0].name = "John Allwork";
personnelList[9].salary = 9999.99;
```

Note we use the dot notation to access the data just as we did with properties for our controls.

You might want to have some actions for your personnel such as change name or increase age or salary – these would be its methods. This leads us to classes and object oriented programming, which we will cover later.

5.4.1 • The public declaration

We covered the public keyword briefly in the previous chapter. In the above code we have declared the individual variables in the structure as 'public'. If we had not done this, the items would only exist within the structure's block of code (i.e. within the curly brackets). Obviously we want to use these items outside the structure and declaring them as **public** allows this to happen. We will cover this in more detail in the chapters on classes and objects.

See the self assessment exercises for more on structures.

5.5 • Character arrays and strings

Characters are variables of type char that hold a keyboard character (e.g. letters, numbers and symbols). Characters are held in UTF-8 format, which enables any language character to be used and is backward compatible with ASCII. UTF-8 is a way of encoding the more universal Unicode characters.

Strings are a special type of array that holds characters.

As we have seen the data held in a text box is a string and individual characters from a text box can be treated as an array element as follows:

```
char aChar;                          // declare a char
aChar = textBox1.Text[2];            // read 3rd character from textbox
textBox1.Text = aChar.ToString();    // convert char to string
                                     // and display in the textbox
```

Note the conversion from the char to the string to allow us to write back to the text box.

You can declare an array of chars as follows:

```
char[] charArray;
charArray = new chr[20];           // 20 elements in the array - 0 to 19
                                   // or you can use
char[] chrArray = { 'a', 'b', 'c', 'd' };   // use single quote
chrArray[2] = '4';                          // change 'c' to '4'
```

5.6 • String manipulation

C# .NET provides a number of methods to manipulate strings such as compare, split, search, change case etc.

Remember we declare a string using double quotation marks:

```
string welcomeString = "Hi there!";
```

We have already seen how we can concatenate strings (add one string onto the end of another) using the + operator, e.g.:

```
MessageBox.Show("This string has" + " this string added to it");
```

Of course the strings could have been previously declared and used as follows:

```
string firstString = "This string has";
string secondString = " this string added to it";
MessageBox.Show(firstString + secondString);
```

We can determine the length of a string with the Length property:

```
int intLength;
string strOfChars = "This string has 29 characters";
intLength = strOfChars.Length;
MessageBox.Show(intLength.ToString());   // will display 29
```

Or we could have had:

```
MessageBox.Show((("This string has 29 characters").Length).ToString());
```

5.7 • String conversion

Just to remind you how to convert between strings and numbers, you can convert from integers or floating point numbers to strings using the .ToString( ) method:

```
int i = 10;
float f = 123456.22f;
double d = 123.567;
MessageBox.Show(
"int= " + i.ToString() + " float= " + f.ToString() + " double= " + d.ToString());
```

To convert from a string to a number, use the **Parse** method. There are many Parse methods. int.Parse and Int32.Parse convert from a string to an integer and float.Parse and double.Parse convert from a string to a floating point number, etc. For example:

```
string strFpNo = "123456.22";
string strIntNo = "12345";
MessageBox.Show("decimal= " + decimal.Parse(strFpNo));
MessageBox.Show("float= " + float.Parse(strFpNo));
MessageBox.Show("integer= " + int.Parse(strIntNo));
```

5.8 • String methods

5.8.1 • The Contains( ) method

You can determine if a character or string is within another using the **Contains( )** method. It returns a Boolean 'true' or 'false'. We saw this in the Array section.

The following code displays 'false':

```
string strFpNo = "123456.22";
MessageBox.Show(strFpNo.Contains("7").ToString());
```

5.8.2 • The Substring( ) method

Part of a string can be retrieved using the **Substring()** method. The start position and number of characters is passed to the method and it returns the string. The first character is 0. For example:

```
MessageBox.Show(("Mary had a little lamb").Substring(0, 4));
// displays 'Mary'
MessageBox.Show(("Mary had a little lamb").Substring(2, 5));
// displays 'ry ha'
```

You might like to see what happens if you try to extract data past the end of a string.

5.8.3 • The IndexOf and IndexOfAny( ) methods

You can determine the position of one string within another using the **IndexOf( )** method. The string you wish to find is passed to the method and it returns the index of the string or -1 if it isn't found. This method is case sensitive. For example:

```
MessageBox.Show(("Mary had a little lamb").IndexOf("ry ha").ToString());
// displays 2
MessageBox.Show(("Mary had a little lamb").IndexOf("mar").ToString());
// displays -1. "mar" not found
```

This method can also be called with an integer starting index and a number of characters to search. For example:

- IndexOf(searchString);
- IndexOf(searchString, startIndex);
- IndexOf(searchString, startIndex, numberOfCharsToSearch);

Examples:

```
MessageBox.Show(("Mary had a lamb").IndexOf("ry ha", 1).ToString());
// finds 'ry ha' at second index and displays 2
MessageBox.Show(("Mary had a lamb").IndexOf("ry ha", 6).ToString());
// starts searching at index 6, doesn't find 'ry ha', and displays -1
MessageBox.Show(("Mary had a lamb").IndexOf("ry ha", 1, 2).ToString());
// starts at index 1, looks for 2 characters,
// doesn't find 'ry ha' and displays -1
MessageBox.Show(("Mary had a lamb").IndexOf("ry ha", 1, 6).ToString());
 // starts at index 1, looks for 6 characters, finds 'ry ha' and displays 2
```

The **IndexOfAny( )** method returns the first occurrence of any letters specified in a char array. For example:

```
string letters = "abcedfghABC %^ &";
char[] searchLetters = { 'c', 'A', '$' };
int charPos = letters.IndexOfAny(searchLetters);  // finds 'c' at index 2.
```

The methods **LastIndexOf( )** and **LastIndexOfAny( )** perform the same operations but start at the end of the string.

5.8.4 • Dealing with spaces– the Trim and Remove methods

The IndexOf( ) method could be used to find spaces, but the following methods are available to find and deal with spaces:

Trim( )	Removes spaces from the beginning and end of a string.
TrimEnd( )	Removes spaces from the end of a string.
TrimStart( )	Removes spaces from the beginning of a string.
Remove( )	Removes a specified number of spaces from a position in a string.

Try these out for yourself.

5.8.5 • The Replace method

Strings can easily be replaced using the Replace( ) method. The text to be replaced and the new text are both passed to the method. The string is searched and the text replaced. For example:

```
string strMaryText = "Mary had a little lamb";
string strReplacedText = strMaryText.Replace("little lamb", "black sheep");
MessageBox.Show(strReplacedText);
// displays "Mary had a black sheep"
```

Note that <u>all</u> occurrences are replaced, so the following code replaces every letter 'a' with the letter 'i':

```
string strMaryText = "Mary had a little lamb";
string strReplacedText = strMaryText.Replace("a", "i");
MessageBox.Show(strReplacedText);
// displays "Miry hid i little limb"
```

5.8.6 • The Split method - parsing strings

Strings can be parsed and individual words extracted by using the **Split( )** method. This uses delimiter characters as markers. This method takes an array of chars containing the chars to be used as delimiters, e.g. spaces, commas colons etc. and the individual words between these are extracted.

The following code uses the delimiter characters: space, comma, full stop, colon and tab to extract the individual words from the string: 'Delimiters are:colon\ttab space,comma. fullStop end'

It displays the original text and finds 8 words as shown in Figure 5-1 and Figure 5-2. It then displays them individually.

```
char[] delimiterChars = { ' ', ',', '.', ':', '\t' };
//delimiter characters are: space, comma, full stop, colon and tab
string text = "Delimiters are:colon\ttab space,comma.fullStop end";
MessageBox.Show("Original text: " + text);
// get words from string 'text' and place in an array called 'words'
string[] words = text.Split(delimiterChars);
// display number of words found
MessageBox.Show("Number of words in text:" + words.Length);
// and display the individual wordsl
for (int i = 0; i < words.Length; i++)
{
    MessageBox.Show(words[i]);
  }
```

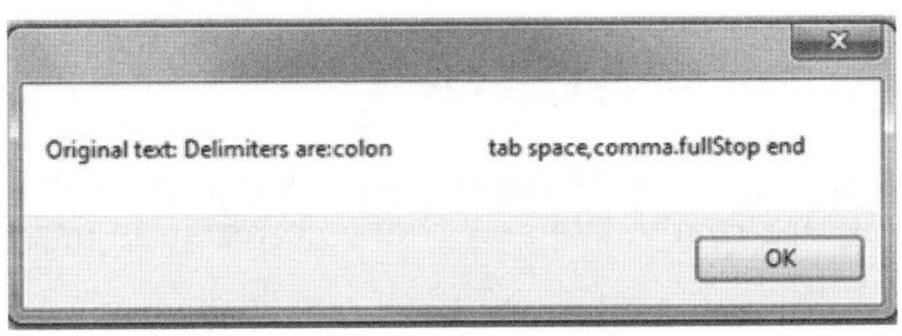

Figure 5-1 Delimiter text

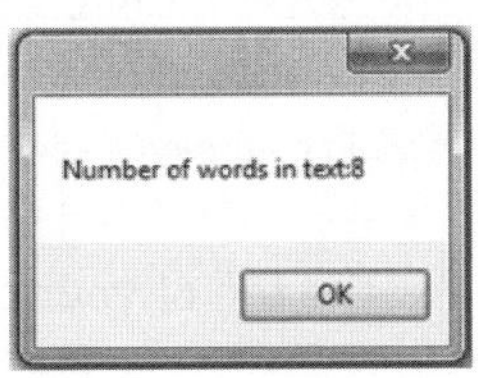

Figure 5-2 Number of words found

Notice that the size of the string array 'words' was calculated by the program.

As a way of introduction, a foreach loop could have been used instead of the for loop to display the strings, as follows. We will see this later.

```
foreach (string s in words)     // we'll see the foreach statement later
{
    MessageBox.Show(s);
}
```

5.8.7 • Upper and lower case methods

The **ToUpper()** and **ToLower()** methods convert a string to upper case and to lower case respectively. For example:

```
text = text.ToUpper();
```

5.8.8 • Padding strings

You can fill strings (pad them out) with spaces or a character on the left or the right using

myString.PadLeft(Int32),

myString.PadLeft(Int32, paddingChar),

myString.PadRight(Int32), and

myString.PadRight(Int32, paddingChar).

For instance:

```
string myString = "7_chars";
char paddingChar = '.';
string 9_chars = myString.PadLeft(9, paddingChar);  // 9_chars is ..7_chars
```

Finally you might want to check if your string is null or empty. This is achieved with the **String.IsNullOrEmpty( )** method. The following code tests string 's', and sets it to `"is null or empty"` if it is null or empty.

```
if (string.IsNullOrEmpty(s)) s = "is null or empty";
```

You can also test if the string is empty: `if (s == string.Empty) s = "is empty";`

5.9 • Dynamic Arrays: The ArrayList Class

We will now move on to some more in-depth data structures. If you don't need this yet, come back when you are ready. We saw these commands used with the List box in Section 2.4 on page 44.

If you don't know how big your array will be you can use a dynamic array. Dynamic arrays change their size as required as the program runs. They are implemented using an **ArrayList**. The ArrayList is found in the System.Collections namespace (library) and an ArrayList (here it is called arrayOfItems) is declared as follows:

```
System.Collections.ArrayList arrayOfItems =
    new System.Collections.ArrayList();
```

If you add 'using System.Collections;' at the top of your code, you can dispense with it here.

You do not have to specify a data type for an ArrayList; any data type can be stored at any index. They also have properties and methods. The most useful property is Count. The Add and Remove methods are used to add and remove items from the list. They can be searched to see if they contain a particular item and also cleared. As any data type can be stored in an ArrayList, a GetType( ) method is available to determine the data type. A list of the more important properties and methods is shown in Table 5-1 on page 87. We saw these when we looked at the List box.

Table 5-1 ArrayList properties and methods

Property	Description
Capacity	Set or get the maximum size
Count	Gets the number of elements in the arraylist
Method	
Add	Adds an item to the end of the list
Clear	Deletes all the elements from the list
Contains	Determines if an element is in the list
Insert	Inserts an element at the specific index
Remove	Removes first occurrence of the object
ToArray	Copies the arraylist to an array

Here's some example code using ArrayLists:

```
System.Collections.ArrayList arrayOfItems =
    new System.Collections.ArrayList();
arrayOfItems.Add(10);                  // add an integer to the list
arrayOfItems.Add(3.141);              // add a double to the list
arrayOfItems.Add("string");           // add a string to the list
int listCount = arrayOfItems.Count; // How many items?
arrayOfItems.Remove(3.141);            // remove first occurrence of 3.141
arrayOfItems.RemoveAt(1);              // remove second item - now ("string")
arrayOfItems.Insert(0, "I'm first");          // new first item
arrayOfItems[1] = (int)arrayOfItems[1] + 1;  // add 1 - note cast to int
foreach (var i in arrayOfItems)              // display list - only 2 items
{
    MessageBox.Show(i.ToString() + " is type: " + i.GetType());
}
arrayOfItems.Clear();                    // Clear the arrayList
```

This time we've used, 'foreach' to loop through the ArrayList.

See the Self Assessment Exercises for more examples.

As well as the ArrayList class, the System.Collection namespace contains other classes that deal with collections of data, including:

- Stack (a last-in, first-out collection),
- Queue (a first-in, first-out collection),
- SortedList (a collection that can be sorted by a key and can be accessed by key or data) and
- HashTable (a sparsely populated collection of data that can be accessed by a key).

5.10 • Collections – the System.Collection.Generic namespace

The System.Collection.Generic namespace contains the classes mentioned above. With collections, you specify the data type stored. This provides a check at compile time rather than at run-time. Consequently, there is less coding needed to check for run-time errors, and as casting the objects is not needed, there is improved efficiency.

The classes are:

- Dictionary<K, V> An unordered collection of key and value pairs <K, V> that can be accessed by a key.
- LinkedList<T> A list containing a data type <T> where each item points to the previous and next ones. Items can be removed from or added to the lists.
- List<T> A generic ArrayList containing a data type <T>.
- Queue<T> A generic Queue containing a data type <T>.
- SortedDictionary<K, V> A Dictionary with binary-tree sorted values <V>, accessed by key <K>.
- SortedList<K, V> A generic SortedList of values <V>, accessed by key <K>.
- Stack<T> A generic Stack.

The <T> means you have to specify the type, and the <K, V> means you have to specify a Key type and a Value type. Let's explain with a few examples.

Example 1: List<T>

This creates a list of declared data type (<T>). This is has an interface known as **ICollection**, which basically provides the properties Capacity and Count, as well as the methods we have seen (Add, Clear, Contains, CopyTo, Remove), but you define the data type in the list. It also provides methods to search, sort, and manipulate lists.

The following code snippet shows the code for two buttons that add and remove items.

See the self assessment exercises if you wish to try this.

Don't forget you will need using System.Collections.Generic; at the top of your code. But it should already be there.

The List is declared with the data type it is to hold:

```
List<int> numberList = new List<int>();
private void btnAdd_Click(object sender, EventArgs e)
{
    // adds a random number to the list and displays list
    Random randomNumber = new Random(); // new random number
    int rndNo = randomNumber.Next(10);      // number from 0 to 9
    // Add the number to the list
    numberList.Add(rndNo);
    // display the list items
    string strItems = string.Empty;
    for (int i = 0; i < numberList.Count; i++)
    {
        strItems += "random number " + numberList[i].ToString() +
            " is position " + i.ToString() + "\r\n";
    }
```

```
        MessageBox.Show(strItems);
    } // end of btnAdd
    // Remove button code
    private void btnRemove_Click(object sender, EventArgs e)
    {
        // removes an item at a random postion from the list
        Random randomNumber = new Random(); // new random number
        // remove a random item from the list
        if (numberList.Count > 1)
            numberList.RemoveAt(randomNumber.Next(numberList.Count));
        // display the list items
        string strItems = string.Empty;
        for (int i = 0; i < numberList.Count; i++)
        {
            strItems += "random number " + numberList[i].ToString() +
               " is position " + i.ToString() + "\r\n";
        }
        MessageBox.Show(strItems);
    } // end btnRemove
```

Note that if you try to add a non-integer value as follows, a compile-time error occurs.

```
numberList.Add("A string"); // will not compile
```

At this point we should mention LINQ (Language Integrated Query) which provides and method of querying, selecting and sorting data without the need for any database. There is more on LINQ in section 15.7 on page 224

Example 2: Dictionary<K, V>

A Dictionary holds two linked types, they are a unique **key** <K>, used to lookup the table and a corresponding **value** <V>. For instance a Dictionary could hold two strings: a word and its definition, synonym, antonym or foreign language equivalent. It could hold an integer and a double, say for a lookup table. In the following example we'll use a stock list with the key the item in stock (a fruit) and the value the number in stock.

The advantages of using a Dictionary over a 2D array are that they can be manipulated, added to, removed, sorted etc.

The key and the value is also a data structure, called a **KeyValuePair**.

Firstly, don't forget to add using System.Collections.Generic; at the top of the code if it isn't already there.

The dictionary is declared using the code:

```
Dictionary<string, int> myStock = new Dictionary<string, int>( );
```

Note the data types are declared between the '<' and '>' brackets, and the '( )' brackets are also used.

The key is a string containing the fruit and the value is the amount in stock.

Items are added using the Add method:

```
myStock.Add("apples",1);
myStock.Add("oranges", 2);
myStock.Add("bananas", 3);
```

The new fruits (the keys) will automatically be created. If a key already exists, an error will occur.

Once added to the dictionary, the value can be read using:

```
int stockValue = myStock["oranges"] ;
```

The value can be changed or incremented as follows:

```
myStock["oranges"] = 4;     // four in stock now
myStock["oranges"]++;       // increment stock
```

To take an item from stock the value is decremented using:

```
myStock["apples"] = myStock["apples"] -1;     // or
myStock["apples"] --;                         // (minus, minus) decrement stock
```

Items can be removed from stock completely using the code:

```
myStock.Remove("bananas");
```

New items can also be added using the key as follows:

```
// If a key does not exist, a new key/value pair is added.
myStock["pineapple"] = 12;
```

The easiest way to access the dictionary (stock) is to use the **foreach** code:

```
foreach (KeyValuePair<string, int> kvPair in myStock)
{
   MessageBox.Show("Key = " + kvPair.Key + " Value = " + kvPair.Value);
}
```

The keys and values can be displayed as follows:

```
// display keys
foreach (string s in myStock.Keys)   // myStock.Keys is a string
{
   MessageBox.Show("Keys = " + s);
}

// display values
foreach (int i in myStock.Values)       // myStock.Values is an int
{
   MessageBox.Show("Values = " + i);
}
```

You can't find the keys using code such as 'myStock.Keys[0]', you have to copy them to a List of myStock.Keys for example:

```
List<string> keys = new List<string>(myStock.Keys);
// the List 'keys' data type is a string
// keys are now in the list keys[i]
// display them and their values
for (int i = 0; i < keys.Count; i++)
{
   MessageBox.Show("Key is " + keys[i].ToString() +
 ", Value is " + myStock[keys[i]].ToString());
}
```

Finally items can be removed and the dictionary checked if it contains a key as follows:

```
// remove the bananas from stock
myStock.Remove("bananas");

// see if they are still there using 'ContainsKey'
if (myStock.ContainsKey("bananas"))
  MessageBox.Show("Banana stock is " + myStock["bananas"].ToString());
else
  MessageBox.Show("Yes, we have no bananas");
```

You can also use myStock.ContainsKey().

There is more in the Self Assessment exercises.

5.11 • Self Assessment Exercises

1. Watch the Virtual Academy video #10 on 'Creating arrays of Values' and #22 'Working with Collections'
2. Declare an array of 5 double values and then instantiate it using:

   ```
   double[ ] myDblArray;
   myDblArray = new double[5];
   ```

   Write a program to fill the array with data in a 'for' loop using the .Length property.
3. Watch the Virtual Academy video #13 on 'Working with Strings'
4. Declare a string array and fill it with data in one statement using:

   ```
   string[ ] myStrArray = { "str1", "str2", "str3", "str4", "str5" };
   ```

   Write a program to display the values using a 'for' loop, then using a foreach loop (see next chapter)
5. Declare a multidimensional array of students' scores for 5 students and 3 scores. *Hint: see section 5.3 on page 79*:

Fill the table for the first and second scores and calculate the third score as 60% score1 + 40% score2.

Extend the program to display the total score (score3).

See if you can use the array method 'Average' to display the average mark.

6. Structures - 1

   a. You might find this useful to do as we start on object oriented programming.

   b. Create a new Windows application called Structures and place a button on the form. Declare the structure and add the button click code, so that the code is as follows:

```
struct personnelRecord
{
    public string name;
    public int age;
    public double salary;
    public char gender;
    public personnelRecord(string name, int age,
                                    double salary, char gender)
    {
        this.name = name;
        this.age = age;
        this.salary = salary;
        this.gender = gender;
    }
} // end declaration of struct
private void button1_Click(object sender, EventArgs e)
{
    personnelRecord[] PersonnelList = new personnelRecord[10];
    PersonnelList[0].name = "Freda Bloggs";
    PersonnelList[1].age = 21;
    PersonnelList[5].salary = 20000;
    PersonnelList[9].gender = 'F';
    MessageBox.Show("Name is " + PersonnelList[0].name +
      "\n\rage is " + PersonnelList[1].age +
      "\n\rsalary is " + PersonnelList[5].salary +
      "\n\rgender is " + PersonnelList[9].gender);
} // end button click
```

Modify this code so that the information for each person is requested and then displayed.

7. Structures - 2

   a. Create a structure for a car dealership with 3 items, Car Name (string), Car mileage (int) and Price (float).

   b. Create an array of 5 cars and set the name, mileage and price for some of the cars.

c. Display all the car's information on a button click, using messageBox. Show( );

8. Strings

Declare a string called 'str29Chars' and set it to: "This string has 29 characters".

Display the length of the string using the .Length property.

a. 7.1 Use the substring method to display the first eleven characters in the string, e.g:

MessageBox.Show(("Mary had a little lamb").Substring(0,4));

// displays 'Mary'

b. 7.2 Determine the starting index of the number 29 using the IndexOf( ) method, e.g:

MessageBox.Show(("Mary had a lamb").IndexOf("ry ha").ToString( ));

// displays 2

c. Declare a new string 'str33', copy the 'str29Chars' string to it and replace the number 29 with 33 in 'str33' using the Replace( ) method, e.g:

string strMaryText = "Mary had a little lamb";

string strReplacedText = strMaryText.Replace("lamb", "sheep");

d. Use the .CompareTo( ) method to compare the strings 'str33' and 'str29Chars'and note the value that is returned.

9. Dynamic arrays using Arraylist

To show how we declare, add and clear an ArrayList, try this exercise which randomly adds an integer, a number or a string to an ArrayList and copies to a listbox.

Start a new project and add a ListBox and two buttons on the form, Change the Text for button 1 to 'Add item' and for button 2 to 'Clear'. See Figure 5-3.

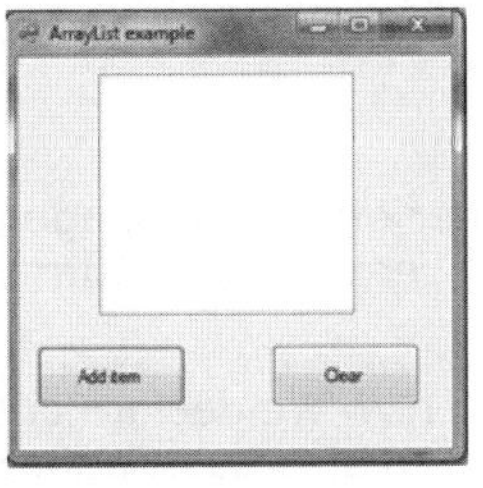

Figure 5-3 ArrayList example

The code to declare the ArrayList and for the button clicks is as follows:

```
private System.Collections.ArrayList arrayOfItems
    = new System.Collections.ArrayList();
private void button1_Click(object sender, EventArgs e)
{
    Random randomNumber = new Random();      // new random number
    int rndNo = randomNumber.Next(3);        // number from 0 to 2
    switch (rndNo)  // get random item to add to arrayOfItems
```

```
            {
                case 0:
                    arrayOfItems.Add(randomNumber.Next(10));  // add integer
                    break;
                case 1:
                    arrayOfItems.Add(randomNumber.Next(10) * Math.PI); // add fp
                    break;
                case 2:
                    arrayOfItems.Add("string");              // add string
                    break;
            }
            listBox1.Items.Clear();  // clear listbox of old items
            // and copy arrayOfItems to listbox
            for (int i = 0; i < arrayOfItems.Count; i++)
            {
                listBox1.Items.Add(arrayOfItems[i]);  // add items to the listbox
            }
        }
        private void button2_Click(object sender, EventArgs e)
        {
            arrayOfItems.Clear();
        }
```

10. Using a Dictionary

    Create a stock inventory using a Dictionary. Place a list box containing stock items (e.g. fruit) and add buttons and code to increment and decrement stock by choosing items from the list box. Add a button to remove an item completely and also to add a new item to the list box and the stock. Use a List to display all the keys in the Dictionary.

5.12 • Summary

This has been a very detailed chapter on the language and used some commands (such as foreach) that we will cover later. Feel free to return to read the parts you want and return to this when you need.

We have looked at arrays, and seen how we declare and use single and multi-dimensional arrays. We have seen how to declare a structure, an array that contains different data types, which will lead us into object oriented code later. We have seen character arrays and strings, and some of the many string handling operations have been seen.

We have seen some advanced data handling techniques in creating dynamic arrays with the ArrayList object, and some of the generic Collections items such as List and Dictionary.

Chapter 6 • Program Flow, Loops and Decisions

6.1 • Introduction

We have done quite a lot so far, but not written any detailed C# code. We will do this now and start by making some decisions.

Sooner or later your program will need to make a decision and alter its course. There are five basic ways a C# program controls the flow of the program, they are:

- if .. else
- switch .. case
- for and foreach
- while
- do-while

We shall look at each of these in turn and also look at exception handling.

6.2 • The if statement

The simplest decision making construct is the 'if' statement. It takes the form of:

```
if ( condition )
{
  statement(s)
}
```

The condition is a logical comparison e.g. equal, less than, greater than, which produces a true or false (a Boolean) answer. The condition must be enclosed in brackets, for example:

```
if ( bankBalance > 1000000 )
{
  MessageBox.Show ("I'm a millionaire");
}
```

If there is only one statement (as above) it doesn't need to be in curly brackets, but if there is more than one statement they must be enclosed in curly brackets, so it's good practice to use them.

The test does not have to be a simple one; it can test complicated expressions so long as there is a true or false result.

The logical comparisons take the following forms as shown in Table 6-1 on page 96:

Table 6-1 Operators

Operator	English	Example
==	is equal to	(two + two) == 4
!=	is not equal to	(one + two) != 4
<	is less than	X < 2
<=	is less than or equal to	Y <= 3
>	is greater than	X > Y
>=	is greater than or equal to	(X+Y) >= Z

6.2.1 • The if .. else statement

The 'if' statement can be extended by using an 'else' clause. This is the if .. else statement and takes the form of:

```
if ( condition )
{
  statement1
}
else
{
  statement2
}
```

Here statement1 is executed if the condition is true and statement2 is executed if the condition is false. For example:

```
if ( expenditure > income )
{
  MessageBox.Show ("Miserable");   // if expenditure > income
}
else
{
  MessageBox.Show ("Happy");                 // if expenditure =< income
}
```

You can have multiple statements for either statement1 or statement2, so long as they are contained within curly brackets.

Additional if .. else statements can be included within other if .. else statements. However you can still have only one ending else statement, e.g.:

```
if ( condition )
{
  statement(s)
}
```

```
else if ( condition )
{
  statement(s)
}
else if ( condition )
{
  statement(s)
}
. .
// more of the same
else
{
  last statement(s) – executed if all the above fail
}
```

6.2.2 • The if .. else shortcut

You can use, or may see, the question mark and colon shortcut for if else: ' ? : '

The shortcut is:

condition ? [true statements] : [false statements] ;

For example the code:

```
if (x != 0.0)
  s = Math.Sin(x)/x;
else
  s = 1.0;
```

becomes:

```
s = x != 0.0 ? Math.Sin(x)/x : 1.0;
```

I'll let you decide which is more readable.

6.2.3 • The ?? null-coalescing operator

The **??** operator is called the null-coalescing operator. It returns the left-hand side if it is not null, otherwise it returns the right-hand side. This is a useful test if you are likely to get a null somewhere in your program. Consider the following. If string s is not null, the Show() method will display the string, otherwise (s is null) "**s is null**" will be displayed.

```
// Display the value of s if it's NOT null otherwise,
// display the string "It's null".
MessageBox.Show(s ?? "s is null");
```

In other words: X ?? y evaluates to y if x is `null`, to x otherwise.

6.2.4 • The ?. and ?[] operators

This has been added in C# version 6.0. Like the ?? operator, they test for a null but are used before performing accessing a member (dot notation) or index operation. They help in writing shorter code. For instance:

```
// assuming int array of words
int? length = words?.Length; // null if words is null or empty
int? firstWord = words?[0];  // null if words is null or empty
```

see: *https://msdn.microsoft.com/en-us/library/dn986595(v=vs.140).aspx*

6.3 • The switch statement

There may come a time when there you have multiple if or if.. else statements, e.g.

```
int age = input;
string s;
if(age == 12) { s = "you are nearly a teenager"; }
if(age == 13) { s = "you are a teenager"; }
if(age == 18) { s = "you can vote"; }
if(age == 20) { s = "you are no longer a teenager"; }
if(age == 21) { s = "you're an adult - congratulations"; }
```

The switch statement makes programming this slightly easier and more readable. The format is:

```
switch ( expression )
{
case statement(s)
default statement
}
```

The expression must be an integer or a string which evaluates to one of the case or the statements. The statement(s) that match the case are executed. If there is no match, the default statement is executed, but you don't have to have a default statement block.

The code above would become:

```
switch (age)
{
    case 12:
        {
            MessageBox.Show("You are nearly a teenager "); break;
        }
    case 13:
        {
            MessageBox.Show("You are a teenager"); break;
        }
    case 18:
        {
```

```
                MessageBox.Show("You can vote"); break;
            }
        case 20:
            {
                MessageBox.Show("You are no longer a teenager"); break;
            }
        case 21:
            {
                MessageBox.Show("You're an adult now"); break;
            }
        default:
            {
                MessageBox.Show("You are not 12, 13, 18, 20 or 21.");
                break;
            }
    }
```

Note the break statement. The break ends the case statement. C# does not support an implicit fall through from one case label to the next. You will get an error if the case statements do not end with either a break or a goto statement. The only exception is if a case statement has no code. For example, you can have:

```
case 6:         // no code  – will go to next case
case 7:         // no code  – will go to next case
case 8: MessageBox.Show ("executed for values of 6, 7, or 8"); break;
```

You can't have more than one condition in a case. You can't have the following:

```
case 6, 7, 8 : MessageBox.Show ("You are 6, 7, or 8") ;
// This will error
```

You can however use the goto statement to change the flow. For instance you could have:

```
case 6:
 {
  MessageBox.Show ("You are 6");
  goto case 8;
 }
case 7:
 {
  MessageBox.Show ("You are 7");
  goto case 8;
 }
case 8:
 {
  MessageBox.Show ("executed for values of 6, 7, or 8");
  break;
 }
```

6.3.1 • The goto statement

You may be surprised to see the goto statement. C# allows a goto jump to a labelled statement, but the label must be within the scope of the jump. This means you can jump out of a statement block, loop, class or 'finally' block.

6.3.2 • Switching on a string variable

As stated earlier, you can also switch on a string variable, for example:

```
switch (textBox1.Text)
{
    case "cut": MessageBox.Show("cut"); break;
    case "copy": MessageBox.Show("copy"); break;
    case "paste": MessageBox.Show("paste"); break;
}
```

6.4 • Looping - The for (and forr) statements

The for loop statement is used when you know the start and finish points of the loop. The construct is:

```
for (variable = start expression ; end condition ; increment expression )
 {
  statement(s)
 }
```

The first statement is executed once only at the beginning of the loop and is normally an initialization statement (e.g. int i = 1;). The end condition determines when the loop terminates - this is evaluated at the beginning of each loop. Finally, the increment (or decrement) expression is executed each iteration of the loop. If the increment expression is an empty statement (a semicolon by itself) the loop will never terminate. You can use the break statement to terminate the loop early.

Example: Initializing an array

Suppose you wish to set an array with its index: a loop will easily do it. The loop code is

```
for (int count = 0 ; count <10 ; count++)
 {
  intArray [count] = count;
 }
```

This declares and sets the loop variable 'count' to 0. The end condition (count < 10) is performed, and count is incremented by one each time around the loop (count ++). This continues until count reaches the value 10. The loop will be executed ten times with values for count from 0 to 9.

You can change the loop variable by a value other than one if you change 'count++' to say 'count=count+3, or 'count=count-5'.

Note that the increment/decrement expression does NOT end with a semicolon, and the editor will highlight this as an error.

If the loop variable is declared within the loop as above (int count =0) it only exists within the loop. Remember what we said about scope.

The editor automatically indents the code which helps to show the content of a loop. It is also a good idea to add a comment at the end of loops to aid documentation (e.g. // end of count loop). As mentioned you can use the break statement to finish the loop early.

Points to note:

- The loop variable can only be an integer.
- The loop variable is initialized inside the 'for' loop; you don't have to initialize it beforehand.
- The loop variable can start with any integer number.
- You should not alter the loop variable within the loop.
- The terminal value does not have to be a number; it can be a variable, say N, as long as it is defined before entering the loop.
- **Hint:** Using the tab key will display the for loop **code snippet**. Type 'for' and hit the tab key twice, then just change the parts you need:

```
for (int i = 0; i < length; i++)
```

- The loop variable may be decremented rather than incremented by using count-- or count=count-n as the increment expression. You can type forr and press the tab key for this code snippet:

```
}
// typing forr and hitting the tab key twice provides
for (int i = length - 1; i >= 0 ; i--)
{
```

6.4.1 • Code snippets

As seen Visual Studio will provide the outline of code for you – just type the keyword and hit the tab key twice. Try it now, say for 'switch' and 'while' code snippets.

Other default code snippets are detailed at:

http://msdn.microsoft.com/en-us/library/z41h7fat%28VS.80%29.aspx

6.4.2 • The foreach statement

C# provides a 'foreach' loop. This provides a simple way to iterate through all the elements of an array or collection of objects such as a List. You do not have to specify an end condition or an increment. Typing 'foreach' and pressing the tab key twice produces the code snippet:

```
foreach (var item in collection)
{

}
```

The following example creates an array called numbers and iterates through it with the foreach statement:

```
int[] numbers = { 4, 1, 6, -5, 3, 2, -2, 1, 0 };

  foreach (int i in numbers)
  {
      MessageBox.Show(i.ToString());
  }
```

When this program runs it displays the values in the array, (4, 1, 6 etc.) not the value of i. This should be used for reading arrays and object data only, not setting values.

We saw this in the chapter on arrays and collections and you might like to revisit that example.

6.5 • The while and do-while statements

The while or do-while loops are used when the loop variable has to be changed by a varying amount or a test occurs within the loop.

The while loop

The format of the while loop is:

```
while (expression)
{
   statement(s)
}
```

The expression is evaluated at the beginning of the loop, and the statements are executed while the expression is true.

The do-while loop

This is similar to the while loop except that the expression is evaluated at the end of the loop:

```
do
{
   statement(s)
}
while (expression);                         // Note the semicolon
```

The **do-while** is convenient to use when the statements within the loop must be executed at least once. For example, when reading information from a file, keyboard or some input, you know that you will always read at least one character:

6.6 • Exceptions. The try-catch code

Your programs may error at run-time. These are known as exceptions. For instance, exceptions can happen on something as simple as a divide by zero, converting a blank textbox field into a number, or opening a file that doesn't exist or is already in use by another application. The operating system will trap exceptions and display a message, but your program should really deal with your exceptions and display relevant messages to your user.

C# provides 'try' and 'catch' code (along with 'throw' and 'finally') to deal with exceptions, trapping them out and allowing your code to deal with the exceptions. Your program can 'try' a section of code and if any exceptions occur, deal with them in the 'catch' code.

Let's see how we can trap a divide by zero error.

Exercise: Try and catch code

Start a new project and add a button to the form. Add the follow exception code to the button click:

```
int number1 = 123, zero = 0;
try
{
    number1 = number1 / zero; // will error
}
catch (DivideByZeroException)
{
    MessageBox.Show("You divided by zero!");
}
```

You can leave out the 'DivideByZeroException' part of the catch statement, in which case all exceptions will be trapped. There are lots of different types of exceptions. To view them all, type any letter after the opening bracket for the catch and the IntelliSense will display them, see Figure 6-1.

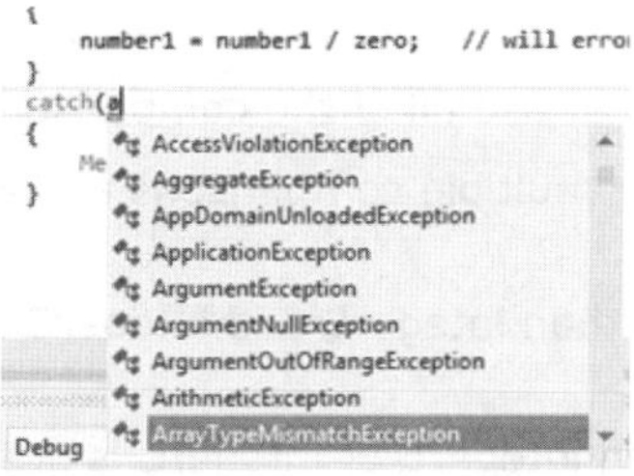

Figure 6-1 Catch exceptions

The numbers to be divided might have been read from a text box. To ensure a valid number has been entered into the text box, you could check for a FormatException as well as the DivideByZeroException as follows:

```
try
{
    int number1 = Convert.ToInt32(textBox1.Text);
    int number2 = Convert.ToInt32(textBox2.Text);
    textBox3.Text = (number1 / number2).ToString();
}
catch (FormatException)
{
    MessageBox.Show("Please check your numbers");
}
catch (DivideByZeroException)
{
    MessageBox.Show("You divided by zero!");
```

```
        }
    }
```

There are two extensions to the try-catch code. They are throw and finally. The throw statement passes the exception to the calling method and the finally statements are always executed and can be used to tidy up.

C#6.0 includes exception filters which let you specify a condition for a catch block.

6.7 • Application.DoEvents method

You might have a situation where your program is looping but you want to check if something else has happened. In this case you should really use threads which we will discuss later, but you can let any outstanding Windows processes run using the code:

```
Application.DoEvents();
```

This is frowned upon by some programmers however, as results can be unpredictable.

6.8 • Self Assessment Exercises

1. Watch the Virtual Academy's video #7, #9 and #12 on **if, for** and **while** statements. #20 covers enumerated values and **switch**. It may also be useful at this stage to watch #21 on exception handling.
2. If exercise

   Write if statements that use all of the comparison operators (==, <=, >=, etc.)

   Extend this to include multiple comparisons and test your programs. For example, test for:

   if integerA is greater than integerB and integerC is less than integerD, and test for:

   if integerA is less than integerB or integerC is greater than integerD.
3. If then else exercise.

   Write a program that requests an income value and determines the Tax due to the Government, if its tax system is as follows:

   Income:

   £0-1999: 0%,

   £2k-2999: 10%,

   £3k-39999: 22%,

   Over 40k: 40%.
4. Switch exercise

   Remove the default statement and complete the switch statement in section 6.3 so that a message is displayed for every teenage year. Combine years 14 to 17 so that the program drops through years 14 to 16 and displays a message for year 17: "You are between 14 and 17".

5. 'for' loop exercises:

Exercise: Two times table

Start a new project and place a list box on a form.

Add a button and change its Caption property to 'Two Times Table'. Add the following code for the button click and run the code:

```
private void button1_Click(object sender, EventArgs e)
{
    for (int count = 1; count <= 12; count++)
    {
        listBox1.Items.Add(count + " times 2 is " + count * 2);
    }       // end of for loop
}
```

Your output should be similar to the following:

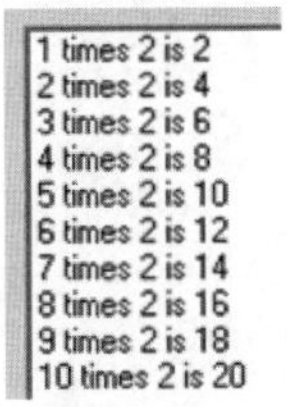

More times tables

Display the three times table, starting at 1 x 3 going up to 12 x 3.

Display the four times table, starting at 12 x 4 going down to 0 x 4.

6. While loop

Declare and set an integer to zero.

Use a while loop to loop while the integer is less than 3, displaying the value in a message box. Increment the integer in the loop.

7. Do-while loop

Declare and set an integer to three.

In a do-while loop, display the integer value in a message box while the integer is more than zero. Decrement the integer in the loop.

8. The Fibonacci series – while and do-while loops

The Fibonacci series occurs widely in nature and is the sum of the previous two numbers in the series starting with 0 and 1: 0, 1, 1, 2, 3, 5, 8, 13, 21 etc. The ratio of the last two numbers approaches the golden ratio (1.618), for example 21/13 = 1.615.

The following code displays the Fibonacci series whilst the sum is less than 10.

Place a button on a form and give it the caption: 'Fibonacci Series'

Add a list box to display the series. Add the following code for the button:

```
private void button1_Click(object sender, EventArgs e)
{
    int old, next, sum;
```

```
        old = 0;
        next = 1;
        sum = old + next;
        while (sum < 10)
        {
            sum = old + next;
            listBox1.Items.Add(old + " plus " + next + " is " + sum);
            old = next;
            next = sum;
        } // end of while sum<10
}
```

Run the program to display the first few numbers of the Fibonacci Series, see figure 6.2.

Figure 6-2 Fibonacci series

Exercise: Modify the code to show more numbers in the sequence.

You might like to try the do.. while version:

```
int old, next, sum;
old = 0;
next = 1;
sum = old + next;
do
{
    sum = old + next;
    listBox1.Items.Add(old + " plus " + next + " is " + sum);
    old = next;
    next = sum;
}
while (sum < 10); // end of do .. while sum<10
```

If you want a loop to continue forever you can use while (true), but make sure there is some way to break out of the loop!

9. Replace the code in section 5.9 on page 86 that checks for a stock item (copied below), with try and catch code

```
if (myStock.ContainsKey("bananas"))
  MessageBox.Show("Banana stock is " + myStock["bananas"].ToString());
else
  MessageBox.Show(«Yes, we have no bananas»);
```

6.9 • Summary

This chapter has covered different ways of changing program flow and looping. These are the commands:

- if .. else
- switch .. case
- the for loop
- while
- do .. while loops.

These statements use a test (a comparison) that provides a true or false result to determine the program code to execute.

The **for** loop is used when the loop conditions are known. The **while** and **do .. while** statements are used when the loop variable has to be changed by a varying amount or a test occurs within the loop. The while loop tests at the beginning of the code, whilst the do .. while statement tests at the end of the code statements.

We also saw how to use the editor to write code snippets for us.Finally we considered exception handling code using the try-catch, throw and finally statements.

Chapter 7 • Object oriented programming: Classes and methods

7.1 • Introduction

By now you may have realised that the programs written so far have been broken up into small portions of code, such as a button click or a timer tick event. We have used other code which we haven't written such as MessageBox.Show. Modules of code like these are called **methods**.

It is good practice to break your program into small parts which have a specific function and consequently are easier to get debugged and working. These smaller methods can be used in other programs, in turn saving memory space and possible errors and making those run faster and easier to write.

If you have programmed in other languages you might call these functions, procedures or subroutines.

When we deal with object oriented code later we shall introduce **classes**, which are a combination of data and methods. We have already seen the DateTime and Math classes and their methods (e.g. AddDays( ) and Sqrt( )).

By convention, method and class names begin with a capital letter, whereas variables begin with a lower case letter. Hence just by looking at the name you can tell if it's a method or a variable. You should use this scheme for your names.

7.2 • Method declaration

Let's see how we write a method and use it in our program. Methods may have data passed to them and returned from them.

A method declaration starts with the data type of the value returned or the keyword **void** if none. It is followed by the method's name and then a list of parameters passed in brackets (their data types and name to be used in the method). The items in the parameter-list are called **arguments**. The method's own data and code is encased in a block within curly brackets:

```
return-data-type   Method-name            ( parameter-list in brackets)
{
  // Method declarations and statements
}
```

As an example, let's see how we would define an integer square root method. We will pass an integer and return a double value.

The declaration starts with the return data type (double) followed by the method name (SquareRoot) and then the data type of the parameters passed and a name that will be used inside the method. If there is more than one parameter, each is separated by a comma and needs its own data type.

The method's code is:

```
double SquareRoot ( int intRoot)
{
  double root = Math.Sqrt(intRoot);
  return root ;                              // squareRoot returns a double
}
```

Note that the integer value that is passed is called 'intRoot' in the method but may have another name in the calling program. The return keyword followed by the variable's name must be used to state which variable is to be passed back to the calling program.

If nothing is returned the keyword 'void' is used for the return data type in the method declaration, and of course no 'return' statement is needed. If nothing is passed to the method, the brackets are still needed but left empty.

The method cannot be placed inside a method and is placed at the same level as other methods, such as a button click.

To run (or call) the method from the main program, we use the method's name followed by the parameters we want to pass to it. In this case as the method returns a value, the result will need to be assigned somewhere so it is placed after an equals sign, e.g.:

```
double dblSqRoot = SquareRoot ( integerNumber ) ;
```

You do not have to state the data type of the parameters passed when the method is called; that will have been declared before the call is made.

You can of course declare variables to be used within the method.

Exercise: A Simple method

Let's try an example before we go any further. We'll start with a method that doesn't accept or return any values. Although this may seem an odd thing to do, it might be useful if you want a method to initialize some values or reset all the controls on a form. A further example (Move) is on page 126. We'll create a method that just waits for a short time.

Start a new windows application; call it 'Wait'. Place a button on the form and give it a suitable name (I've used btnWait). Double-click the button and change the code to be:

```
private void btnWait_Click(object sender, EventArgs e)
{
    Wait();
}
```

To declare the Wait method, place the following code before the button click method:

```
void Wait()
{
    int i = 0;
    while (i < 10)
    {
        i = i + 1;
    }
}
```

Note that even though nothing is returned, we have to state that fact using the keyword 'void' in the method declaration.

Run the program and click the button to call the method. Of course your computer won't wait for very long. In fact the VS2015 debugger (which we will see later) says it takes less than 1ms, see Figure 7-1.

Figure 7-1 The Wait code

Here's a complete copy of the code:

```
namespace Chapter7_2Methods
{
    public partial class Form1 : Form
    {
        public Form1()
        {
            InitializeComponent();
        }
        void Wait()
        {
            int i = 0;
            while (i < 10)
            {
                i = i + 1;
            }
        }
        private void btnWait_Click(object sender, EventArgs e)
        {
            Wait();
        }
    }
}
```

We shall discuss this in a later chapter, but if you really want your program to pause, you can use the code: System.Threading.Thread.Sleep(1000);

7.3 • Parameter passing

We will want to pass data to and from our methods. For our example, we may want to wait for different amounts of time or pass a message back when it's done waiting.

Let's look at all the possibilities. We can:

1. Pass nothing, return nothing,
2. Pass something, return nothing,
3. Pass nothing, return something,
4. Pass something, return something.

The first case we have just seen. Take another look at the method declaration now 'void Wait( )' and see how the method is called using its name: Wait( );

Let's look at the second case and pass a variable which will be an integer value that will be used as a delay time.

To the above code, declare a new method called PassWaitingTime as follows. Add this before your 'void Wait( )' line of code.

```
void PassWaitingTime(int delayTime)
{
    int i = 0;
    while (i < delayTime)
    {
        i = i + 1;
    }
}
```

This method is passed an integer which is called delayTime within the method.

To call the method, add the following code after the Wait( ); in the button click code:

```
PassWaitingTime(100);
```

Run the code. It should wait a bit longer this time – but of course you still won't notice it.

This isn't much use if we can only pass the value of 100 each time and of course we can pass a variable.

Change the PassWaitingTime(100); to the following:

```
int longTime = 10000;
int shortTime = 10;
PassWaitingTime(longTime);
PassWaitingTime(shortTime);
```

Run the code again. This time it waits 10000 loops followed by 10 loops. You still won't notice the delay.

Note the variable name is longTime or shortTime in main program, but always called delayTime in method. You can declare a variable called delayTime in the button click, but it is different from the one in the Wait method.

What if we want to pass nothing, but return a value? Let's look at our first Wait( ) method but now return a string "done" when it's finished. As this method is going to return a string, the word 'void' will be replaced by 'string' in the method's declaration. We will also have to do something with the string that is returned.

Add the following method before the void PassWaitingTime(int delayTime) code:

```
string ReturnWait()
{
    int i = 0;
    while (i < 10)
    {
        i = i + 1;
    }
    return "done";
}
```

In our button click code, let's display the string it returns. Add the following code after the PassWaitingTime (shortTime); line of code:

```
MessageBox.Show(ReturnWait( ));
```

Run the code. The MessageBox.Show method will call ReturnWait and display 'done' when the waiting is over.

The important code is shown in Figure 7-2:

```
private void btnWait_Click(object sender, EventArgs e)
{
    Wait();
    PassWaitingTime(100);
    int longTime = 10000;
    int shortTime = 10;
    PassWaitingTime(longTime);
    PassWaitingTime(shortTime);
    MessageBox.Show(ReturnWait());
}

string ReturnWait()
{
    int i = 0;
    while (i < 10)
    {
        i = i + 1;
    }
    return "done";
}

void PassWaitingTime(int delayTime)
{
    int i = 0;
    while (i < delayTime)
    {
        i = i + 1;
    }
}

void Wait()
{
    int i = 0;
    while (i < 10)
    {
        i = i + 1;
    }
}
```

Figure 7-2 Method code

Finally let's pass a variable and return a value:

Add a new method called PassReturnWait. (I'll let you think about where to put this)

```
string PassReturnWait(int delayTime)
{
    int i = 0;
    while (i < delayTime)
    {
        i = i + 1;
    }
    return "done";
}
```

And add the following code in the button click method:

```
// shortTime should already be declared: int shortTime = 10;
MessageBox.Show(PassReturnWait( shortTime));
```

Check that it works.

We may want to pass or return more than one value. We can pass many variables, but generally only return one. Parameters are passed as a list between the brackets and we've seen an example of this in the button click method itself:

```
private void button1_Click(object sender, EventArgs e)
```

Here the object (in this case the button) and the type of event (e.g. a mouseEvent) are passed to the method. You can test for this in the button click code, but more of that later.

7.4 • Pass by reference – ref and out keywords

In the examples we have seen, a **copy** of the parameter is passed to the method and the original remains intact. This is known as 'pass by value' (a value type). However, it is possible to let the called method access and permanently change the value. This is known as 'pass by reference' (a reference type). In this case the keyword **ref** is used. The keyword **out** is also used for methods that also initialize and return a variable.

Consider the following code. In the first part of the button click code, PassNotRef is called, which alters x in the method, but doesn't change the value of y which is passed, and so y's initial value of 1 is displayed.

However in the second part, when the method PassByRef is called, y is passed by reference. Now when x is changed to zero, this is reflected in y's original value, and consequently y=0 is displayed.

```
void PassNotRef(int x)
{
    x = 0;  // value passed won't be changed
}
void PassByRef(ref int x)
{
    x = 0;  // value passed will be set to zero
}
private void button1_Click(object sender, EventArgs e)
{
    int y = 1;
    PassNotRef(y);
    MessageBox.Show("y=" + y); // displays y=1
    y = 1;
    PassByRef(ref y);
    MessageBox.Show("y=" + y); // displays y=0
}
```

Note neither a **return** statement nor an assignment statement in the main code is needed.

It's important to remember this when using arrays and methods. A whole array is passed by reference (a single pointer to the start of the array), whereas an array element is passed by value, for example if we have a method called 'Modify':

```
public void Modify (int  intModify)
 {
   intModify  = intModify *2;
 }
```

This might be called by the code:

```
int [ ] intArray = { 1, 2, 3, 4, 5, 6 };
Modify (intArray[3]);
```

This does not change the original value in the array, as it was passed by value.

However, if we have a method that squares an array:

```
public void SquareArray(int[] anArray)
{
   for (int j = 0; j < anArray.Length; j++)
   {
     anArray[j] = anArray[j] * anArray[j];
   }
}
```

which is called using:

```
int[] intArray = { 1, 2, 3, 4, 5, 6 };
SquareArray(intArray);
```

The whole array is passed by reference and squared, even though the ref keyword isn't used.

7.5 • Scope of a method – private and public

As we have seen in section 4.10 on page 71, the block of code to which variables are available is known as the **scope**. Eventually your programs will consist of many methods and classes and you will need to consider their scope. The main types of scope are private and public; **private** is the least permissive access level and items are accessible only within the body of the class in which they are declared; **public** is the most permissive access level, with no restrictions their access.

Individual variables can be defined as public or private, and we shall see some other modifiers such as 'static' and 'protected' later.

7.6 • Recursive methods

Methods can call themselves, this is known as recursion. A recursive method simply calls itself. This can't go on forever of course and there must be a way of eventually stopping the recursive call and if necessary return a value.

Consider a method that works out the factorial of a number. The factorial of a number, N, is the multiplication of all the numbers up that number. It is denoted by N! and defined for N>0 as N! = N x (N-1)! where 0! =1.

For example the factorial of 4 is 4*3*2*1*0

4! = 4*3! = 4*3*2! = 4*3*2*1! = 4*3*2*1*0! = 4*3*2*1*1.

A recursive method can then be defined which calls itself with a number one less than the number passed until the number is one. A method that performs this is shown below.

```
int Factorial(int factorialNo)
{
  if (factorialNo == 0)
  {
    return 1;
  }
  else
  {
    return factorialNo = factorialNo * Factorial(factorialNo - 1);
  }
}
```

The method is passed and returns an integer.

In the 'else' code, the return statement calls the Factorial method itself with the number one less than the one passed. This continues until the number 0 is passed, when the value 1 is returned. The calls then undo themselves calculating the required value. See the Self Assessment exercises for another example.

7.7 • Calling an event

As we have seen events such as a button click are written as a method, and your program can call these methods and hence cause an event to occur, e.g. to force a button click. The correct parameters need to be passed to the method of course.

Let's take an example. Place two buttons on a form and write the following code for the button clicks. Clicking button 1 displays "Button 1 clicked" and clicking button 2 displays "Button 2 clicked" followed by "Button 1 clicked".

```
private void button1_Click(object sender, EventArgs e)
{
  MessageBox.Show("Button 1 clicked!");
}
private void button2_Click(object sender, EventArgs e)
{
  MessageBox.Show("Button 2 clicked!");
  button1_Click(null, e);
}
```

Clicking button2 has calls the button1 click event. Note that the button click event expects an object and EventArgs data types to be passed to it (object sender, EventArgs e). You must pass (null, e) or (sender, e) to it in this case.

7.8 • Classes and Namespaces

We shall see in the next chapter that a **class** contains both data and methods to manipulate that data. It is used as a template to create an **object**. A **namespace** is a collection of classes and their methods. Think of it as a library.

The .NET library is composed of many namespaces. We have seen some of them such as System, System.IO, and System.Windows.Forms. They are included in our program with the 'using' keyword. Namespaces are stored in dynamic link locate (DLL) files called assemblies. We shall see how to create our own DLL program and include them in our own libraries in chapter 18.

Visual Studio 2015 greys out any unused namespaces, and you can remove them by right-clicking the code area and selecting Organize Usings > Remove Unused Usings, Figure 7-3.

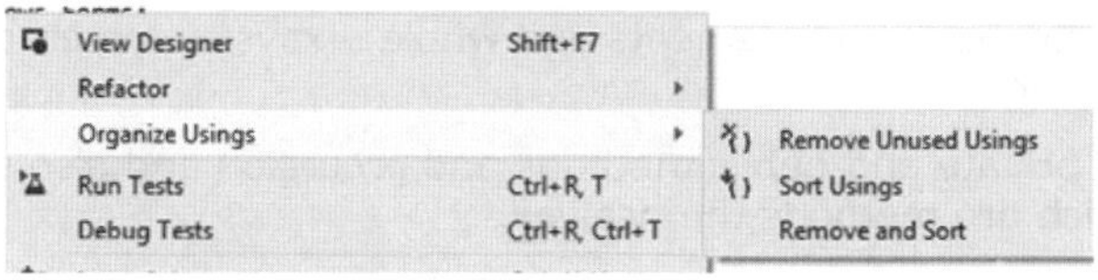

Figure 7-3 Removing unused usings.

7.9 • Self Assessment Exercises

1. Don't forget to look for any of my supporting videos on YouTube.
2. Place some text boxes on a form, and write a method that clears the text in the boxes. This method isn't passed or returns any data. Call this method from a button click and try it out.
3. Create a method that when called 'rolls' a die (a single dice) and returns the number displayed. It's not passed anything but returns an integer value from 1 to 6.
4. Write a method that rolls a number of dice. It is passed the number of dice to roll and returns the total number thrown.
5. Write a method that rolls up to three dice. It is passed the number of dice to roll and returns a number 1 to 6 for each of the dice rolled and zero for the dice not rolled. You will have to pass four parameters and either use the out or ref keyword or pass an array.
6. Create a method that rolls a number of dice and returns the values. This time pass one variable - an array. The first value in the array holds the number of dice to roll and the rest of the array returns the dice values. In this case the array will be passed by reference, i.e. the whole array is passed (or more accurately the address of the array is passed). See the array examples in section 7.4 to see how a whole array is passed to a method.
7. Try writing a similar method that passes one array value only. See if the value is changed in the calling program. It shouldn't be. If you want it to be changed pass the value with the ref keyword and prove it.
8. Write a program that requests a number and calculates its factorial using recursive calls. Change the method so that it deals with long integer data types and large factorials.

9. Write a program that requests a number and using recursive calls, returns the sum of numbers up to that number.
10. If you want to find out more about namespaces, watch the Virtual Academy video #18 'Understanding namespaces'.
11. The video #24 'Understanding Event-Driven Programming' can also be watched but it may be a bit too soon.

7.10 • Summary

This chapter has looked at breaking your program down into smaller more manageable parts called methods. We have seen how to declare a method and how to pass data to the method from our program and how to return values from method using the return keyword.

We have seen how to pass array elements and whole arrays to a method and discussed the ref and out keywords.

We have discussed private and public methods and recursion and also seen how we can call our events, which are methods themselves.

Chapter 8 • Object oriented programming – creating objects

8.1 • Introduction

We have covered a lot of programming concepts so far, so now is a good time to look at Object Oriented Programming (OOP). It may seem a little early to talk about this subject so if you want to skip this and come back, but it does fit in well with the ideas we've been covering and may actually make your programming easier.

First of all, don't panic. Object Oriented Programming was devised to relate computer programs more closely to real items such as a person, car or house and simplify complex applications. We have seen some objects already: the button and the form are objects. We have seen that these objects have methods, properties and events. In this chapter we will see how to create our own objects.

I do not intend to cover OOP in great detail, but simply to give you an idea of what it is and how to use OOP and to create your own objects and use them.

Firstly, let's deal with some terminology.

Class

A class contains both data and methods to manipulate that data, and is a template for an object. The code and its data are integrated (or in OOP terms, **encapsulated**). The data can only be manipulated by the class code and this obviously leads to more structured and reliable code. It is from the class that we instantiate (create) our objects using the 'new' keyword that we have seen and used. Objects created in this way are all different from each other.

Object

An object is a specific **instance** (or creation) of a class, created using 'new'. You have created buttons, which are instances of class Button, and in their own right are different from each other. An object normally has its own data and the only way to change deal with that data is to use the object's own interfaces – via its own methods, properties and events.

Properties

You should be happy with properties by now. We have seen that our controls have properties and how we access the properties using the dot notation. In this chapter we will create an object with methods and properties and be able to access them with the dot notation.

Methods

We discussed methods in the previous chapter. In OOP terms you can think of a method as an action that an object can perform. In a Transport example it might be start, drive, stop, reverse etc. We call an object's method using the dot notation and if necessary pass data to the method in brackets, e.g. MessageBox.Show("message");

Inheritance, encapsulation and **polymorphism** are the three primary features of object-oriented programming. **Encapsulation** means that properties, methods and other members are treated as a combined unit. **Inheritance** enables you to create and extend new classes. **Polymorphism** is the capability to have multiple classes, with each class interpreting properties or methods in different ways.

8.2 • Creating Objects

Let's start creating our own objects. We'll create a simple object, a Point. It will have properties: X and Y. We start by writing a class which has X and Y variables and then instantiate our own Point objects based on this class. We will be able to set and read the X and Y values as properties. We'll add a Move method that will move the point. Later we'll extend this point to a new class called Circle by extending Point and adding a further property, radius. The new class will 'inherit from' the original class.

Exercise: Our first object

Start a new project – I've called it OOP1. Now add a new class using **Project > Add Class** or Project > Add New Item > Class. Give it the name **Point** and click Add, see Figure 8-1.

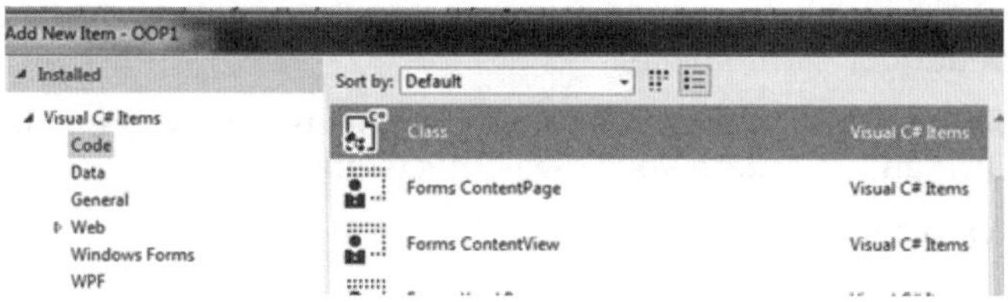

Figure 8-1 Adding a Class

A new tab entitled **Point.cs** appears in the design and has the code as follows:

```
namespace OOP1
{
    class Point
    {
    }
}
```

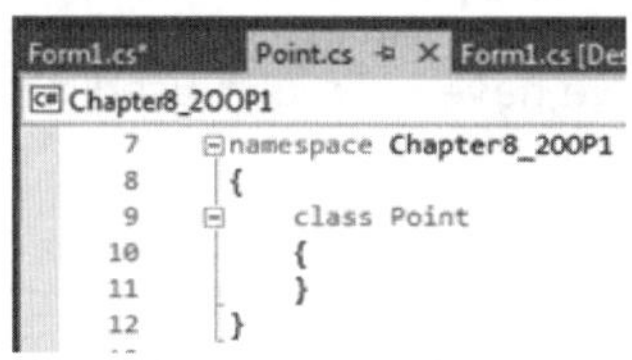

If you forget to change its name when you create it, a class called Class1 will be created. You can delete this by selecting it in the Solution Explorer and choosing delete.

That's it - we can now create some new points from this Point class template.

Return to the form design and add a button to the form. Change the button click code to the following:

```
private void button1_Click(object sender, EventArgs e)
{
    Point point1;
    point1 = new Point();
}
```

Notice how the IntelliSense knows about the class Point and variable point1 as you type code, see Figure 8-2 below and Figure 8-3 on page 121.

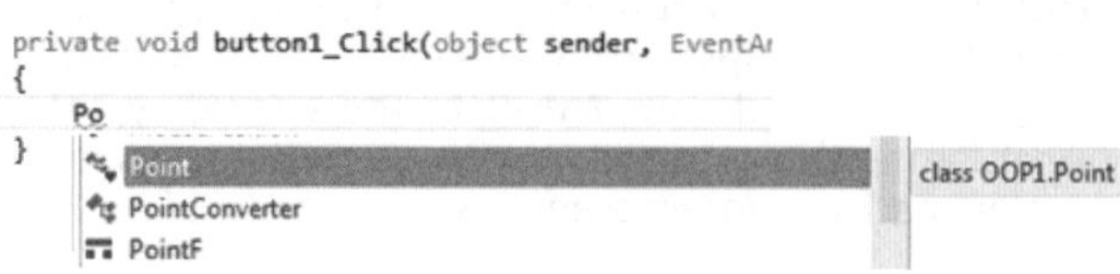

Figure 8-2 IntelliSense display of class

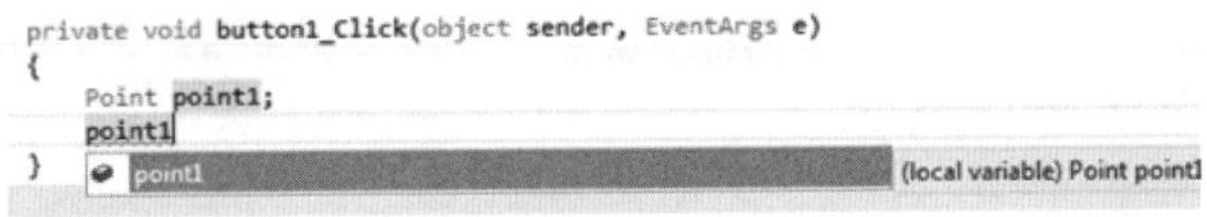

Figure 8-3 IntelliSense display of variable point1

You can also create a new object in one line of code as follows:

```
Point point1 = new Point( );
```

Clicking the button will create new point objects. You have just created your own objects! Of course they don't do anything yet.

Let's add X and Y properties to give a position for the Point. For external code to access them the points must be declared **public**, but to ensure the integrity of the data there must also be internal private variables; we shall call these privateX and privateY. The public X and Y properties will be accessed using the dot notation, which will in turn read and write the internal privateX and privateY values using the **get** and **set** keyword commands.

Change the Point class code (Point.cs) to the following:

```
namespace OOP1
{
    // Point class definition
    class Point
    {
        // private Point coordinates
        private int privateX, privateY;
        // constructor - runs when a new Point is instantiated - see later
        public Point()
        {
        }
        // property X
        public int X
        {
        // allow users to read X property - use lower case for get and set
            get
            {
                return privateX;
            }
            // allow users to set X property
            set
            {
                privateX = value;
            }
        } // end property X
        // ditto for property Y
        public int Y
        {
            get
            {
```

```
                return privateY;
            }
            set
            {
                privateY = value;
            }
        } // end property Y
    } // end class Point
}
```

Let's explain this before we run the code.

Every Point object you create will have its own privateX and privateY values, these are declared with the code private int privateX, privateY;.

As they are declared private, they can only be accessed within the class so to allow access using the dot notation, public properties X and Y are declared which access the private values with the get and set code:

```
public int X
{
   get { return privateX; }              // same code on one line
   set { privateX = value; }             // same code on one line
} // end property X
```

The **get** code returns the privateX variable and the **set** code changes the privateX variable with the value passed. See below for example code that sets and gets values.

Note the variables X and Y have been declared public, and so can be accessed from outside of the class. Once a point has been instantiated, the dot notation code can be used to access X and Y, for example:

```
firstPoint.X = 32;                       // set X value
int Yposition = firstPoint.Y;            // get Y value
```

To see this in action, change the button code to the following:

```
private void button1_Click(object sender, EventArgs e)
{
    Point point1;
    point1 = new Point();
    Point firstPoint = new Point();
    firstPoint.X = 23;
    firstPoint.Y = 345;
    int y = firstPoint.Y;
    MessageBox.Show("X value = " + firstPoint.X.ToString() +
        " Y value = " + y.ToString());
}
```

Run the program, the code and output should look like Figure 8-4 on page 123.

```
private void button1_Click(object sender, EventArgs e)
{
    Point firstPoint = new Point( );
    firstPoint.X = 23;
    firstPoint.Y = 345;
    int y = firstPoint.Y;
    MessageBox.Show("X value = " + firstPoint.X.ToString( ) +
        " Y value = " +     y.ToString( ));
}
```

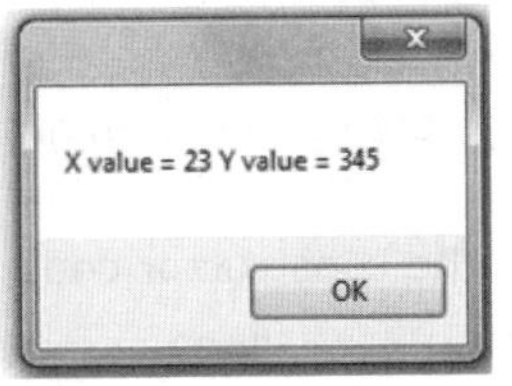

Figure 8-4 Button click code and display

Exercise: Create more point objects

Change the button click code so that new Point objects called 'secondPoint' and 'thirdPoint' are created and then set and display their X and Y values.

8.3 • Constructors

We may want a way of initializing our objects or to set initial default values, say for X and Y. This is done in the **constructor** code and an empty constructor was included in the code you typed:

```
// constructor - runs when a new Point is instantiated - see later
public Point()
{
 }
```

The constructor is called whenever a new object is instantiated. If you don't write constructor code a default one is provided. Note the constructor has the same name as the class and even though it has no return value or type, it doesn't include the 'void' keyword.

The constructor code creates a new Point object when the **new** code is executed, e.g.:

```
Point firstPoint = new Point();
```

Now I hope you understand why we write this code when we create a new object and what it does. In this case it just creates the Point – it doesn't have any X or Y values at this time.

We could add some lines of code in the constructor to set X and Y to specific values, e.g. set them to zero, as follows:

```
public Point()
{
    privateX = 0;
    privateY = 0;
}
```

This will set the X and Y values of a new Point to zero. Change your constructor code and prove it.

We may also want constructor code that sets X and Y values points passed when we instantiate the object, i.e. we might write:

```
Point newPoint = new Point(123,456);
```

This will create the object with the properties passed as parameters. Our constructor code won't currently do this, and we will add another constructor and code to do this. This means there will be two constructors, one for default or initialised values and one where we want to set the values.

Before adding the code you might like to think what the second constructor contains. Consider:

a. Is the constructor code public or private?

b. What's it called?

c. What are the parameters passed (what are their type and name)?

d. What values do we set in the code?

Let's try it. Add the following code after the closing bracket } of the public Point ( ) constructor:

```
public Point(int xValue, int yValue)
{
    // set x and y
    privateX = xValue;
    privateY = yValue;
}
```

We have two constructors now, one will be called if no parameters are used and the other if two parameters (X and Y) are passed. The correct one will be executed depending on the number of parameters used when the object is instantiated.

Add the following code for the button click and see it create the new point with the values passed:

```
Point setPoint = new Point(987, 654);
MessageBox.Show("X value = " + setPoint.X.ToString() +
    " Y value = " + setPoint.Y.ToString());
MessageBox.Show(setPoint.ToString());  // see below
```

Notice that the intelliSense editor knows about both constructors (2 of 2) and provides a prompt, see Figure 8-5.

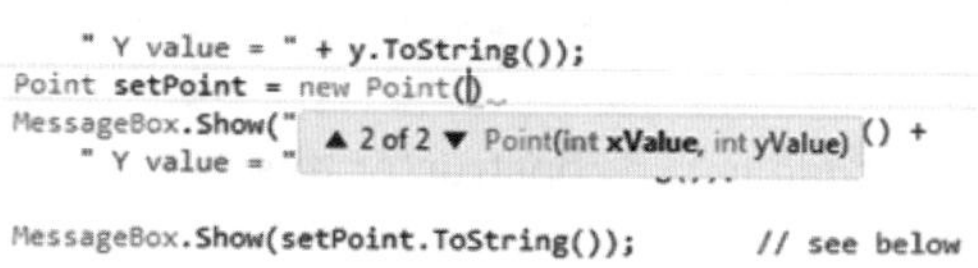

Figure 8-5 IntelliSense Constructor Prompt

Note the setPoint.ToString() code. When this is executed, it gives information about the object - see the next section.

Exercises:

- If you didn't do so, add code in the default constructor so that initial values of X and Y are set to zero.
- Take a look at the code we used when we created our structures in chapter 5.3. You can see that the personnelRecord structure has constructor code and is very similar to our class code.

Incidentally, we can use just setPoint.X instead of setPoint.X.ToString( ) in the **ShowMessage** method.

8.4 • The object's ToString method

Note the setPoint.ToString( ) method we have just used. This shows information about the object itself. Even though we haven't written any code for it, all objects have a default .ToString( ) method. At the moment, this code simply returns 'Object.Point', see Figure 8-6.

Figure 8-6 The ToString( ) method

This method is defined within the original C# object class code and we have used that code. Three other methods are also available by default. They are: **Equals**, **GetHashCode** and **GetType**.

8.5 • Overriding

The ToString method doesn't provide much information. We will now write our own ToString method to provide more useful information about our class, overriding the default one. We create our own 'ToString' method and use the keyword **override** to ensure this method runs, rather than the default one.

Add the following code to the Point class (after '// end property Y'):

```
public override string ToString()   // note the keyword 'override'
{
    return "My Point Object is at : " + privateX + " " + privateY;
}
```

Run the program. The message box now shows Figure 8-7.

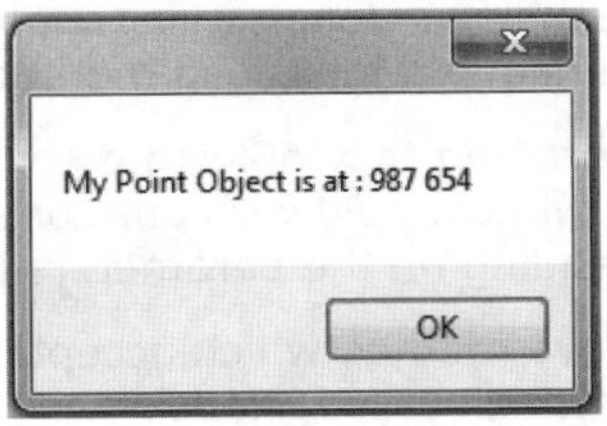

Figure 8-7 The overriden ToString( ) display

8.6 • Adding Methods to a class

Apart from the ToString method, we haven't added any methods to our Point class yet. Let's now add a method called **Move** which moves the point a fixed distance one unit in both the X and Y directions.

We want the method to be accessible from everywhere, so it will be declared **public**. Add the following code at the end of the Point class code, i.e. **before** '} // end class Point'.

```
public void Move()  // move by one in both X and Y directions
{
    privateX++;
    privateY++;
}  // end move
```

Add the following code to the end of the button click code to move our setPoint values. See Figure 8-8. The code is:

```
    setPoint.Move();
    MessageBox.Show(setPoint.ToString());
```

Run the code to see that setPoint is moved by one in the X and Y direction as shown in Figure 8-8.

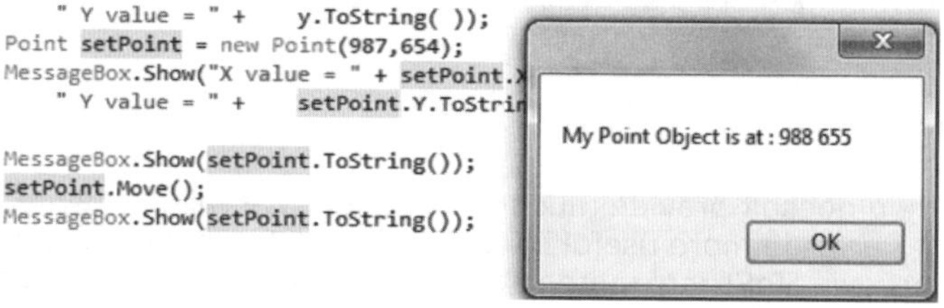

Figure 8-8 Result of the Move method.

We can of course have private methods which would be accessible only from within our Point class. For instance we could check if x and y were the same, if they were within a certain range, or if one was zero, change its value.

8.7 • Method overloading

As we did with the ToString method, we can also define methods with the same name but different parameters so that the method does similar actions. This time we are declaring a second version of our own method and it's called method overloading.

This is slightly different from overriding the ToString method which completely replaced the original code. It is similar to what we did with our constructors, having the same name, but different actions depending on the parameters passed.

We shall now define a second Move method which accepts a distance to move passed to it as X and Y values. Remember it is still called 'Move'.

Add the following code to the Point class

```
public void Move(int Xdistance, int Ydistance)
{
    privateX = privateX + Xdistance;
    privateY = privateY + Ydistance;
}
```

You should know by now where to put this, if not, remember all the code is available via Elektor's web site.

And add the following to the end of the button click code:

```
setPoint.Move(-3, 345);
MessageBox.Show(setPoint.ToString());
```

Run it to observe that the point does move, see Figure 8-9.

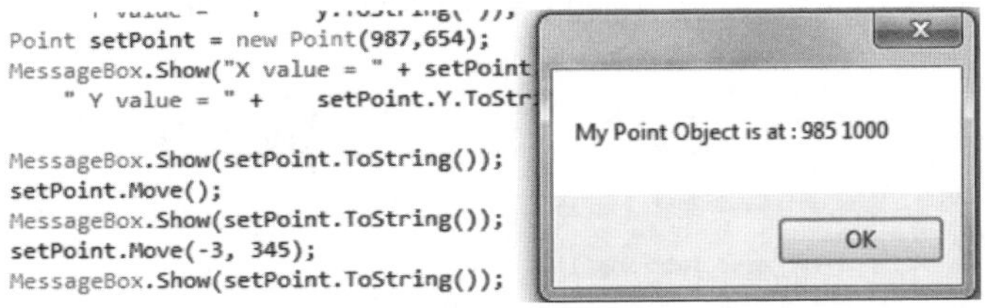

Figure 8-9 Overloaded Move method

Notice how the intelliSense editor knows about both of the Move methods as you type, see Figure 8-10.

Figure 8-10 IntelliSense method display

We will add some more methods later when we have extended our Point class to a circle.

8.8 • Static classes

You may have noticed that we don't have to instantiate some objects with the **new** keyword; we can just use them. For example we didn't instantiate the Math or MessageBox classes. They are considered to be commonly used objects and so they don't have to be instantiated before use; they have been declared with the keyword **static**.

A **static** class is useful for methods, like the Math class that just performs an operation or read parameters and does not use **get** or **set**.

We could do same for our Point class, but it doesn't make sense as we want to create different points. However it might be useful if we wanted a 'Distance to origin' calculation available to all our objects.

We will create a new static class called Calculate to do this.

Add a new class to the project called Calculate (Project > Add class). Within the class add a method called DistanceToOrigin. This will be our static class; note how this is declared in the code below. It will accept an X and Y position and return a double.

The complete object code is:

```
class Calculate
{
    public static double DistanceToOrigin(int x, int y)
    {
        return Math.Sqrt(x * x + y * y);
    }
}
```

Now add the following at the end of the button click code, to display the distance of our point from the origin:

```
MessageBox.Show("Distance to Origin = " +
    Calculate.DistanceToOrigin(setPoint.X, setPoint.Y).ToString());
```

Note we do not have to instantiate Calculate or DistanceToOrigin. The result is shown in Figure 8-11.

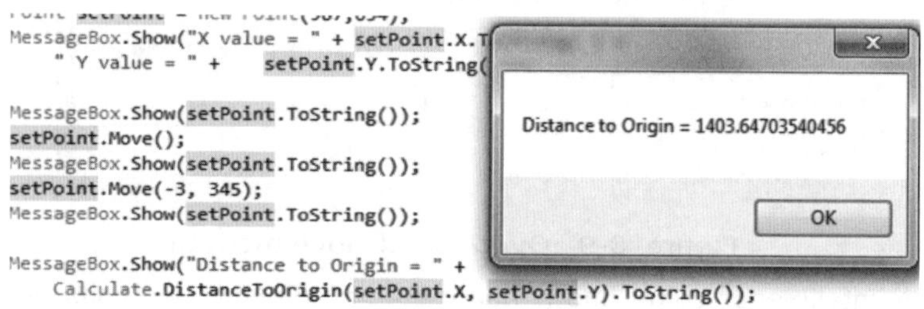

Figure 8-11 Static class

Without the **static** statement, DistanceToOrigin would have to be placed in the Point class code and called using the Point's name, e.g. firstPoint.DistanceToOrigin( )

Exercise: Remove the 'static' declaration and note the error message.

All the above code is available at the Elektor's web site. (Chapter8_2OOP1)

8.9 • Inheritance

Inheritance is a key concept in OOP. It allows you to create a new class that extends (or inherits from) the behaviour of an existing class. We shall take our tried and tested Point code and create a new Circle class. A circle can be defined with three parameters: the centre at points X and Y and a radius. Instead of creating a completely new Circle class which might introduce errors and take time to debug, we can use the Point class we have defined and extend it to create our Circle class. In other words the Circle object we create **inherits** the Point class's data and behaviour (and hopefully bug-free code).

To inherit from a class, the new class is defined followed by a colon and the class name to inherit from.

You've already seen this. If you look at the definition of Form1 in your C# code, you'll see the line of code:

```
public class Form1 : Form
```

The Form1 : Form part indicates that your Form1 inherits from the class Form.

Exercise: A Circle class

Let's add a new class called Circle. Select Project > Add class. Name it Circle.

To define a class Circle which will inherit all the Point class information, we type:

```
class Circle : Point

    {
    }
```

Change the code that has been written for you from class Circle to class Circle : Point, as above.

We can now instantiate a Circle object on the button click. To the button click code, add:

```
Circle smallcircle = new Circle();
```

The code will run and create a circle (actually a Point – a circle with zero radius).

What we really want is to be able to define a Radius property for our circle and add methods such as Area or Circumference. Let's add constructor code, get and set Radius property code and an Area method code. Add these to your code as follows:

```
class Circle : Point
{
    // declare an internal, private radius variable
    private double _radius;
    public Circle()     // implict constructor call comes here
    {
    }
    public Circle(int xValue, int yValue, double radiusValue)
    {
        // Circle constructor code privateX and privateY
        // obtained from Point class
        privateX = xValue;
        privateY = yValue;
        // privateX and privateY must now be declared
        // protected in Point class
        _radius = radiusValue;
    }
    // property Radius
    public double Radius
    {
        get
        {
            return _radius;
        }
        set
        {
            if (value >= 0) _radius = value;    // check for positive radius
        }
    }
    // method Area
    public double Area()
    {
        return Math.PI * _radius * _radius;
    }
    // override default ToString method
    public override string ToString()
    {
```

```
return "Circle at x," + privateX + " y,"
                    + privateY + " radius," + _radius;
        }
}
```

We have now added a Radius property for the circle. The **get** method reads the radius and in the **set** method we check for a non-zero value passed. We have a method that calculates the Area and also an overridden ToString method. Finally we have two constructors for Circle – the default and one that sets X, Y and a radius.

However, for the Circle class to be able to access the Point variables privateX and privateY, their declaration has to be changed to **protected** in the Point class code. You may have noticed the error messages when you typed the code. **Protected** is halfway between public and private declaration and allows access from with the class it is declared, but also any class derived from it.

Therefore, you have to change the point class privateX and privateY declaration to protected, as follows:

```
// Point coordinates - changed to protected so that Circle can access them
protected int privateX, privateY;
```

We can now instantiate a default circle with no X, Y or Radius properties defined, or instantiate a circle with X, Y and Radius values. We can alter the X, Y and Radius properties and calculate the circle's radius. Try the following code for the button click

```
Circle smallCircle = new Circle();          // default circle
Circle largeCircle = new Circle(12, 34, 56);    // set x,y and radius
smallCircle.X = 98;                     // set smallCircle X
smallCircle.Y = 87;                     // set smallCircle Y
smallCircle.Radius = 11;                    // set smallCircle Radius
                                            // and display
MessageBox.Show("Small circle = " + smallCircle.ToString());
MessageBox.Show("Large circle = " + largeCircle.ToString());
MessageBox.Show("Circle area = " + smallCircle.Area().ToString());
```

Notice also that your circle object has access to the Point class Move method. You can move your circle around the same way you can move your points.

And of course you can use the DistanceToOrigin method for your circle points.

8.10 • Overriding methods

We have seen how we can override the ToString method. If we want to allow any of the class methods we have defined to be overridden, their declaration must be changed to **virtual**. For instance, we might want to calculate to overall surface area of a cylinder. The Area method we defined could be overridden.

You might want to do this if for instance you had a selection of shapes - e.g. cylinder, cone, sphere, box etc. - all of which have a surface area, but is calculated in different ways. You can use a common method 'SurfaceArea' for each shape and the correct method will be used to calculate the surface area for each shape. This is worked out at run-time and is particularly helpful if you have an array of those (different) objects.

Let's try it now.

Start a new project and place a button on the form.

Add new class, call it Shape. Its code is:

```
class Shape
{
    // private coordinates
    private double privateX, privateY, privateZ;
    public Shape()
    {
    }
    public double X
    {
        get { return privateX; }
        set { privateX = value; }
    } // end property X
    public double Y
    {
        get { return privateX; }
        set { privateY = value; }
    } // end property Y
    public double Z
    {
        get { return privateZ; }
        set { privateZ = value; }
    } // end property Z
    public Shape(double xValue, double yValue, double zValue)
    {
        privateX = xValue;
        privateY = yValue;
        privateZ = zValue;
    }
    public virtual double SurfaceArea()
    {
        return privateX * privateY * privateZ;
    }  // end SurfaceArea
    public override string ToString()   // note the override
    {
        return "Shape's ToString() method";
    }
} // end class Shape
```

Test it out. Add the following code for a button click on the the form:

```
private void button1_Click(object sender, EventArgs e)
{
    Shape box = new Shape(1.0, 2.0, 3.0);
    MessageBox.Show("Surface Area = " + box.SurfaceArea().ToString());
```

```
            MessageBox.Show(box.ToString());
        }
```

You should get a message saying Surface area is 22, followed by the Shape's ToString method message.

Now create another new class Sphere which inherits from Shape with a different ToString() method.

```
    class Sphere : Shape
    {
        private double privateX;
        public Sphere (double xValue)
        {
            // set radius
            privateX = xValue;
        }
        public override double SurfaceArea()
        {
            return 4 * Math.PI * private * privateX;
        }
        public override string ToString()
        {
            return "Sphere's ToString() method";
        }
    } // end Sphere
```

We can now create a new Sphere (earth) and a Shape (another Sphere) both having the Sphere's SurfaceArea method. Add this to the button click code:

```
            Sphere earth = new Sphere(2.0);
            MessageBox.Show("earth's surface Area = " +
                                  earth.SurfaceArea().ToString());
            MessageBox.Show(earth.ToString());
            // Shows Surface area of a Sphere (50.265..)
            Shape newSphere = new Sphere(2.0);
            MessageBox.Show("newSphere's Surface Area = " +
                                  newSphere.SurfaceArea().ToString());
            MessageBox.Show(newSphere.ToString());
            // Shows Surface area of a Shape (50.265..)
```

Now when you run the code, you get the earth's surface area (50.265) with the Shape's ToString message, followed by the newSphere's surface area (50.265) and the Sphere's ToString message.

Now we can create an array of Shapes containing Spheres and Shapes and display their surface areas:

```
            Shape[] allShapes = new Shape[4]; // keep it simple
            allShapes[0] = new Shape(2, 3, 4); // a box
            allShapes[1] = new Sphere(2); // a sphere
```

```
        allShapes[2] = new Sphere(3); // another sphere
        allShapes[3] = new Shape(1, 3, 4); // a another box
        foreach (var item in allShapes)
        {
            MessageBox.Show(item.SurfaceArea().ToString());
        }
```

Exercise: Add a further shape, say a cone

Incidentally if you copy a class from a different namespace, use the complete name.

If your Circle was created in the project OOP1, the full namespace OOP1.Circle is used in a different project:

```
    class Cylinder : OOP1.Circle
    {
        public Cylinder()      // implict constructor call comes here
        {
        }
    }
```

You can also add 'using OOP1;' and just use Cylinder : Circle

8.11 • GetType methods

You may now see the use of the GetType method you will have seen. You can determine the type of your object. You can add the following to your code:

```
        MessageBox.Show(earth.GetType().ToString());
```

You will get the message: Namespace.sphere

8.12 • Interfaces

While OOP lets us write reusable and easily maintained code, it only goes so far. Interfaces allow your classes to inherit from multiple parents and provide a universal structure to your properties and methods. Interfaces are beyond the scope of this (supposed) beginner's book but a search for C# Interfaces will soon find more information and examples.

8.13 • Self Assessment Exercises

1. Hopefully I will have produced some videos to support this. Find them at Elektor's web site.
2. Watch the 11th, 15th, 16th, 17th and 18th Virtual Academy videos on Creating and Calling methods, Classes and Inheritance, and Namespaces at: http://www.microsoftvirtualacademy.com
3. Create a class for a Rectangle with properties Height and Width and a method Area(). Write the code to get and set the Height and Width and calculate the Area. Provide some checks, so that negative values can't be used.
4. Create objects of your Rectangle class and change the rectangle's properties in the code. Call the Area method and display it.

5. Overwrite the default .ToString() method to provide more useful information on your object.
6. Create a new class called 'Box' which inherits from Rectangle and has an extra property 'Depth' and a new method called 'Volume' which overrides the Area method.
7. Create an object called Vehicle. It could have properties such as Bus, Car, Train, etc. Each could have a make, number of wheels and passengers etc. You could declare a public variable called 'PetrolPrice' and a static method PricePerKm.
8. Can you think how this might be overloaded to produce a Transport object with say a method PassengerPricePerKm?
9. Look at the other methods that are inherited from the Class code (Equals, GetHashCode, GetType) and find out what they mean.
10. Create a new class 'Cylinder' which inherits from the Circle and has an extra property 'Height' and method 'Volume'. Override the Area method to create a Volume method.
11. If you want to find out more about OOP, look up the terms: base class and derived class and polymorphism. And if you didn't do so, see:

    www.codeproject.com/Articles/1445/Introduction-to-inheritance-polymorphism-in-C

8.14 • Summary

This chapter has covered writing classes and creating objects from a class. We defined a class called Point and created objects of this class using the keyword 'new'. The class has properties and methods which are parts of the object. The class properties are altered by the get and set methods and accessed from the main code using the dot notation. We have seen how an object is instantiated using a default constructor and we have created our own constructor that initializes the object's properties. The default ToString method was overridden by our own ToString method.

We created a method called Move for our class and saw how the methods runs. We added a further Move method that was passed a distance to move. This overloaded the original Move method.

Static classes were then covered. These don't have to be instantiated and are useful for methods which just access values or perform calculations.

Inheritance was then covered. Circle objects were created from a Circle class which inherited from the Point class. To do this we had to declare protected variables and virtual methods.

Finally we saw how to override our own methods by creating a Shape class and extended this to Sphere class. We added surface area methods which were called depending on the shape created.

This has been a fairly intense chapter and congratulations if you have understood it all. If not don't worry, we'll cover some easier subjects in the next chapters. Return to this chapter as and when you need to.

Chapter 9 • File handling and menu dialogs

9.1 • Introduction

After the fairly intensive chapter on Object Oriented Programming let's return to more practical work.

Sooner or later you will want to save or read information on a file. Disk files are used for a wide variety of reasons; to hold temporary or permanent data, set-up or user information etc. Some applications can easily collect large amounts of data which may be saved on disk before analysed. Sometimes it is easier to save data on a disk than to deal with databases. In this chapter we will look at file types and the C# controls to handle them. We will look at databases later.

9.2 • File Types – Text or Binary

Files are either text files (ASCII, Unicode or similar) or non-text (binary) files.

9.2.1 • Text Files

Text files simply contain ASCII or Unicode characters, i.e. those that can be typed from the keyboard. These are often strings terminated with Carriage Return (CR, 0x0D or '\r') and Line Feed characters (LF, 0x0A or '\n'). Basic text editors create this sort of file. Most applications can handle text files and it is a good way of transferring data between applications. These files are normally handled in a line-by-line or sequential manner. We will see that these are handled by StreamReader and StreamWriter classes.

9.2.2 • Binary Files - Typed and Untyped files

Binary files contain all values (i.e. printable and non-printable characters) and can't be displayed directly on the screen. Binary files are either typed or untyped. Typed files have a known format using data types, e.g. the Personnel record structure seen in section 5.3 on page 79. Untyped files have no rigid structure and record sizes can vary. Application program files (.EXE) and bitmap graphic files (.BMP) are good examples of these. In this case the application dealing with the file knows about the file structure and how to deal with it. We will see that these are handled by BinaryReader and BinaryWriter classes.

9.3 • File Dialog Boxes and MenuStrip control

We shall start by looking at the C# File handling controls and Menus which make it easy to open and save files.

The .NET framework provides File and Directory classes which can be used to read and write files and these are covered later. Before that however, we shall look at the controls available to handle files.

Visual Studio environment provides dialogs to open, save and print files on the dialogs and printing toolbox. These are normally displayed using a menu system, and the MenuStrip control is used to create these. The relevant controls are shown in Figure 9-1 on page 136.

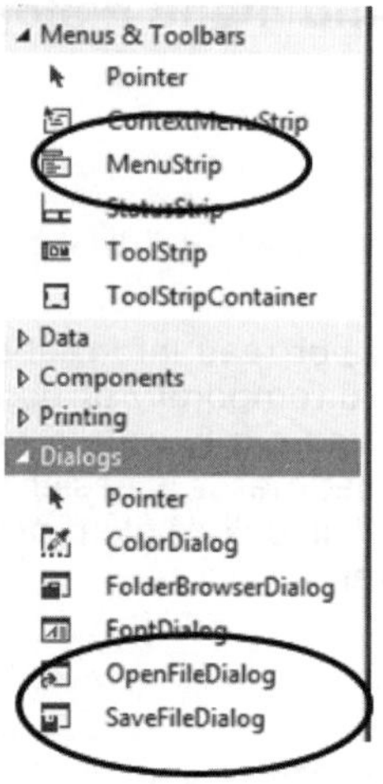

Figure 9-1 The MenuStrip and FileDialog controls

To open and save files, place the OpenFileDialog and SaveFileDialog controls on the form. You have used these whenever you have opened or saved files. They are not part of the form, so will be placed at the bottom of the form's display area. They are displayed by executing code and we will create a menu which will do this.

9.3.1 • The MenuStrip control – a simple RichTextBox editor

The MenuStrip control on the 'Menus and Toolbars' toolbox group is used to create the typical 'File, Edit, View .. Help' menu that many Windows programs have.

Let's study these with an exercise and create a simple text editor using the RichTextBox control. This application use a MenuStrip control to display a main menu like Word with File > Open and File > Save options, and use the familiar File handling dialogs.

- Start a new Windows Application and give it a suitable name (e.g. TextEditor).
- Add the OpenFileDialog and SaveFileDialog controls to the form (they will be placed in the status area)
- Place a MenuStrip control on the form. This invites you to type a heading, or you can add further MenuItems, a ComboBox or a TextBox, see Figure 9-2.

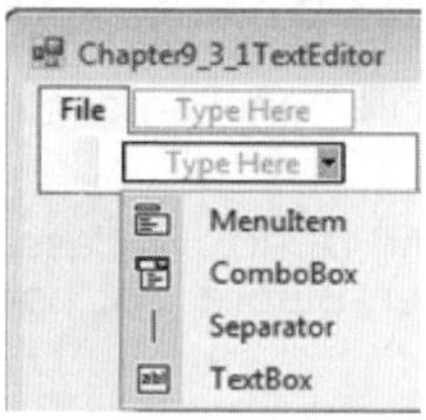

Figure 9-2 Menu Designer

We want to have a File heading here, so just type 'File' and press return. You can now enter the items for this drop down menu. Type 'Open' and 'Save'. If you hold the mouse over the menu item you will see a down arrow which as before, allows you to add further menu items, combo boxes, and text items or a separator.

If you want to delete an item in the menu, just right-click it and select 'delete'.

- Add a separator and a File > Exit option. If you want to you can add a File > New option. If you make a mistake clicking away from the menu will tidy things up for you.

Let's add an Help > About menu. Add a further menu item to the right of the File menu and type '&Help'. You will notice that the ampersand causes the 'H' in Help to be underlined and can be used as a short-cut item when your program runs. Add an '&About' item under the Help menu.

- Finally add a Rich Text box from the Common Controls toolbox group. This is where the file that is opened will be displayed. A Rich Text box provides more functionality than a text box including edit methods such as Find, Cut, Copy and Paste, and file handling methods LoadFile and SaveFile.

Your design should be similar to Figure 9-3:

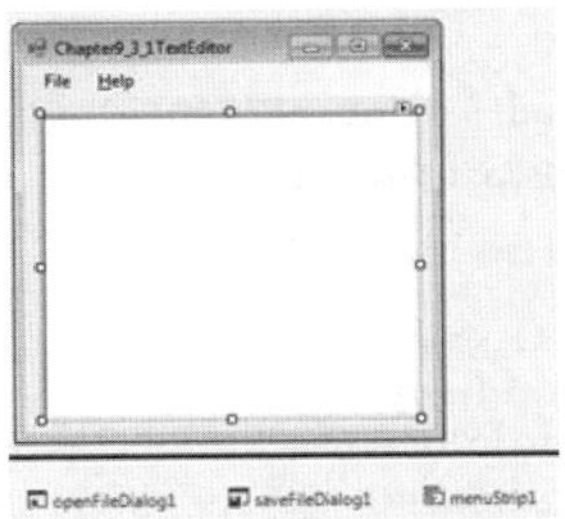

Figure 9-3 Text Editor User interface

Now we have to write the code for each of the menu items (File > Open) etc. Let's see how we can use the menu to open and save a file.

9.3.2 • The OpenFileDialog

The OpenFile and SaveFile dialogs appear when an application such as Word opens or saves a file, so your user should be familiar with them, see Figure 9-4. They are not permanently visible controls and appear when a 'ShowDialog' method is executed.

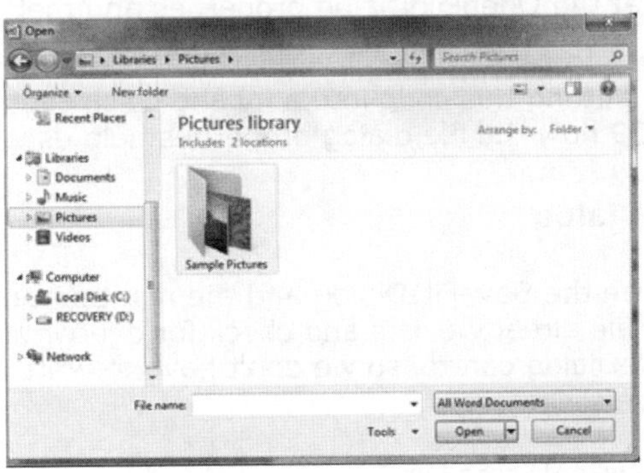

Figure 9-4 File Open Dialog

To add the File Open dialog, on the MenuStrip control click 'File' then double-click 'Open' to display the code for openToolStripMenuItem_Click.

The following code clears the richTextBox, sets up the openFileDialog properties and displays the open file dialog. Add this for the menuStrip 'File>Open' click code.

```
private void openToolStripMenuItem_Click(object sender, EventArgs e)
{
    // clear rich text box
    richTextBox1.Clear();
    // Set the open file dialog initial directory, filename and title
    openFileDialog1.InitialDirectory = @"C:\";
    openFileDialog1.FileName = "";
    openFileDialog1.Title = "Please select a file";
    // open the dialog and check for cancel
    if (openFileDialog1.ShowDialog() != DialogResult.Cancel)
    {
        // not cancelled - read file
        richTextBox1.LoadFile(openFileDialog1.FileName,
RichTextBoxStreamType.PlainText);
    }
    else
    {
        MessageBox.Show("You pressed cancel");
    }
}
```

This code sets the initial directory of the open file dialog to C:\ and gives a title prompt. The @ symbol is used to treat the string literally (it means you don't have to use a double backslash). The dialog is displayed when the openFileDialog.ShowDialog( ) method is executed. If the operation isn't cancelled, the file is read using the RichTextBox 'LoadFile' method.

If you want to, try this now and see what happens.

We have written code to set up the open file dialog properties such as InitialDirectory in the code, but of course we could set the properties at design time. You might like to take this opportunity to look at the OpenFileDialog properties and methods.

As the user should browse to select a file, it is unlikely there will be any errors. We could check for user errors by putting this code into a try and catch construct. But we will see in section 9.3.5 on page 139 how the file dialog properties help us with this.

9.3.3 • The SaveFileDialog

To save the file we will use the SaveFileDialog and the rich text box method 'SaveFile'. We might want to see if the file already exists and check for overwriting the file. These are properties of the SaveFileDialog control so we don't have to write code for them. Add the following for the File Save click:

```
private void saveToolStripMenuItem_Click(object sender, EventArgs e)
{
    if (saveFileDialog1.ShowDialog() != DialogResult.Cancel)
    {
        // not cancelled - write file
        richTextBox1.SaveFile(saveFileDialog1.FileName,
RichTextBoxStreamType.PlainText);
```

```
        }
        else
        {
            MessageBox.Show("You pressed cancel");
        }
    }
```

Finally, for the File > Exit commands add the following code:

```
    private void exitToolStripMenuItem_Click(object sender, EventArgs e)
    {
        Application.Exit();   // but you might like to give a warning
    }
```

Save the project and run the program. Select a text (.TXT) file to see it displayed in the list box. You can save the file under another name, or change the text in the memo box and save it. You have created a simple editor.

If you want to see how a binary file is displayed, try selecting an Application (.EXE) file.

9.3.4 • Open and Save Dialog Box properties

At this stage, the dialog boxes display all the file types. You might want to limit the file types that the user can see. It's not really necessary for our editor program to display anything other than text files and possibly 'All files'. To select specific files such as *.TXT, the filter property is used. The filter can be set in the properties or by code. To select files in code, try the following code:

```
    openFileDialog1.Filter = "All files (*.*)|*.*|Text files(*.TXT)|*.txt";
```

The same string is entered into the Filter property if you want to set it at design time.

You can try adding word documents to the list. Add: Word docs (*.DOCX) |*.DOCX) to the filter and open one to see how it is displayed.

Repeat the above for the Save Dialog component and save the project. You can now run the program, select only text files and open them in your editor.

Save the file with a different name and directory. Close the application using File > Exit and using your favourite editor, prove to yourself that the file has indeed been copied to a different directory.

9.3.5 • File error handling

If the user types in an invalid filename an error message is shown. This is because the OpenFileDialog's CheckFileExists property is set 'true'. You don't have to do any checks to see if the file selected exists.

The SaveFileDialog property CheckFileExists is set to False, so it is possible to overwrite an existing file. If this property is set true, a warning message appears when you try to overwrite an existing file. Again there is no need to write any checking code.

There are many other properties which you might find useful to try out, including 'CheckPathExists', 'DefaultExt' and 'AddExtension' You might like to see the default values for these.

9.4 • Adding Menu items – About box

The Help > About menu item hasn't been added. Let's do that. An About form is one of the forms available from the Visual studio menus.

Select Project> Add Windows Form and select About Box from the offerings.

An About Box is displayed, which you can modify to suit, see Figure 9-5.

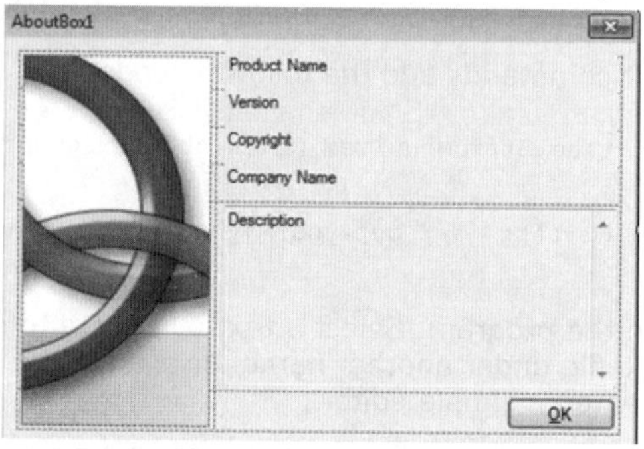

Figure 9-5 The About Box

The About box does not display the changes made to it at design time. The compiler uses the project's assembly information in AssemblyInfo.cs, see Figure 9-6. You should change the project assembly information using Project > Application > Assembly Information.

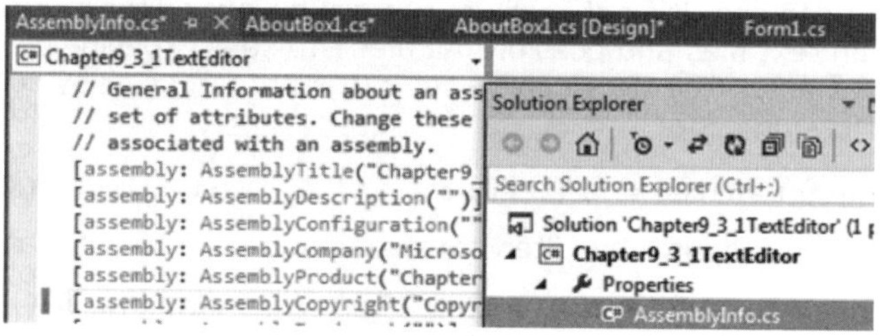

Figure 9-6 The About box information

The About box is displayed the same way we displayed a second form in Chapter 3 on page 53. Add the following code for the Help > About menu item

```
private void aboutToolStripMenuItem_Click(object sender, EventArgs e)
{
    AboutBox1 frmAbout = new AboutBox1();
    frmAbout.Show();
}
```

You also need to write code to close the AboutBox. Click the OK button and change its code to the following:

```
private void okButton_Click(object sender, EventArgs e)
{
    this.Close(); // or just Close();
}
```

The full program is available on Elektor's web site.

9.5 • PrintDialog boxes

You must control the printing process. PrintDialog and PrintDocument controls are on the toolbox and help the user specify items such as the printer, page orientation, font etc. The PrintDialog is displayed with the ShowDialog( ) method. The PrintDocument contains the event that prints the document.

Printing the text involves writing your own print event handler. A short code snippet is shown here. If you want further information on this, search for the PrintDocument Class and the Print method in MSDN library.

```
        private void printDialogToolStripMenuItem_Click(object sender,
    EventArgs e)
        {
         printDialog1.ShowDialog();
        }
        private void printDocumentToolStripMenuItem_Click(object sender,
    EventArgs e)
        {
          // Select filename (not used)
          printDocument1.PrinterSettings.PrintFileName =
    openFileDialog1.FileName;
          // Set printer
          printDocument1.PrinterSettings.PrinterName =
        "Microsoft XPS Document Writer";
          // Add Print event (we add our code for this below)
          printDocument1.PrintPage += printDocument1_PrintPage;
          // and print
          printDocument1.Print();
        }
        // Add this event code – called when printing
        private void printDocument1_PrintPage(object sender,
    System.Drawing.Printing.PrintPageEventArgs e)
        {
          richTextBox1.SelectAll();     // Example – select RTB text
          string textToPrint = richTextBox1.SelectedText;
          // and print
          e.Graphics.DrawString(textToPrint, new Font("Arial", 12),
        new SolidBrush(Color.Black), new PointF(15, 15));
        }
```

We will see the DrawString command in the Graphics chapter.

9.6 • RichTextBox editor: cut, paste copy and find

The rich text box also has methods for cut, copy and paste. All you have to do is add menu items for these, e.g. Edit> Cut and Edit >Paste, and add the following code:

```
private void cutToolStripMenuItem_Click(object sender, EventArgs e)
{
    richTextBox1.Cut();
}
private void pasteToolStripMenuItem_Click(object sender, EventArgs e)
{
    richTextBox1.Paste();
}
```

Run your program, type some text into the rich text box and select some of it. Edit > Cut will remove the selection and Edit > Paste will replace it. Edit > Copy works in a similar way.

For Edit > Find, you have to choose the text to find. Add an Edit > Find menu item and the following code for the click event. The code finds the text 'Text', matching its case and changes the selection to Verdana, 12, italic, blue.

```
private void findToolStripMenuItem_Click(object sender, EventArgs e)
{
    richTextBox1.Find("Text", RichTextBoxFinds.MatchCase);
    richTextBox1.SelectionFont = new Font
            ("Verdana", 12, FontStyle.Italic);
    richTextBox1.SelectionColor = Color.Blue;
}
```

Exercise: 1. Add an Edit > Copy command and 2. Add a box to request text to be found for the Edit > Find.

9.7 • File and Directory classes

You may not want to use the Open and Save file dialogs. Your program can create its own files and folders using the File and Directory classes. These provide methods for the creation, copying, deletion, moving and opening of files. They are **static** methods and (as we now know) don't have to be instantiated.

Note that some of the methods return another I/O type (e.g. StreamReader) when the file is created or opened. This is then used to access the file.

The main File methods are:

AppendText	Creates a StreamWriter that appends text to an existing file.
Copy	Copies an existing file to a new file.
Create	Creates a file in the specified path.
Delete	Deletes the specified file.
Exists	Determines whether the specified file exists.
Move	Moves a file to a new folder.

Open	Opens a FileStream on the specified path.
OpenRead	Opens an existing file for reading.
OpenText	Opens an existing text file for reading.
OpenWrite	Opens an existing file for writing.
ReadAllBytes	Opens a binary file, reads the file into a byte array and closes the file.
ReadAllLines	Opens a text file, reads all its lines into a string array and closes the file.
ReadAllText	Opens a text file, reads all lines of the file into a string and closes the file.
Replace	Replaces the contents of the file with the contents of another file, deleting the original file and creating a backup.
WriteAllBytes	Creates a new file, writes the specified byte array to the file and then closes the file. If the target file exists, it is overwritten.
WriteAllLines	Creates a new file, writes the specified string to the file and then closes the file. If the target file exists, it is overwritten.
WriteAllText	Creates a new file, write the contents to the file and closes the file. If the target file exists, it is overwritten.

The main Directory methods are:

CreateDirectory	Creates all the directories in a specified path.
Delete	Deletes a specified directory.
Exists	Determines whether the directory exists.
Move	Moves a file or a directory and its contents to a new location.

The FileStream class is used to read from, write to, open and close files on a file system. It provides access to a Stream, a class that provides byte read and write to a file, but could also be an I/O device, or as well shall see later, an internet socket.

StreamReader and StreamWriter classes are used to read and write text files and BinaryReader and BinaryWriter classes are used for binary data.

Remember, 'using System.IO' is needed at the top of your code to use these classes.

9.8 • File handling example

Here are two examples of writing and reading to files using the File and Directory classes. The first uses StreamWriter and StreamReader classes to create a text file and read it back, and the second uses File and Directory classes to check if they exist and then FileStream, BinaryWriter and BinaryReader to write binary data to a file, then read it back. These classes are in the System.IO namespace, so make sure that at the top of your code, you have

```
Using System.IO;
```

9.8.1 • Using StreamWriter and StreamReader objects

The following example creates a StreamWriter object to write text to a file and then creates a StreamReader object to read it.

```
// add using System.IO; at the top
// Create a stream to write to the file
StreamWriter sw = new StreamWriter("Test.txt");
// Add some text to the file.
sw.Write("Hello ");          // no CRLF
sw.WriteLine("World!");      // add CRLF
sw.WriteLine("-------------------");
// and close the file so others can access it
sw.Close();
// Here the 'using' statement also closes the StreamReader.
using (StreamReader sr = new StreamReader("Test.txt"))
{
    MessageBox.Show(sr.ReadLine());   // Displays 'Hello world!'
    MessageBox.Show(sr.ReadLine());   // Displays  '-----------'
}
```

The file will be saved in the same folder as the .EXE file, and can be checked by reading it in Notepad (or the editor you have just created!)

9.8.2 • Using BinaryReader and BinaryWriter objects

The following example creates a BinaryWriter object to write binary values text to a file and then creates a BinaryReader object to read the data. Make sure you have access rights to the folder you use, or use the default folder as above.

```
// add using System.IO; at the top
string dirPath = @"C:/Temp";
// Create the folder C:\temp if it doesn't exist
if (!Directory.Exists(dirPath))
{
    Directory.CreateDirectory(dirPath);
}
string fileName = @dirPath + "/TestFile.bin";
// create and binary file if it doesn't exist
if (!File.Exists(fileName))
{
    // file doesn't exist - create file
    FileStream fs = new FileStream(fileName, FileMode.CreateNew);
    BinaryWriter bw = new BinaryWriter(fs);
    byte[] byteArray = { 0x48, 0x45, 0x4C, 0x4C, 0x4F }; // hello!
    for (int i = 0; i < byteArray.Length; i++)
    {
        bw.Write(byteArray[i]);
    }
    bw.Close();
    fs.Close();
}
// Read it back and display binary and character.
```

```
FileStream fsRead = new FileStream(fileName, FileMode.Open);
BinaryReader br = new BinaryReader(fsRead);
for (int i = 0; i < fsRead.Length; i++)
{
    byte byteRead = br.ReadByte();
    MessageBox.Show(byteRead.ToString() + " " + (char)byteRead);
}
br.Close();
fsRead.Close();
```

Note that as this file contains ASCII characters 'HELLO', it can also be read by notepad.

9.9 • Self Assessment Exercises

1. Watch video #12 at Microsoft's Virtual Academy on Reading data from a text file if you haven't seen it already.
2. Add Print commands to the menu strip and your editor. If you need more information try searching in Help.
3. Add the cut, copy, paste commands to your editor.
4. Add Find and Replace commands to your editor.
5. Write a program to open a text file and save the individual high and low 4 bit nibbles of each byte and in a binary file. Write a program to do the reverse, i.e. reads two bytes from a binary file, combines them and writes them as a text file.

9.10 • Summary

In this chapter we have looked at text and binary file types. We have seen the MenuStrip component and looked at the openFileDialog and saveFileDialogs. A simple editor was created using the versatile rich text box to load and save files. The editor was extended to provide print, cut, paste and find commands. Finally we looked at File and Directory classes and saw how to read and write both text and binary files using StreamWriter and StreamReader classes and FileStream, BinaryWriter and BinaryReader classes. We shall use these classes again when we look at Internet communication.

Chapter 10 • Graphics and Multimedia

10.1 • Introduction

Your user interface can be made more impressive if it uses images and graphics. We have seen the picture box control which can display images. There are no toolbox controls such as rectangle or ellipse that can be placed directly on the form; they have to be drawn by your code. In this chapter we will see how to draw graphics objects. We shall also look at the Media Player control.

10.2 • Drawing Graphics

The basic procedure for drawing text or graphics is as follows: A **Graphics object** is created on a form or container such as a panel where the graphics is to be drawn. A pen or brush object is defined and then Graphics methods are called to draw or paint lines and shapes. The pen is used to draw lines and the brush to fill areas. The Graphics object is in the **System.Drawing** namespace.

Exercise: Line Drawing

Let's see how we draw lines with an example that draws a line on a panel on a form.

Start a new application and place a panel on the form. So you can see the panel, change its BorderStyle property to FixedSingle. Find the panel's MouseDown event and change it to the following code:

```
private void panel1_MouseDown(object sender, MouseEventArgs e)
{
    System.Drawing.Graphics grpObject;
    grpObject = this.panel1.CreateGraphics();
    Pen objmyPen = new Pen(System.Drawing.Color.Blue);
    grpObject.DrawLine(objmyPen, 0, 0, 100, 100);
}
```

In this code the graphics object (grpObject) is created on panel1. A Pen object is created (objmyPen) in Blue. Note the American spelling for colour. The DrawLine method uses the Pen object to draw between two points. In this case from 0, 0 to 100, 100. Make sure that 'using System.Drawing' is at the top of your code.

Run the program and click on the panel. A blue line should be drawn from top left to bottom right of the panel as shown in Figure 10-1. Note that point (0,0) is the top left, with increasing X values moving right and increasing Y values moving down the screen.

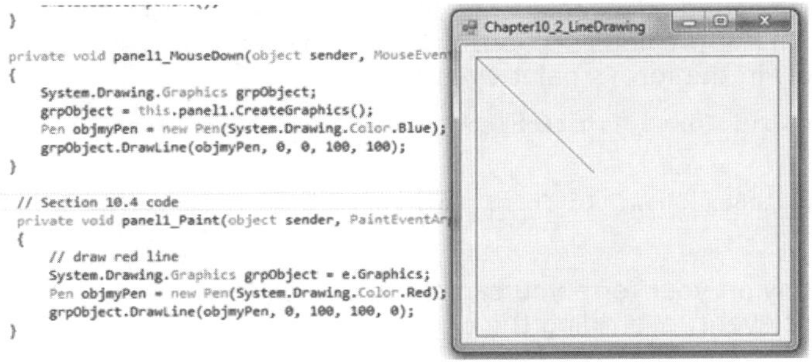

Figure 10-1 Drawing on a panel

10.3 • The Paint event

Unfortunately the line doesn't stay drawn if the form is minimized and then redisplayed. (Try it now). In this example the line is only drawn when the panel is clicked and not when the panel is redisplayed. We may need to draw the line when our form is redrawn. The panel and the form controls have a paint event which occurs when the control is redrawn. We will now use this event to draw a line.

Find the paint event for the panel in the properties window and change it to the following code:

```
private void panel1_Paint(object sender, PaintEventArgs e)
{
    // draw red line
    System.Drawing.Graphics grpObject = e.Graphics;
    Pen objmyPen = new Pen(System.Drawing.Color.Red);
    grpObject.DrawLine(objmyPen, 0, 100, 100, 0);
}
```

The paint event is the default event when you click the panel.

You might have noticed when you declared the Pen object that you can choose a Brush type instead of a Color. We'll see the brush types soon.

Run the code. When the panel is drawn, its Paint event occurs and a red line is drawn on the panel from bottom left to top right. Click the panel to draw the blue line. Now minimize and redisplay the form; the original blue line disappears, but the red line is still drawn by the paint event.

Note how the graphics object (e.Graphics) was obtained from the PaintEventArgs parameter passed to the panel's paint event.

If you need to redraw your graphics from your code you should not call the Paint event, but instead call the Invalidate method. This invalidates the object which will then be redrawn by Windows, e.g.:

```
panel1.Invalidate( );
```

You should dispose of your objects when you have finished with them. To do so use the code:

```
objmyPen.Dispose( );
```

10.4 • Drawing on the form

When the form is opened or revealed, the objects on it are drawn by the paint event. We saw this happen in the previous section. You can prove this by displaying a message using MessageBox.Show in the form's paint event:

```
private void Form1_Paint(object sender, PaintEventArgs e)
{
    MessageBox.Show("In Form1_Paint");
}
```

If you wish to draw on your form you can either add code to this event or you can write your own OnPaint event, overriding the original.

For example, add the following OnPaint method

```
protected override void OnPaint(PaintEventArgs e)
{
    Graphics grpObject = e.Graphics;
    Pen objmyPen = new Pen(System.Drawing.Color.Blue);
    grpObject.DrawLine(objmyPen, 0, 0, 100, 100);
}
```

We saw the **override** command in section 8.5 on page 125. The Paint event (now your OnPaint code) is triggered when the form is opened or displayed and hence the graphics is drawn every time; it doesn't disappear. It will draw the blue line on the form, behind the panel.

You can still call the original Form's Paint code from your OnPaint method if you add the following code:

```
base.OnPaint(e);
```

In this code the term 'base' refers to the base class, in this case the Form. This code calls the form's original Paint code, which we had previously overridden.

If you want to prove it, add the base.OnPaint(e); code to the protected override void OnPaint event and see what happens. The message only appears if the base.OnPaint(e); code is present and appears when the form is resized or redisplayed.

Here's the full code:

```
private void panel1_Paint(object sender, PaintEventArgs e)
{
    // draw red line
    System.Drawing.Graphics grpObject = e.Graphics;
    Pen objmyPen = new Pen(System.Drawing.Color.Red);
    grpObject.DrawLine(objmyPen, 0, 100, 100, 0);
}
protected override void OnPaint(PaintEventArgs e)
{
    // base.OnPaint(e);  // uncomment to see the "In Form1_Paint" message
    Graphics grpObject = e.Graphics;
    Pen objmyPen = new Pen(System.Drawing.Color.Blue);
    grpObject.DrawLine(objmyPen, 0, 0, 100, 100);
}
private void Form1_Paint(object sender, PaintEventArgs e)
{
    MessageBox.Show("In Form1_Paint");
}
```

Exercise: Try using OnPaint(e); instead of base.OnPaint(e); and see what happens. Can you also use Form1_Paint(null, e); instead of base.OnPaint(e); ?

If you need your graphics to stay on the form then you can do it in one of two ways:

- Place all the code in the form's Paint event. This is best if you are drawing only a few items.

- Draw to a memory bitmap and copy the bitmap to the form in the form's Paint event. This is more complicated and better if you are doing a lot of drawing, but beyond the scope of this book.

If you want to find out more on how **base** works, see the MSDN reference at: *https://msdn.microsoft.com/en-us/library/hfw7t1ce.aspx*

10.5 • The Pen

As we have seen, the Pen is used to draw lines and we shall use it to draw shapes such as rectangles, circles, ellipses and polygons later. A Pen object is created and it controls the appearance of the lines drawn. The main Pen properties are:

- Color – as we have seen, we can use the System colors or we can specify the individual values for Alpha, Red, Green and Blue (ARGB). Alpha defines the transparency of the colour and is optional. Each ARGB value can be from 0 – 255. For the RGB values 0, 0, 0 (0x0) is black and 255, 255, 255 (0xFFF) is white.
- Width - The width in pixels of the line drawn.
- DashStyle - Specifies the pattern of the line (Solid, Dash, Dot, DashDot, Custom, etc.)

Once a pen object has been created its colour, width, style etc can be changed as shown in the following example code fragment:

```
System.Drawing.Graphics grpObject;
grpObject = this.panel1.CreateGraphics();
// create blue pen 5 pixels wide
Pen objmyPen = new Pen(System.Drawing.Color.Blue, 5);
grpObject.DrawLine(objmyPen, 0, 0, 100, 100);


// change Width
objmyPen.Width = 3;


// change style to dashed
objmyPen.DashStyle =
        System.Drawing.Drawing2D.DashStyle.DashDotDot;
// change to semi-transparent red
objmyPen.Color = System.Drawing.Color.FromArgb(128, 255, 0, 0);
grpObject.DrawLine(objmyPen, 0, 100, 100, 0);
```

Note that the FromArgb( ) method is used to set the alpha and RGB values. The program output is shown in figure 10.2.

10.5.1 • Line end caps

You can have different start or end to your lines, e.g. rounded, or triangular. These are known as end caps. They can be arrow, diamond, flat, round or square.

Try the following code

```
objmyPen.Width = 20;
objmyPen.DashStyle =
   System.Drawing.Drawing2D.DashStyle.Solid;
objmyPen.StartCap =
            System.Drawing.Drawing2D.LineCap.RoundAnchor;
objmyPen.EndCap = System.Drawing.Drawing2D.LineCap.Round;
objmyPen.Color = System.Drawing.Color.DarkBlue;
grpObject.DrawLine(objmyPen, 30, 150, 150, 150);
```

The code and output is as seen in Figure 10-2.

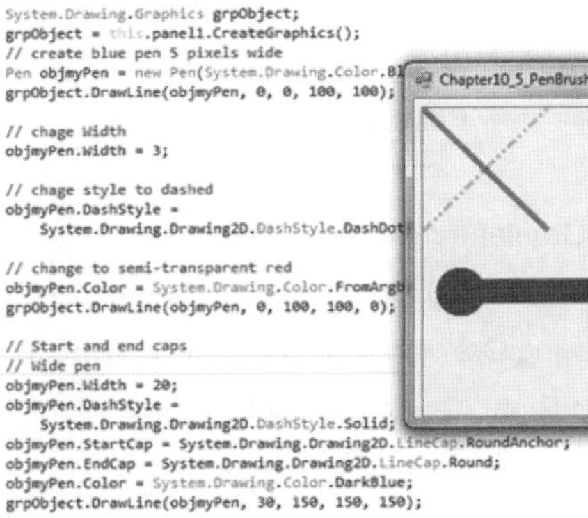

Figure 10-2 Pen drawing program and output

10.6 • The Brush

The Brush object defines how areas are filled. Like the Pen, the Brush object has to be created and its main properties are its colour (color) and style.

- The Color determines the colour of the filled shapes, including foreground and background colours.
- The Style determines if the area is filled with a solid colour or a line style. Some styles are:

  HatchBrush (uses a foreground and background colour),

  LinearGradientBrush (blends one colour into another along a line or rectangle),

  SolidBrush (fills with one colour),

  TextureBrush (uses an Image).

The Brush is defined in the **System.Drawing** namespace. When you declare the Brush you want to use, you don't use 'Brush', as it is a class (from which all the other Brush types come), you declare the type of brush you want to draw with, e.g. SolidBrush or HatchBrush and use that.

The HatchBrush and the LinearGradientBrush are found in the **System.Drawing.Drawing2D** namespace, so include this at the top of your code.

The LinearGradientBrush uses **Point** objects as its arguments; consequently we need to define new instances of Point to use them.

Some examples of declaring a brush are:

```
// Fill with a solid brush
SolidBrush mySolidBrush = new SolidBrush(Color.Red);
// A blue to red HatchBrush
// – add 'using System.Drawing.Drawing2D'
HatchBrush myhBrush = new HatchBrush
(HatchStyle.Horizontal, Color.Blue, Color.FromArgb(255, 0, 0));

// declare some points
Point topLeft = new Point(0, 0);
Point bottomRight = new Point(100, 100);

// declare a linearGradientbrush red to blue
System.Drawing.Drawing2D.LinearGradientBrush myLGBrush =
 new System.Drawing.Drawing2D.LinearGradientBrush
    (topLeft, bottomRight, Color.Red, Color.Blue);
// get a bitmap
Bitmap imageBitMap = new Bitmap(@"grandDad.bmp");
// declare a TextureBrush
TextureBrush myTBrush = new TextureBrush(imageBitMap);
// Draw the picture in a rectangle
grpObject.FillRectangle(myTBrush, 0, 0, 270, 370);
```

10.7 • Drawing Text

Text is drawn with graphic object's **DrawString()** method. You state the text string, the Font and Brush together with the X and Y position of the text, for example:

```
private void panel1_Paint(object sender, PaintEventArgs e)
{
// get the graphics object used to paint
Graphics grpObject = e.Graphics;
Font myFont = new Font("Arial", 16);
SolidBrush myBrush = new SolidBrush(Color.Green);
grpObject.DrawString("Mystring", myFont, myBrush, 20, 30);
}
```

If you are drawing with a simple Brush, you can choose one from the **Brushes** class. For example:

```
grpObject.DrawString("Mystring", myFont, Brushes.Green, 20, 30);
```

If you want to rotate text, use the **RotateTransform** method. If you want to move its position, use **TranslateTransform**, for example:

```
e.Graphics.RotateTransform(30);
e.Graphics.TranslateTransform(50.0F, 50.0F);
e.Graphics.DrawString
("Rotated and moved text", myFont, Brushes.Gold, 100, 0);
```

10.8 • Basic Shapes

Methods are provided for graphics objects to draw ellipses and rectangles (and hence circles and squares). A graphics object is created and the shape methods are used. We have seen the DrawString( ) method. You can let the IntelliSense prompt display them, see Figure 10-3.

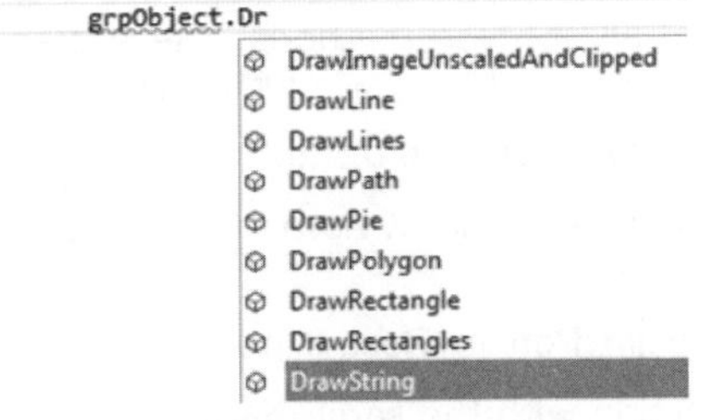

Figure 10-3 Graphics object drawing methods

The basic graphic methods are:

```
DrawRectangle (Pen p, int X, int Y, int width, int height);
```

This draws a rectangle with a Pen p, at X, Y, with width and height.

```
DrawEllipse (Pen p, int X, int Y, int width, int height);
```

This draws an ellipse with Pen p, bounded by the rectangle defined by top left hand point X, Y with width and height.

```
FillRectangle (Brush b, int X, int Y, int width, int height);
```

This draws a filled rectangle with Brush b, bounded by the rectangle defined by top left hand point X, Y with width and height.

```
FillEllipse(Brush b, int X, int Y, int width, int height);
```

This draws a filled ellipse with brush b, bounded by the rectangle defined by top left hand point X, Y with width and height.

For more detail on drawing shapes, refer to the self assessment exercises. This has an example which draws a different shape and colour each time the form is painted as shown in Figure 10-4 on page 154. The code for this and above is on Elektor's web site.

Figure 10-4 Shape program output

10.9 • Other shapes – arcs, pies, polylines and polygons

Other shapes such as arcs, pie, filled pie, polylines, polygons and filled polygons can also be drawn. The methods for these are defined as follows, but aren't simple.

DrawArc(Pen p, int X, int Y, int width, int height, int startAngle, int sweepAngle);

This uses the Pen and draws an arc of an ellipse from startAngle in degrees, sweeping by sweepAngle, bounded by the rectangle defined by top left hand point X, Y with width and height.

There are many variations of all of these methods. The Rectangle object can also be used as the bounding area. This replaces the 'x, y, width, height' code, for instance:

Rectangle myRect = new Rectangle(0,0,200,100);

This defines a rectangle with at 0, 0 and a width of 200 and height of 100. The DrawArc code becomes:

grpObject.DrawArc(objmyPen, myRect, 0, 45);

The DrawPie draws a pie section with the same parameters as the DrawArc.

DrawPie (Pen p, int X, int Y, int width, int height, int startAngle, int sweepAngle);

Arcs and Pies are drawn in a clockwise direction, with 0° being along the +X-axis. The following code draws the pie section shown in figure 10.5, bound by a box at x=0, y=0, width = 100, height=100, start angle = 0 and sweep angle =45°.

DrawPie(objmyPen, 0, 0, 100, 100, 0, 45);

The code in Figure 10-5 shows how to draw a Pie shape directly on the form when it is clicked.

```
private void Form1_Click(object sender, EventArgs e)
{
    System.Drawing.Graphics graphics = this.CreateGraphics();
    // create red pen 5 pixels wide
    Pen objmyPen = new Pen(Color.Red, 5);
    graphics.DrawPie(objmyPen, 0, 0, 100, 100, 0, 45);
}
```

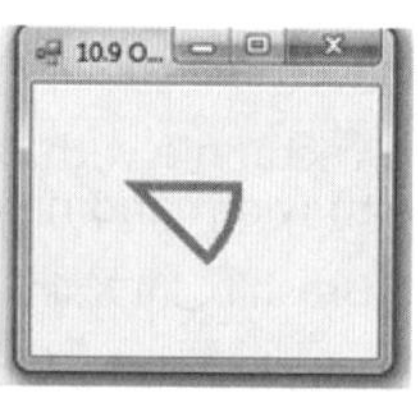

Figure 10-5 A Pie section

FillPie (Brush b, int X, int Y, int width, int height, int startAngle, int sweepAngle);

FillPie is Similar to DrawPie, except a filled Pie is drawn using a Brush.

Polylines and Polygons (a closed series of Polylines) are best drawn using the **Polyline** and **Polygon** methods. These methods draw a series of lines connecting points which are passed to the method in an ArrayList.

A filled polygon can also be drawn using the FillPolygon method.

The self assessment exercises have an example on drawing Polygons. In the exercise the user clicks the mouse to define the X and Y positions for the polygon's points, and produces a display similar to Figure 10-6.

Figure 10-6 Polygon program output

10.10 • Drawing Graphs and Charts

C# now includes a chart control, so you no longer have to draw your own or rely on external software. We will look at drawing graphs and charts in Chapter 17 on page 239.

10.11 • Multimedia applications

The MediaPlayer control is used to control playing or recording devices such as audio or video CD-ROM/DVD player.

The MediaPlayer control provides a screen and controls to manage the media (play, pause, stop, etc.), see Figure 10-7.

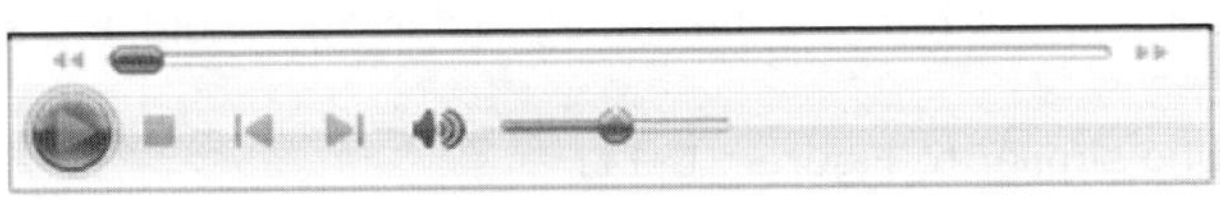

Figure 10-7 MediaPlayer control

The mediaPlayer control needs to be added to the toolbox before it can be used - right-click the Toolbox menu and select 'Choose Items', see Figure 10-8.

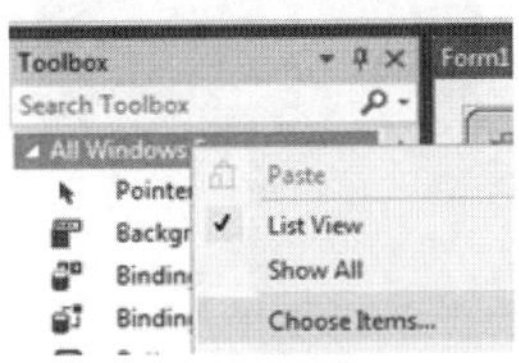

Figure 10-8 Choose Toolbox items

This displays 'Choose toolbox items'. Select the COM (component object model) controls tab and scroll to Windows Media Player, see Figure 10-9 on page 156.

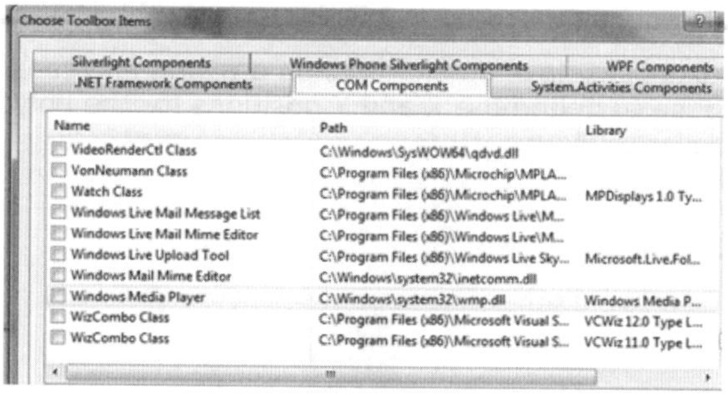

Figure 10-9 COM Component Toolbox items

Tick the box and click OK to add the component. It should appear in the toolbox, see Figure 10-10.

Figure 10-10 Adding Media Player control

Add the Player to the form and resize it to show the controls and the screen. Its default name is 'axWindowsMediaPlayer1'.

Add a button and change its Text to 'Load Video'. Find a video and add the following code for the click event:

```
axWindowsMediaPlayer1.URL = @"myVideo.mp4";
```

The @ symbol instructs the compiler to ignore backslashes which would otherwise be interpreted as an escape sequence. Make sure the file exists, that you are allowed to access it and if necessary put it in the bin/debug folder. You could add a file dialog box to search for media files.

Your design should be similar to Figure 10-11:

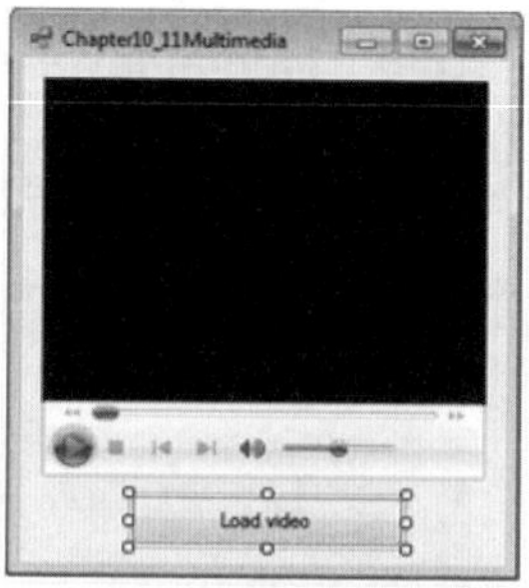

Figure 10-11 The MediaPlayer User Interface

The media will start when you set the URL, but you can control the video from your application, for example you could have:

```
axWindowsMediaPlayer1.Ctlcontrols.stop( );
```

or

```
axWindowsMediaPlayer1.Ctlcontrols.play( );
```

If you don't want the player controls to be displayed, set the uiMode property to 'none'. You can also turn the screen off if by making it invisible. E.g:

```
axWindowsMediaPlayer1.uiMode = "none";
axWindowsMediaPlayer1.uiMode = "invisible;
```

You can also have a mini or custom controls display.

Note: if you copy the multimedia file to your program folder, you can move files between computers if you use relative addressing.

You don't have to add a Windows Media Player control to your form. You can play music using the following code:

```
WMPLib.WindowsMediaPlayer wmplayer =
        new WMPLib.WindowsMediaPlayer();
wmplayer.URL = @"C:\Temp\MyMusic.mp3";
wmplayer.controls.play();
```

If you have problems installing the Media Player, or want to distribute your multimedia application, you need to add a couple of files to your application. See the following reference for more details:

http://msdn.microsoft.com/en-us/library/dd564585(VS.85).aspx

You can also use the **System.Media.SoundPlayer** to play WAV files, see section19.4 on page 267.

10.11.1 • MediaPlayer events

If you want to loop your sound or video, you have to detect the event which tells you the media has finished playing and restart your media. Find the **PlayStateChanged** event and add the following code to loop the media:

```
private void axWindowsMediaPlayer1_PlayStateChange
 (object sender, AxWMPLib._WMPOCXEvents_PlayStateChangeEvent e)
    {
      axWindowsMediaPlayer1.Ctlcontrols.play( );
    }
```

If you do add this code, note that you cannot use the pause button because the playing state changes (you've paused it) triggering this event, which starts it again!

All the code is available via Elektor's web site.

10.12 • Launching Windows applications

As we have just seen how to run Mediaplayer, this might be a good place to explain how to launch external windows applications such as Word or Excel from your program.

The **ProcessStartInfo** system call is used. It's in System.Diagnostics so add using System.Diagnostics; at the top of your code. The following code launches Google Earth on my computer:

```
// Prepare the process
ProcessStartInfo startInfo = new ProcessStartInfo();
// Enter the full path and name
startInfo.FileName = @"C:\Program Files (x86)\Google\
                        Google Earth\client\googleearth.exe";
int exitCode;
// Run application and wait for it to end
using (Process process = Process.Start(startInfo))
{
    process.WaitForExit();
    // Get the exit code if you need it.
    exitCode = process.ExitCode;
}
```

You may also want to pass any arguments (e.g. filename of Word or Excel file), password, or state which Window style you want (e.g. none, single or 3D border), etc. These parameters can all be set before launching.

10.13 • Self Assessment Exercises

Try the following exercises

1. The Paint method

   Place a panel on the form. Add MessageBox.Show methods to the panel's paint event and the form's paint event and observe the paint's operation. Override the form's paint event with your own OnPaint method, which should also have a MessageBox.Show method. Notice that the original form's paint method no longer runs. Add a base.OnPaint(e); code and see that the form's paint method is now called.

2. Drawing shapes

   As an exercise in drawing the different shapes, type in the following code for the form's OnPaint overridden event. It draws a different shape and colour each time the form is painted as shown in Figure 10-6 on page 155.

```
protected override void OnPaint(PaintEventArgs e)
{
  Graphics grpObject = e.Graphics;   // create Graphics object
  Pen objmyPen = new Pen(System.Drawing.Color.Blue);   // define Pen
  SolidBrush myBrush = new SolidBrush(Color.Red);           // and brush
  Font arial = new Font("Arial", 12);     // and font
  Random RandomNumber = new Random();// define random number
  int rndNo = RandomNumber.Next(4);       // get random value 0 to 3
  switch (rndNo)          // get random brush color
  {
      case 0: myBrush.Color = Color.Red; break;
      case 1: myBrush.Color = Color.Blue; break;
      case 2: myBrush.Color = Color.Orange; break;
      case 3: myBrush.Color = Color.Green; break;
  }
```

```
rndNo = RandomNumber.Next(4);     // get random value 0 to 3
switch (rndNo)          // get random pen color
{
    case 0: objmyPen.Color = Color.DarkOrchid; break;
    case 1: objmyPen.Color = Color.Tomato; break;
    case 2: objmyPen.Color = Color.Peru; break;
    case 3: objmyPen.Color = Color.AliceBlue; break;
}
rndNo = RandomNumber.Next(7);     // get random number 0-6
int rndX = RandomNumber.Next(100);    // get random X and Y
int rndY = RandomNumber.Next(100);    // values for end point
string drawnstr = null;       // string for DrawString
switch (rndNo)        // draw random shape at 0,0
{
    case 0:           // draw line
        grpObject.DrawLine(objmyPen, 0, 0, (float)rndX, (float)rndY);
        drawnstr = "Line to ";
        break;
    case 1:           // draw rectangle
        grpObject.DrawRectangle(objmyPen, 0, 0, (float)rndX, (float)rndY);
        drawnstr = "Rectangle ";
        break;
    case 2:           // fill rectangle
        grpObject.FillRectangle(myBrush, 0, 0, (float)rndX, (float)rndY);
        drawnstr = "Filled rectangle to ";
        break;
    case 3:           // draw ellipse
        grpObject.DrawEllipse(objmyPen, 0, 0, (float)rndX, (float)rndY);
        drawnstr = "Ellipse to ";
        break;
    case 4:           // fill ellipse
        grpObject.FillEllipse(myBrush, 0, 0, (float)rndX, (float)rndY);
        drawnstr = "Filled ellipse to ";
        break;
    case 5:           // draw square x = y
        grpObject.DrawRectangle(objmyPen, 0, 0, (float)rndX, (float)rndX);
        drawnstr = "Square to ";
        break;
    case 6:           // draw circle x = y
        grpObject.DrawEllipse(objmyPen, 0, 0, (float)rndX, (float)rndX);
        drawnstr = "Circle to ";
        break;
} // end switch
// draw string
grpObject.DrawString((drawnstr + rndX + "," + rndY),
arial, myBrush, 0, 100);
```

```
    base.OnPaint(e);  // call form's paint event
}
```

3. Drawing Polygons

   Let us study a filled polygon example. In this example the polygon is drawn as the user clicks on a panel. The mouse X and Y coordinates are added to an ArrayList and the panel is invalidated to force a redraw. Refer to Chapter 5 on page 77, Arrays and Strings, for more details of the ArrayList.

   Start a new project and place a panel on the form. We shall draw the polygon on the panel. Place a button labeled 'Reset' on the form (named btnReset here)

   Add the following code for the panel's mouseDown event, the paint event and the button click event, so the complete code is as follows:

```
private System.Collections.ArrayList aryPoints =
    new System.Collections.ArrayList();
SolidBrush myBrush = new SolidBrush(Color.Gold);
private void panel1_MouseDown(object sender, MouseEventArgs e)
{
    aryPoints.Add(new Point(e.X, e.Y));
    // x and y postion of mouse passed
    panel1.Invalidate();
    // Invalidate to call panel's paint event
}
private void btnReset_Click(object sender, EventArgs e)
{
    // create a new arrayList
    aryPoints = new System.Collections.ArrayList();
    panel1.Invalidate();
    // and make sure paint is called
}
private void panel1_Paint(object sender, PaintEventArgs e)
{
    Graphics myGrpObject = e.Graphics;
    // get panel's graphics object
    if (aryPoints.Count > 1)
    // 2 points or more - draw shape
    {
        Point[] arrayofPoints =
            (Point[])aryPoints.ToArray(aryPoints[0].GetType());
        myGrpObject.FillPolygon(myBrush, arrayofPoints);
    }
}// end method paint
```

This may need a short explanation. An ArrayList (aryPoints) and brush are created with the lines:

```
System.Collections.ArrayList aryPoints = new
        System.Collections.ArrayList();
```

When the mouse button is clicked, the mouse X and Y points are added to the dynamic ArrayList (aryPoints). The X and Y position of the mouse is passed with the MouseEventArgs (e) and obtained from e.X and e.Y. The panel is invalidated, which causes it to be repainted by calling the panel's paint event.

The panel's paint event draws a filled polygon if there are more than 2 points. The FillPolygon method fills a polygon defined by an array of Points, so the ArrayList has to be converted to an array. This is done with the line of code:

```
Point[ ] arrayofPoints = (Point[ ])aryPoints.ToArray(aryPoints[0].GetType());
```

The ArrayList can hold different types of data, so GetType is used to pass that information to the arrayofPoints array. We have seen GetType used before.

Finally when the Reset button is clicked a new ArrayList is created and the panel invalidated creating a new blank panel.

Your program should produce a display similar to Figure 10-6 on page 155 when the form is clicked.

4. A Scribble program.

   Write a program that draws a line which follows the mouse movement. Hint: you will have to use the mousemove event.

5. Find out more about rotating and translating text. Can you do it for an image too?

6. Search MSDN for **ProcessStartInfo** to find out more about launching apps.

10.14 • Summary

In this chapter we have seen how to draw graphics. We have seen how to use the pen and brush to draw lines and basic shapes such as ellipse and rectangle, as well as more complicated shapes such as arcs, pie and filled pie. We have seen how the Paint method works and how to override the Paint method to ensure our drawings are always redrawn. Finally we have seen how we can add multimedia controls to our programs and launch external applications from our programs.

Chapter 11 • Debugging

11.1 • Introduction

Sooner or later your programs will have a problem that causes a run-time error, hangs the computer, or just fails to work as you expected. I imagine that has already happened to you by now. You will need to debug the program to find out why it's not working. The development environment has tools to help you debug your program and get it working. It should be noted that there may be some differences depending on the version of Visual Studio you have.

The compiler will detect syntax errors and anything else it can't understand and it does go a long way to removing many errors so that it will compile, but your program may still fail due to a run-time or logic error. Typical run-time errors are: divide by zero, text box type conversion error, or opening a non-existent file. We have seen how to trap run-time exceptions using try and catch code, but in this chapter we shall study how to use the debugger within the development environment.

11.2 • Writing to the Debug Window

Before we study the debugger, let's see how we can write a variable's value to the debug window using a C# command. We do this using the Debug.WriteLine method which is held in the System.Diagnostics namespace.

Start a new project and place a textbox and a button on the form. Set the text box's multiline property to true and add some text to the box (e.g. 'line 1', 'line 2' etc.). We shall display this in the debug output window.

Change the button click code to the following:

```
private void button1_Click(object sender, EventArgs e)
{
    // Create a string array and save the content of the lines.
    string[] tempArray = textBox1.Lines;
    // Loop through the array and write the array to the debug window.
    for (int count = 0; count < tempArray.Length; count++)
    {
        System.Diagnostics.Debug.WriteLine(tempArray[count]);
    }
}
```

You can also use Console.WriteLine(); you will see used this for Console applications.

Run the program. The following should appear in the debug window (see Figure 11-1 on page 164). If the Output window isn't displayed, click Debug>Windows>Output.

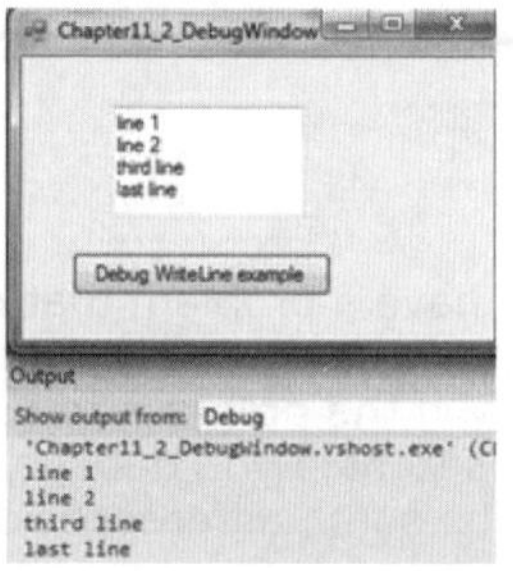

Figure 11-1 The Debug Window Output

Instead of adding code to display your variable's values in the Debug Window, you can also display then using the IDE's menus, e.g. Debug > Windows > Local.

You may also see that the Diagnostic Tools window opens. We will look at that later.

11.3 • Using the Debugger

The debugger provides options to:

- Run the program to the cursor position or specified points (known as a breakpoint).
- To view, disable, enable and delete breakpoints.
- To set conditions on breakpoint operation.
- To pause the program.
- To restart in different ways after meeting a breakpoint or pause.
- To view, evaluate and modify variables.

But as we will see, VS2015 has a new Diagnostic Tools window which includes the Output window; an intelligent trace option (IntelliTrace) which records and traces your code's execution history (Call Stack and Locals); and CPU and Memory usage tools. Performance Tips (perfTips) also provide an indication of how long it takes your code to execute. IntelliTrace is only available with the Enterprise version of Visual Studio.

11.3.1 • Setting a breakpoint

If you want stop the program at a specific line of code, you can run to the cursor position or set a breakpoint. To run to the cursor, right-click the line you want to stop at and select 'run to cursor'. Alternatively, you can set as many breakpoints as you want by clicking the grey area to the left of the line of code where you want the breakpoint. A red circle is displayed and the line of code highlighted, see Figure 11-2 on page 165. The breakpoint is removed if the red circle is clicked a second time.

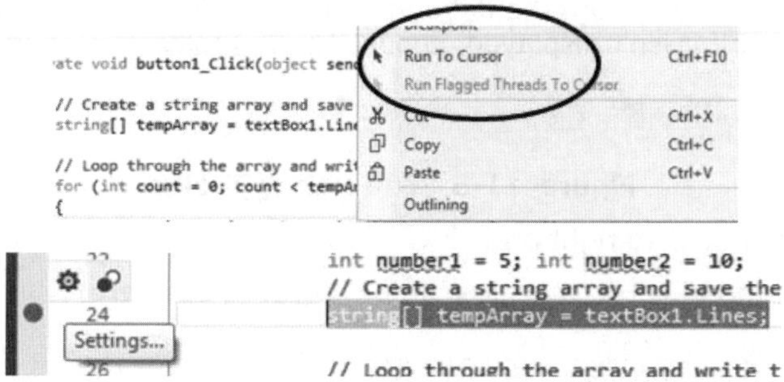

Figure 11-2 Setting a breakpoint

We will look at the Settings option later.

The program will stop when it reaches the breakpoint. The line of code about to be executed is highlighted in yellow with an arrow pointing to it. If the cursor is now hovered over a variable its value will be displayed, see Figure 11-3.

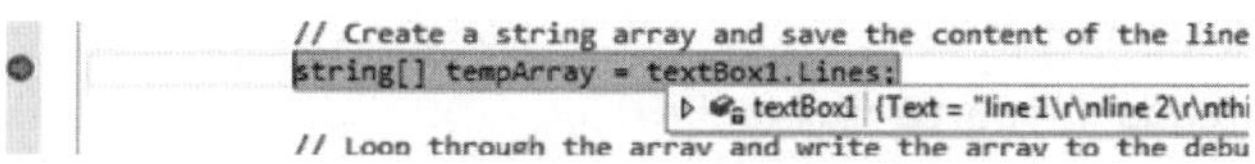

Figure 11-3 Program stopped at breakpoint and displaying a value

If the item is an object (as it is in Figure 11-3), you can also expand its detail ('drill down') by holding the cursor over the object and then moving to the arrow symbol. Figure 11-4 shows the textBox object expanded to show its properties. You can drill down further if items have more arrow symbols (e.g. BackColor).

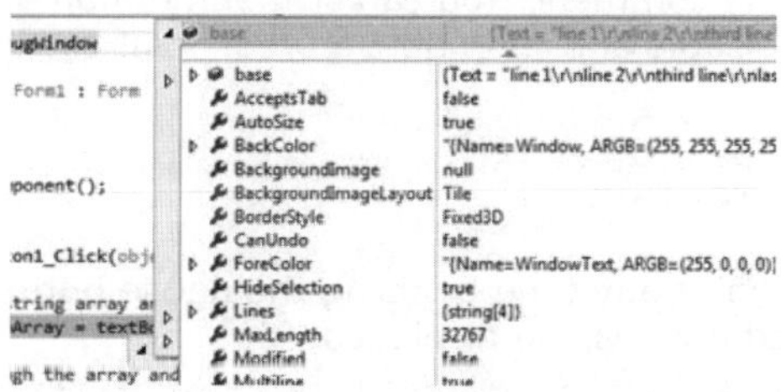

Figure 11-4 Displaying expanding object items

Note that you will have to completely stop the program running if you want to make any changes to your program.

When the program is paused you can stop debugging (click the red square, or Shift-F5), inspect your variables, run the program at full speed (press the F5 key), or a line at a time (press F10 or F11). If you step your code the debugger PerfTips will tell you how long it took to execute the code (≤ 1ms elapsed).

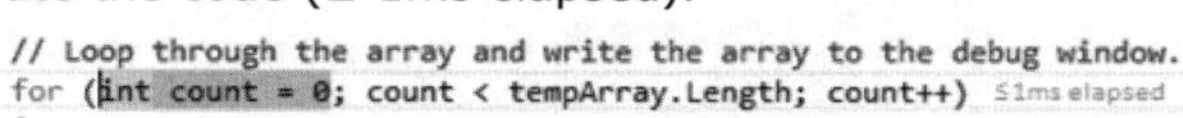

You can also change which line of code is to be executed next by dragging the yellow arrow to that line, but heed the warning!

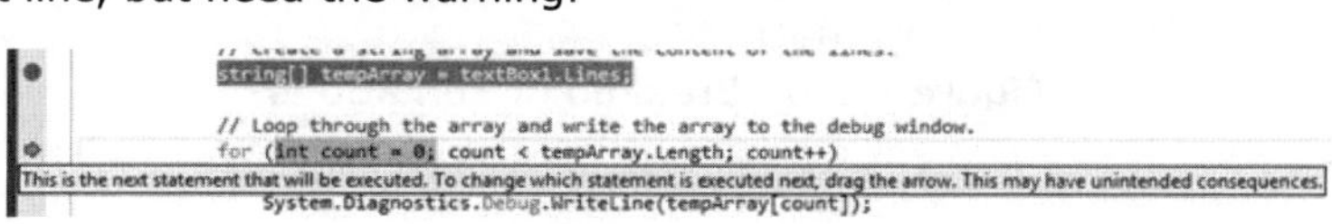

You can select these options from the debug toolbar, see Figure 11-5. This appears when the program runs but if it isn't displayed, choose View>Toolbars>Debug.

Figure 11-5 The Debug Toolbar

The toolbar icons from left to right are:

- pause, or break all (ctrl + alt + break) (greyed out here)
- stop debugging (shift + F5)
- restart, (ctrl + shift + F5)
- refresh windows app
- show next statement, (alt + Num *)
- step into, (F11)
- step over, (F10)
- step out, (shift + F11)
- show threads in source (see below)

The continue button is on the left hand side of the toolbar.

The down arrow allows you to add or remove buttons, so you could add the Continue button here. The 'Show Threads' button helps determine which thread caused a breakpoint. We will discuss threaded applications later.

Breakpoints can be set before or at run-time but they must be on executable code; you cannot set a breakpoint at a comment. You can switch them on and off with the F9 key. Remember, you can also disable and re-enable a breakpoint by right-clicking the red circle.

11.3.2 • Pausing the Program

The program can be paused at any time by using the pause button on the toolbar; the line of code to be executed next will be displayed.

11.4 • Conditional Breakpoints

If your breakpoint is in a loop, you may not want to break every time around the loop. You can set breakpoints on a number of passes through a breakpoint, or when a variable has a certain value. You set the conditions by right-clicking the red circle, or choosing the settings icon (see Figure 11-2 on page 165). The Setting options are shown in Figure 11-6.

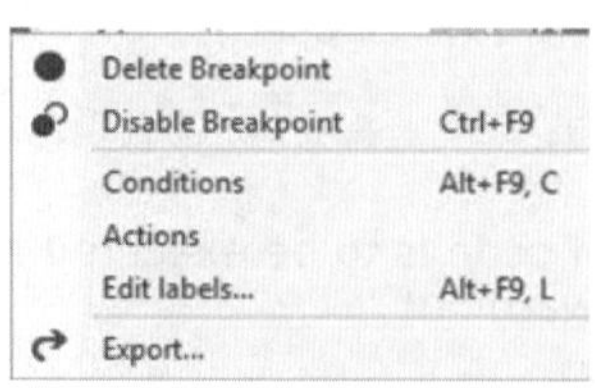

Figure 11-6 Breakpoint conditions

Earlier version of VS also had slightly different options which have been incorporated into the Conditions setting.

Selecting Conditions displays a window which prompts for the breakpoint's conditions and action to take, see Figure 11-7. This also appears when clicking the Settings icon.

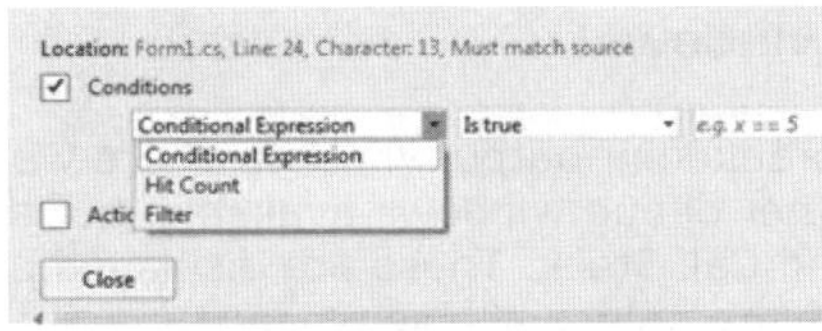

Figure 11-7 Breakpoint condition options

You can change the location – i.e. break when the program reaches a line and character location in a file (this doesn't have to be the current code file)

You can set the following:

- Condition – the breakpoint is executed if the condition is true or has changed.

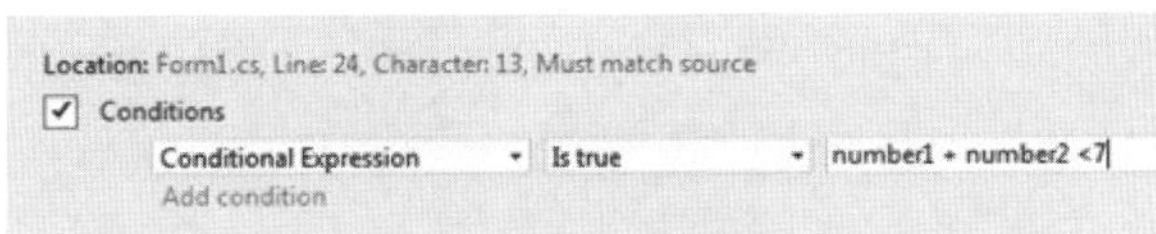

- Hit Count – the breakpoint is executed if the hit count is either: always, equal to, multiple of, or greater than or equal to, a value set.

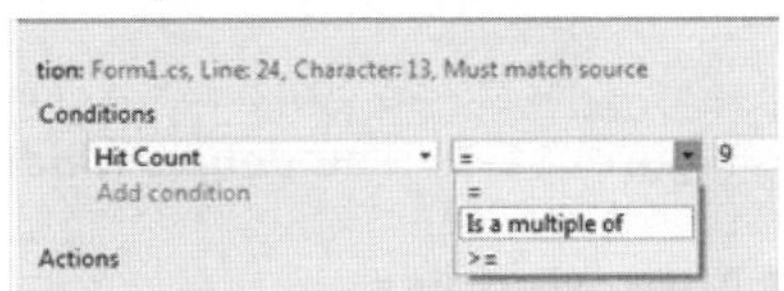

- Filter – e.g. Thread ID or name or even a Machine name or Process ID.

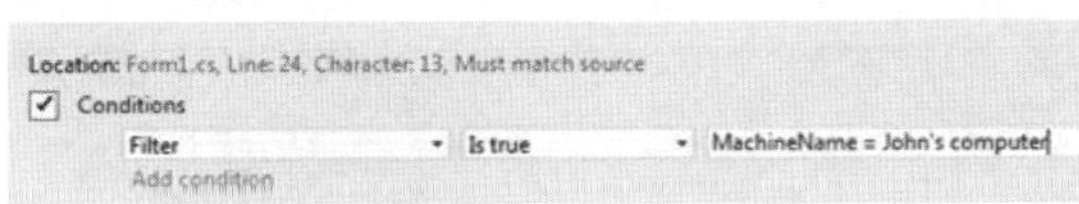

- Action. Set the action you want (Display a message) and break or continue:

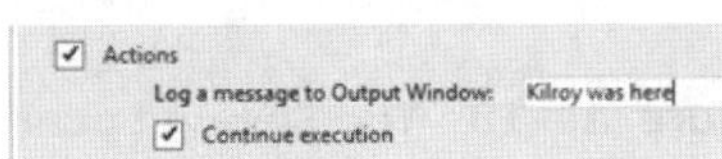

Notice the red circle changes to a red diamond when these are set.

11.5 • Restarting – Stepping through your code

To step the program a line at a time use 'Step Into' or 'Step Over'. Step Into (F11) steps the program a line at a time including any method calls. Step Over (F10) steps the program a line at a time, but runs any methods at full speed (unless they contain a breakpoint) and pauses at the line after the method call. You can also use Step Out, which takes you out of any methods you are debugging.

To use the Step Into, Step Over or Step Out commands press F11, F10 or Shift+F11, or click the icons on the debug toolbar, see Figure 11-8 on page 168.

Figure 11-8 Restart option icons

11.6 • The breakpoint windows

We have already seen the breakpoint output window where we can display variable values. There are a lot of other debug windows available, but the common ones are: Local, Watch, Immediate and Call Stack. These are displayed using Debug > Windows, see Figure 11-9. Note these are only available when you are debugging.

Figure 11-9 The debug windows

11.6.1 • The Local and Auto windows

The Local window displays the currently available local variables, see Figure 11-10.

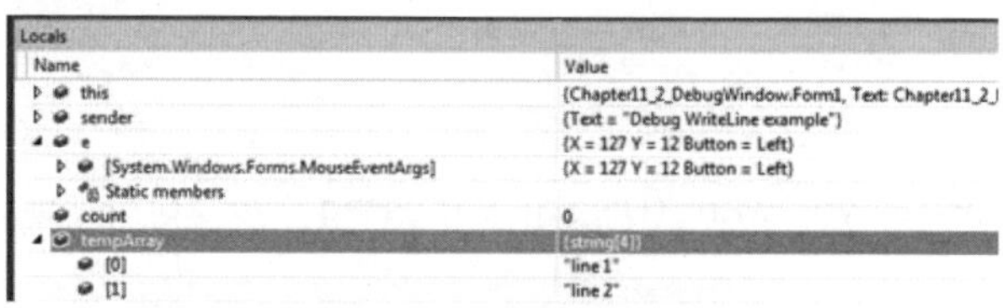

Figure 11-10 The Debug Local window

In this example the window is showing all the parameters available to this method:

'this' - the current object (Form1 in this case);

'sender' – the button that called the method (and its text 'Debug WriteLine..');

'e' - the sender's arguments (in this case the mouse position X, Y and left-click);

'count' – an integer variable with the value 0;

'tempArray' – a string array. This has been expanded to see the contents.

The Autos window provides a quick way to display variables used in the current statement and changes as the program is stepped. It automatically recognizes these, hence the name.

The Live Visual Tree and Live Property Explorer are new options for debugging WPF applications, see *http://bit.ly/1KgoXR0*.

11.6.2 • Watch window

The watch window is used to examine variables and is enabled when the program is at a breakpoint. The variables or expressions to be watched are set by entering them in the name field, see Figure 11-11.

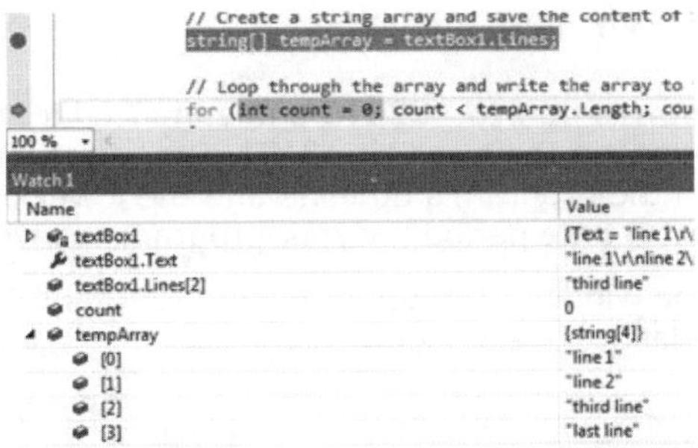

Figure 11-11 The Debug Watch window

In this example, five items are being watched; textBox1, textBox1.Text, textBox1. Lines[2], count and tempArray. tempArray has been expanded to see its contents. Remember if an item is not declared within this block of code (out of scope), its value cannot be displayed.

11.6.3 • The Immediate window

This window lets you type in an expression to evaluate. I've added variables number1 and number2 to the code; see Figure 11-12.

Note that you can use the Math class in this. You can also use this window to assign values or create new ones, and then continue debugging.

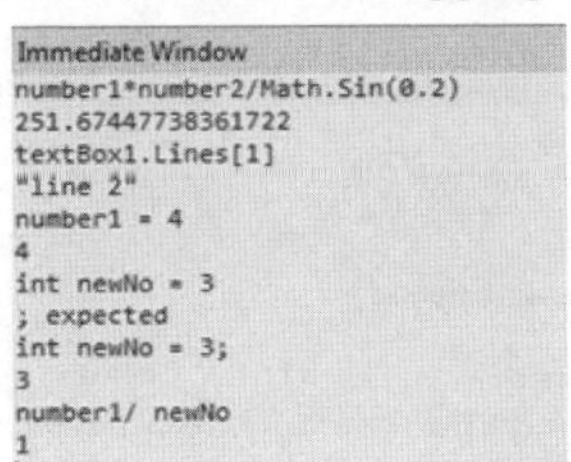

Figure 11-12 The Debug Immediate window

11.6.4 • The Call Stack

This window lists the calls that were executed to get to the current code position. It can be useful to find out how your program got where it is. Figure 11-13 on page 170 shows the current location came from button1_Click, which came from the Main() code, line 19.

Figure 11-13 The Call Stack window

11.7 • Diagnostic Tool Window

The Diagnostic Tools window is new to VS2013 and enhanced in VS2015. It is displayed using Debug > Show Diagnostic Tools or Ctrl-Alt-F2. The window has two parts. The upper part adds graphs to the program's timeline and the lower part contains detailed information. You can select a time period for your program to investigate further.

There are three tools in the window: Debugger Events, CPU and Memory Usage tools. You can enable or disable the last two, see Figure 11-14.

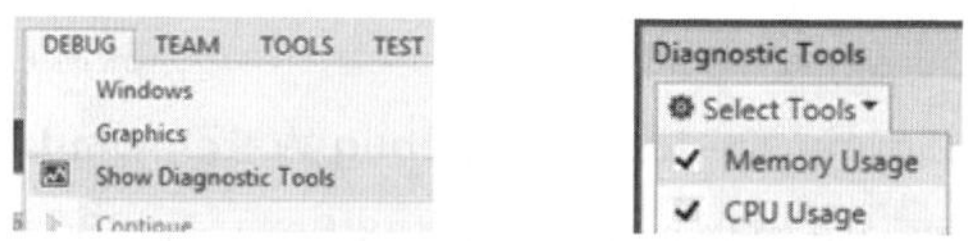

Figure 11-14 Diagnostic Window

The Debugger Events window has multiple tracks that represent events that occur during debugging: Break, Output Window and IntelliTrace events. The last two only display if you have the Enterprise version.

The CPU and Memory window provide an insight into how much processor time and memory is being used (and when), Figure 11-15.

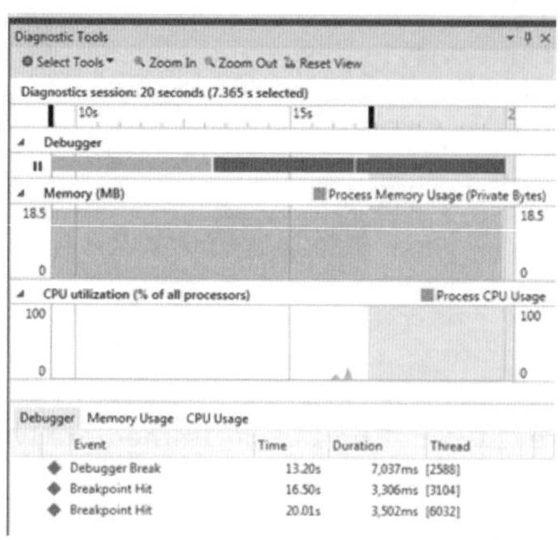

Figure 11-15 Diagnostic Tools display

Clicking on a time period in the in Debugger will zoom in on it. You can use the Zoom In, Zoom Out or Reset View to change the view. You can also click and drag and Zoom In on a selected time frame, see Figure 11-16 on page 171.

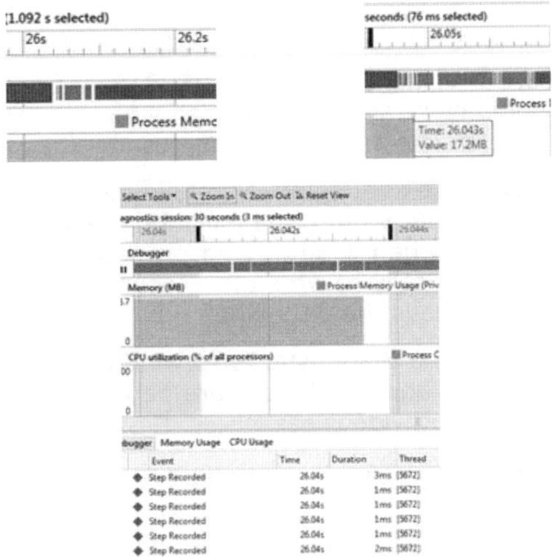

Figure 11-16 Diagnostic Tools display

The Enterprise version also shows the Output and IntelliTrace events (see section 11.9), Figure 11-17.

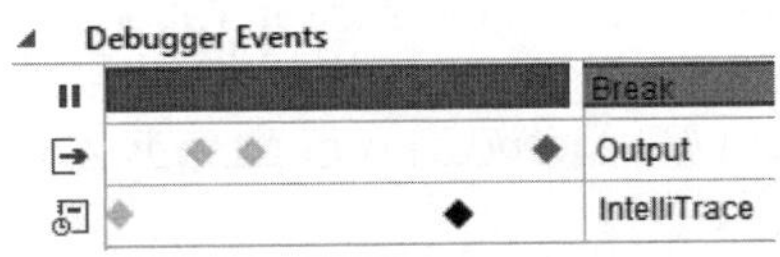

Figure 11-17 Output and IntelliTrace display

Please see the MSDN blog at: *http://bit.ly/1CxaAQB* for more information and look at the MS Channel9 video on the debugger features at: *http://bit.ly/1dxboyP*

11.8 • Performance Tips (PerfTips)

PerfTips (ToolTips with Performance information) indicate how long the program takes during a step or since the last breakpoint. You will have seen these and we mentioned them in section 11.3.4. You may not have noticed that the time displayed is in fact a link that will open the Diagnostic Tools window where more information can be found.

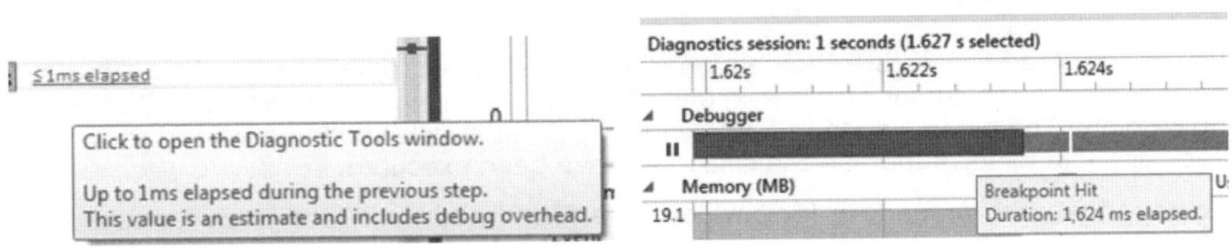

By using PerfTips you can find out any sections of code that are taking a long time and try to shorten them.

For more information on PerfTips see the MS information at: *http://bit.ly/1rRbYrP*

11.9 • IntelliTrace

IntelliTrace has been a part of Visual Studio since VS2010. It provides Historical Debugging, which means you can trace back through your program to find faults, rather than continually setting breakpoints and debugging.

It now provides Non-Live and Live debugging. Non-Live debugging occurs when your program executes outside of Visual Studio; the execution is recorded to a file that can be debugged. Live debugging is when you run your program as we have been doing. If IntelliTrace is enabled it automatically records the execution of your program (events, stack calls, timing etc.) and displays the data when a breakpoint is executed.

IntelliTrace is incorporated into the Diagnostic Tools window in VS2015 Enterprise edition, and as both the Diagnostic Tools and IntelliTrace are better shown dynamically, please see the Microsoft walkthrough and videos at:

IntelliTrace: *http://bit.ly/1Ap8m3f*. This has a link to both a walkthrough and a video at the end.

11.10 • Self Assessment Exercises

You will get plenty of chances to debug your programs! But you might like to try some of the following:

1. If you didn't watch the debugging section (about 10 minutes in) of the fifth Virtual Academy 'Quick Overview of the Visual C# IDE' at:

   http://www.microsoftvirtualacademy.com/training-courses/c-fundamentals-for-absolute-beginners
2. If you haven't done so, read the MS blogs and watch the videos on the new Diagnostic Tools and features mentioned in this chapter and try their features.
3. See the run to cursor command.
4. Try the breakpoint conditions.
5. Once stopped at a breakpoint, examine variables and know how to 'drill down into objects.
6. Step through your code using Step Into, Step Over and Step Out.
7. Try all the breakpoint windows.

11.11 • Summary

We have covered how to use the debugger to correct your program errors. You can run the program to the cursor or a breakpoint. You can set, view, edit, enable and disable breakpoints. The debug windows help you view, evaluate and modify data and show the stack providing information on the calls that have been executed.

We have also seen Diagnostic Tools window, PerfTips and IntelliTrace - new features in VS2015.

Chapter 12 • Threading

12.1 • Introduction

So far our programs have been running a single program or task at a time. You can split some programs into separate tasks called threads and run these tasks at the same time (concurrently) and for the threads to communicate with each other. You may have noticed this in the MS videos mentioned in the previous chapter. Threading can speed up programs that use different resources such as files and networking but may also create resource sharing problems. Threads can be run on different processors in multiple processor chips. We will use threads to perform networking tasks in the next chapter.

12.2 • Threads

You can split your program into individual tasks, or threads. The .NET environment allows concurrent programming by controlling the execution of the threads. Your main code is run under the .NET environment as a thread.

Each thread is allocated a priority and runs either until it finishes, runs out of its allocated time, or is held up for some reason (e.g. waiting for some data, say from the internet or another thread). This operation is controlled by the operating system. You do not need a multiple processor system to run threaded programs.

Threads move between states. The thread states are:

- Unstarted – created, but waiting for Start
- Started – wait for Run
- Running – it runs when a processor is assigned to it (dispatched)
- Stopped – Thread is terminated or aborted
- Blocked – when making I/O request, waits for I/O
    - WaitSleepJoin
    - Waiting for something else to happen (e.g. other code to complete)
    - Sleep for a specific time
    - Join (waiting for another thread to terminate)
- Suspend – a method call; goes to Started on Resume

A simplified flow diagram of a threaded program is shown in Figure 12-1 on page 174.

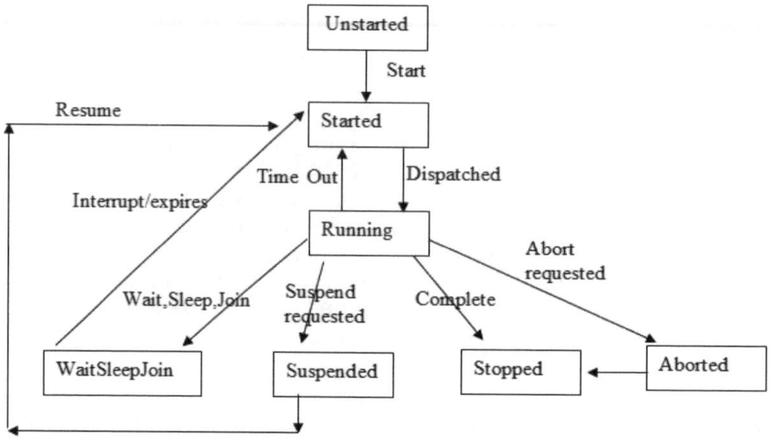

Figure 12-1 Thread states

12.3 • Writing Thread Code

As you might expect the thread code is written as a class and a Thread object is instantiated the same way as any other object. Once a thread class is written, you can then instantiate and start as many threads as you want, just like you do with objects.

Threading code needs the System.Threading namespace (using System.Threading;) added to your code.

The thread code is in its own class, which can have its own methods. It is defined just like a class e.g.

```
Class MyThreadCode {
 // declarations
 public MyThreadCode ( )
  {
  // constructor
  }
 private myThreadMethods ( )
  {
  // methods go here
  }
} // end of thread code
```

The thread is instantiated and started using ThreadStart as follows:

```
MyThreadCode myThread = new MyThreadCode();
Thread thread1 =
    new Thread (new ThreadStart (MyThread.StartMethod));
```

ThreadStart is a **delegate** - an object that refers to a method, and is used to call the method. It's like a pointer which allows a third-party access to a method. We won't go into any more detail, just use the code provided.

Delegates are also used for events. They provide notification from a component to "listeners" about changes in that component, e.g. a button click.

The thread's properties can be accessed if necessary, e.g.:

```
thread1.Name = "first Thread";
```

And then the thread can be started:

```
thread1.Start();
```

12.4 • Thread sleeping example

Let's explain this with an example. Let's start by writing a thread that puts itself to sleep for a random amount of time and when it wakes up displays its name. We will later run as many of these threads as we want.

Start a new project. Add a new class (Project > Add Class) and call it 'MySleepThread'

Add 'using System.Threading;' at the top of the thread class code. Here's the full code for the MySleepThread class:

```
namespace Chapter12_4ThreadSleep
{
    class MySleepThread
    {
        // private declarations for each thread
        private int sleepTime;
        private Random random = new Random();
        // constructor
        public MySleepThread()
        {
            sleepTime = random.Next(5000);  // random time to 5s
        }
        // Thread method
        // - displays name, sleeps and when woken, displays 'awake'
        public void MySleepMethod()
        {
            // get a reference to the current Thread
            Thread current = Thread.CurrentThread;
            // display message - sleeping for threadSleep time
            System.Diagnostics.Debug.WriteLine
                (current.Name + " sleeping for " + sleepTime);
            Thread.Sleep(sleepTime);            // Sleep
            // Wake up ! -  display message
            System.Diagnostics.Debug.WriteLine(current.Name + " awake !");
        }
    } // end ThreadCode
} // end namespace Chapter12_4ThreadSleep
```

The sleeping time (SleepTime) is initialized in the constructor code. The thread's method (MySleepMethod) simply outputs a message that the thread is going to sleep, then puts the thread to sleep, and when it wakes up displays that fact.

Note that the program **writes to the console debug window**, so it needs to be displayed if you want to see the output from the program (Debug > Windows > Output). If the program had used MessageBox.Show to display its output, the program would wait for input from the user, which isn't what we want. You could also write this as a console application.

As you can imagine, if there are multiple threads all trying to write to the same label or textbox to display their information (or update a database!), there can be a problem.

The thread needs to be instantiated and started. We shall do this when the form loads. Add the following code for the form load event. It will also need a using System.Threading; declaration.

```
private void Form1_Load(object sender, EventArgs e)
{
    // Display message
    MessageBox.Show("Thread will start when OK is pressed");
    // Instantiate MySleepThread - run constructor code, get random time
    MySleepThread sleepThread = new MySleepThread();
    // Instantiate thread with method to run
    Thread thread1 = new Thread
        (new ThreadStart(sleepThread.MySleepMethod));
    // We can now refer to thread
    thread1.Name = "first Thread";
    // and finally start the thread
    thread1.Start();
}
```

Run the program. Be patient – it may sleep for up to 5 seconds. The Debug output window will be similar to Figure 12-2:

```
first Thread sleeping for 44
first Thread awake !
The thread 0x1010 has exited with code 259 (0x103).
```

Figure 12-2 Thread output

Incidentally, if you see a message like '`The thread 0x6e8 has exited with code 0 (0x0).`' this is nothing to do with your thread - it occurs occasionally. Exit code 0 means that the thread terminated correctly and code 259 means thread is still running.

As you will see that although the thread is terminated the form is still active. You can use Application.Exit() to close all the threads and windows. You can stop a thread running by using the Abort(); method (see Figure 12-1 on page 174)

Current.Abort();

12.5 • Multiple Threading example

Now that we have some idea how threads start and run, let's expand the previous example to run multiple threads. We will simply change the form load code to create threads on a button click. We can then create as many as we want.

Repeat the above exercise (new project, add class and code). This time, instead of writing the form load code, add a button to the form. We will add a count to identify each thread. Add the following count declaration before 'public Form1 ( )' .

```
int count = 0;
```

Don't forget to add 'using System.Threading;' to the code and type the following code for the button click:

```
private void button1_Click(object sender, EventArgs e)
{
    count++;   // unique value for each thread
    MySleepThread sleepThread = new MySleepThread();
    Thread thread1 = new Thread
        (new ThreadStart(sleepThread.MySleepMethod));
    thread1.Name = "Thread " + count.ToString();
    thread1.Start(); // and finally start the thread
}
```

Run the program and click the button quickly a few times to run several threads. The output should be similar to Figure 12-3:

```
Thread 1 sleeping for 7531
Thread 2 sleeping for 7077
Thread 3 sleeping for 4464
Thread 4 sleeping for 5339
Thread 3 awake !
The thread 'Thread 3' 0xf1c has exited with code 259 (0x103).
Thread 4 awake !
The thread 'Thread 4' 0x1204 has exited with code 259 (0x103).
Thread 2 awake !
The thread 'Thread 2' 0x131c has exited with code 259 (0x103).
Thread 1 awake !
The thread 'Thread 1' 0x580 has exited with code 259 (0x103).
```

Figure 12-3 Multiple thread output

The threads run and put themselves to sleep for different lengths of time. Each thread has its own value for count which is displayed.

You have created a multi-tasking, concurrent program environment.

12.6 • Accessing form controls from threads

You might get a situation where you want your thread to access a control such as write to a TextBox on a form. If you try to do this from a thread, you will get a 'cross-thread error' at run-time.

You cannot directly access an object owned by one thread from another thread. Your program has to request that the owning thread does the work for you and to do so you call the control's invoke method (Control.Invoke) and pass it the data needed.

There are two ways to solve this problem.

1. In File Load event, add the code to ignore the error:

   CheckForIllegalCrossThreadCalls = false;

But this isn't really good programming.

2. Provide the correct coding checks and call the Invoke method. We shall do this. If you really want to find out more about how Invoke works, you can refer to the Microsoft web site.

We shall expand the previous example so that the threads write to a textbox when they wake up.

Start a New Project and add a button and a text box on the form. Set the text box's Multiline property 'true'. We will write a new thread that will write to this text box.

Add the using statements and declare the count variable before 'public Form1 ( )' as before:

```
int count = 0;
```

For the button click type the following code:

```
private void button1_Click(object sender, EventArgs e)
{
    count++;
    // use 'this' to pass a reference to this form
    MyWriteThread writeThread = new MyWriteThread(this);
    Thread thread1 = new Thread
        (new ThreadStart(writeThread.MyWriteMethod));
    thread1.Name = "Thread " + count.ToString();
    thread1.Start(); // and finally start the thread
}
```

This is almost the same as we had before, but now we have used 'this' to pass the Form's reference to the thread. See the constructor in MyWriteThread class below. If you are unsure about this, place a breakpoint after writeThread has been instantiated and look at 'this' with the debugger – it will have the form's information, see Figure 12-4.

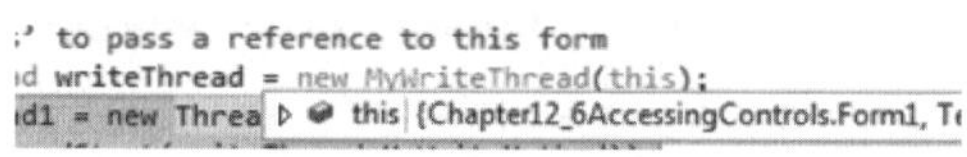

Figure 12-4 The Form's reference

We will now add the Invoke method so that we can write to the textbox from the thread.

Before public Form1() add the delegate declaration.

```
delegate void SetTextCallBack(string text);
```

Now add the code to check if it is OK to write to the text box, using cross threaded code. Add this before private void button1_Click. The code is:

```
int count = 0;
delegate void SetTextCallBack(string text);
public void WriteToTextBox(string strText)
{
    // InvokeRequired compares the thread ID of the
    // calling thread to the thread ID of the creating thread.
    // if different, it calls Invoke (when it will be the same).
    if (this.textBox1.InvokeRequired)
    {
        SetTextCallBack d = new SetTextCallBack(WriteToTextBox);
```

```
            this.Invoke(d, new Object[] { strText });
        }
        else // it's OK  - add text to text box
        {
            this.textBox1.Text += strText;
        }
    }   //end WriteToTextBox
```

Add a new class (MyWriteThread) and type the following code:

```
class MyWriteThread
{
    // declarations
    private int sleepTime;
    private static Random random = new Random();
    private Form1 f;          // Reference to Form1
    // constructor
    public MyWriteThread(Form1 f)
    {
        sleepTime = random.Next(10000);  // random time to 10 s
        this.f = f;         // Assign a reference to form1
    }
    // Thread method
    public void MyWriteMethod()
    {
        // get reference to current Thread
        Thread current = Thread.CurrentThread;
        Thread.Sleep(sleepTime);        // Sleep
        // Wake up ! -  display message on text box
        f.WriteToTextBox(current.Name + " awake !\r\n");
        // f is reference to form1
    }
}   // end ThreadCode
```

Run the program and click the button a few times. The output should appear on the text box, similar to Figure 12-5.

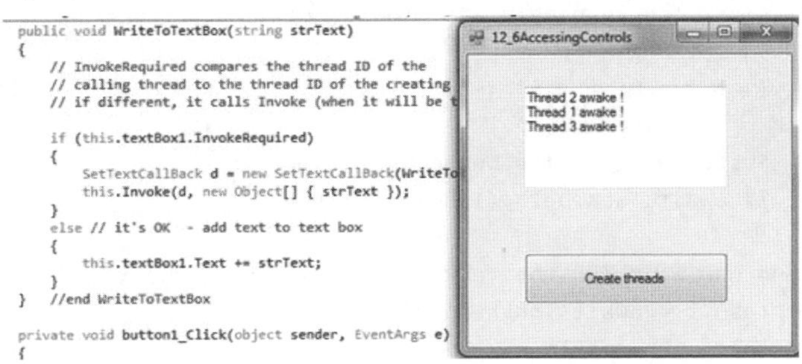

Figure 12-5 Accessing form controls

If you think this is a bit too complicated, don't try to understand it - just copy and modify the code. All the code is available via Elektor's web site.

If your threads don't stop naturally, you should terminate your threads when you have finished with them. The easiest way to do this is to use the Abort() method. This begins the process of terminating the thread and 'usually terminates it'. For example use:

```
thread1.Abort();
```

12.7 • Asynchronous programming - await, async

VS2012 C# introduced asynchronous programming with the **await** and **async** commands. These enable you to define an asynchronous method which will run concurrently with other methods. The **await** instruction is used to wait if the calling process cannot continue until the async method has finished.

Consider writing a program that performs analysis of a very large file over a slow internet link. This could be defined as an async method which would then allow other processing to be performed. The user won't then think the program has crashed. If the calling code has to wait for a result, it uses the await command.

Any method declared as async has to have a return type of:

- void (avoid if possible)
- Task (no response except for notification of completion or failure)
- Task<T> (for a logical response of type T), e.g. Task <int>

In the following example we have declared an asynchronous SlowTask which returns an integer value of 1 when completed. It is called from an asynchronous MyTask, which in turn is called from a button click. They will all run concurrently. The output window displays 0,1,2,3,4 followed by "Done" and finally the result value 1. Try removing the comment from `await Task.Delay(1000);` and see when "Done" is output.

Place a button on a form and add the following code:

```
private void button1_Click(object sender, EventArgs e)
{
    Task myTask = MyTask();
    System.Diagnostics.Debug.WriteLine("Done!");
}
private async Task MyTask()
{
    Task<int> longRunningTask = SlowTask();
    //Do something here
    for (int i = 0; i < 5; i++)
    {
        System.Diagnostics.Debug.WriteLine(i);
        // await Task.Delay(1000); //wait
    }
    //and now wait for the task to finish - call await
    int result = await longRunningTask;
    //display the result
    System.Diagnostics.Debug.WriteLine(result);
}
```

```
private async Task<int> SlowTask() // returns an int
{
    await Task.Delay(5000); //wait 5 seconds
    return 1;
}
```

12.8 • Other thread considerations

We have only touched on threading, but we have covered the basics here. For instance we haven't seen how to communicate between threads or use buffers. There can be problems running threaded programs; not least of all that high priority threads can starve low priority ones and threads may hang waiting on each other. This will be enough for us to deal with internet communications in the next chapter.

12.9 • Self Assessment Exercises

1. Change the code in 12.4 on page 175 so that it uses MessageBox.Show() rather than write to the debug output window and see what happens.
2. Write Invoke code to write to other controls, say a listbox or label.
3. Find out more about delegates. See the delegates tutorial and read about 'delegates and events' at: *https://msdn.microsoft.com/en-us/library/aa288459%28v=vs.71%29.aspx*
4. Find out how to pass data and communicate between threads.
5. Read the MS article on Async and Await at:

   https://msdn.microsoft.com/en-us/library/hh191443.aspx
6. Read the blog on threaded v. async code at: *http://bit.ly/1AAIM1r*

12.10 • Summary

This has been a brief introduction to threaded programming. We have seen why we need threaded programs. We have seen the various states a thread can take and how they move from one state to another. We have seen how to write a threaded program and how to put them to sleep. We have run a multi-threaded program, each of which can access the same form control to report its progress. We have seen the **async** and **await** commands that provide concurrent programming. We have also mentioned possible problems with threaded programs. All of this provides the background for internet communications that we will cover next.

Chapter 13 • Internet Applications

13.1 • Introduction

Now that we have some idea about how we use threads, we can see how to apply that to an internet application. In this chapter we will write internet communication programs using threads that will wait for data to be received from the internet and at the same time be able to send data to the internet. Without threads the programs would hang waiting for data to be received. We shall look at programs using the internet communication protocols Transmission Control Protocol (TCP) and User Datagram Protocol (UDP). We will end up with an internet chat program.

13.2 • Client-Server communication

We will start by looking at client-server internet communication. In this case the client (e.g. a user typing a web request) sends a request to a server which responds with the data. This response could be an HTML page, a file transfer, an ASP.NET page request or other communication. Initially we will look at a TCP server application that receives data and then expand this to respond with data. We will then study a TCP client application which sends data and finally to display the server's response. Having produced this TCP communication program, we will write a similar program using UDP protocols.

Networking capabilities are provided through the System.Net.Sockets namespace. There are no controls to be placed on the form. The communication sockets are created at run-time.

13.3 • TCP and UDP

The two main communication protocols used by the internet (TCP/IP) are TCP (Transmission Control Protocol) and UDP (User Datagram Protocol). The main difference is that TCP implements a connection and re-transmissions whereas the UDP protocol just sends data in packets and has no guarantee of delivery, ordering of packets or even reception. UDP is useful in streaming technology when re-transmission is irrelevant.

TCP communication is based on streaming (similar to disk I/O streaming we have seen). A connection is established and data transfers occur in continuous streams. The alternative UDP communication uses packet based transmissions known as datagram sockets. This protocol is a connectionless service in which packets are sent and can arrive in any order. This requires more programming, but may result in a faster performance.

We shall start with TCP communications and, as our server will wait for connections and client requests, we will use threads. If you are unsure about these read the chapter on threads again.

13.4 • Creating a TCP server

Note that these examples use IPv4 addresses; IPv6 is the new addressing mechanism. See the MS blog on Dual Mode sockets at: *http://bit.ly/1dAkeM5* for more information.

A TCP server simply listens on the internet at a port and at the computer's IP address. There are five steps to creating a TCP streaming server:

1. Create a server using a **TCPListener** with the code which sets up the IP and port addresses. A TCPListener object is created with the following code:

```
Int32 port = 5000;
IPAddress localAddr = IPAddress.Parse("127.0.0.1");
TcpListener server = new TcpListener(localAddr, port);
```

The program 'listens' at the port number and the computer's IP address. Port values below 1024 are reserved. The IP address 127.0.0.1 or "localhost" refers to the host computer, so you can run the client and server applications on any PC and you don't need to know or change the IP address for different PCs.

2. Start listening at the port. The TcpListener we called 'server' is started with the command:

```
server.Start( );
```

The server simply listens at this address. The server creates a connection to the client when a client request is received via a socket.

3. Establish the connection between client and server. To start the TCPListener, use the code:

```
Socket connection= server.AcceptSocket( );
```

Socket is defined in the System.Net.Sockets namespace so you will need to add: using System.Net.Sockets;

4. Communicate with the client. Create the network stream and use the Socket methods Send( ) and Receive( ). Methods BinaryReader() and BinaryWriter() are used to read and write objects. By contrast the UDP communications use SendTo() and ReceiveFrom() methods.
5. Terminate the connection. Use the Socket method Close( ).

13.5 • Threads

As we have said, without threads the program would hang waiting for data to be received. We will put the Receive method into a thread allowing other sections of our program to run; the thread will continue when data is received. We shall see how this all works in the following example. Remember if we want to write to a textbox or other control from a thread we will have to deal with cross-thread exceptions.

13.6 • Creating a TCP client

The **TcpClient** makes the connection to the server via the server's port and IP address. Four steps have to be taken to create a TCP client:

1. Create a TcpClient client and connect to the server using the code:

```
TcpClient client = new TcpClient();
Client.connect (serverAddress, serverPort);
```

The Client code will connect to a server, so the serverAddress is either the IP address of the server of type 'IPAddress' (e.g. 127.0.0.1, see above) or a string containing its name (e.g. "localhost"). The serverPort is the port number of the server, i.e. the one we used when we created the server. To run code on your PC, use the local IP address 127.0.0.1 or "localhost", otherwise you will need to know the IP address of your computer. You can find this in Control Panel or you can run the command 'ipconfig'. IPv4 is a number like 192.168.1.7.

2. Create the network stream using the TcpClient getStream( ) method.

3. Create BinaryWriter and BinaryReader objects. Communicate with the server using the NetworkStream methods ReadString( ) or Read( ), ReadByte( ), Write( ) or WriteByte( ).
4. Finally close the connection using the method Close( ).

13.7 • TCP Client-Server application

We shall develop a program with a TCP server that receives and echoes data sent to it and then add a TCP client that sends data to the server and displays the data returned. We could extend this so the server does some useful work such as squaring any numbers sent to it, or retrieving data from a file.

Start a new project. I've called it Server. On the form place a list box (called lstRxdData) and buttons to listen and disconnect (btnListen and btnDisconnect). Your design should look similar to Figure 13-1.

Figure 13-1 Server application

At the following to the using statements at the top of the code:

```
using System.Net.Sockets;
using System.Net;
using System.IO;
using System.Threading;
```

Before the code public Form () add the declarations:

```
private Socket connection;
private NetworkStream socketStream;
private BinaryReader reader;
private BinaryWriter writer;
```

Now add the following method:

```
public void RunServer()
{
    try //    and catch (Exception error)
    {
        // create listener
        Int32 port = 5000;
        IPAddress localAddr = IPAddress.Parse("127.0.0.1");
        TcpListener server = new TcpListener(localAddr, port);
        // defined in System.Net.Sockets
        server.Start();   // start listening
```

```
                // establish and accept connection
                connection = server.AcceptSocket();
                // Create a NetworkStream for the socket
                socketStream = new NetworkStream(connection);
                //create read and write objects to send data through stream
                writer = new BinaryWriter(socketStream);
                reader = new BinaryReader(socketStream);
                // display on listBox this will cross thread error
                lstRxdData.Items.Add("connection made");
                // and tell client
                writer.Write("Message from Server: connected OK");
                // now loop reading and displaying data received
                string msgFromClient = null;
                do
                {
                    try
                    {
                        // read the string sent by client and terminate if QUIT
                        msgFromClient = reader.ReadString();
                        lstRxdData.Items.Add(msgFromClient);
                        // won't hang because it'll be in a thread
                        // and echo data
                        writer.Write(msgFromClient);
                    } // end try
                    catch (Exception)
                    {
                        break;
                    } // catch
                }
                while (msgFromClient != "QUIT"); // close if QUIT received
                lstRxdData.Items.Add("Client disconnected");
                // and close connection
                reader.Close();
                writer.Close();
                socketStream.Close();
                connection.Close();
                Application.Exit();      // and close app and threads
            } // end try
            catch (Exception error)
            {
                MessageBox.Show(error.ToString());
            } // catch
        } // end RunServer
```

RunServer will be run as a thread.

For the listen button click we are going to instantiate and start the RunServer thread code:

1. Check that you added the statement: using System.Threading;
2. Add the Thread declaration:

```
private Thread serverThread;
```

3. Change the code for the listen button click to:

```
private void btnListen_Click(object sender, EventArgs e)
{
    serverThread = new Thread(new ThreadStart(RunServer));
    serverThread.Start();
    btnListen.Enabled = false;
}
```

Add the code for disconnect button:

```
private void btnDisconnect_Click(object sender, EventArgs e)
{
    try
    {
        if (connection.Connected)
        {
            reader.Close();
            writer.Close();
            socketStream.Close();
            connection.Close();
            btnDisconnect.Enabled = false;
            serverThread.Abort(); // and terminate the thread
        }
    } // try
    catch (Exception error)
    {
        MessageBox.Show(error.ToString());
    } // catch
}
```

The .NET security won't let a thread write directly to a control on the form, (you get illegal cross thread error) so to make life easy, add this line to the Form1_Load( ) event:

CheckForIllegalCrossThreadCalls = false;

If you want to do it the correct way, see the chapter on threads and use the Invoke method.

Check the code runs. You will get an error on disconnecting because a connection hasn't been made by a client. (I'll let you write the error code for that!) Save and close the project. We now create a TCP client that sends data to the server.

13.8 • TCP Client Code

We will now create a second application which will act as a TCP client. Both this and the TCP server can be tested on the same PC. I've called this one Client.

1. Create a form as before with listBox (lstRxdData) and two buttons: Disconnect as before, but this time name the second button 'btnConnect' (with the Text: 'Connect').

   Also add a textbox and name it txtSendData.

   The design should be similar to Figure 13-2 on page 190.
2. Add the **using** statements as before (IO, Net, Net.Sockets and Threading)
3. Add the private declarations as follows:

```
private NetworkStream clientStream;
private BinaryReader reader;
private BinaryWriter writer;
private Thread clientThread;
private string message = null;
TcpClient client;
```

4. Now add the client code and thread code:

```
public void RunClient()
{
    //TcpClient client;
    // init tcpClient
    try
    {
        // 1. Create client and connect to server- give
        client = new TcpClient();
        // give IP address and port to talk to
        client.Connect("localhost", 5000);
        // get network stream
        clientStream = client.GetStream();
        // create read and write objects
        writer = new BinaryWriter(clientStream);
        reader = new BinaryReader(clientStream);
        lstRxdData.Items.Add("connecting to server");
        // we will ignore cross-thread errors in form load,
        do
            try
            {
                // read message from server until QUIT received
                message = reader.ReadString();
                lstRxdData.Items.Add(message);
            } // try
            catch (Exception error)
            {
                MessageBox.Show("Error reading from server " +
```

```
error.ToString());
                    } // catch
                while (message != "QUIT");
                // close connection
                lstRxdData.Items.Add("Closing connection");
                writer.Close();
                reader.Close();
                clientStream.Close();
                client.Close();
                Application.Exit();     // and close app and threads
            } // end try
            catch (Exception error)
            {
                MessageBox.Show("Error creating connection " + error.
ToString());
            }
        } // end RunClient
```

5. To start the thread when the connect button is clicked, change the button click code to following:

```
        private void btnConnect_Click(object sender, EventArgs e)
        {
            clientThread = new Thread(new ThreadStart(RunClient));
            clientThread.Start();
            btnConnect.Enabled = false;
        }
```

6. Let's ignore cross-thread errors. Add this line to the Form1_Load( ) event:

```
            CheckForIllegalCrossThreadCalls = false;
```

7. Add the code for the disconnect button:

```
        private void btnDisconnect_Click(object sender, EventArgs e)
        {
            try
            {
                if (client.Connected)
                {
                    reader.Close();
                    writer.Close();
                    clientStream.Close();
                    client.Close();
                    btnDisconnect.Enabled = false;
                    clientThread.Abort(); // and terminate the thread
                }
            } // try
            catch (Exception error)
```

```
            {
                MessageBox.Show(error.ToString());
            } // catch
        }
```

8. Finally add the code for the KeyDown event to send data when enter is pressed in text box:

```
private void textBox1_KeyDown(object sender, KeyEventArgs e)
{
    if (e.KeyCode == Keys.Enter)
    {
    // Enter key pressed - write to writer (binaryWriter to ClientStream)
        writer.Write(txtSendData.Text);
        // and clear text box
        txtSendData.Clear();
    }
}
```

Run this client code from the Visual Studio environment and the previous TCPserver .EXE code from its bin>Debug folder.

Press Listen to start the server listening and press Connect on the client. You may be trapped out by your firewall, but the server should display the message 'connection made' and the client the message: 'connecting to server' and 'Message from Server: connected OK'

You can now type messages in the client (don't forget to press 'return') and they are echoed back. Your program displays should be similar to Figure 13-2.

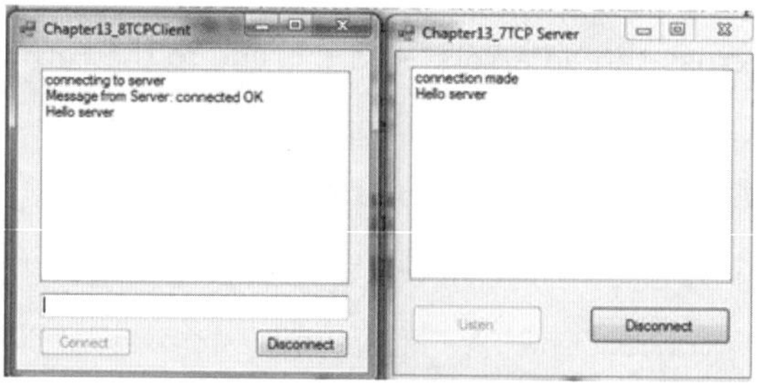

Figure 13-2 TCP Client and Server displays

Typing QUIT will close both programs. You will get an error message if you try the Server's disconnect button. You might like to solve this problem. You can observe any running thread using Windows Task Manager.

Note that we don't need to know the IP address of our machine because we have used 'localhost' as the IP address.

13.9 • UDPClient communications – A chat program

Let's now design a chat communication program using the UDP protocols. This time we will use the UDPClient class. This both sends and receives; there is no Listener or Client class. This is different from the TCP example which had individual Server and Client applications.

We will start with one program that both sends and receives (to itself). Then we will modify this slightly and run two versions of this program that will chat to each other.

We shall use the UDPClient's Send and Receive methods to send and receive data. When we run the second copy of this program to make a chat program will just send to an IP address and port. We will see how the Receive method finds out the IPaddress and port of the sending PC, and consequently to reply to.

13.9.1 • UDPClient.Send( )

The UDPClient Send method sends a datagram packet. Its parameters are in order: a byte array containing the data, the number of bytes to be sent, the destination host name and port address.

The datagram packet to be sent is a byte array. A string is converted to a byte array using System.Text.Encoding's GetBytes method as follows;

```
byte[ ] sendData = System.Text.Encoding.ASCII.GetBytes(string);
```

This will be sent to the server using the code:

```
client.Send(sendData, sendData.Length, "IPaddress", int.Parse("port"));
```

'IPaddress' and 'port' are the IP address and port of the destination computer.

13.9.2 • UDPClient.Receive( )

The UDPClient.Receive method accepts a datagram packet. Our program will be put in a loop waiting to receive data and this is put in a thread so our program won't hang waiting for data. We will be able to send and receive at the same time.

The Receive method has one parameter, an IPEndpoint. The IPEndpoint is a combined IP address and port number of the remote host from which the data was sent. We can use this to send the data received back to the client using the Send method.

The Receive method returns the datagram packet received as a byte array. We shall use the following code to accept the data:

```
byte[ ] rxdata = client.Receive(ref this.rxPoint);
```

Note that the 'ref' keyword is used. This allows the Receive method to update and return the IPEndpoint, rxPoint, consequently we know where to respond. We will use rxPoint in the Send method.

13.9.3 • UDP program threads

Let's try our UDP chat program. Remember, we will start with just one application which uses only UDPClient classes to both send and receive; I will call them 'client' and 'server'. The client will send data typed into a textbox to the server, the server will display this data and reply echoing the data back to the client. As both the server and client will have to wait for data there will be two threads, we'll call them WaitForDataFromClient and WaitForDataFromServer.

As we will see later, the client will send data via port 5000 to port 5001 on a KeyDown event; the server will listen for packets on port 5001, display the message and reply to the sending port, port 5000, when the client will display the echoed data.

The communication will be set up as shown in Figure 13-3.

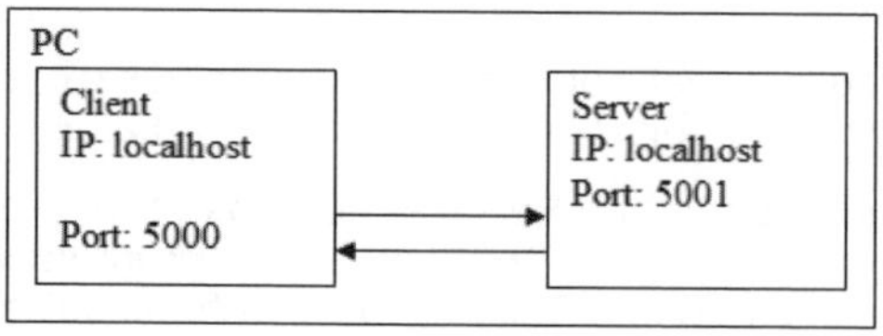

Figure 13-3 UDP Client - Server communications

Rather than ignoring IllegalCrossThread errors as we did previously, we shall correctly write from the threads to the list box display.

Initially we will run the application on our PC using the IP: 'localhost', but later we will run a second version of the program so a true chat will run. It could then be run on separate PCs, so long as the IP addresses are known.

13.9.4 • UDP design

Start a new project (UDPChat) and place a list box (lstRxdData) and a text box (txtData) on the form. The list box will display the data received. The text box will contain the data to be sent when the return key is pressed.

The IP and port values are declared at the start of the program. Port values less than 1024 are reserved; we will use 5000 and 5001.

Your interface should be similar to Figure 13-4.

Figure 13-4 UDP Chat application

We will start by writing the server thread code that waits for data from the client using the UDPClient.Receive method.

13.9.5 • UDP server code

Add the following at the top of your code:

```
using System.Net;
using System.Net.Sockets;
using System.Threading;
```

We have to declare a UdpClient which will be the server and create and start a thread which waits for data from the client and puts this in the list box.

Declare an UdpClient and an initial IPEndPoint for the server; this will be overwritten with the IPEndPoint of the client. We'll also declare the delegate so we can write to the listbox. Add the following code before the declaration: public Form1( ).

```
// Server
UdpClient server = new UdpClient(5001);
IPEndPoint rxPoint = new IPEndPoint(new IPAddress(0), 0);
// add the thread call to allow us to write to the list box as well:
delegate void SetTextCallBack(string text);
```

Follow this with the method that waits for the data from the client:

```
// Server code
private void WaitForDataFromClient()
{
    while (true)
    {
        // receive data from server
        byte[] ClientData = server.Receive(ref rxPoint);
        // display on list box
        ListBoxDisplay("Server received: " +
       (System.Text.Encoding.ASCII.GetString(ClientData)));
        // and echo back
        ListBoxDisplay("Sending back");
        server.Send(ClientData, ClientData.Length, rxPoint);
    } // end while true
} // end WaitForDataFromClient
```

To write to the list box from the thread add the following code after the code you have just entered:

```
private void ListBoxDisplay(string message)
{
    this.SetListBox(message);
}
private void SetListBox(string strText)
{
    if (this.lstRxdData.InvokeRequired)
    {
        SetTextCallBack d = new SetTextCallBack(SetListBox);
        this.Invoke(d, new Object[] { strText });
    }
    else // it's OK
    {
        this.lstRxdData.Items.Add(strText);
    }
} //end SetListBox
```

We covered all this before in threading. Revisit that chapter if you need to.

Now we need to start the server's thread.

Add the following after Form1's InitializeComponent( );

```
// start server
Thread serverThread = new Thread
        (new ThreadStart(WaitForDataFromClient));
serverThread.Start();
Thread clientThread = new Thread
        (new ThreadStart(WaitForDataFromServer));
clientThread.Start();
```

You can now run the program to check it. You may have to give your firewall access to your program.

Now we need to declare the UdpClient 'client' and use the Send method to send the data.

Add the following code to declare the 'client' and endpoint after the 'UdpClient server' declaration:

```
UdpClient client = new UdpClient(5000);
IPEndPoint txPoint = new IPEndPoint(new IPAddress(0), 0);
```

Change the KeyDown event for the text box to the following:

```
private void txtData_KeyDown(object sender, KeyEventArgs e)
{
    if (e.KeyCode == Keys.Enter)
    {
        // create a string datagram packet
        string packet = txtData.Text;
        // convert packet to byte array
        byte[] sendData = System.Text.Encoding.ASCII.GetBytes(packet);
        // send to server on port 5001
        this.client.Send(sendData, sendData.Length, "localhost", 5001);
        // and clear text box
        txtData.Clear();
    }
}
```

Check the program runs. Your firewall may block your program, but you should be able to type into the text box and see the message 'Server received:' followed by the message in the list box.

Note that although the server code echoes the data using the server.Send code, it's not accepted by the client (yet) and there is no error message. That is what is expected by the UDP protocol. We'll write the code to accept the data now.

The thread that was started continues when you close the window. You will have to stop debugging to add further code. If you run the .EXE file the only way to stop the process is to use the Task Manager. If you want to, see if you can add code that terminates the thread.

13.9.6 • UDP client code

Now we have to add the client code to accept the data echoed from the 'server'. This will be put in a thread so that the program won't hang. We have already declared the

UDPClient object and transmit IPEndPoint for the client.

Add the thread code to wait for data sent by the server. This will echo the data sent by the server.

Add the following code after the WaitForDataFromClient method:

```
private void WaitForDataFromServer()
{
    while (true)
    {
        // receive data from client
        byte[] rxdata = client.Receive(ref this.txPoint);
        // cross-thread exception if lstRxdData.Items.Add ( ) is used
        // so call
        ListBoxDisplay("Client received: " +
            System.Text.Encoding.ASCII.GetString(rxdata));
    }
} // end of wait for data from server
```

Now we will declare and start the thread 'WaitForDataFromServer' which waits for data. Add the following code after InitializeComponent( );

```
Thread clientThread = new Thread
        (new ThreadStart(WaitForDataFromServer));
clientThread.Start();
```

You can now run the program, data typed into the text box is sent to the 'server', echoed back and displayed by the 'client' on the list box, see Figure 13-5.

Figure 13-5 UDPChat Display

13.10 • A Local Chat program

We can now try to run our program as a true chat program. We will run two copies of our chat program on the same PC. To do this we have to use two different ports. They will communicate as shown in Figure 13-6 on page 196. We can't run the same program twice, as they will both try to use the same port and an error would occur.

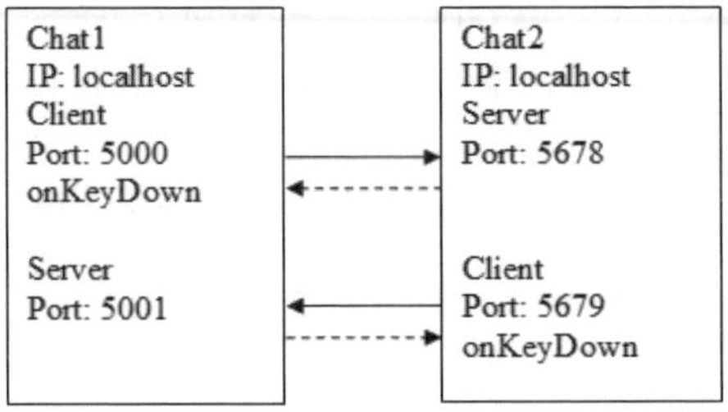

Figure 13-6 Remote chat program communications

This is how it will work:

Chat1 onKeyDown sends data out (using Client.Send) via port 5000 to (server) port 5678. Chat2 'server' receives this and sends back to the sending port (5000) using information sent in rxPoint. Chat1 receives this and displays the message received.

Chat2 onKeyDown sends data out (using Client.Send) via port 5679 to port 5001 (Chat1 server code) which sends back to the rxPoint (5679). This is received by Chat2 (in wait for data from server) and displays message in the listBox.

We will make two copies of our first program and change the port addresses so they can communicate on the same PC, but via different ports.

13.10.1 • The Second Chat program

It's easiest to run a second Visual Studio application. Make a copy of your first program. Using Windows Explorer, copy all the files and folders from the folder where you are saving your files.

I kept the original solution and made two copies, so that I had a file structure as follows:

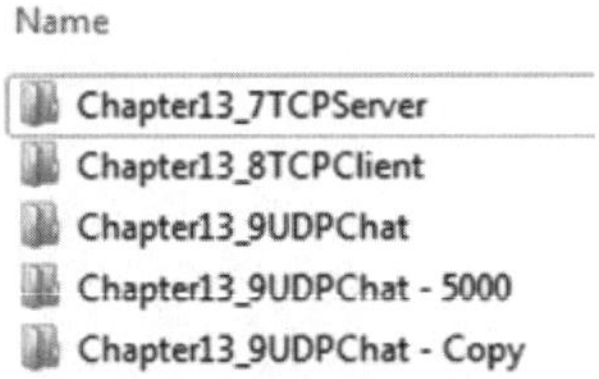

Notice I changed the top level folder names, so I know which is which.

Open one copy of the code by double-clicking its .sln file, and change the following line from:

```
this.client.Send(sendData, sendData.Length, "localhost", 5001);
```

to:

```
this.client.Send(sendData, sendData.Length, "localhost", 5678);
```

Open the second copy of the code by double-clicking its .sln file. This will start a second version of VS2013. Change the server and client declarations for this program as follows:

From: `UdpClient server = new UdpClient(5001);`

to:

```
UdpClient server = new UdpClient(5678);
```

and from: UdpClient client = new UdpClient(5000);

to:

```
UdpClient client = new UdpClient(5679);
```

So that the code is:

```
UdpClient server = new UdpClient(5678);
IPEndPoint rxPoint = new IPEndPoint(new IPAddress(0), 0);

//UdpClient client = new UdpClient(5000);
UdpClient client = new UdpClient(5679);
IPEndPoint txPoint = new IPEndPoint(new IPAddress(0), 0);
```

You can also display the rxPoint. In WaitForDataFromClient, change ListBoxDisplay 'sending back' code to:

```
ListBoxDisplay("Sending back to " + rxPoint.ToString()+"\n");
```

Compile and run both programs (or run the EXE files) and chat, see Figure 13-7.

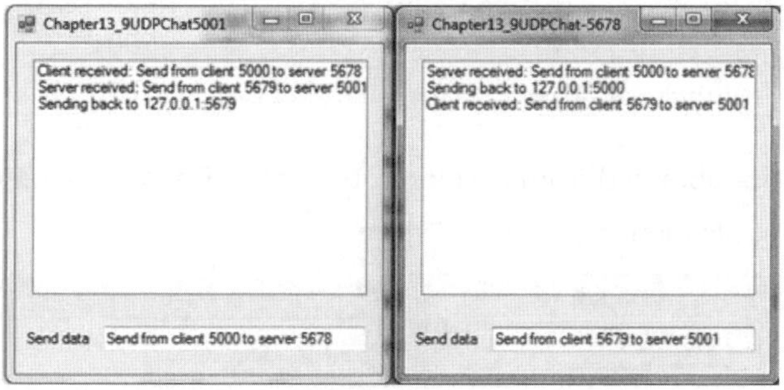

Figure 13-7 Chat program displays

Just to recap, the important lines of code are for one copy program:

```
UdpClient client = new UdpClient(5000);
UdpClient server = new UdpClient(5001);
```

and

```
this.client.Send(sendData, sendData.Length, "localhost", 5678);
```

And for the other copy program:

```
UdpClient server = new UdpClient(5678);
UdpClient client = new UdpClient(5679);
```

and

```
this.client.Send(sendData, sendData.Length, "localhost", 5001);
```

Don't worry; all the software is available at Elektor's web site.

13.11 • Remote Chat program

You can now try to the run the programs on separate PCs, as shown in Figure 13-8 on page 198. You can now have the same server and client port numbers because the IP addresses are different.

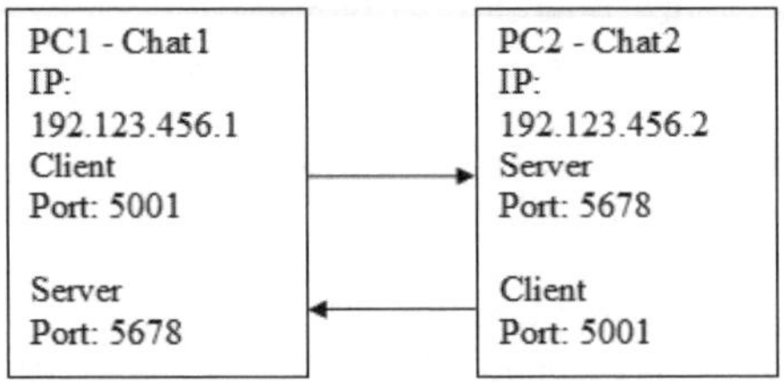

Figure 13-8 Remote chat IP and port connections

You will have to find out your IP addresses and change the code, for example to:

```
this.client.Send(sendData, sendData.Length, "192.168.1.104", 5001);
```

You will also have to check your port addresses. My IP and port addresses were:

	PC	Laptop
IP:	IP: 192.168.1.104	IP: 192.168.1.100
KeyDown sends to IP & port	192.168.1.100, 5001	192.168.1.104, 5001
Server port	5001	5001
Client port	5678	5678

The port to reply to is obtained from rxPoint in the server.Receive(ref rxPoint); code.

The resulting communication is shown in Figure 13-9.

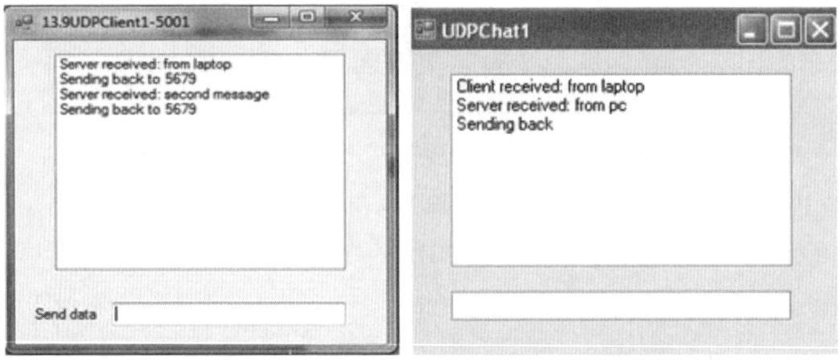

Figure 13-9 PC and Laptop displays

13.12 • Web requests

We have seen that you can display a web page using the WebBrowser control, but you may not want to display data that way, or you might want to deal with data from a web page or file in your program.

You can request data (e.g. a web page or a file) from a host server using a WebRequest.

The procedure is as follows:

1. Create the **WebRequest** using the URI of the server.

   ```
   WebRequest request = WebRequest.Create("http://www.contoso.com/");
   ```

2. Set any values you need, e.g. for authentication.

   ```
   request.Credentials = CredentialCache.DefaultCredentials;
   ```

3. If you need any protocol-specific properties, cast the web request.

   ((HttpWebRequest)request).UserAgent =
   ".NET Framework Example Client";

4. Send the request and get a response from the server using GetResponse.

   WebResponse response = request.GetResponse();

5. Display any information sent.

   MessageBox.Show
   (((HttpWebResponse)response).StatusDescription);

6. Read the data stream sent using GetResponse.

   Stream dataStream = response.GetResponseStream ( );

7. You can now deal with the data.

8. Finally close the stream or WebResponse.

   response.Close( );

For detailed description, see the MSDN library at

https://msdn.microsoft.com/en-us/library/456dfw4f(v=vs.110).aspx

You can try the Microsoft example before writing your own. You don't have to use their Console application. Start a new project, add a button on the form and type in the MS code for the button click. You will have to add 'using System.Net;' and 'using system.IO;' at the top of your code.

The Console output will appear in the Debug Output window, so make sure that is displayed, but you could change the code to use a MessageBox.Show.

The output begins as follows. The OK comes from the StatusDescription, and you should recognize the HTML code.

```
OK
<html><head><title>Microsoft Corporation</title><meta http
```

If you want to try this yourself, start a new project; add the 'using System.Net;' and 'using system.IO;' statements; add a button on a form and for the button click code use:

```
private void btnWebRequest_Click(object sender, EventArgs e)
{
    // Create a request for the URL.
    WebRequest request = WebRequest.Create
            ("http://www.elektor.com/");
    // Get the response.
    WebResponse response = request.GetResponse();
    // Get the stream data returned by the server.
    Stream dataStream = response.GetResponseStream();
    // Open the stream using a StreamReader for easy access.
    StreamReader reader = new StreamReader(dataStream);
    // Read the content.
    string responseFromServer = reader.ReadToEnd();
    // Display the content.
    Console.WriteLine(responseFromServer);
```

```
            // Clean up the streams and the response.
            reader.Close();
            response.Close();
        }
```

It's best to use Console.WriteLine (or Debug.WriteLine) rather than MessageBox.Show as the response can be rather long.

13.13 • E-mail communications

E-mails can be sent from your programs using both a **MailMessage** and an **SmtpClient**.

A **MailMessage** (in namespace System.Net.Mail) is instantiated and includes the items you would expect in your e-mail, e.g.: From, To, Subject, Body etc.

This can be set up in one line as follows:

```
MailMessage Mail = new MailMessage (
"FromEmail@gmail.com",
"ToEmail@gmail.com",
"Email subject",
"Email body");
```

But you can also do it as shown in the example below.

The **SmtpClient** uses simple mail transfer protocol (SMTP) and is in the System.Net.Mail namespace. You will have to log on to your e-mail server to send the e-mail. Your e-mail server (e.g. Google) may also block attempts that do not use modern security standards (as here), so you may need to permit this.

An **SmtpClient** is instantiated and assigned the Host and Port information. The default SMTP port is 25, but it may vary - check with your e-mail provider. It can be instantiated in one line as follows:

```
SmtpClient smtpMailClient = new SmtpClient("smtp.gmail.com", 587);
```

Other smtpClient properties may need to be set such as DeliveryMethod or UseDefaultCredentials.

The MailMessage is sent using the Send command:

```
smtpMailClient.Send(Mail);
```

The following code sets up the smtpClient and MailMessage and sends a message. You will need to add using System.Net.Mail;

You should put it in a try .. catch construct and will have to use your own e-mail set up!

```
MailMessage Mail = new MailMessage( );
SmtpClient smtpMailClient = new SmtpClient("smtp.gmail.com");
Mail.From = new MailAddress("your_email_address@gmail.com");
Mail.To.Add ("Destination@ gmail.com ");
Mail.Subject = "This is a test email from a C# program.";
Mail.Body = "This is the body of the email";
```

```
smtpMailClient.Port = 587;
smtpMailClient.Credentials = new System.Net.NetworkCredential("username",
"password");
smtpMailClient.EnableSsl = true;
smtpMailClient.Send(Mail);
```

Note how the **To** address is added in the example using: Mail.To.Add( ). You can CC or Bcc addressees too, e.g.:

```
Mail.Bcc.Add("destination1@gmail.com");
Mail.CC.Add("destination2@gmail.com");
```

An example is included in the code at Elektor's web site, but you will still have to find out your e-mail settings.

13.14 • File transfer protocol

Files can be uploaded and downloaded using the FTP protocol with the **FTPWebRequest** and **FTPResponse** classes, which are derived from the **WebRequest** and **WebResponse** classes we have seen in 13.12 on page 198 and are in the System.Net namespace.

The procedure is similar to the WebRequest

1. Create the FTP request:
   ```
   FtpWebRequest request =
       (FtpWebRequest)WebRequest.Create("host and filename");
   ```
2. Set the method (upload or download)
   ```
   Request.Method = WebRequestMethods.Ftp.DownloadFile;
   ```
3. Set Credentials, e.g. login information
   ```
   request.Credentials = new NetworkCredential
           ("username","password");
   ```
4. Get the response
   ```
   FtpWebResponse response =
           (FtpWebResponse)request.GetResponse();
   ```
5. Create the Stream, StreamReader and read the data
   ```
   Stream responseStream = response.GetResponseStream();
   StreamReader reader = new StreamReader(responseStream);
   string responseFromServer = reader.ReadToEnd()
   ```
6. Close the reader and response
   ```
   reader.Close( );
   response.Close( );
   ```

If you want further information on this, look at the Microsoft site:

https://msdn.microsoft.com/en-us/library/ms229718%28v=vs.110%29.aspx

13.15 • Self Assessment Exercises

1. TCP Server:

Having created the first TCP client and server applications, make the server to do a useful task such as return the area of a circle for that radius, sent to it. You will need to think about the data string you receive, how to check that it is a (positive) number and how to reply with either the square of the number or an error message.

2. Change the TCP server and client code so that it reads the IP and port address from text boxes.

   Basically, the TcpListener will be instantiated as follows:

```
TcpListener server = new TcpListener
        (IPAddress.Parse(txtIp.Text), int.Parse(txtListenerPort.Text););
```

   Change the client connect code to:

```
client.Connect(txtIP.Text, int.Parse(txtServerPort.Text));
```

3. Change UDP code so that it reads the IP and port address from text boxes.

   You will have to read the port values before instantiating the server and client UdpClient objects and then start the 'serverThread' and 'clientThread' threads.

   The Client.Send method should send to the IP address entered into a text box.

   Remember the port values are integers, whereas the IP address is a string

4. Expand this to the remote chat program, so that one program only needs to be used for can be used.

5. Can the programs be run as await and async Tasks instead of Threads?

13.16 • Summary

In this chapter we have seen the TCP and UDP communications and programs. The TCP program uses separate TCPListener and TCPClient objects and a server which listens on the internet and a client which connects to the server. The code is put into threads and the communication uses Read and Write methods. The UDP application uses UDPClient objects only and connectionless communication using Send and Receive methods.

Both TCP and UDP communication chat programs were developed. The UDP program initially started with a single application that communicated via the internet and 'localhost'. This was extended to two separate applications which communicated on the same PC, and then extended further to communicate across the internet to any internet address.

Web requests were studied, enabling data from a web site to be accessed, e-mail communications and finally FTP transfers were covered.

Chapter 14 • Introduction to Databases

14.1 • Introduction

Databases themselves are a vast subject. The following few chapters intend to give you a feel for databases, how to display the data in a database, how to create your own databases and access database data from code.

A database is an integrated collection of data. The most popular database systems are relational databases which consist of separate but linked, tables of data. In this way an item of data is held in only one place. Databases are often manipulated and queried using a language called SQL (structured query language).

In this chapter we will firstly view data in an existing database and secondly create our own database from within the Visual Studio environment. In the next chapter we will see how to display this data on a UI and then finally access the database using code. All the necessary items to deal with databases should have been loaded when you installed Visual Studio.

14.2 • A typical database

Before we start let's look at a typical database; we shall look at Microsoft's Northwind database. Instructions on downloading this are in the next section. It's a typical relational database that might be used by a company and has separate tables for customers, orders, products, suppliers, etc., all of which are linked together. Figure 14-1 shows a portion of the employees table, which shows the table's rows (the individual employee's data), and columns (or fields): Last Name, First Name etc.

E...	LastName	FirstName	Title	Titl...	BirthDate	HireDate	Address	City
1	Davolio	Nancy	Sales Represent...	Ms.	08/12/19...	01/05/19...	507 - 20th ...	Seattle
2	Fuller	Andrew	Vice President, ...	Dr.	19/02/19...	14/08/19...	908 W. Capi...	Tacoma
3	Leverling	Janet	Sales Represent...	Ms.	30/08/19...	01/04/19...	722 Moss B...	Kirklanc
4	Peacock	Margaret	Sales Represent...	Mrs.	19/09/19...	03/05/19...	4110 Old Re...	Redmo
5	Buchanan	Steven	Sales Manager	Mr.	04/03/19...	17/10/19...	14 Garrett ...	London
6	Suyama	Michael	Sales Represent...	Mr.	02/07/19...	17/10/19...	Coventry H...	London

Figure 14-1 The Northwind Database

A particular row of a table is called a record and consists of columns or fields of data (e.g. LastName). To link tables, there must be a unique item in each record which is known as the primary key field; in this case it is the employee's ID. Other columns are allowed to have duplicate data though, for example one employee's first name, date of birth or department may be the same as another employee.

Structured Query Language (SQL) provides a set of commands that enable programmers to define complex queries to select the required information from a database. For instance one user might want to know the names of all the employees working in a department but another user, employees over the age of 60, or paid a certain salary. We will look at the basic SQL commands later, but won't get involved in extracting specific data.

14.3 • Dealing with Databases

In this chapter we shall look at the following:

1. Inspect and view data in an existing database
2. Creating our own database

In the following chapters we shall see how to use the controls to display data and finally we will see how to access database from our code.

14.3.1 • Viewing a database in C#

We will start by creating an application that will simply view the Microsoft Northwind database. If it's not already on your PC, instructions for downloading it are at Microsoft's site:

http://msdn.microsoft.com/en-us/library/8b6y4c7s.aspx

Or you can find it by searching for 'Northwind database'.

We will go through the steps here, but this is not a trivial process and if you have difficulties you might like skip to Creating Your Own Database, section 14.4.

1. Download the SQL Server 2000 version.

   This is found at: www.microsoft.com/en-us/download/details.aspx?id=23654

   Run the downloaded file. The Northwnd.mdf database will be installed in the C:\SQL Server 2000 Sample Databases folder.

   Note the Microsoft comment:

   'The .MDF database file cannot easily be converted to a format that you can use in current versions of SQL Server, so it's best to use the script to create the database.'

   Note the SQL script for the Northwind database, **instnwnd.sql**

2. Start a new project and display the Server Explorer (View > Server Explorer).

   We will be using a Microsoft SQL Server (SqlClient) database and connection, and will use the SQL Server that is installed with Visual Studio. To do so, we will use **(localdb)\v11.0** as its name (don't ignore the backslash).

   We need to make a connection to the database (to an instance of the SQL Server).

   Right-click Data Connections in the Server Explorer and choose 'Add Connection'

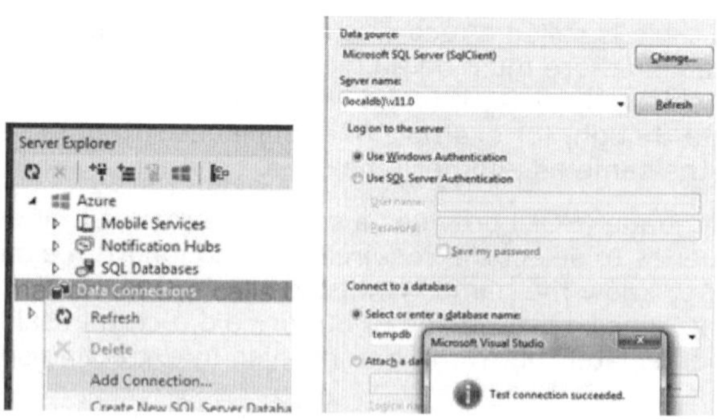

Figure 14-2 Adding a Data Connection

In the Add Connection dialog, choose **MicroSoft SQL Server** and check the Data source is **Microsoft SQL Server (SqlClient).** Enter **(localdb)\v11.0** for the Server name (or the name of SQL Server where you want to create the database). If you don't have this, check that you selected **MicroSoft SQL**

Server and NOT MicroSoft SQL Server Database File.

Leave the authentication as Windows and select tempdb as a temporary database. Test the connection. If it is successful, click OK to add the connection, see Figure 14-2 on page 204.

3. We now need to run the SQL query to extract the Northwind database.

   Right-click the connection to your database in Server Explorer and select 'New Query'. Copy the text from the **instnwnd.sql** file and paste it in the SQLQuery1.sql window. The file has to be modified. This is explained at (5) in the Microsoft link, at *https://msdn.microsoft.com/en-us/library/8b6y4c7s.aspx* but here's the short version.

   Having pasted the instnwnd.sql text, modify the following lines as follows:

   Delete the following lines (they're about line 23):

```
exec sp_dboption 'Northwind','trunc. log on chkpt.','true'
exec sp_dboption 'Northwind','select into/bulkcopy','true'
```

   and replace with the following:

```
ALTER DATABASE Northwind SET RECOVERY SIMPLE
```

   This code sets up a backup model for the database.

   What Microsoft doesn't say is now to **execute the script**. Click the green triangle.

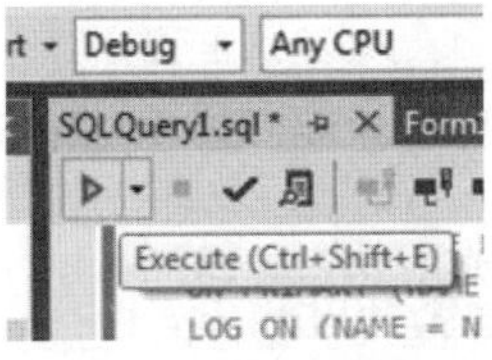

   Once executed, you should get a message: 'Query executed successfully at: '

You should now be able to add a new Data Connection (Data Connection > Add New Connection) and Northwind should be in the list of names to connect to. If not, try adding (localdb)\v11.0 to the Server name list and refreshing it.

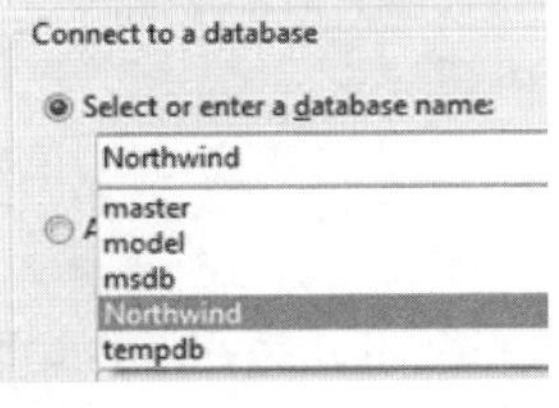

You can delete the original tempdb data connection you made.

Now that the connection has been made, we can use this in our projects. Close this solution.

Having created the database, let's add this to a project and display the data.

Start a new windows application. I've called it 'ViewingADb'. Display the Server Explorer (View > Server Explorer). Older versions of Visual Studio call it Database Explorer, but the procedure is the same.

The Northwind database may already be included as a Data Connection. If not, right-click 'Data Connections', and select Add Connection. Make sure you have **Microsoft SQL Server (SqlClient)** as the Data source, select or type in **(localdb)\v11.0** as the Server name, use Windows authentication and in 'Connect to a database' select Northwind from the drop-down box (or another database if you have one). If the database is shown, but it has a red cross on it, just click on it to reconnect to the database. If it's not shown, check you have run the SQL query as explained above. If you find you can't access the database, make sure you have access rights.

Click OK to connect to the database.

You can now expand the tables in the database. Figure 14-3 shows the Data Connections and the Northwind database tables in the Server Explorer.

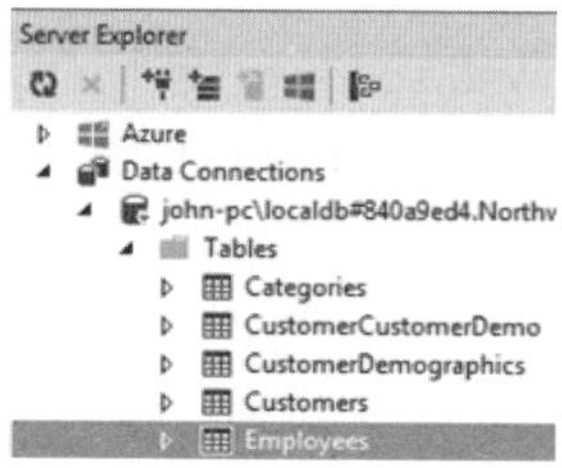

Figure 14-3 Server Explorer database

There are different database files: Access database files have an MDB file extension, SQL Server compact database files have an SDF extension and SQL Server database files which have a MDF file extension. There are others too, such as Oracle database files.

You can now expand the Northwind database in the Explorer. There are a number of Tables and Views. Expand the 'Tables' to see all the individual tables that make up the database.

We can inspect, add or delete the data in the tables by right-clicking the table name in the explorer and selecting 'Show Table Data', see Figure 14-4.

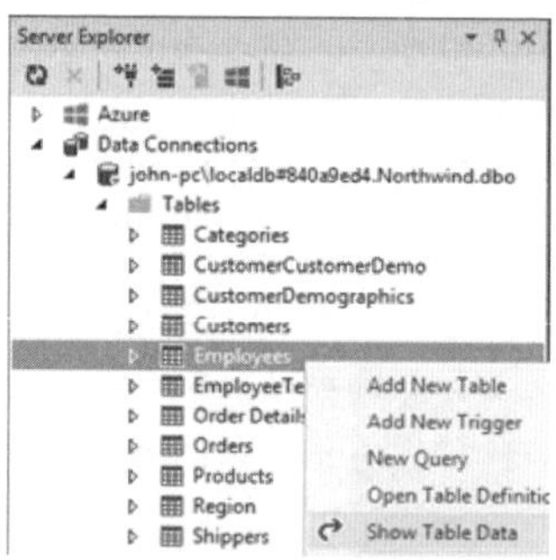

Figure 14-4 Retrieving database data

If you do this for the Employees table, you will see data similar to Figure 14-5. This is of course the same data as we saw in Figure 14-1 on page 203.

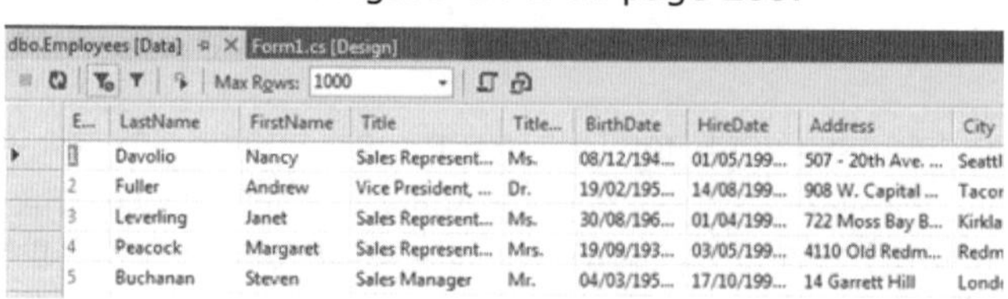

Figure 14-5 Table Data

You can change the data or add more employees by typing directly into the cells. You must obey the data type and can't type anything into the ID column – in this database this is generated automatically for you. Right-click the cell for the options, see Figure 14-6. You may need to execute the SQL command to update the database.

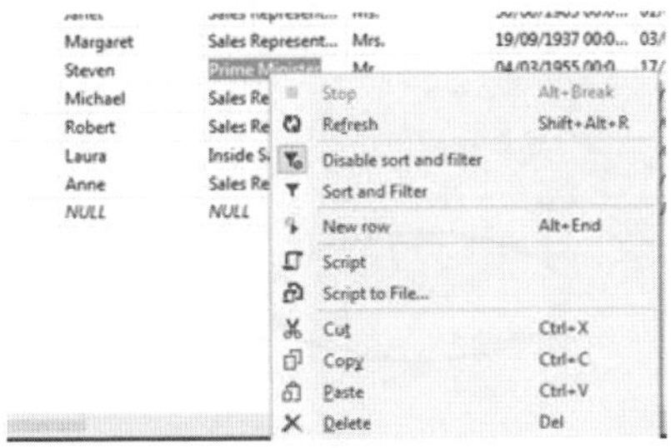

Figure 14-6 Updating database

You can add or delete a row, but note that if you now add more employees, the ID you deleted isn't used again.

We'll see this in more detail in section 15.3 on page 215, but if you want to run a program to see the data, drag a DataGridView from the Toolbox onto the form. The DataGridView tasks will prompt you to choose a Data Source. Select Add Project Data Source and Database, DataSet, select Northwind.dbo and save the connection String.

You are then asked for the objects you want to see, select Tables and click Finish.

Return to the DataGridView tasks and now you should be able to use the Other Data Sources > Project Data Sources > NorthwindDataSet > Employees to show the employee's data.

You can now run the program and the employee's data will be displayed.

Before moving on you might like to look at some of the other tables in this database.

14.4 • Creating a new database

Let's create our own record collection database. It will have two tables, called Artist and Recording. We will provide a link from the recording to the artist so that on adding a new recording, the user will have to select an artist from the Artist table.

Start a new project. I've called it CreatingADbase.

To add a new database select Project > Add New Item. Scroll down and select the Service-based Database, see Figure 14-7 on page 208. If you have a different version of Visual Studio you may see a local database option (e.g. MS Access). This provides a simple data storage and manipulation solution, whereas a service-based database (e.g. SQL server) provides a multi-user solution with the ability to search and manage large amounts of data. Confusingly, Service-based database have an MDF file extension, whereas Local databases have an SDF file extension.

Select a Service-based database (MDF file), give it a suitable name (e.g. 'Recordings') and add the database.

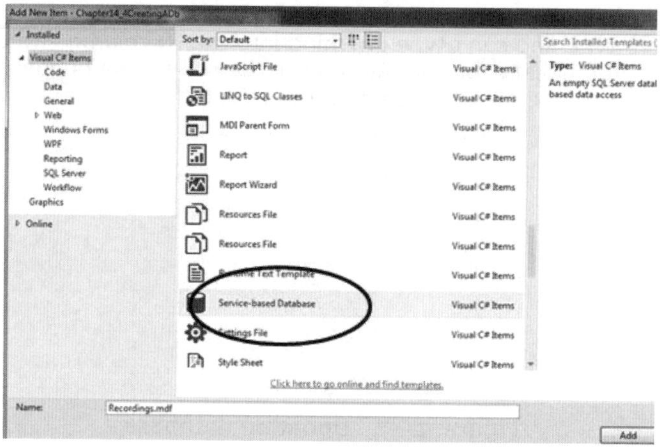

Figure 14-7 Adding an SQL database

The database connection has been made and appears in the Server Explorer, see Figure 14-8.

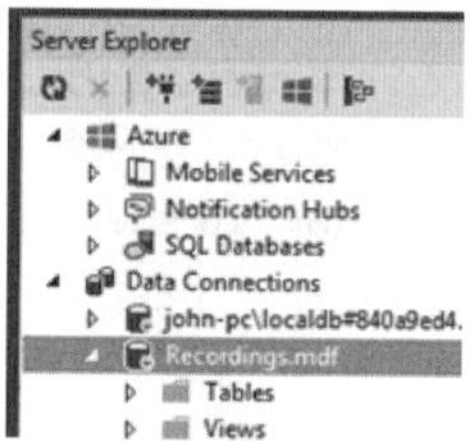

Figure 14-8 Adding a database

Remember, to display the Server Explorer you can double-click the database name in the Solution Explorer or use View > Server Explorer as you did in section 14.3.1 on page 204.

As we have seen, if you already have a database you can right-click Data Connections in Server Explorer and browse for the database. You can also delete the connection to the Northwind database.

At this stage you can use the Data Source Configuration Wizard to create a connection to the (future) database but will do that in the next chapter (15.3 on page 215).

14.4.1 • Adding the database tables

Now we need to add the tables, columns and data to our database. We will link the tables in database together.

Expand the database and right-click Tables and select Add New Table. The design surface appears, Figure 14-9 on page 209. We can now add the names and data types for each column of our database.

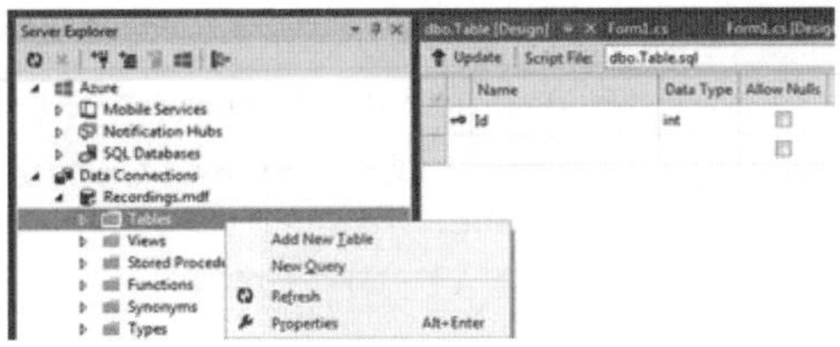

Figure 14-9 Adding tables to a database

If you are using a different version of Visual Studio and the correct icons don't appear, check you have selected and MDF database and not an SDF database.

Let's create a database for our record collection. We will create tables for Artist and Recording, but we could also add group/solo artist, date, playing time, genre, record label etc. At a later date we could search for (say) a solo rock and roll artist, dated before 1980 whose playing time is longer than 3 minutes.

The first table we are going to create is for our Artists. It will have a unique ID for the artist.

This database will simply have an ArtistID (an integer variable) and an Artist Name (a number/name variable).

Type in ArtistID for the first Column Name with data type 'int' and clear the 'allow Nulls' checkbox. To link with other tables, one of the items in the table has to be unique. In this case we will use the ArtistID. This has to be the Primary Key. If the Primary Key isn't already set (Key symbol) right-click the ArtistID row and select Primary Key or set it in the Identity Specification in Properties.

It would be useful to automatically generate and increment the ArtistID number when the user adds an artist so, in **Properties** expand the **Identity Specification** and set **(Is Identity)** to **True**. The auto-increment value and seed can be changed if necessary. You don't have to do this, but whatever you choose must match in the linked table.

Add 'Name' for the next Column item and select nvarchar(50) for the data type (it's a variable-length Unicode character data) and again remove the tick so don't Allow Nulls, see Figure 14-10.

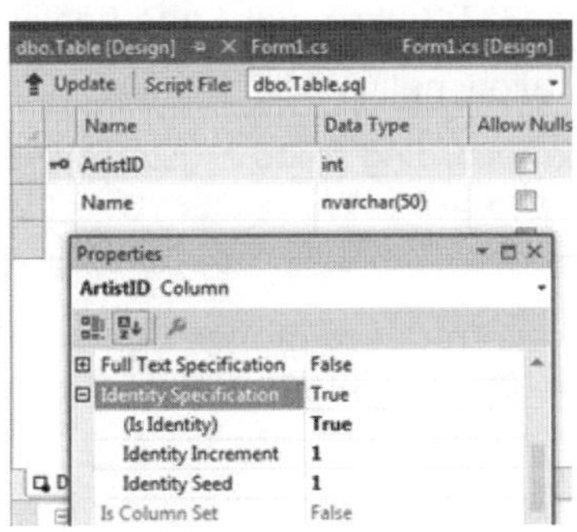

Figure 14-10 Artists database

If you want to change the default value of nvarchar(50), just change the value in the brackets to a value of your choice.

If you want to delete a row, select it, right-click and choose delete.

Give the table a name by changing the first line (in the T-SQL tab) of the script (from

CREATE TABLE [dbo].[Table]) to:

CREATE TABLE [dbo].[Artists]

Click Update (in the top right hand corner) to preview and Update the Database. The changes are saved to the local database file.

The table is added to the database. Right-click tables in Server Explorer and choose 'Refresh' if the Tables don't appear. You can now see the Artists table in the Server Explorer.

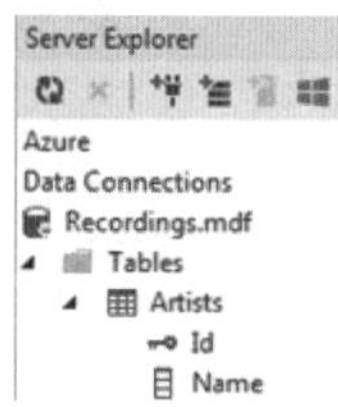

Add a second table (in Server Explorer, right-click Tables > Add New Table). Add the following column names and data types, see Figure 14-11 on page 211:

- ID, int, no nulls. Add the primary key and identity as before:

  (Identity Specification and set (Is Identity) to True)

- Title, nvarchar(MAX) – type 100 in place of MAX, no nulls
- PlayingTime, datetime2(7), allow nulls, and finally
- Date, datetime2(7), allow nulls.

Finally add a column to link the recording to its artist. This is given the same name and data type as the primary key **ArtistID**.

- ArtistID, int, no nulls

The data type datetime2(7) was introduced in SQL Server 2008. It is an extension to datetime, but has a larger date range, a larger default fractional precision and an optional user-specified precision.

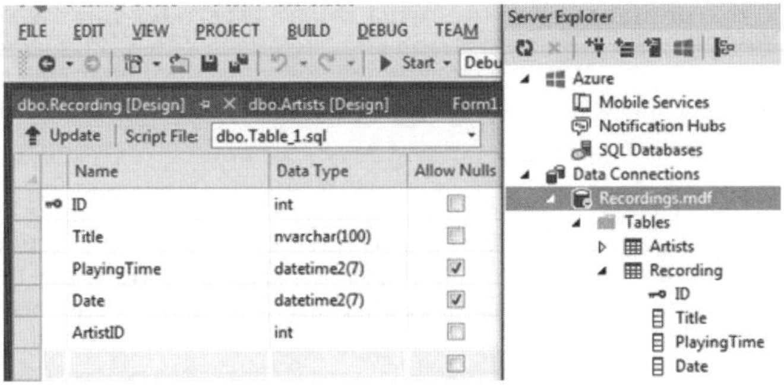

Figure 14-11 Recording table

Change the first line of the script to:

```
CREATE TABLE [dbo].[Recording]
```

Click Update to preview the database update and click Update Database.

Refresh the Recordings.mdf database to see both tables. Your table should be similar to Figure 14-11.

We now have two tables defined: **Artists** and **Recording**.

14.5 • Adding relationships – linking the tables

We have created two separate tables. We now need add a relationship from the recordings to their artist. To do this we provide a link from the Recording table to the Artist table. This link is known as a foreign key and points from the Recording table to the primary key of the Artist table. Now you can see why the link in the Recording table that matches the primary key ArtistID is in the Artist table. When a new recording is added to the database the user will be forced to select an Artist for the recording from the Artist table.

Earlier versions of Visual Studio had a Database Diagram which could be used to visually add the link, but to quote Microsoft: *'In previous versions of Visual Studio, you could use Visual Database Tools to create tables, queries, and views, and to create and maintain database diagrams. In Visual Studio 2013, Visual Database Tools have been deprecated, but SQL Server Database Tools provide replacement features to help you create tables, queries, and views'*

Ensure the Recordings [Design] table is displayed and right-click 'Foreign Keys' and select 'Add New Foreign Key', Figure 14-12.

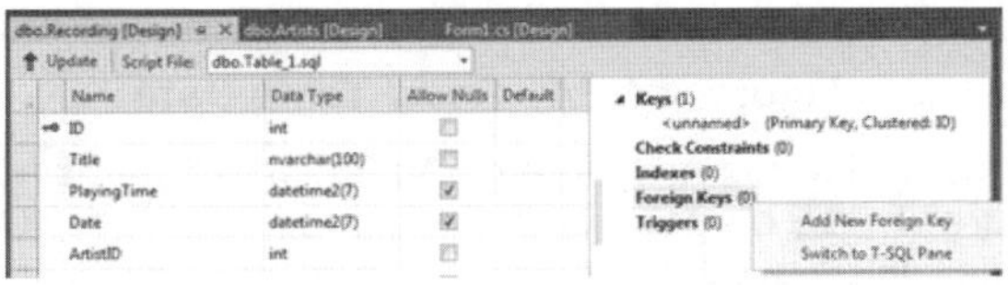

Figure 14-12 Linking the tables

The prompt **FK_Recording_ToTable** appears. We want to make the Foreign Key (**FK**) link from the **Recording** to the **Artist** table. We will worry about which row in a minute.

Replace **ToTable** with **Artist** so that it says: `FK_Recording_Artists`

We want to link to the primary key in the Artist table (ArtistID) so in the script panel change the last line so that it reads:

```
CONSTRAINT [FK_Recording_Artists] FOREIGN KEY ([ArtistID]) REFERENCES
[Artists]([ArtistID])
```

Update the database.

The (now deprecated) database diagram would have shown the connection between the tables, see Figure 14-13. Note the 'one to many' connection. The Artist table has the primary key, and the Recording table the 'infinity' sign, indicating that one unique artist can have unlimited recordings.

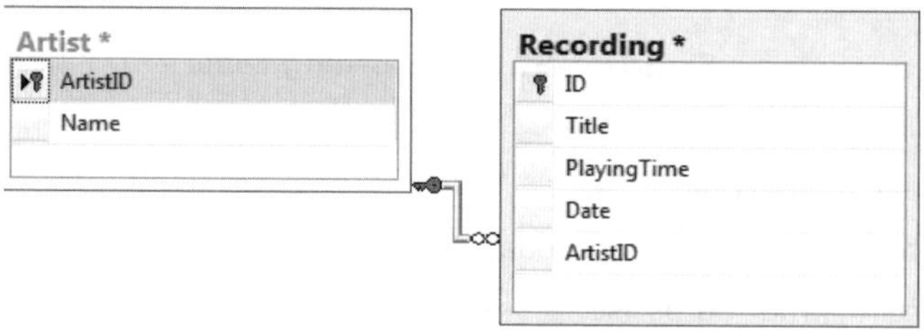

Figure 14-13 One to Many database diagram connection

We will see a similar diagram when we look at the XSD (XML Schema Definition) file in Figure 15-18 on page 220.

14.6 • Adding data to the tables

Now let's add some data to our tables. We will add our artists first and then we will be forced to select one when we add our recordings.

Expand the Server Explorer tables to show the Artist and Recording tables. Right-click the Artist table and select 'Show Table Data', see Figure 14-14. We can now add our artists.

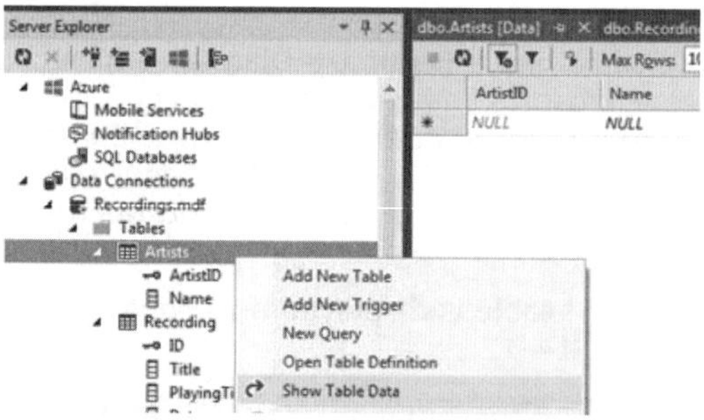

Figure 14-14 Show Table Data

Click the Name field and add some artists, e.g.: Van Morrison, Rolling Stones, Bob Dylan, The Who etc, see Figure 14-15 on page 213. Remember the ArtistID number will be generated for you. This will be used when we link from the recording table.

	ArtistID	Name
	1	Van Morrison ...
	2	Rolling Stones ...
	3	Bob Dylan ...
	4	The Who ...
▸*	NULL	NULL

Figure 14-15 Adding Artists to Tables

Now we can add some recordings. Choose 'Show Table Data' for the Recording table and add some titles and artists. You have to use the number you want for the required artist in the ArtistID column, not the artist's name. You will get an error if you try typing in a non-existing number for ArtistID. If you didn't allow nulls, you will have to add a complete DateTime data type (8/7/2008 12:59:59, or 1:23:45).

Of course we could have used a different data type for the ArtistID (say nvarchar(20)) and matched that in the recordings table. An example of that is used in the Microsoft database walkthrough suggested in the Self-Assessment Examples.

Add the data as shown in Figure 14-16, or make up your own titles.

ID	Title	PlayingTime	Date	ArtistID
1	Best of Van Morr...	04/09/2007 01:03:00	01/01/1999 00:00:00	1
2	Veedon Fleece	04/09/2007 00:56:00	01/01/1978 00:00:00	1
3	Live at Leeds	04/09/2007 01:03:00	01/01/1972 00:00:00	4
4	Quadrophenia	04/09/2007 01:20:30	01/01/1970 00:00:00	4
5	Sticky Fingers	04/09/2007 00:50:45	01/01/1972 00:00:00	2
NULL	NULL	NULL	NULL	NULL

Figure 14-16 Adding recordings

You will see that you are forced to select a matching ArtistID and perhaps a better choice could have been made for the PlayingTime data type.

If you now try to delete 'The Who' from the Artist table you will get an error message, because you have links to it from the Recording table, Figure 14-17.

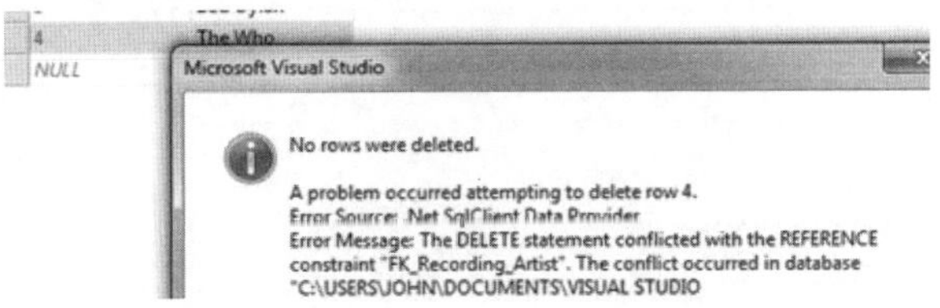

Figure 14-17 Error message

Save the solution, we will return to this in the next chapter. The Recordings database is an MDF file (Recordings.mdf) and has been saved in the project's folder.

What we now need to do is display our data in our projects. We'll do that in the next chapter.

14.7 • Self Assessment Exercises

1. Follow the Microsoft walkthrough at:

   https://msdn.microsoft.com/en-us/library/ms233763.aspx

2. Hopefully I will have some videos on YouTube to support all this. Watch them.
3. Open up your Recording database in a new project. Remember it's a Microsoft SQL Server Database (MDF) file (called recordings.mdf) and has been saved in the CreatingADb folder.
4. Create another database this time with three dependent variables. You could extend your record collection to add a third table that holds a library shelf where it is stored.
5. Create a database using names as the primary key. You will of course not need a unique number as an ID, so experiment with the Identity Specification

14.8 • Summary

We have discussed databases and looked at a detailed database, Microsoft's Northwind. We have seen how we can include this database in our Visual Studio projects. We have created our own database with two tables (Artist and Recording) from within Visual Studio. Each of these tables has had a primary key and a relationship was established so that when data is added, the user is forced to select an artist for each recording.

We now want our programs to display the data in the database and also write code to access the database to read, write and update the database. In the first case we want a UI so that a user can see the items in the database and in the second case, code to access the database and add delete or search the database. We'll do that in the next chapters.

Chapter 15 • Displaying databases

15.1 • Introduction

So far we have looked at an existing database (Northwind) and also created our own database with linked tables from within Visual Studio. Now we want to design a user interface and write a program to display the database information. We will introduce the UI database controls, but before we do that, we'll cover some terminology.

15.2 • The dataset, data binding and ActiveX Data Objects (ADO.NET)

ADO.NET objects create the connection to the database, manage the communication (the requests, updates etc.) between your application and the database and manage the data that is retrieved as a result of a database query.

The **dataset**: Database programs do not deal directly with the database when they run; they use a copy known as a dataset and update the database only when required. The dataset can be the whole database or a subset, and holds a collection of data tables related to each other. The DataSet is a class within ADO.NET and we will create a dataset for our program.

Data binding allows data to be retrieved and displayed automatically using the database controls. These controls know how to automatically display and update the various types of data, relieving the programmer of the task.

The binding source is responsible for displaying the current row of data on the form and making sure all the items have the correct and matching data.

We will use a wizard to add all these controls for us. They will appear in the designer tray.

To recap, the dataset is populated from the database. This is controlled by the TableAdapter which provides the connection and knows how to update the data. The BindingSource is responsible for displaying the current row of data on the form and making sure all the items have the correct and matching data, see Figure 15-1.

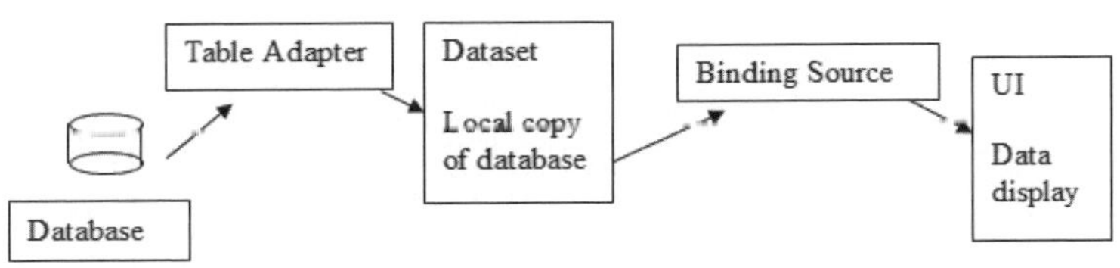

Figure 15-1 Database data transfer

You can choose to display a media-player like navigator which enables you to scroll through and update the database data. These are all in the toolbox and you can add them yourself, but there is a wizard that does it all that for you. We will use that.

15.3 • Displaying database information

Let's return to the Northwind database and display its information. If you haven't downloaded the Northwind database, use the Artist/Recording database you created in the previous chapter (or use mine from the code provided).

Start a new project and call it DisplayNorthwind. This time we'll use the Data Source Configuration Wizard to add the database. Remember, Access database files have an MDB file extension; SQL Server compact database files have an SDF extension and SQL Server database files have a MDF file extension. The Northwind database is an SQL Server database file (Northwnd.mdf).

Display the Data Sources window (View > Other Windows > Data Sources) and click the icon or choose the Add New Data Source link. If the Data Sources window isn't available, displaying the Form design window should make it so.

The Data Source Configuration Wizard is displayed. Select Database > Dataset > New Connection, see Figure 15-2.

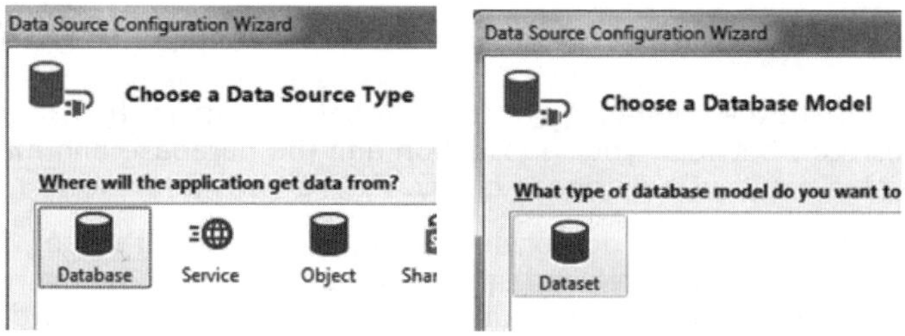

Figure 15-2 Data Source Configuration Wizard

Make sure Microsoft SQL Server (SqlClient) is selected as the Data source, if not click Change and select it.

You now need to add your server name. In our case it is **(localdb)\v11.0** but of course you might eventually have a different server. Click Refresh. Under 'Select or Enter a database name', use the drop down box to select the Northwind database, see Figure 15-3. If it doesn't appear make sure you followed the instructions in section 14.3.1 on page 204, or use the SQL Server Object Explorer tab to locate it. Finally test the connection.

Figure 15-3 Adding a database

The data connection and connection string are displayed. Click Next and save the Connection string, see Figure 15-4 on page 217.

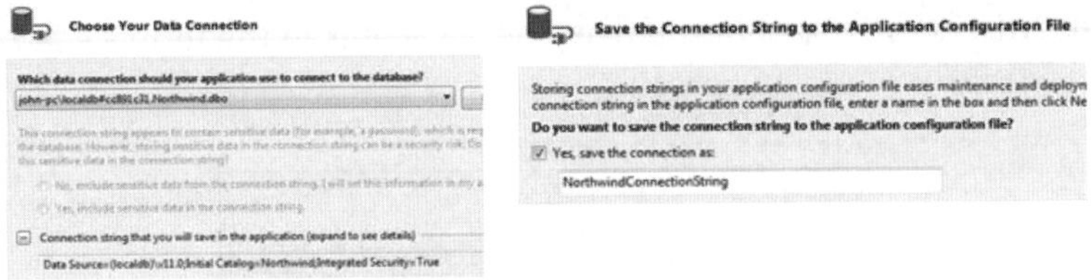

Figure 15-4 Data connection

We now choose the database objects we want for our program. We only want the Tables information. Select Tables (the expanded tables are shown below) and click Finish. See Figure 15-5.

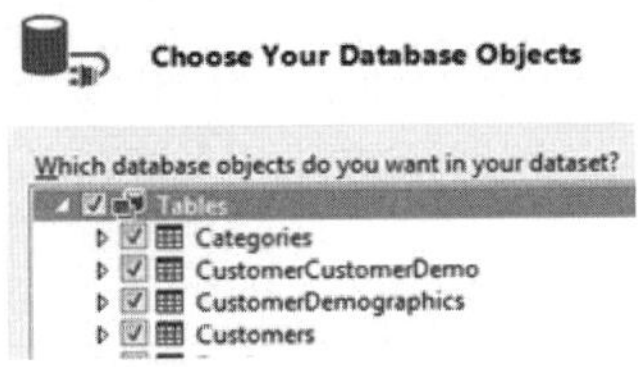

Figure 15-5 Adding a data source

The dataset is displayed in the Data Sources window.

We now want to select the data sources that we want to display on our form. Display the Data Sources tab (Shift+Alt+D) to see the dataset, see Figure 15-6. If the database isn't displayed, check you have completed the Data Source Configuration Wizard as above.

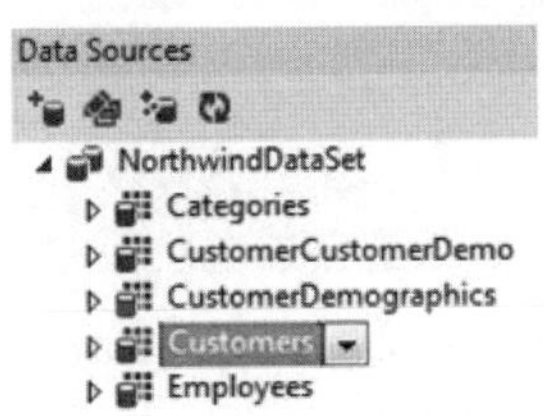

Figure 15-6 Customer Data Source

15.3.1 • DataGridView

This time, we'll look at the Customers table instead of the Employees table. Click the down arrow by Customers table and you will see you have the option of DataGridView or Details View, see Figure 15-7.

The DataGridView will display all the data in a grid form. Alternatively, the Details view displays the individual data rows one at a time - we'll see that later.

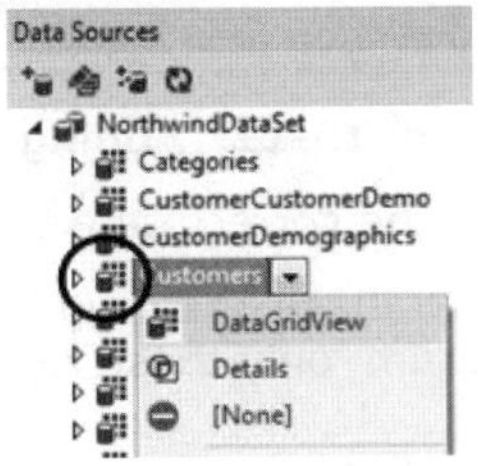

Figure 15-7 DataGrid view

Make sure the DataGridView is selected by the side of 'Customers' and drag the icon onto the form. This will add a DataGridView and Navigator to the form - see Figure 15-8.

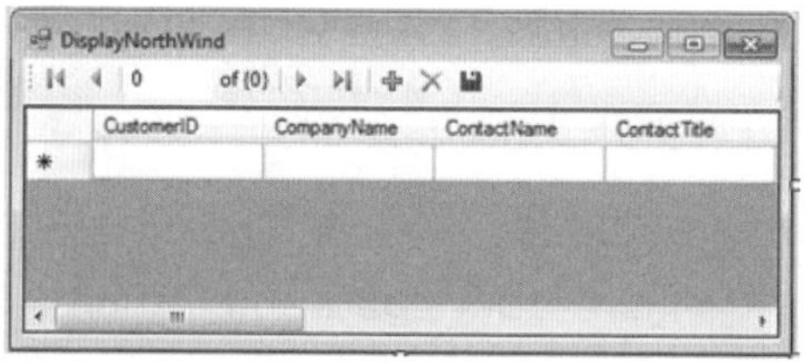

Figure 15-8 DataGrid view and Navigator

This action has also added the database controls: DataSet, BindingSource, TableAdaptor, TableAdaptorManager and BindingNavigator to the status bar, see Figure 15-9. Don't worry about what these do for now, we will use some of these when we start to access the data from our program.

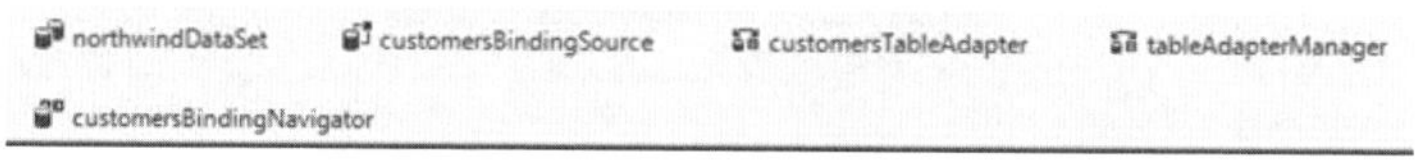

Figure 15-9 Database controls

You can now run the program and see the customer database displayed in a grid format, see Figure 15-10.

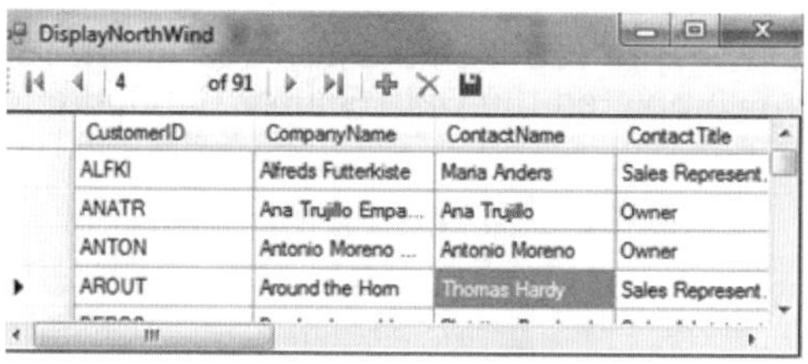

Figure 15-10 Customer DataGrid display

It's as easy as that! We have done all this without writing a single line of code.

You can now use the Navigator at the top of the form to step through the database and also add new customers and delete the customers you added, see Figure 15-11.

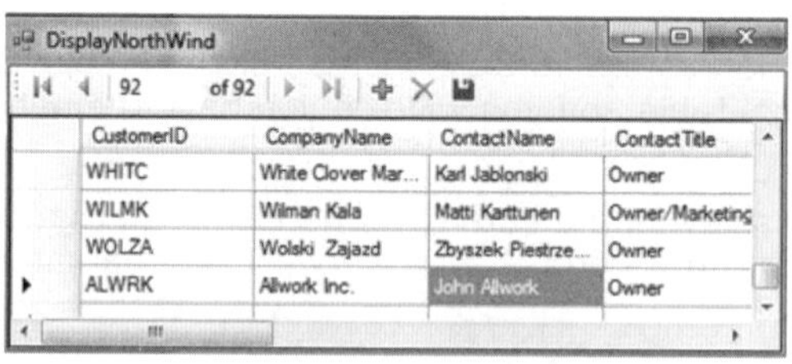

Figure 15-11 Adding Data

The individual fields are checked for the correct data type when you add a new customer.

If you do this with the Recordings database and drag both the artist and recordings tables to the form, when you run the program, only those recordings for the selected artist are shown, Figure 15-12 on page 219.

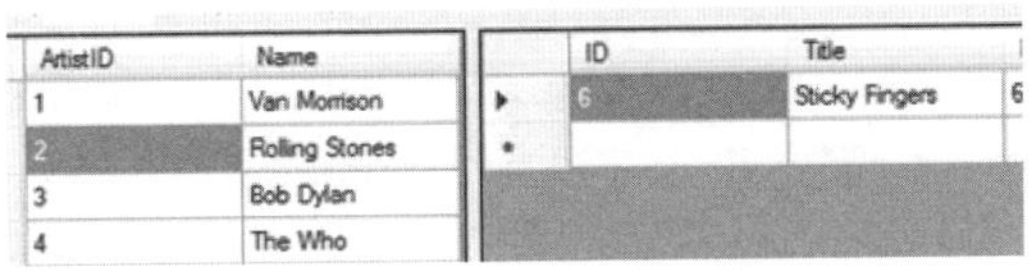

Figure 15-12 Linked data display

Stop the program and click the tiny box with the arrow in the top right hand corner of the DataGridView control to display the DataGridView tasks, see Figure 15-13. It is here that the data source and editing options can be selected.

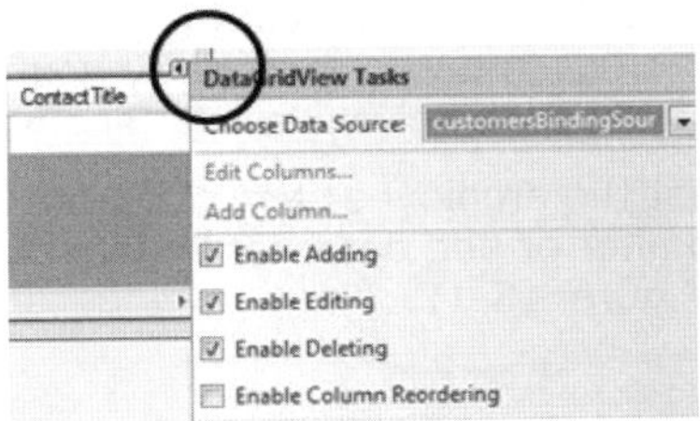

Figure 15-13 DataGridView tasks

You can edit and add columns, and enable adding, editing, deleting and reordering of database entries by your user.

15.3.2 • Details view

If you want to see how the Details view works and displays the items repeat the above exercise and select Details instead of the DataGridView from the drop-down box. You can either do this in a new project, or add the details to the current form.

Figure 15-14 shows the Employees Details selected, note the icon is different from the DataGridView.

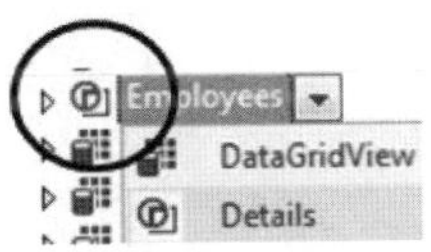

Figure 15-14 Details view and icon

Drag this to the form to show the details view on the form, see Figure 15-15.

Figure 15-15 Details display

Each of the controls has its own task that can be selected by clicking the right arrow. For instance you can change the textbox properties to multiline, Figure 15-16 on page 220.

Figure 15-16 Control task options

We will see how to use the Add Query option later. Preview Data and see what appears.

If you want to navigate through your employees you will have to add a navigator.

Add a BindingNavigator from the ToolBox Data controls tab. You will have to add the link to the binding source. We'll see this in detail later, but if you want to do it now select employeesBindingSource from the BindingNavigator's BindingSource property.

Run the program and note that the employees are displayed one at a time. The correct option appears if you want to alter or add data, for instance the birth date appears as a DateTimePicker control, see Figure 15-17.

Figure 15-17 DateTimePicker

You can also display individual items from the table on the form. Stop the program and in the Data Sources expand the Employees table. Select PictureBox from the available items. Drag a PictureBox onto the form and click the right-arrow to see the PictureBox tasks, see Figure 15-18.

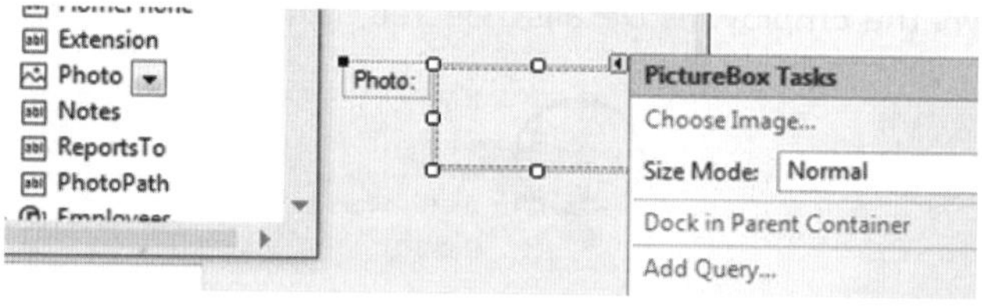

Figure 15-18 PictureBox display

Run the program to see the photographs of the employees, see Figure 15-19.

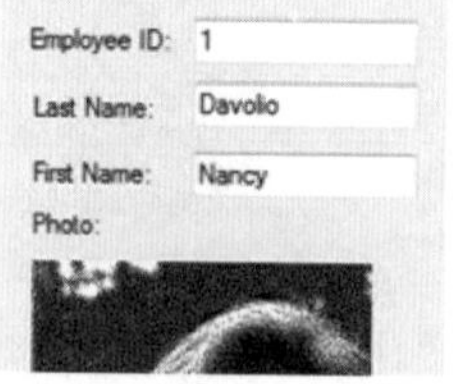

Figure 15-19 Photo Data

15.4 • Viewing the data set

The dataset is the memory resident copy of the database. The individual tables of the database and how they are linked can be viewed by double-clicking the XSD (XML Schema Definition) file displayed in the Solution Explorer, see Figure 15-20.

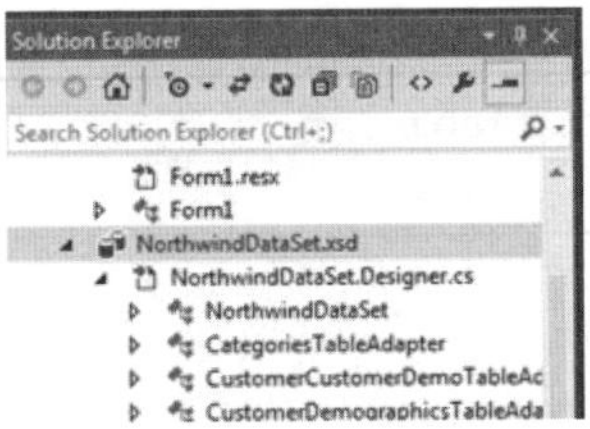

Figure 15-20 Dataset XSD file

The database tables and the links between the tables are displayed, see Figure 15-21.

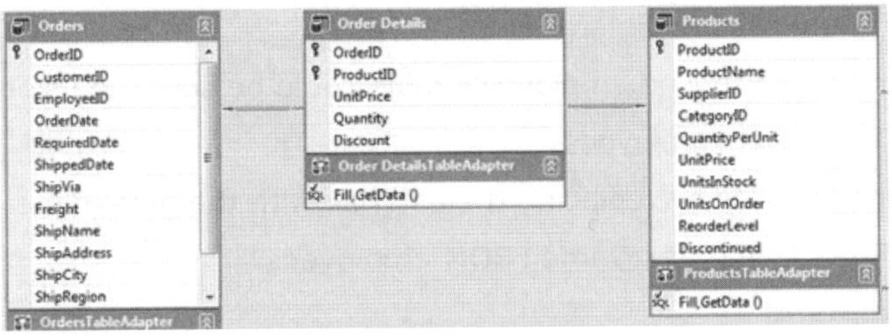

Figure 15-21 The DataSet

Here you can see the primary key fields and the relationships (remember our Artist/Recording relationship diagram).

15.5 • Structured Query Language (SQL)

Finally we will take a look at how we might extract information using Structured Query Language (SQL) commands. In fact we did this with the instnwnd.sql file we used to extract the Northwind database.

If you looked at the SELECT command you would have seen how it defines the fields to extract from the database. You can search in your code for 'SELECT' to find some examples. It's something like:

```
SELECT CustomerID, CompanyName, ContactName, Phone FROM Customers
```

The SELECT command can be qualified in many ways and the basic SQL commands are shown in Table 15-1. We won't use any of these commands, letting the wizard generate them instead, but you might find it useful to know some of the commands to see how the data is extracted from the database.

Table 15-1 SQL commands

SQL keyword	Description
SELECT	Selects fields from one or more tables
FROM	Specifies the table(s) from which to retrieve the data. - Required for SELECT and DELETE commands
WHERE	Specifies criteria that determines the rows to be retrieved
GROUP BY	Specifies criteria for grouping records
ORDER BY	Specifies criteria for ordering records

SQL keyword	Description
INSERT	Inserts data into a table
UPDATE	Updates data in a table
DELETE	Deletes data from a table

We shall briefly discuss these commands.

The SELECT command

The SELECT query is used to select or get information from a table. The basic form is:

```
SELECT fields FROM tableName
```

All the fields from the Northwind employee's table could be selected using:

```
SELECT * FROM employees
```

We can select specific fields by replacing the asterisk with the field name. For example:

```
SELECT firstName, lastName FROM employees
```

The WHERE command

In most cases users want to look for specific data with the fields. The WHERE command is used to specify the selection. The simplest format of the WHERE command is:

```
SELECT field FROM tableName WHERE criteria
```

For example to select all the users called John from the database you might use:

```
SELECT firstName, lastName FROM employees WHERE firstName = John
```

The WHERE condition can contain the usual operators (<,>, <=, >=, ==, <>) as well as LIKE. LIKE can be used with a wildcard, for example, to get first names beginning with J, as follows:

```
SELECT firstName, lastName FROM employee WHERE firstName LIKE 'J*'
```

The INSERT command

The INSERT command inserts a new record in a table. The simplest form for this is:

```
INSERT INTO tableName (fieldname(s)) VALUES (value(s))
```

For example:

```
INSERT INTO employees(firstName, lastName) VALUES ('Joe', 'ALLWORK')
```

The UPDATE command

Changes are made only to a local copy of the database. The UPDATE command is used to save these changes. The simplest form is:

```
UPDATE tableName SET fieldname = value WHERE criteria
```

For example:

```
UPDATE employees SET lastName = 'ALLWORK'

WHERE lastName = DOE and firstName = 'Jane'
```

This will change the last name of the record for Jane DOE to ALLWORK.

The DELETE command

The DELETE command will delete data from a table. The simplest form is:

DELETE FROM tableName WHERE criteria

For example we could delete the record for Jane ALLWORK using the command:

DELETE FROM employees WHERE firstName = 'Jane' AND lastName = 'ALLWORK'

15.6 • Query Builder

Now that we now slightly more about SQL, we can briefly return to the 'Add Query, we saw in section 15.3.2 on page 219 and Figure 15-16 on page 220. If you clicked on this you saw an SQL criteria builder dialog appear, see Figure 15-23.

Figure 15-22 SQL Criteria Builder

Clicking on Query Builder, displays the dialog shown in Figure 15-23.

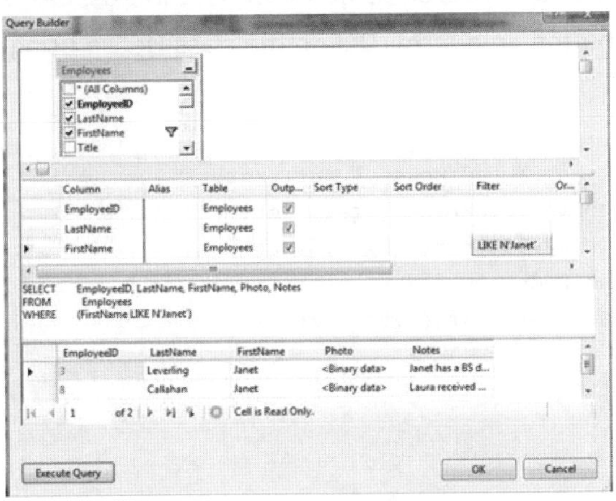

Figure 15-23 Query Builder

Here you can select and deselect the fields you want included in the query, order them by dragging their details, add a filter (LIKE 'Janet') and the query is built for you. By clicking Execute Query, you can see the result. In this example an employee's first name has been changed, so that two Janet's are displayed.

Incidentally, if you try this and get the error message: *'The schema returned by the new query differs from the base query'*, this is because the query returns a table which has a different number of columns from the original database. If you leave the number of

Employees records alone in the query (the top selection) it should work.

When you run the program you now get another query button, in this case called by its default name 'FillBy', which when clicked fills the relevant boxes with the data. Figure 15-24 shows only the two records displayed; those with the name Janet.

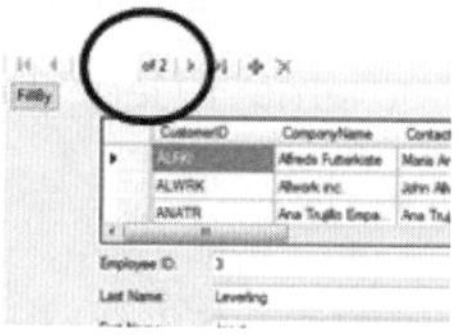

Figure 15-24 The Query Builder results

15.7 • LINQ Queries

You may have noticed by now the '**using System.Linq**' statement. As this is included by default, you might think that Microsoft consider it important.

LINQ (Language INtegrated Query) provides a way of selecting data from within your code. You can then perform work on that data. LINQ has commands and works in a similar way to SQL, but you don't need a database to use LINQ.

The steps in a LINQ query are to specify the data source (using **from**, **in** and **select** commands), filter the query (using **where** and Boolean operators), order the results (using **orderby**, **ascending** and **descending**) and group results based on a keyword.

Here is a short exercise that might be used by an estate agent. We define a class 'House' and use **enum** to limit the choices for a roof. A List<> of class House is then created and displayed on a list box. Items are selected from the list and displayed, and finally further selection of just SalePrice and Bedrooms items within the class takes place.

Place a listbox and a button on a form. Define the class House using the code:

```
class House
{
    public string TypeOfHouse { get; set; }
    public double SalePrice { get; set; }
    public string District { get; set; }
    public int Bedrooms { get; set; }
    public material Roof { get; set; }
}
enum material
{
    slate,
    stone,
    tile,
    thatch
}
```

For the button click code, type:

```
        private void btnSelectedList_Click(object sender, EventArgs e)
        {
            listBox1.Items.Clear(); // clear the list box
            // define the a List of House - note enum limits roof type
            List<House> forSale = new List<House>() {
                new House()
                { TypeOfHouse = "Semi", SalePrice = 150,
District = "SK3", Bedrooms = 2, Roof = material.tile},
                new House()
                { TypeOfHouse = "Semi", SalePrice = 300,
District = "SK8", Bedrooms = 4, Roof = material.slate},
                new House()
                { TypeOfHouse = "Semi", SalePrice = 200,
District = "SK3", Bedrooms = 3, Roof = material.stone},
                new House()
                { TypeOfHouse = "Bungalow", SalePrice = 100,
District = "SK8", Bedrooms = 2, Roof = material.thatch},
                new House()
                { TypeOfHouse = "Detached", SalePrice = 250,
District = "SK3", Bedrooms = 2, Roof = material.slate}
            }; // end of List house
            // Display the list
            listBox1.Items.Add("Original List:");
            foreach (var home in forSale)
            {
                listBox1.Items.Add
                    (home.TypeOfHouse + " in " + home.District +
     " with " + home.Bedrooms + " bedrooms for sale at " +
home.SalePrice);
            }
            // Use LINQ to select only semi-detached houses in district SK3
            var semis = from house in forSale
                where house.TypeOfHouse == "Semi" && house.District == "SK3"
                select house;
            // Display the list
            listBox1.Items.Add("List of Semi-detached available:");
            foreach (var home in semis)
            {
                listBox1.Items.Add
                    (home.TypeOfHouse + " in " + home.District +
                    " with " + home.Bedrooms + " bedrooms for sale at " +
      home.SalePrice);
            }
            // Select only semi-detached houses with tiled roof
            // and just extract SalePrice and Bedrooms
            var selectedSemis = from house in forSale
```

```
            where house.TypeOfHouse == "Semi" && house.Roof == material.tile
            select new { house.SalePrice, house.Bedrooms };
        listBox1.Items.Add("These extracted homes found:");
        foreach (var home in selectedSemis)
        {
            listBox1.Items.Add
                (home.Bedrooms + " bedrooms for sale at " + home.SalePrice);
            // note using home.TypeOfHouse now will cause an error
        }
    }
```

The program's output is shown in Figure 15-25.

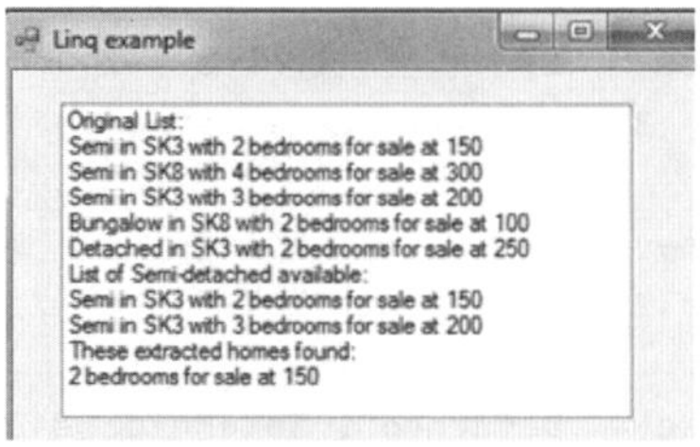

Figure 15-25 LINQ output

An introduction to LINQ and a walkthrough are available at:

https://msdn.microsoft.com/en-us/library/bb397927(v=vs.140).aspx,

and

https://msdn.microsoft.com/en-us/library/bb397900(v=vs.140).aspx

This is also covered in the Virtual Academy video #23.

15.8 • Self Assessment Exercises

1. Display the Artist and Recording tables from last chapter's database using both DataGridView and Details views.
2. Add a selection of individual items for the same item to the form, for example: for the recording date display a DateTimePicker, a TextBox, a Label etc.
3. Look at the code examples provided at Elektor's web site.
4. Create your own database from within Visual Studio.
5. Read the MS articles on LINQ.
6. Watch the Virtual Academy video on #22 and #23 on Data Collections and Filtering and Managing Data Collections Using LINQ.

15.9 • Summary

In this chapter we have seen how data is extracted from the database with a table adaptor creating a local memory resident copy of the database (the dataset), the items of which are displayed using controls which are binding sources, i.e. 'bound' to the data, and change automatically as the user interacts with them.

The DataSource configuration wizard was used to select the DataGridView to display all the data in a grid form and the database information was displayed. The Details view shows the individual items. We saw the DataGrid view tasks such as adding, editing and deleting. A navigator was placed on the form and as the user scrolled through the database the views automatically change; they are bound to the data.

The SQL language which is used to access the data in the database has briefly been covered. In our case the wizard created the SQL statement we needed, and we also saw how to add and display the results of a query using the SQL query builder.

We also saw the LINQ instructions which let you select data from within your code and perform work on that data.

In the next chapter we will see how to extract the data from the database and deal with this in our code, for example to save data collected from a database.

Chapter 16 • Accessing a database with code

16.1 • Introduction

We have seen how to display the contents of a database, create our own database and display the data in a UI using DataGrid and Details views. We will now see how to access the data in a database from code and either extract or add data to the database.

We shall create our own single table database with integer, floating point and datetime data types, and we will write code to read the data and then extend it to add data from our code.

There is also an example of a single table database using Northwind on the Microsoft website at: *http://msdn.microsoft.com/en-us/library/0f92s97z.aspx*.

16.2 • Creating the database

We will create a simple single table database from within Visual Studio and write code to navigate and update the database. We will add our own navigation buttons rather than use the Navigator tool or grid view tasks, so that you understand the process in adding, deleting and updating a database.

Start a new project and add a service-based Project > Add New Item > Service-based Database and call it Logger, see Figure 16-1.

Figure 16-1 Adding a database

Remember that the database is an SQL Server database files MDF file. The logger.mdf file appears in Server Explorer.

We will add the dataset file to our application later, so if it appears cancel the rest of the Data Source Configuration Wizard.

The (empty) database will appear in the Server Explorer. Display the explorer, expand the Logger database and right-click Tables to add a new table, see Figure 16-2.

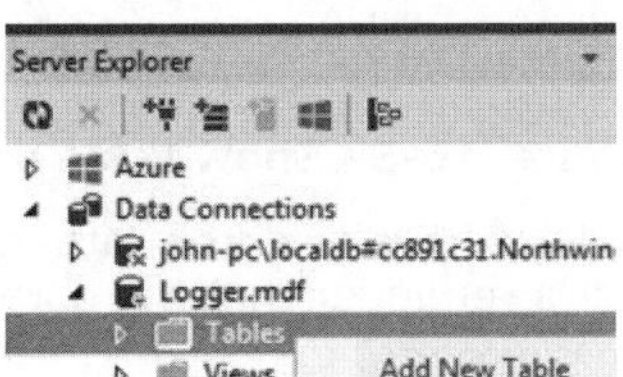

Figure 16-2 Adding a New Table

The table design tab appears. Add the data types as shown in Figure 16-3 on page 230. Don't allow any nulls.

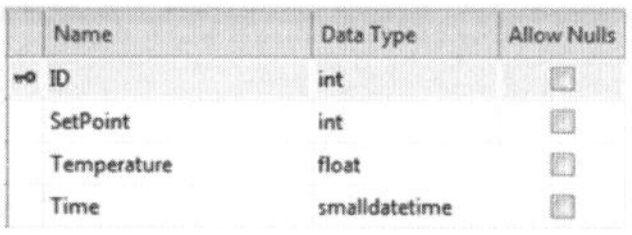

Name	Data Type	Allow Nulls
ID	int	☐
SetPoint	int	☐
Temperature	float	☐
Time	smalldatetime	☐

Figure 16-3 Table data types

Set the ID field's **Identity Specification** 'Is Identity' to 'True'. Make it a primary key if it isn't already set.

To give the table a name, change the first line in the T-SQL tab of the script from `CREATE TABLE [dbo].[Table]` to:

```
CREATE TABLE [dbo].[LoggerTable]
```

See Figure 16-4.

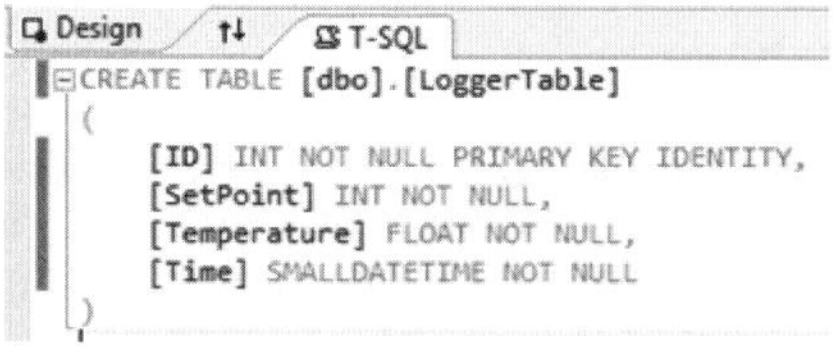

```
CREATE TABLE [dbo].[LoggerTable]
(
    [ID] INT NOT NULL PRIMARY KEY IDENTITY,
    [SetPoint] INT NOT NULL,
    [Temperature] FLOAT NOT NULL,
    [Time] SMALLDATETIME NOT NULL
)
```

Figure 16-4 SQL Script

Click Update to preview and Update the database. The tables are added to the Logger database. You can expand this to see the table's columns.

Save everything. The (empty) Logger.mdf file is saved in program's folder.

We can now add data to our database. We have done this before in section 14.5 on page 211.

Expand the Tables, right-click LoggerTable and select Show Table Data, see Figure 16-5. This will enable you to add data.

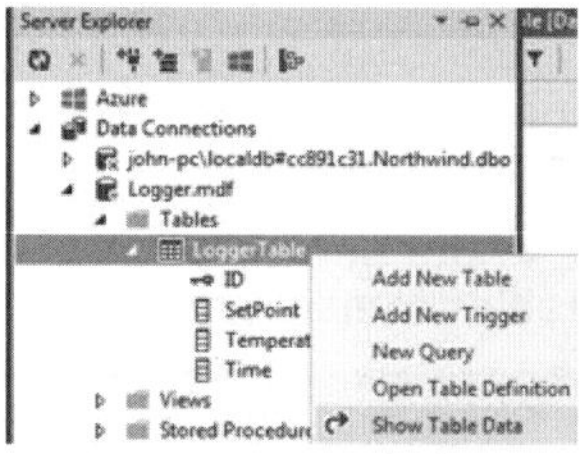

Figure 16-5 Show table data

Add some data. Remember you don't have to enter data into the ID field. Ignore the exclamation marks which are just a reminder that the data hasn't been saved.

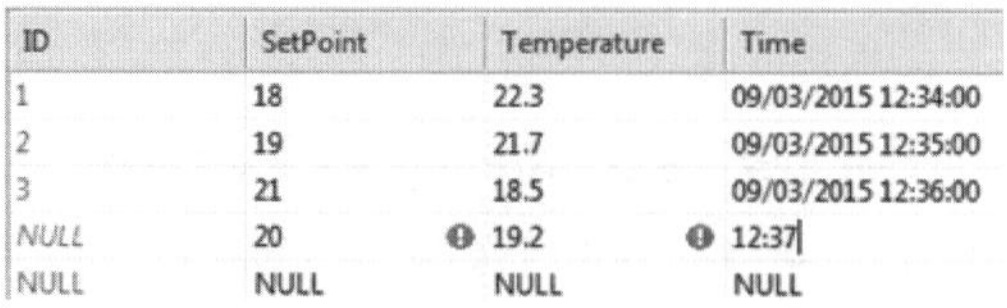

ID	SetPoint	Temperature	Time
1	18	22.3	09/03/2015 12:34:00
2	19	21.7	09/03/2015 12:35:00
3	21	18.5	09/03/2015 12:36:00
NULL	20	19.2	12:37
NULL	NULL	NULL	NULL

Figure 16-6 Adding data

Save All and close the solution. The database will be saved in the program's folder.

16.3 • Displaying the database

Now that we have a database, let's display the items before moving on to change the database. This is slightly different from before as we are connecting to the database we have just created which is in a different folder.

Start a new project.

Display Server Explorer, Right-click Data Connections and Add Connection. Type **(localdb)\v11.0** for the Server name (click 'Refresh') but this time, choose 'Attach a database file', see Figure 16-7.

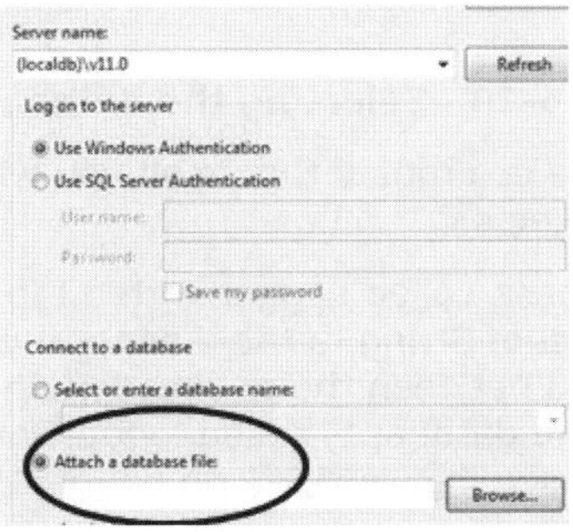

Figure 16-7 Attaching a database file

Browse for your Logger.mdf file. Test the connection and click OK. Your Logger.mdf file should now appear in Server Explorer and you should be able to expand it and see the data you created earlier on, see Figure 16-8. If you get a server version error, you may have to update your SQL server.

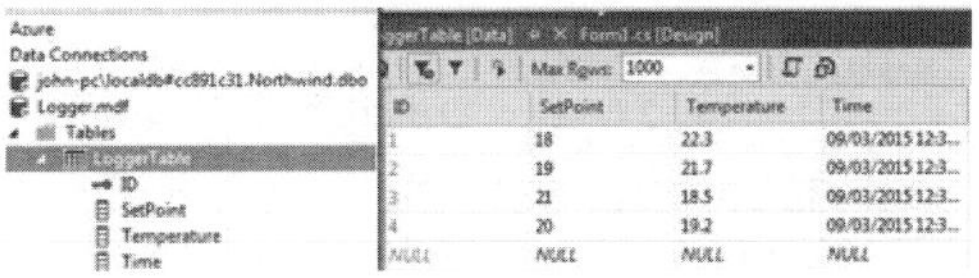

Figure 16-8 Table data

Remember, all we have done here is to make the connection to the database; we still need to choose the database objects we need. We will use the Data Configuration Wizard again to do this. We did this before in section 15.3 on page 215, but it is slightly different this time.

Display the Data Sources window (Shift+Alt+D) and choose add New Data Source. This displays the Data Source Configuration Wizard. Choose Database, Dataset as we did before but select Logger.mdf from the data connection drop down box, see Figure 16-9.

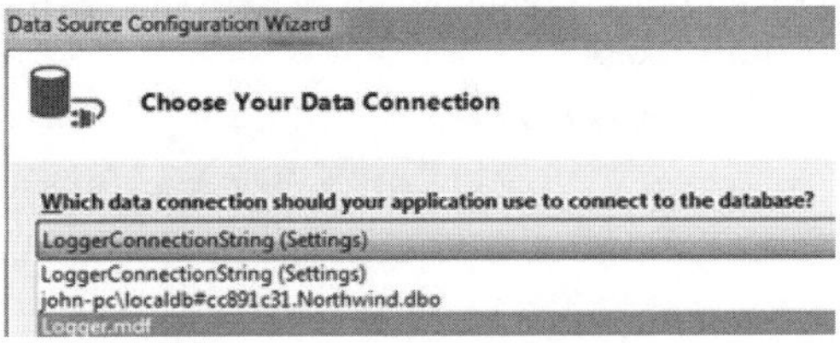

Figure 16-9 Selecting the database

Copy the file to your local folder when requested (unless you want to use the original). Save the connection string and select all the table columns from the option, see Figure 16-10.

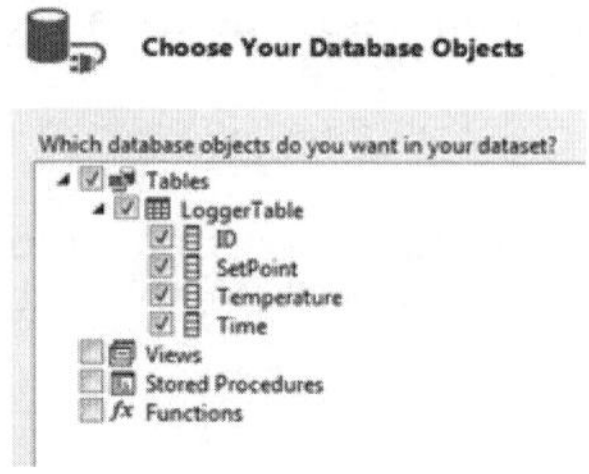

Figure 16-10 Selecting the database objects

You can select only some of the columns if that is all you want in your program. Click 'Finish' to add the database objects.

To recap, we now have a database called Logger with a table called LoggerTable, a connection called loggerConnectionString, a table adaptor called LoggerTableTableAdapter (which provides communication between the application and the database) and a dataset (memory resident version of the database) called loggerDataSet. To refresh your memory on how these all link together, see Figure 15-1 on page 215.

To see the individual database fields, expand the database in Server Explorer, see Figure 16-11.

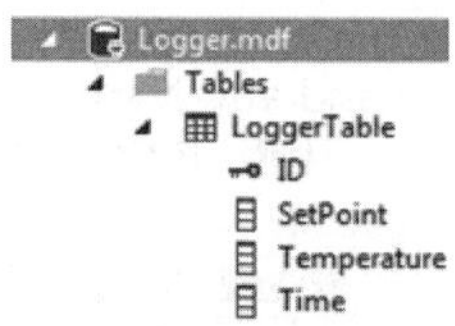

Figure 16-11 Database fields

Before we add individual Details view controls check your database access works by displaying the items in a DataGridView as we did before. Display the DataSources tab, select the Logger table and ensure DataGridView option is selected. Click and drag the Logger table to the form, see Figure 16-12.

Figure 16-12 Data Sources Window

Check the DataGridView tasks (click arrow in top right-hand corner) and check the editing options are as shown in Figure 16-13.

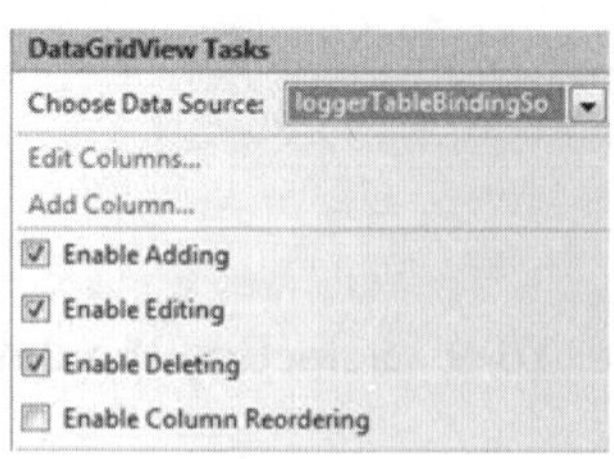

Figure 16-13 DataGridView tasks

Run the program. Because editing was allowed, you can now add data to your database by typing in the fields, see Figure 16-14.

ID	SetPoint	Temperature	Time
1	18	22.3	09/03/2015 12:34
2	19	21.7	09/03/2015 12:35
3	21	18.5	09/03/2015 12:36
4	20	19.2	09/03/2015 12:37
5	19	22.2	09/03/2015 12:53
6	18	19.5	09/03/2015 12:54

Figure 16-14 Database display

Note: Negative numbers are displayed for the ID whilst entering new data, but on saving the correct ID is recorded.

If you run the program from Visual Studio when you restart the program the original database is obtained (because we told it to copy), not the updated one. However, this does not happen if you run the .EXE file.

16.4 • Accessing the database from code

To see how we can display the database items from our code we'll add our own navigation controls, even though the navigator toolbar is available. We shall read the database values and display them using a MessageBox and add new values to the database from textboxes.

Start by adding controls so we can add data to the database. Add two labels and two textboxes to allow the user to add a new set point and temperature (call them txtSP and txtTemp).

Add buttons First, Next and Add (btnFirst, btnNext and btnAdd) so that your design is similar to Figure 16-15.

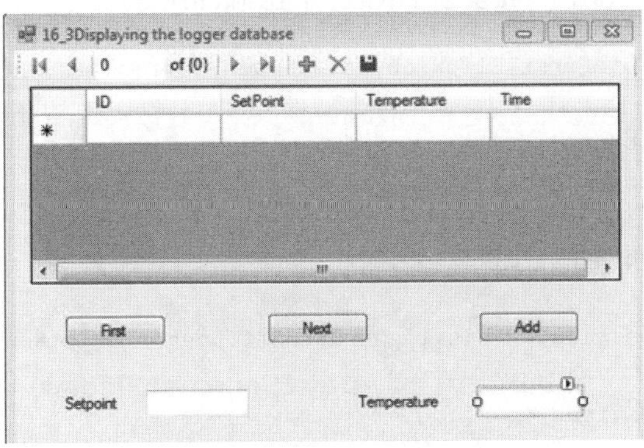

Figure 16-15 Program UI

The DataRow object is used to retrieve, insert, delete and update values in a DataTable. The DataRow's fields are filled with data and then the new row can be added. See the Self Assessment examples for an example of creating a DataTable, creating its columns and adding the Rows.

In your code declare a pointer to the current database row and a DataRow type:

```
public int rowPosition = 0;
public DataRow drAdd ;                // see later
```

The cells in the database are accessed by the row position and the column name or index, like a two dimensional array. So the ID of the a row is accessed using:

loggerTable.Rows[rowPosition]["ID"]

and the first row's ID would be:

loggerTable.Rows[0]["ID"]

Add the following method to display the rows. We shall call this from the First and Next button clicks.

```
        private void ShowCurrentRecord()
        {
            if (this.loggerDataSet.LoggerTable.Rows.Count != 0)
            {
                MessageBox.Show("ID=" +
this.loggerDataSet.LoggerTable.Rows[rowPosition]["ID"].ToString() +
            ", Setpoint=" +
this.loggerDataSet.LoggerTable.Rows[rowPosition]["Setpoint"].ToString() +
            ", Temperature=" +
this.loggerDataSet.LoggerTable.Rows[rowPosition]["Temperature"].ToString() +
            ", Time=" +
this.loggerDataSet.LoggerTable.Rows[rowPosition]["Time"].ToString());
            }
        }
```

If you get errors when you enter this code, it's most probably upper/lower case errors, so check the names and the case of identifiers (e.g. LoggerTable v. loggerTable). Let the IntelliSense prompt you.

Add the following code for the First and Next button click events:

```
        private void btnFirst_Click(object sender, EventArgs e)
        {
            rowPosition = 0;
            ShowCurrentRecord();
        }
        private void btnNext_Click(object sender, EventArgs e)
        {
            if (rowPosition < this.loggerDataSet.LoggerTable.Rows.Count - 1)
            {
                rowPosition++;
            }
            ShowCurrentRecord();
        }
```

I'll let you work out how you might add 'Previous' and 'Last' buttons.

Now let's add code to add data. We use the DataRow we declared at the top and add the contents for each field. I have also added the current time.

```
        private void btnAdd_Click(object sender, EventArgs e)
        {
            // check we have something to add
```

```
        if ((txtSP.Text != String.Empty) || (txtTemp.Text != String.Empty))
        {
            drAdd = this.loggerDataSet.LoggerTable.NewRow();
            drAdd["ID"] = this.loggerDataSet.LoggerTable.Rows.Count + 1;
            drAdd["Setpoint"] = int.Parse(txtSP.Text);
            drAdd["Temperature"] = float.Parse(txtTemp.Text);
            DateTime theTime = new DateTime();
            theTime = DateTime.Now;
            drAdd["Time"] = theTime.ToShortTimeString();
            this.loggerDataSet.LoggerTable.Rows.Add(drAdd);
        }
    }
```

Run the and add data to the database from your code. When you click the First or Next buttons, data is retrieved from the database and displayed in a MessageBox, see Figure 16-16.

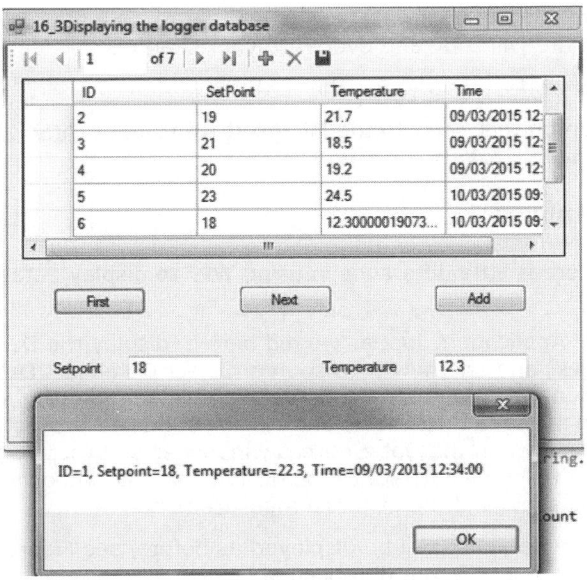

Figure 16-16 Adding and Retrieving data

16.4.1 • Update the Database

At the moment only the memory resident dataset is updated. You can delete the original rows, but data you have added is not saved (even if you click the save icon). To update the database on the disk, add an Update button and the following code:

```
private void btnUpdate_Click(object sender, EventArgs e)
{
    try
    {
        // validate control
```

```
            this.Validate();
            // end the editing to allow update
            this.loggerTableBindingSource.EndEdit();
            // Update all the changes in the dataset
            this.tableAdapterManager.UpdateAll(this.loggerDataSet);
        }
        catch (SystemException ex)
        {
            MessageBox.Show("Update failed" + ex.ToString());
        }
    }
```

Check it compiles, now for this to work and save data, **run the .EXE file.**

Note: On running the application from Visual Studio, the original database is copied and you will not see your updates. You can see this if you display the files in the Debug folder. You will see the logger.mdf file date change back to the original. This means that even if you correctly run and update your database (running the .EXE file), running from Visual Studio at any later date will copy and overwrite your changes.

For your program to work correctly, run the .EXE file.

For more information on this, refer to the Microsoft web site at: *http://msdn.microsoft.com/en-us/library/ms233817.aspx*

16.5 • A WPF database

Just to show that there is little difference in using WPF to display databases, here's an exercise.

Start a new C# WPF Application. Just as we did before, display the DataSource Window (View > Data Sources) and add new data source. Select Database, Dataset, New Connection. Add **(localdb)\v11.0** for the server, refresh and find the Northwind database. Save the connection string. Select tables and Finish. **Build the project**. The Northwind database tables are shown in the DataSources window as before. I've dragged the Customers and the Employees table onto the design surface. The only difference is the handles to move and skew and the distance measurements.

Run the program. The database will be displayed as before, see Figure 16-17. Microsoft have a walkthrough with a different database at:

https://msdn.microsoft.com/en-us/library/dd547149.aspx

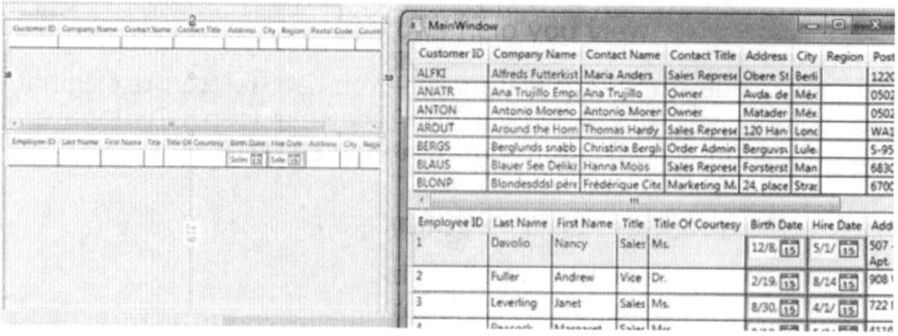

Figure 16-17 WPF Design and database display

16.6 • Self Assessment Exercises

1. There an example of a single table database using Northwind on the Microsoft website at: *http://msdn.microsoft.com/en-us/library/0f92s97z.aspx*.
2. An excellent example of creating a DataTable, adding its columns and finally adding a row is shown at:

   https://msdn.microsoft.com/en-us/library/system.data.datacolumn(v=vs.90).aspx
3. Watch the supporting videos pointed to at Elektor's web site or via YouTube.
4. Add buttons in the program for Last and Previous commands.
5. Write a program that automatically generates a set point, a temperature and a time, say on a Timer event, and adds these values to the database.
6. Create your own database and add values to it.
7. Follow the Microsoft 'Saving Data to a Database (Multiple Tables) walkthrough at: *https://msdn.microsoft.com/en-us/library/4esb49b4.aspx*

16.7 • Summary

In this chapter we have seen how to create a database from within Visual Studio and to add this data source to a program. Initially the data was displayed using a DataGridView and navigator controls as we did in the last chapter, but this time we have added our own navigation controls and read the database using the database table property with row and column, and written to the database using DataRow data type. We have also seen how to create a WPF database design.

Now we know how to access data in a database, we will now see how to plot data, from a program or a database.

Chapter 17 • Plotting and Charts

17.1 • Introduction

A chart control was included in VS2010 (.NET v4) - before that a third party application had to be used (and took up a long chapter in my previous book). The chart control is in the Data section of the Toolbox:

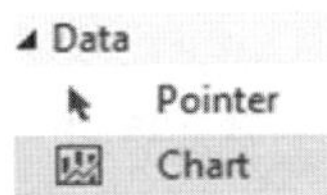

If the Chart control isn't displayed in the Toolbox, right click inside the Toolbox, select Choose Items and from the .NET Framework Components tab add the namespace: *System.Windows.Forms.DataVisualization.Charting*

17.2 • The Chart control

When you drag a chart onto a form a sample chart is displayed, see Figure 17-1. You can now run the code but the sample data is removed and only an empty chart is shown.

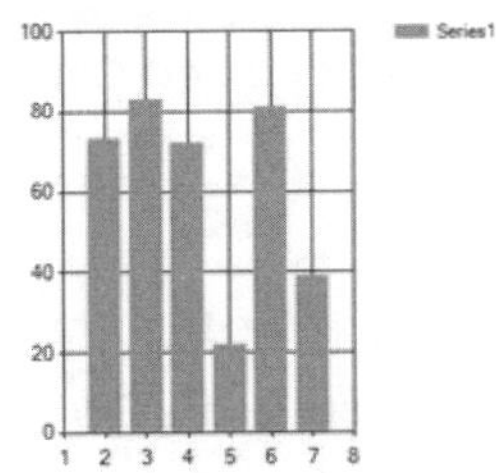

Figure 17-1 Sample chart

A wide selection of charts is available as shown in Figure 17-2. This includes Point, Line, Bar, Column and Pie charts. It is important to note that the chart type is a property of the **Series** (called ChartType) and not a property of the Chart.

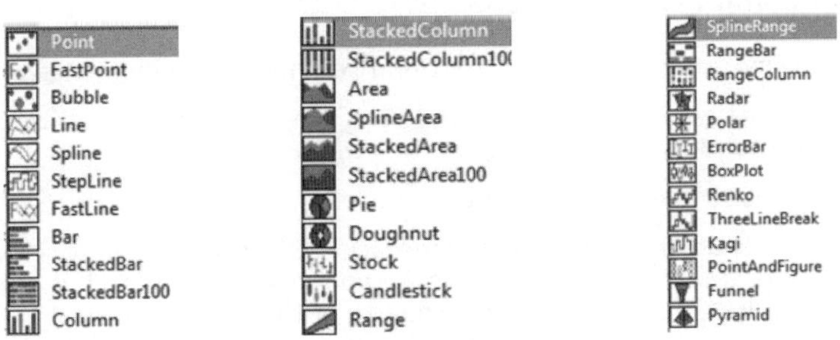

Figure 17-2 Chart types

We shall see how the Series is used to define the type of plot, appearance, data, labels, axes, scales etc.

17.3 • Chart elements

A chart is made up of various elements. Some of the main ones are:

- Chart Area: An area used to draw the series, labels, axes, grid lines etc.
- Series: A group of related data points with associated chart type and display information.
- Plot Area: An area used to draw the series and gridlines. Labels and titles are outside this area.
- Title, legends and annotations: A title and labels for your axes and highlights for your chart.

If you categorize the Chart properties, the important properties are grouped into: Annotations, ChartAreas, Legends, Series, and Titles, see Figure 17-3.

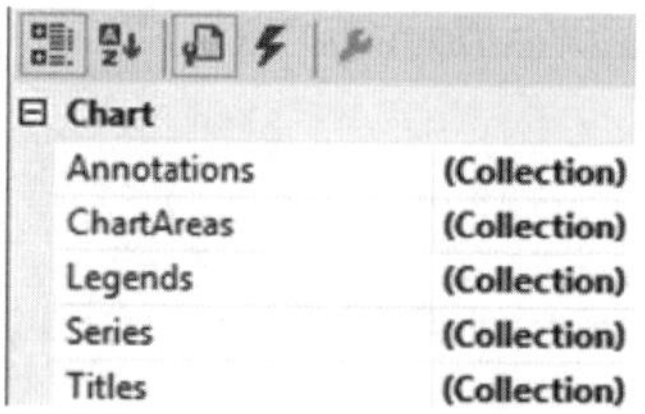

Figure 17-3 Categorized Chart Properties

The process is to:

a. Place a chart on the form
b. Select the appearance of the chart – the ChartArea properties
c. Select the appearance of the data – the Series properties
d. Add data to the chart
e. Add a legend(s)
f. Add a title

17.4 • Column Chart example

Let's start by drawing a simple column chart and see how these elements work.

Microsoft has a tutorial which can be followed as a Self Assessment exercise. We will create a simple 2D column chart and extend this to a 3D one.

Start a new project and place a chart on a form.

First let's study the ChartArea. You can change 2D or 3D display, the Appearance (background color or image, border styles etc), the Axes, the Cursor, but not the type of chart itself. Find **ChartAreas** in the **Chart** property of the chart (Figure 17-3). Click the ellipsis button [...] to display the ChartAreas Collection Editor, see Figure 17-4 on page 241. Change some of the properties and see how the chart changes.

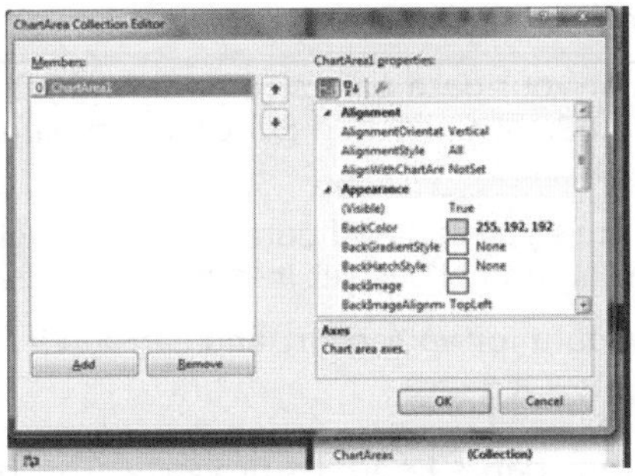

Figure 17-4 The ChartAreas Collection Editor

You can also add new ChartAreas with different properties. In this case, the original chart will shrink to make room for it but until some data is added the new chart won't be displayed. Close the Collection editor when you are happy.

Now we will add some data for our chart. Find the chart **Series** property and open the Collection by clicking the ellipsis button. Here you can change the Appearance, Axes, Chart, Data series and this is also where the series links to the chart area.

If you added a new ChartArea, check that the **ChartArea** property points to the one you want to use. Otherwise just use ChartArea1.

Select the **ChartType** as Column and change the **Name** to **'Column chart'**, see Figure 17-5. This will be used as the legend. Move this so that you can see the chart.

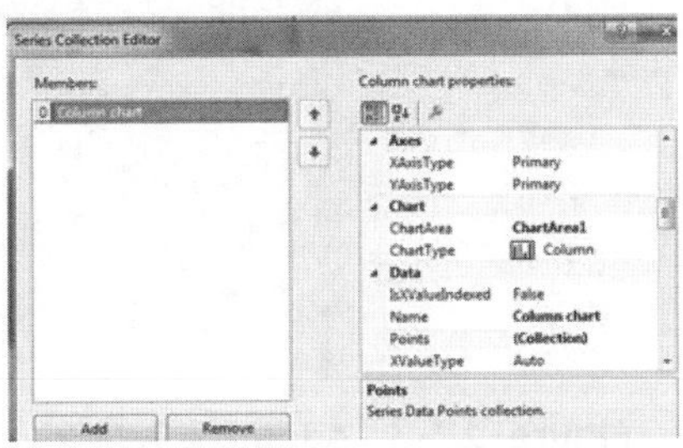

Figure 17-5 Series Collection Editor

Now we will add some data for our chart.

Staying with the Series Collection Editor, find the **Points** property and click the ellipsis button to open the DataPoint Collection Editor. Click **Add** and type in a value for the **YValue** property, click Add again and repeat until you have added as many YValues as you want, see Figure 17-6.

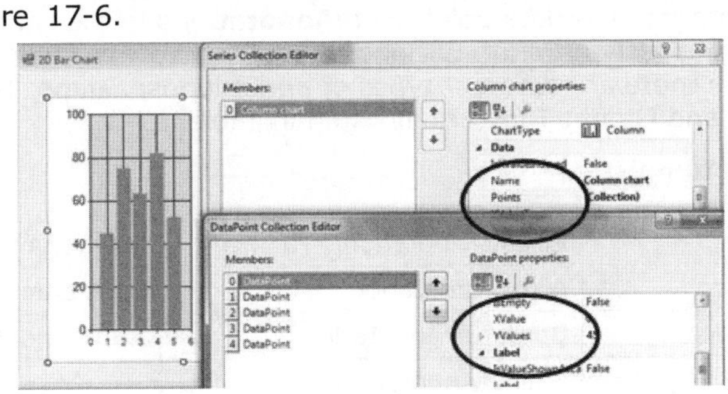

Figure 17-6 Adding data points.

The values are added to the chart and it changes to suit as you enter them.

You can add labels for each of your data points (e.g. George, Bill, John, Helen, Joanna) by selecting Points in the DataPoint Collection Editor and typing in the **Label** property for your DataPoint.

If you have a second chart area you can add data to this as well. This will display a second column of data with the properties set in the Chart Area. We will do this soon.

At this point you have some data for your chart and can run it to see how it is displayed.

Now we will add a legend to our chart.

Click the ellipsis button for the chart's **Legends** property. This opens the Legends Collection Editor. Here we can change the Appearance, Cell Columns data, Docking and Title.

Select ChartArea1 for the **DockedToChartArea** property. If you have more than one Chart Area, you can add a second Legend and dock it to that chart area. Select a position for the Docking property (Left, Right, Top or Bottom) and add a **Title** for your legend: 'My Chart'

The Title and legend 'Column chart' appears on the chart where we have docked it, figure 17.7. Close the editor.

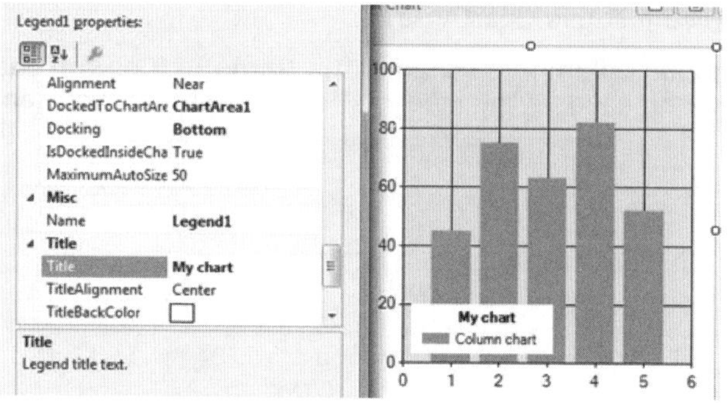

Figure 17-7 Adding a legend

Add a title to the chart. Find the **Titles** property of the Chart and open the Title Collection Editor. Click Add to add a new title. The default is Title1, but you can change this in the Name property. Type in the title you want for your chart in the **Text** property (e.g. 'My Column Chart'). Dock the title to your chart. You can also change the title's Appearance or Docking position, or add a ToolTip. Close the editor.

Finally, add an Annotation to a data point. Find **Annotations** in the chart's property and open the Annotation Collection Editor. Clicking the down arrow by the Add button will display all the types. There are different types of annotations: Shape, Text, Text and Shape (e.g. Ellipse) and Group. They are all listed in Table 17-1.

Table 17-1 Annotation list

LineAnnotation	EllipseAnnotation	PolygonAnnotation
VerticalLineAnnotation	ArrowAnnotation	ImageAnnotation
HorizontalLineAnnotation	Border3DAnnotation	AnnotationGroup
TextAnnotation	CalloutAnnotation	
RectangleAnnotation	PolylineAnnotation	

Let's add a CalloutAnnotation. Select it and change its properties to the following: **Text:** Callout Annotation, **ClipToChartArea**: ChartArea1, **X: 20, Y: 20** (or to suit your chart). I changed a backColor value to Fuchsia too, see Figure 17-8.

If you leave the Width property to NotSet, the size will be automatically calculated.

If you use an ArrowAnnotation, you can point to a specific place on your chart, by choosing the point from the drop-down box in the AnchorDataPoint property, see Figure 17-8. The **Height** property is used to point up or down – a negative values point down.

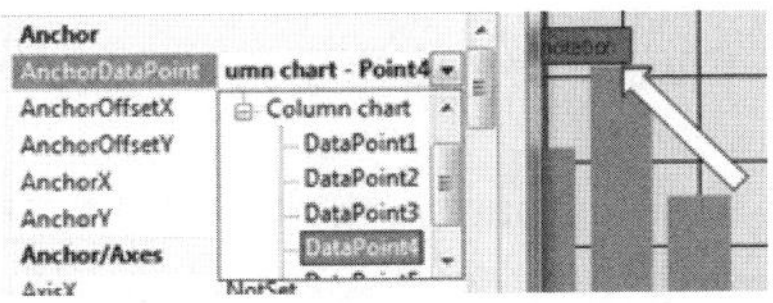

Figure 17-8 Annotation anchor data point

My chart looked like Figure 17-9.

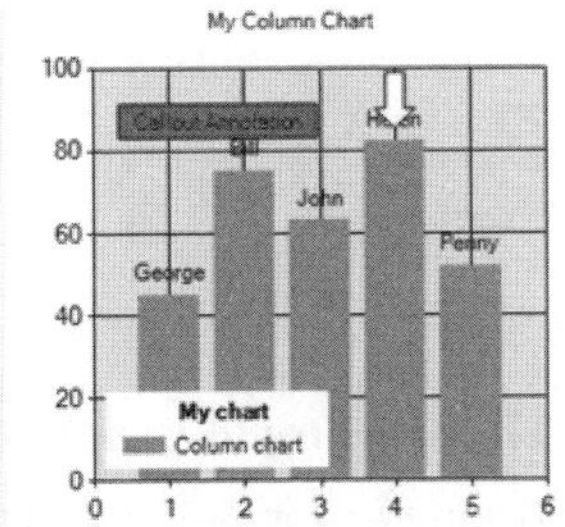

Figure 17-9 The final chart

If you want a 3D chart, display the ChartAreas Collection Editor and from the **Area3DStyle** property, set the **(Enable3D)** property true.

We haven't added titles for our axes. We will do that in the next section, but if you want to try it now, display the Chart Area Collection Editor, find the **Axes** property, open up the Axis Collection Editor, chose the X-axis, find the **Title** property and type in the title you want ('X-axis Title'). Repeat for the Y(Value)-Axis.

If you want more on charts, follow the Microsoft example in the Self Assessment exercises.

17.5 • Plotting points

Before we draw any graphs, let's start by seeing how we can display some random points on a chart. We will use the default settings for the chart using just one series of data.

Start a new project and place a chart on the form. At the top of the code add:

using System.Windows.Forms.DataVisualization.Charting;

We'll run the code when the form loads, so double-click the form and add the following code for the form load event:

```
private void Form1_Load(object sender, EventArgs e)
{
    Random rnd = new Random();
    for (int i = -20; i < 20; i++)
```

```
        {
            chart1.Series["Series1"].Points.AddXY
                (rnd.Next(-10, 10), rnd.Next(-10, 10));
        }
        chart1.Series["Series1"].ChartType = SeriesChartType.Line;
        chart1.Series["Series1"].Color = Color.Red;
    }
```

It's as simple as that! You just use AddXY to add an X and a Y value to the Series DataPoint Collection.

Running the program results in an output similar to Figure 17-10.

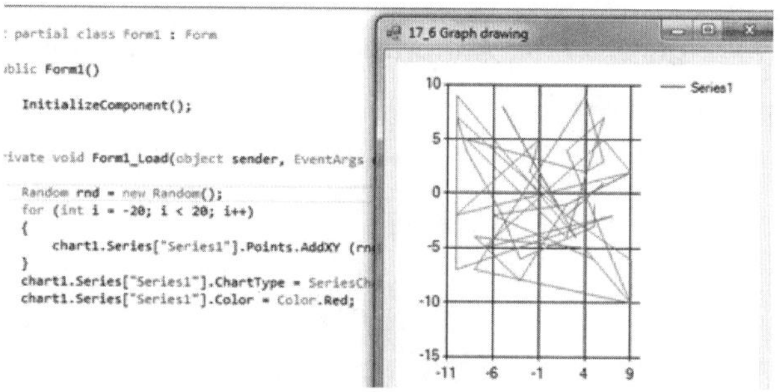

Figure 17-10 Simple Graph drawing

You can have some fun looking at the different SeriesChartType properties. Figure 17-11 shows a Pie, a Funnel and a Radar plot.

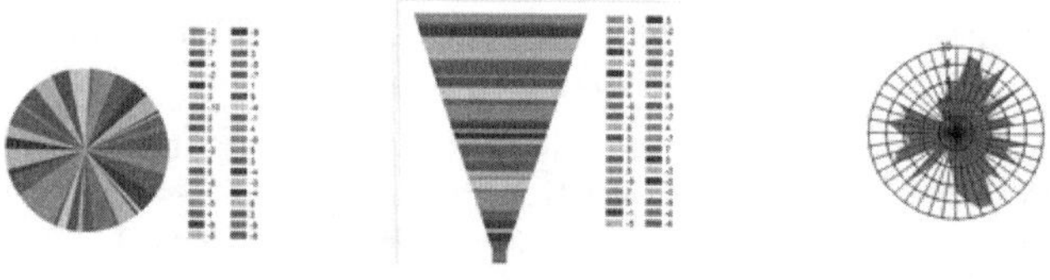

Figure 17-11 Different chart types

17.6 • Drawing a graph

Let's see how we draw a graph by generating the numbers from our code. If you're like me, you most probably haven't thought about the process of drawing a graph since you were at school. You have to work out what the range of values are for the axes, what scales you are going to use and their labels, the grid (both horizontal and vertical), the size, colour (and width) of the pen and the data values themselves. All of these need to be defined in your code (or in the chart design) when drawing the graph. We shall set the ones we need in our code.

Let's try plotting the graph of y = sin(x)/x. This is quite a pretty graph. It has a maximum Y value of +1 when X=0. We shall plot it over ±30 radians.

To see different graph types, we'll start with a Line plot but also add the code to display a Point and StepLine plots.

Start a new project. Place a chart on your form.

At the top of your code add:

```
using System.Windows.Forms.DataVisualization.Charting;
```

Add the following to a button click or form load:

Add a new series and remove the default "Series1" series:

```
chart1.Series.Add("SineX");
chart1.Series.RemoveAt(0); // remove Series1
```

Add a title and remove the SineX legend (this would have said 'Series1'):

```
chart1.Titles.Add("Sine(X)/X");
// Remove SineX (was Series1) Legend:
chart1.Series["SineX"].IsVisibleInLegend = false;
```

Let's add some titles for our X and Y axes:

```
chart1.ChartAreas[0].AxisX.Title = "X value";
chart1.ChartAreas[0].AxisY.Title = "Sine(x)/x";
```

And we might want to change our grid line styles and interval:

```
chart1.ChartAreas[0].AxisX.MajorGrid.LineDashStyle =
        ChartDashStyle.DashDotDot;
chart1.ChartAreas[0].AxisY.MajorGrid.LineDashStyle =
        ChartDashStyle.Dash;
chart1.ChartAreas[0].AxisX.MajorGrid.Interval = 5;
```

The program will automatically work out the maximum and minimum values for the X and Y values, but we will override this. We can also set the interval for our axes:

```
chart1.ChartAreas[0].AxisX.Maximum = 30;
chart1.ChartAreas[0].AxisX.Minimum = -30;
chart1.ChartAreas[0].AxisX.Interval = 10;
chart1.ChartAreas[0].AxisY.Maximum = 1.2;
chart1.ChartAreas[0].AxisY.Minimum = -0.3;
```

Let's change the colour and width of the Pen:

```
chart1.Series["SineX"].Color = Color.DarkBlue;
chart1.Series["SineX"].BorderWidth = 5;
```

And choose a chart type (uncomment the chart type you need):

```
chart1.Series["SineX"].ChartType = SeriesChartType.Line;
//chart1.Series["SineX"].ChartType = SeriesChartType.Point;
//chart1.Series["SineX"].ChartType = SeriesChartType.StepLine;
```

Finally add the code to plot the points:

```
for (int x = -30; x < 31; x++)
{
    if (x != 0)
    {
        chart1.Series["SineX"].Points.AddXY(x, Math.Sin(x) / x);
    }
    else
    {
        chart1.Series["SineX"].Points.AddXY(0, 1);
    }
}
```

That's it. That should give you enough to do most things with the chart. The resulting output is shown in Figure 17-12.

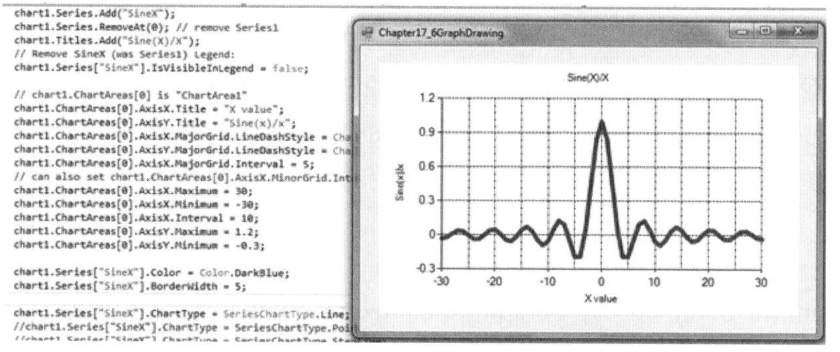

Figure 17-12 Graph plot output

17.6.1 • Adding a second plot

Suppose we want to find a solution to the equation:

sin(x)/x = ln(x);

We can plot both graphs (y = sin(x)/x and y = ln(x)) on the same chart area. As we already have the first graph we just need to add another series and the solution is where they cross.

Add the following code the previous project before the 'for' statement:

```
chart1.Series.Add("LnX");
chart1.Titles.Add("loge(x)");
chart1.Series["LnX"].Color = Color.Red;
chart1.Series["LnX"].ChartType = SeriesChartType.Line;
```

And add the code to draw the ln(x) graph. Again this can be before the 'for' statement:

```
for (int x = 1; x < 31; x++)
{
    chart1.Series["LnX"].Points.AddXY(x, Math.Log(x));
}
```

The code will run and both lines should be drawn, see Figure 17-13 (A).

Let's allow the user to zoom in on the area where the graphs cross by selecting an area of our graph. First allow zooming on your graph. Add this before the 'for' loops:

```
chart1.ChartAreas[0].AxisX.ScaleView.Zoomable = true;
chart1.ChartAreas[0].AxisY.ScaleView.Zoomable = true;
```

Set cursorX and cursorY property IsUserSelectionEnabled true:

```
chart1.ChartAreas[0].CursorX.IsUserEnabled = true;
chart1.ChartAreas[0].CursorY.IsUserEnabled = true;
```

We can also let the user display the X and Y cursors:

```
chart1.ChartAreas[0].CursorX.IsUserSelectionEnabled = true;
chart1.ChartAreas[0].CursorY.IsUserSelectionEnabled = true;
```

The user can now select an area of the graph and zoom in. Enable and disable these properties to see how they work.

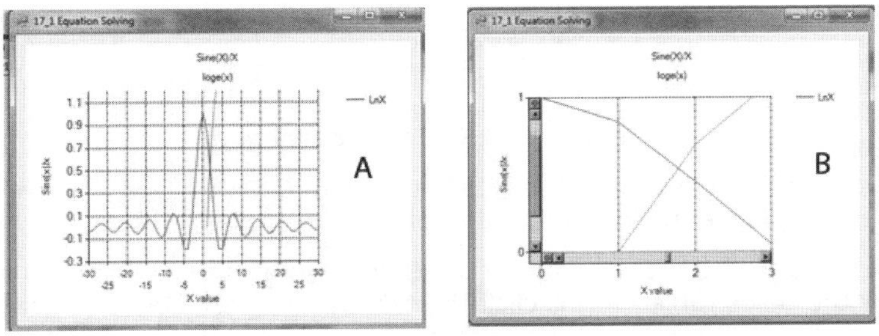

Figure 17-13 The graph (A) and graph zoomed in (B)

We can see that the solution is approximately X = 1.8 and Y= 0.55. It would help if we plotted more data points.

Finally we might like to display the position of the cursor as we move it around the graph

This can be done on the chart's MouseMove event. This passes the X and Y position of the mouse in MouseEventArgs (in **e.location**). The chart's HitTest method can then be used to determine the chart element at that point. This returns information on the chart's properties, such as the ChartArea, ChartElementType, Series, etc. See Figure 17-14.

Axis	null
ChartArea	{ChartArea-ChartArea1}
ChartElementType	DataPoint
Object	{X=-1, Y=0.841470984807897}
PointIndex	29
Series	{Series-SineX}
SubObject	null
Non-Public members	

Figure 17-14 Chart HitTest method

From the X and Y pixel values it can be found if a DataPoint is the object of the click.

```
var results = chart1.HitTest(e.Location.X, e.Location.Y, false,
                             ChartElementType.DataPoint);
```

The full code has been included in the code provided on Elektor's web site.

For more on this, search for Chart.HitTest method in the Microsoft developer Network at:

https://msdn.microsoft.com/

The Self assessment exercises points to an example you can follow.

17.7 • Displaying database data on a chart

Obviously it might be useful to display information in a database in a graphical form. Let's add our own single table database consisting of a Sales person, a sale price and a date of sale. We've added databases before, in section 14.4 on page 207, so we will run through it quickly.

Start a new project. Add a New item – a Service-based Database and call it 'Sales'.

Open the Sales database in Server Explorer, right-click Tables and select Add New Table. Add the columns as shown in Figure 17-15.

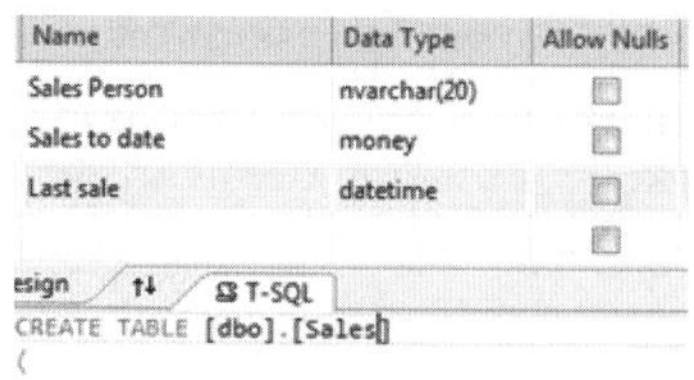

Figure 17-15 Sales database

Change the first line of the script in the T-SQL tab from `CREATE TABLE [dbo].[Table]` to `CREATE TABLE` [dbo].[Sales]. Update the database.

Now add some data to the tables. Refresh the Sales.mdf in Server Explorer, expand tables to show the Sales table. Right-click the table and select 'Show Table Data'.

Add the following data to the fields:

Sales Person	Sales to date	Last sale
Bill	25.3000	09/02/2015 00:0...
Susan	18.3000	11/11/2014 00:0...
Joanna	19.7000	02/01/2015 00:0...
Arthur	29.8000	01/02/2015 00:0...
Helen	45.1000	03/03/2015 00:0...

We now need to choose the database objects we want the chart to display. We will display the Sales Person and their Sale to date.

Display the Data Sources window. (If option isn't shown, click the Form1.cs[design] tab). Add a new data source, (database, dataset and choose Sales.mdf from the drop-down box) and click Next until asked to choose your database objects.

Open the Tables and Sales and select Sales Person and sales to date items, see Figure 17-16.

Figure 17-16 Selected Tables

Click Finish.

Now add a chart to your form.

Open the drop down box for the chart's **DataSource** property. And choose the Sales from the sales dataset in chart dataset properties, see Figure 17-17.

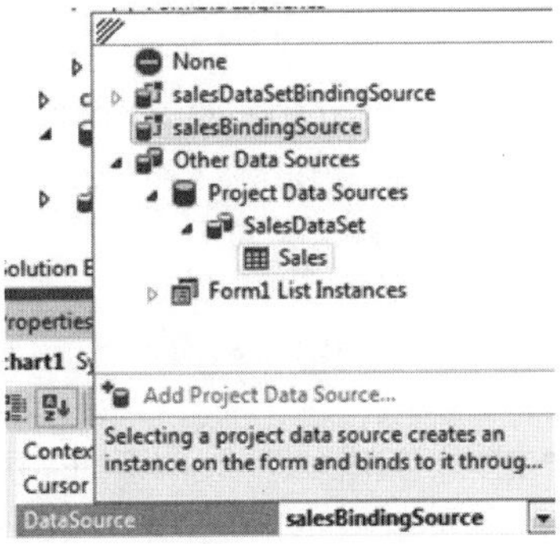

Figure 17-17 Sales DataSource

A DataSet, a BindingSource and a TableAdaptor should appear in the status window.

Open the chart's **Series Collection Editor.** For the Data Source select SalesPerson for the XValueMember, and Sales to date for the YValueMember, see Figure 17-18.

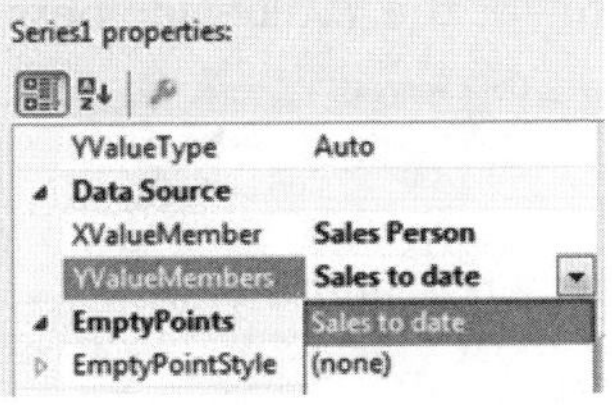

Figure 17-18 Series Collection

Run the program. The sales person and sale is displayed, see Figure 17-19.

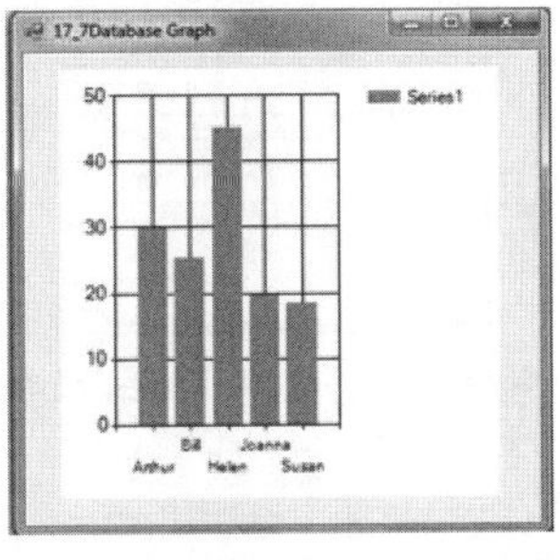

Figure 17-19 Sales database

Just as an example of how dates are displayed, let's change the XValueMember to Date of sale, but leave the YValueMember as Sales to date.

Add a new chart (chart2). I've removed the legend from the charts (Legends > Enabled > False).

First you will need a new set of database objects.

Add a New Data Source from the Data Sources window, then choose Database, Dataset, SalesConnectionString and this time select Sales to Date and Last Sale from the Tables. Note the DataSet name is SalesDataSet1. Click Finish.

A new DataSet (SalesDataSet1) appears in the Data Sources window.

Return to chart2's **DataSource** properties and select Sales from the new dataset.

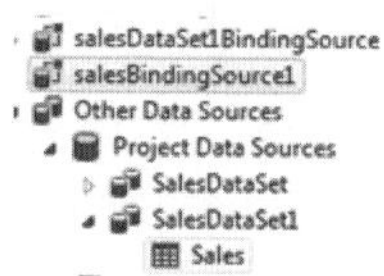

Display the Series Collection Editor and for Series1 select 'Last sale' for the XValueMember and 'Sales to date' for the YValueMembers.

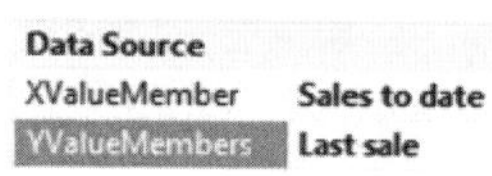

Run the program. The result is shown in figure 17.20.

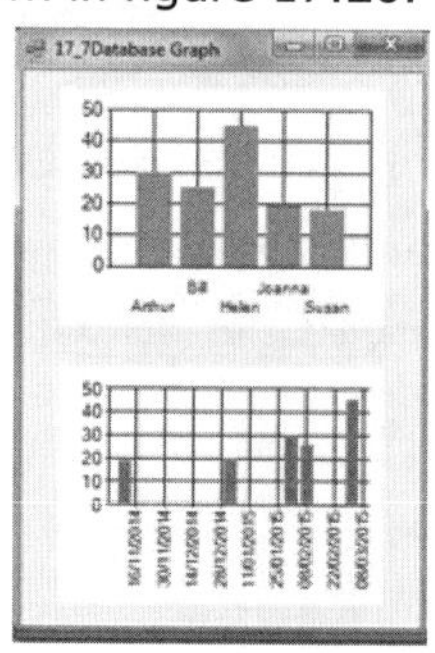

Figure 17-20 Final chart

17.8 • Dynamic data display

We have seen how we can write a program to draw a graph. Now we will place a numericUpDown counter on a form and display its value on a chart, so that when numericUpDown counter value changes, so will the chart's display.

In a new project, place a chart and a numericUpDown counter on a form.

Change the numericUpDown Maximum property value to 10.

Chart Area Collection Editor, find the **Axes** property, open up the Axis Collection Editor

We will also limit the maximum value in for the chart. In the Chart Area Collection Editor, find the **Axes** property, open up the Axis Collection Editor and change the Y (Value) Axis

Maximum property to 10.

Now add the following code for the numericUpDown counter ValueChanged event:

```
decimal? numUpDown = null;   // the ? lets us declare it as a null
private void numericUpDown1_ValueChanged(object sender, EventArgs e)
{
    // run once
    if (!numUpDown.HasValue)
        chart1.Series["Series1"].Points.AddXY(0, numericUpDown1.Value);
    else   // remove old value and add new one
    {
        chart1.Series["Series1"].Points.RemoveAt
             (chart1.Series["Series1"].Points.Count - 1);
        chart1.Series["Series1"].Points.AddXY(0, numericUpDown1.Value);
    }
    numUpDown = numericUpDown1.Value;
    chart1.Update();    // not needed - included for reference
}
```

The bar should move up and down as you change the numericUpDown counter value, Figure 17-21.

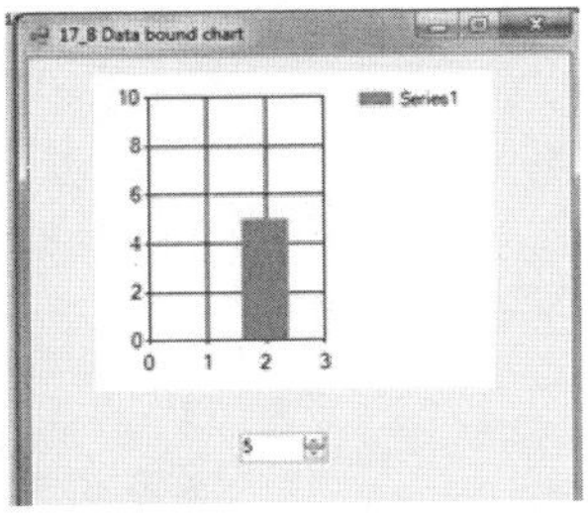

Figure 17-21 Dynamic display

17.9 • Self Assessment Exercises

1. Draw individual graphs of:
   a. y = log(x);
   b. y = x-5;
2. Try to draw the graphs on the same graph and see if there is a solution to the equation:
   x-5 = log(x);
3. Display the graph values when the mouse is moved over them. Look at the code provided or the code project's web site for more information: *http://bit.ly/1KICWf5*
4. Follow the Microsoft has a tutorial at:
   https://msdn.microsoft.com/en-us/library/dd489237%28v=vs.140%29.aspx

17.10 • Summary

We have covered the Chart component. We have seen the types of charts that can be drawn and how to design your own charts with different chart types, colours, styles annotation etc.

We drew a chart that plotted points on a graph and add a second plot to find the solution to an equation.

We followed that by displaying data in a database on a chart, and finally showed how to dynamically display data.

Chapter 18 • Dynamic link libraries (DLL) and using Windows API

18.1 • Introduction

You will soon have written some useful methods which you may want to use in other programs. Of course you could cut and paste the code into each new program, but there is a better way. By saving your code as a dynamic link library (DLL) and providing a link to it from your new program you can just call and use it. The code will be loaded by the program when needed. Be careful however, if at that time it's not available you will get a run-time error so you must include it with your executable.

18.2 • Writing a DLL

Let's try this with a simple example. We will create our own namespace, which we will add to our code with a using statement. This will have a class that contains the methods we will use in our program.

Let's take the method we used in the chapter on Methods, which to take an integer and return its square root. The method is:

```
double SquareRoot ( int intRoot)
{
  return Math.Sqrt(intRoot);
}
```

We create our DLL by starting a new project, but this time choosing **Class Library** instead of a Windows Forms Application, see Figure 18-1. Give it a sensible name. I've used MyMathLibrary.

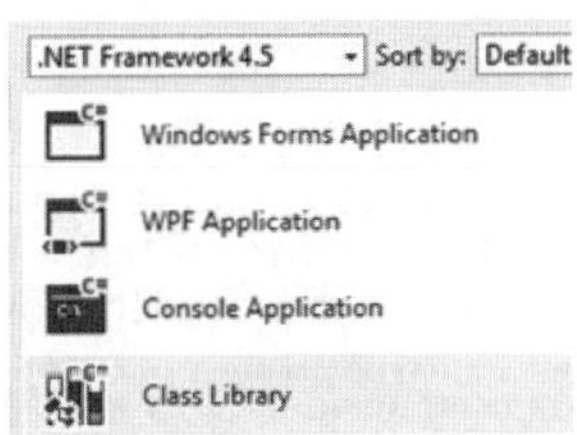

Figure 18-1 Creating a DLL

The following code with Class1 is created. We will add our own class and delete Class1.

```
namespace MyMathLibrary
{
    public class Class1
    {
    }
}
```

Add a new Class (Project>Add Class) and give it the name MyMathClass, see Figure 18-2.

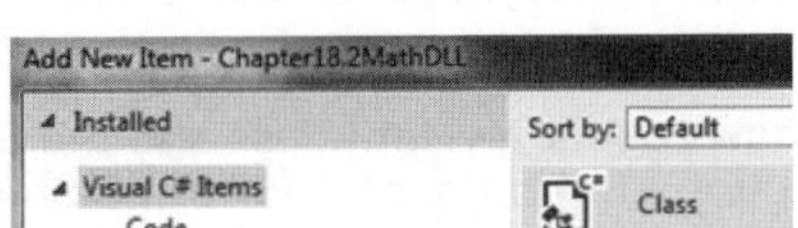

Figure 18-2 Adding a new DLL class

MyMathClass is added to the Solution. Delete Class1.cs by selecting it in the Solution Explorer and pressing the delete key.

Add the SquareRoot method to your class as shown below and save the project. The class must be declared **public**. We could add further mathematics classes in MyMathLibrary. You might want to save all your DLLs in their own folder.

```
namespace MyMathLibrary
{
    public class MyMathClass
    {
        public double SquareRoot(int intRoot)
        {
            return Math.Sqrt(intRoot);
        }
    }
}
```

Build your DLL solution and save the project. Note that if you try to run the program, you will get an error message that says the Class Library cannot be started directly.

18.3 • Calling the DLL

Now we need a program to call our DLL code. Start a new **Windows application** (I've called it MathDLLDemo).

We'll make it really simple and display the square root in a message box when a button is clicked.

You have to let your program know about your DLL. Add the using statement at the top of the code:

```
using MyMathLibrary;
```

Add the DLL to the References. Use Project > Add reference, click the Browse tab, and browse for MyMathDLL.dll (it's in MyMathLibrary > bin > release). You can now see it in References in the Solution Explorer and in the Object Browser, see Figure 18-3.

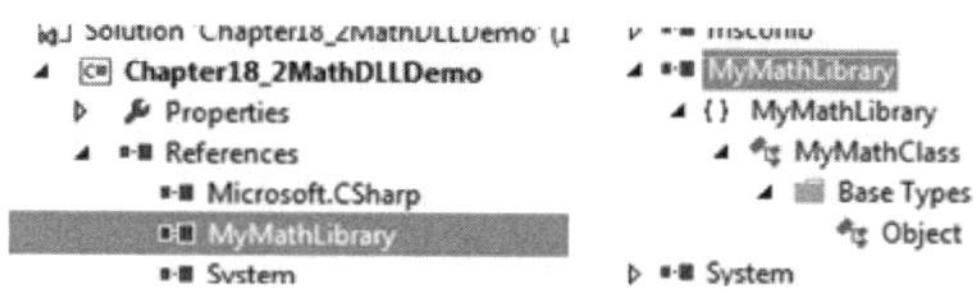

Figure 18-3 MyMathLibrary object

Add a button to a form and for the button click, change the code to the following:

```
private void button1_Click(object sender, EventArgs e)
{
    MyMathClass myMathObj = new MyMathClass();
    MessageBox.Show((myMathObj.SquareRoot(5)).ToString());
}
```

Note that the IntelliSense knows about MyMathClass and the SquareRoot method and prompts as you type; see Figure 18-4 on page 255. If the SquareRoot method isn't displayed, check that both the class and the method were originally declared as public.

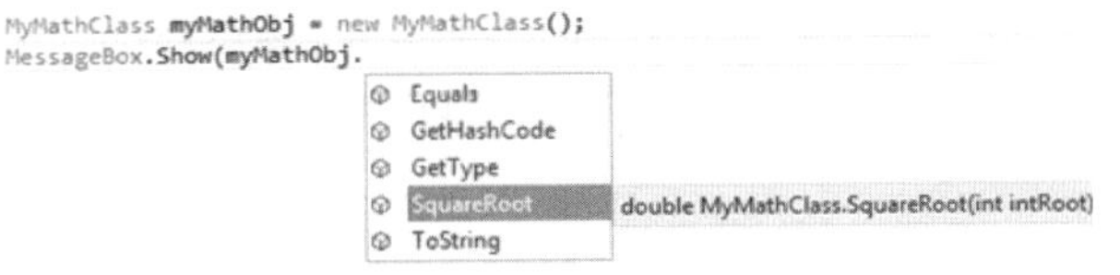

Figure 18-4 The IntelliSense display

Run the program to check it works. Your display should be similar to Figure 18-5.

Figure 18-5 DLL example output

18.4 • Static Classes

In this case we had to instantiate the myMathObj object before we could use it. But we don't have to do this for the normal Math methods, so how can we do this for ours? If you remember, declaring a method as 'static' let's us do this. We'll see how to do this now by adding a Square method and declaring this as **static**.

Return to the MyMathLibrary and add the Square method as follows:

```
static public double Square(double dblSquare)
{
    return dblSquare * dblSquare;
}
```

Build the project and save it.

Return to MathDLLDemo and change the code to the following:

```
private void button1_Click(object sender, EventArgs e)
{
    // declare math object
    MyMathClass myMathObj = new MyMathClass();
    // use Square root method
    double mySqRt5 = myMathObj.SquareRoot(5);
    // square it - no need to instantiate
    double fiveSquared = MyMathLibrary.MyMathClass.Square(mySqRt5);
    // and display
    MessageBox.Show(fiveSquared.ToString());
}
```

We still have to instantiate the myMathObj object from the MyMathClass, but we can now use the Square method without instantiating any objects. We have used this directly with the code:

MyMathLibrary.MyMathClass.Square(mySqRt5);

You don't have to include the MyMathLibrary if it's in the **usings**.

Note that as you type, the IntelliSense knows about the Square method but not the SquareRoot, see Figure 18-6.

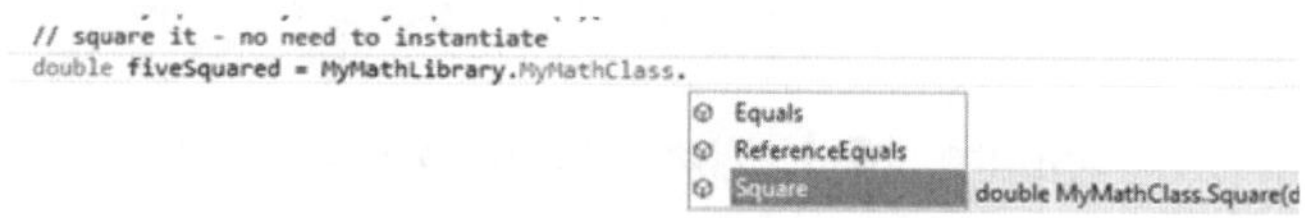

Figure 18-6 Square method

18.5 • Windows Application Program Interface (API)

This is a good point to introduce the Windows Application Programming Interface and the DLL calls provided that enable access to the Windows operating system and Windows services such as file handling, mouse and keyboard interfacing. Of course many of these can be made through the .NET libraries, but .NET programs run slower than truly compiled programs such as C++, and programs that use API calls run faster.

Please note that whenever possible, you should use the .NET Framework to perform tasks (**managed code**) instead of Windows API calls.

The API calls are held in three main namespaces:

- Base services – file systems, threads, error handling (kernel32.dll)
- Graphics devices interface – output to output devices and to draw windows and dialog boxes (gdi32.dll)
- User interface – manages windows and controls, mouse and keyboard inputs (user32.dll)

Platform Invocation Services (Pinvoke) allows managed code to call unmanaged DLL functions. It is easy to use the API calls once you know what calls are available. They are described at the Platform Invoke web site at www.pinvoke.net, which also has examples and a Visual Studio add-in that provides direct access to the calls.

18.6 • Using Win API calls

The API calls are held in an external library, so you must add the namespace:

```
using System.Runtime.InteropServices;
```

Declare the API call. For example to add the call to make your computer beep, add the declaration:

```
[DllImport("User32.dll")]

static extern Boolean MessageBeep(UInt32 beepType);
```

Note that it is DLLImport, not DLLLmport or DIIImport. Also note the square bracket which here are used to specify Attributes. If you want to find out more on this, look in the MSDN library, or the tutorial in the Self assessment exercises.

The MessageBeep is held in the user32.DLL library, it's a static member and is implemented externally (extern). It is passed a UInt32 data type, and returns nothing.

To call the MessageBeep API, use the code:

```
MessageBeep(0);
```

A more versatile API called Beep is also available. This plays a frequency for a specific duration. The declaration is:

```
[DllImport("kernel32.dll", SetLastError=true)]
[return: MarshalAs(UnmanagedType.Bool)]
static extern bool Beep(uint dwFreq, uint dwDuration);
```

Example code to play a 1 kHz tone for ½ second (500 ms) is:

```
Beep (1000, 500);
```

We will return to this when we look at using DirectX for audio output.

18.7 • MessageBox API example

As an example, let's call the MessageBox API. This is similar to the MessageBox.Show call we are familiar with.

Start a new project and add the following using clause at the top of the code:

```
using System.Runtime.InteropServices;
```

Before 'public Form1()', add the DLL declaration code that displays the MessageBox:

```
[DllImport("User32.dll")]
public static extern int MessageBox(int h, string m, string c, int type);
```

Add a button to a form and add the following code:

```
MessageBox(0, "API Message", "API title", 0);
```

Run the program to check it works and displays the message box shown in Figure 18-7.

Figure 18-7 MessageBox API call

You can see how the message and title are passed to the MessageBox display. The final parameter controls the icon and the buttons displayed, for instance the value 1 displays OK and Cancel buttons and 2 displays 'Abort, Retry, Ignore'.

This API call also returns a value, depending on which button was pressed. This can be checked, for example:

```
int returnValue = MessageBox(0, "API Message", "API title", 2);
System.Windows.Forms.MessageBox.Show(returnValue.ToString());
```

Notice how we have put the full definition of the Windows MessageBox call to differentiate between that and the API call.

More information on this and all the other calls can be found on the pinvoke.net web site.

18.8 • Playing sounds

We can play a tone using the Beep call, but we can play WAV files using the PlaySound API. The DLL declaration is more detailed because we can also pass information on how we want the sound to be played (e.g. loop, sync or async - wait for it to finish or not before returning to the user, etc.).

The DLL and Sound flag declarations and usage are as follows:

```
        [DllImport("kernel32.dll", SetLastError=true)]
        [return: MarshalAs(UnmanagedType.Bool)]
        static extern bool Beep(uint dwFreq, uint dwDuration);

[System.Runtime.InteropServices.DllImport
("winmm.DLL", EntryPoint = "PlaySound", SetLastError = true,
CharSet = CharSet.Unicode, ThrowOnUnmappableChar = true)]
        private static extern bool PlaySound
(string szSound, System.IntPtr hMod, PlaySoundFlags flags);
        [System.Flags]
        public enum PlaySoundFlags : int
        {
            SND_SYNC = 0x0000,
            SND_ASYNC = 0x0001,
            SND_NODEFAULT = 0x0002,
            SND_LOOP = 0x0008,
            SND_NOSTOP = 0x0010,
            SND_NOWAIT = 0x00002000,
            SND_FILENAME = 0x00020000,
            SND_RESOURCE = 0x00040004
        }

        private void button1_Click(object sender, EventArgs e)
        {
            Beep(440, 500);
            PlaySound("C:\\WINDOWS\\Media\\tada.wav", new System.IntPtr(),
PlaySoundFlags.SND_SYNC);
        }
```

18.8.1 • Which library?

The MessageBox API is found in the user32.dll library and the PlaySound is in the winmm.dll library, so how do we find out which library holds the DLL call? If you type the call into pinvoke's search, you should find out. For instance the results for the MessageBeep search are shown inFigure 18-8 on page 259; Beep is in the kernel32 library and MessageBeep is in the user32 library.

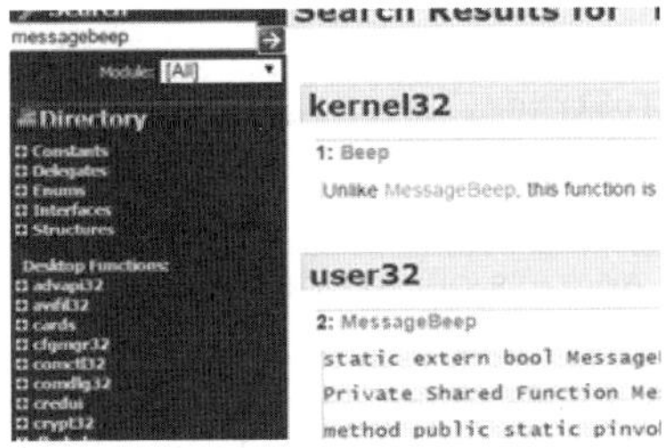

Figure 18-8 Pinvoke search result

A DLL can optionally define an entry point. For instance an open source input / output DLL (inpout32.dll) has two entry points: one for input and one for output.

18.9 • Unsafe code

Unsafe code allows us direct access to memory and generally involves the use of pointers. You should not use unsafe code if you can help it, but sometimes it is unavoidable. For instance:

- When real time applications need enhanced performance
- For external functions and some Windows APIs
- In debugging, when we need to access memory

As an example of using unsafe code, we shall look at the GetComputerName API call.

This uses a pointer to pass both a buffer and the buffer's size. To allow your project to compile and run unsafe code, label the code as unsafe and tell Visual Studio.

In a new project, add using System.Runtime.InteropServices; and add the DLL declaration, before the code public Form1( ):

```
[DllImport("Kernel32.dll")]
static extern unsafe bool GetComputerName(byte* lpBuffer, long* nSize);
```

Add a button on the form, and change its click code to:

```
private void button1_Click(object sender, EventArgs e)
{
    byte[] byteArray = new byte[512];
    long size = byteArray.Length;
    unsafe
    {
        long* pSize = &size;
        fixed (byte* pBuffor = byteArray)
        {
            GetComputerName(pBuffor, pSize);
        }
    }
    System.Text.Encoding textEnc = new System.Text.ASCIIEncoding();
    MessageBox.Show("Computer name: " + textEnc.GetString(byteArray));
    // or use:
    MessageBox.Show("Machine Name is: " +
```

```
    Environment.MachineName.ToString());
        }
```

We've not seen the asterisk and the ampersand before (e.g. long* pSize = &size;). It's C code for a pointer into (or the address of) memory, in this case holding a pointer to a long variable called pSize.

You have to state the size of the data being pointed to (e.g. long*). Pointers can be incremented, and so one pointing to a byte variable would only be incremented by one byte, whereas one pointing to a Uint32 would have to be incremented by four bytes.

To compile the unsafe code, open the project's Properties page. (Project > programName > Properties), click the Build property page and select the 'Allow Unsafe Code' check box, see Figure 18-9.

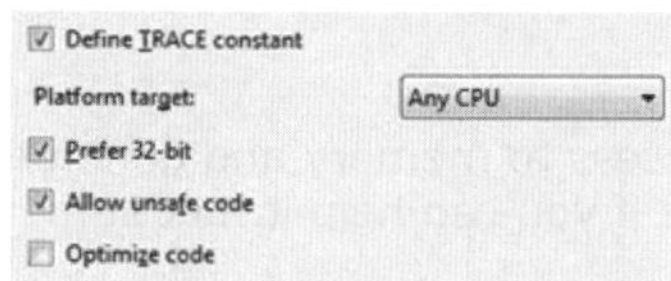

Figure 18-9 Compiling unsafe code

Compile and run the program – it should display your computer's name, see Figure 18-10.

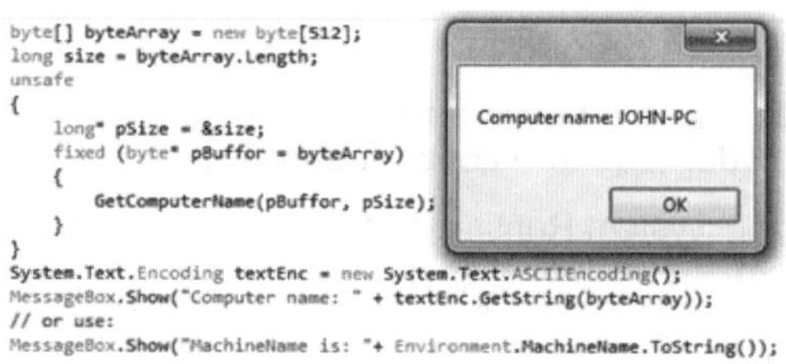

Figure 18-10 GetComputerName display

Incidentally, there is a 'safe' version of this and should really be used. This can be found using Environment.MachineName and the code is:

```
MessageBox.Show("Name is: "+ Environment.MachineName.ToString());
```

This may be a good point for you to investigate the Environment options.

18.10 • Measuring time

There are two ways we know of measuring time: the timer component and the Ticks property of the DateTime structure. The resolution of these is stated as 1 ms and 100ns respectively. But due to overheads you never get this resolution; it's more like 16ms.

If your system supports a high-resolution counter, it is possible to get a better resolution using the QueryPerformanceCounter (QPC) and QueryPerformanceFrequency (QPF) DLLs. These provide a much more accurate measurement of time. For managed code, use the **System.Diagnostics.Stopwatch** class which uses **QPC** as its time reference.

The QPC and QPF calls are defined in the Pinvoke kernel32 library. Detailed information is found on the Microsoft site at: *http://bit.ly/1CIL2o9*. For a discussion on accuracy and resolution, see: *http://bit.ly/1CObPsJ*.

To use these components you need to know the frequency used to clock the counter, then read the counter values and hence calculate the time between values. The following exercise displays the clock frequency and the minimum resolution (the time taken to read the counter).

Start a new project and add using System.Runtime.InteropServices; at the top of your code. Add the following DLL declarations:

```
[DllImport("kernel32.dll")]
extern static short QueryPerformanceCounter(ref long x);
[DllImport("kernel32.dll")]
extern static short QueryPerformanceFrequency(ref long x);
```

The long data types are passed by ref.

For a button click event code add the following:

```
    private void button1_Click(object sender, EventArgs e)
     {
         long count1 = 0, count2 = 0, freq = 0;
// if the Performance counter returns a value other than zero, there must be one
         if (QueryPerformanceCounter(ref count1) != 0)      // Begin timing.
         {
             QueryPerformanceFrequency (ref freq);  // find frequency
             QueryPerformanceCounter (ref count1);   // read counter
             QueryPerformanceCounter (ref count2);   // and read again
             MessageBox.Show("Start Value: " + count1 + ". End Value: " +
  count2 + "\r\n" + "Clock frequency is: " + freq + "\r\n" +
             "Resolution: 1/freq = " + (int)1000000000 / freq +
  " nanoseconds." + "\r\n" + "Time to read counter: " +
  (count2 - count1) * 1.0 / freq + " seconds.");
         }
         else
             MessageBox.Show("High-resolution counter not supported.");
     }
```

Figure 18 11 shows the output for a one of my (old) computers. It shows a clock frequency of 1.9MHz (n.b. this is not the CPU frequency), giving a resolution of 513 nanoseconds and this is the best timing I can get (see the Microsoft references above for a more detailed description).

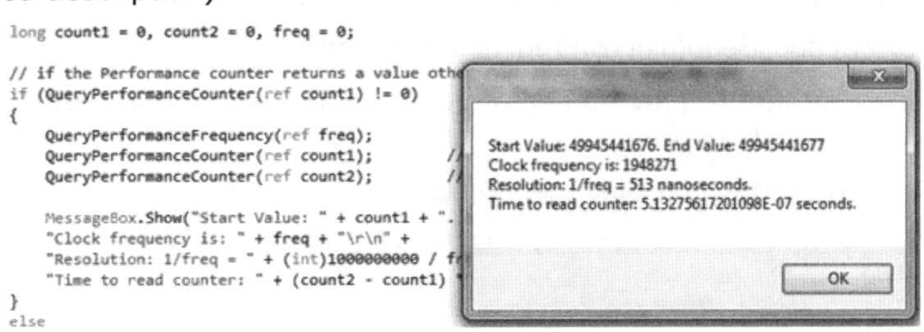

Figure 18-11 Performance frequency and counter

QPC is not synchronised to any external reference. To get a time stamp synchronised to an external reference such as UTC, use **System.Diagnostics.Stopwatch**. This is also managed code, for example:

```
System.Diagnostics.Stopwatch stpWatch = new System.Diagnostics.Stopwatch();
stpWatch.Start();
TimeSpan ts1 = stpWatch.Elapsed;
TimeSpan ts2 = stpWatch.Elapsed;
stpWatch.Stop();
MessageBox.Show((ts2 - ts1).ToString());
```

See Figure 18-12.

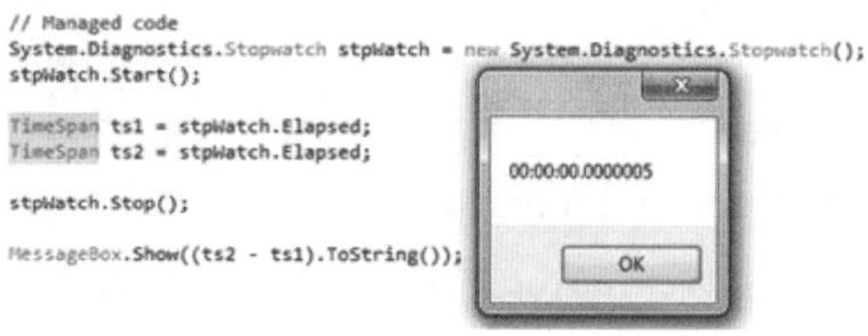

Figure 18-12 Stopwatch code

For Windows 8 computers, GetSystemTimePreciseAsFileTime can be used. This will provide time stamped events across multiple machines.

18.11 • Self Assessment Exercises:

1. Take a look at the BASIC Walkthrough calling Windows APIs at:

   https://msdn.microsoft.com/en-gb/library/172wfck9.aspx

   This is in Basic, but the concepts are the same.

2. Look at the Microsoft Pinvoke tutorial: http://bit.ly/1eZWRvO

   and at: https://msdn.microsoft.com/en-us/library/ms173187.aspx

   DLL

3. Add some extra Math classes. It doesn't matter if they are already defined in the Math namespace. Try adding DLLs that need to be instantiated and some that don't i.e. that are declared as static.

   API

4. Look at some of the API calls at the pinvoke web site. Search for the Beep API. Note that it can be overridden to include a frequency and duration:

   static extern bool Beep(uint dwFreq, uint dwDuration);

5. Write a program to play a beep of your own frequency and duration. Combine this to play a short tune.

6. Look at the (now a bit old) media player example at:

   http://www.codeproject.com/Articles/16316/Audio-Player-using-winmm-dll-and-WPL-File

   Timing

7. Write a program to read find out the resolution of your PC using ticks and DateTime.Now. Compare this with the resolution obtained with the performance APIs.

8. You can also try using GetTimeStamp for timing:

```
// Get the current ticks
        long startTime = System.Diagnostics.Stopwatch.GetTimestamp();
        long endTime = System.Diagnostics.Stopwatch.GetTimestamp();
        MessageBox.Show("Time stamp frequency is: " +
          System.Diagnostics.Stopwatch.Frequency +
          "\r\n" + "Time taken is " + (endTime - startTime).ToString());
```

18.12 • Summary

We have seen how we can create a Windows Library class and add methods, saving them as Dynamic Link and Locate (DLL) code. We have seen how we add the DLL reference and call the DLL code from other projects. We have the use of static methods.

We have covered Windows API calls and seen how they allow us direct access to the operating system using some simple examples. We have discussed using unsafe code.

Finally we have seen how we can use the Performance frequency and Performance counter to obtain timings from our PC.

Chapter 19 • Sound, Video and DirectX drivers

19.1 • Introduction

In this chapter, we will see how we can capture sound and video (and for any Engineers provide analogue input and output from the PC) by using the Microsoft DirectX drivers and software that interfaces to the sound card.

We will start by introducing the DirectX drivers and then see how these are used to generate an analogue output via the headphone / loudspeaker socket.

We will then see how the DirectX drivers are used to read the microphone or line-in input and develop a simple oscilloscope application using the charts seen in Chapter 17 on page 239.

Finally we will see how to use third party software to capture video.

19.2 • DirectX

Microsoft's DirectX is a collection of APIs used for games programming and multimedia (the X stands for the individual applications, e.g. DirectSound). It provides a common interface so that code for each individual sound or graphics card doesn't have to be written. In this chapter we will use the DirectInput API for input and the DirectSound API for output.

For developing games, an apps programmer would use C++/CX and the Windows 8.1 DirectX APIs, DirectX 11, which supports hardware features. Apps can then be published on Windows Store.

The Software Development Kit (SDK) is available from Microsoft DirectX Developer Center (http://www.microsoft.com/en-gb/download/details.aspx - DXSDK_Jun10). It's 571Mb and needs 1.2 GB disk space. Needless to say it takes some time to install and if you already have the DirectX drivers, is most probably unnecessary. I installed the SDK and got the error message 'S1023' (possibly due to the new version of VS) but the drivers I needed had been installed.

Before we start coding, let's take a look at the DirectX classes we will use.

If you don't want to go into great detail here, you might like to skip this and read on from section 19.9 on page 275 which uses third party software that makes it easier.

19.3 • The DirectX components

19.3.1 • The DirectSound class

This provides the interface between your programs the sound card drivers. It provides some advanced techniques such as mixing and adding effects. To play sounds, the DirectSound class needs a DirectSound device object which provides the basic interface and drivers for the sound device (a sound card).

19.3.2 • The DirectInput class

This class collects input from input devices such as the mouse and keyboard. In our case we will be using the microphone or line-in as our input device. We will see how we can determine which input devices are available.

19.3.3 • Cooperative level

The Cooperative level determines how much control of the hardware your program is allowed. The available levels are:

- Normal – The primary buffer (see later) is set to 22 kHz, stereo, 8-bit and it can't be written to.
- Priority – The primary buffer format can be set by the application. This should be used as it gives the most robust behaviour whilst allowing the user some control.
- Write-Primary – The application has direct access to the primary buffer

In the following examples when we play a WAV file, we'll use the Normal cooperative level. If we don't want to be restricted by sampling rate, nor need direct access to the primary buffer, we will use the Priority cooperative level. This provides control over the sound format and allows other programs that use sounds to play.

19.3.4 • The Buffers

The Primary and Secondary Buffers

The buffers hold the sounds being played. The primary buffer is the one that the sound card plays. The secondary buffer (SecondaryBuffer) provides a higher level interface to the device. There may be more than one secondary buffer; these have the effects applied to them and sounds mixed before being transferred to the primary buffer. We will use secondary buffers.

Short sound samples can be loaded completely into the secondary buffer and played, but as audio can take up a lot of memory a few second's worth of data is normally transferred into the secondary buffer and streamed. Your program then fills the buffer as the sound plays. Events can be set to occur when the buffer is nearly empty (or full in the case of capturing data), but we won't use those here.

The Capture Buffer

When it comes to capturing the sound inputs, the opposite happens. A capture buffer (CaptureBuffer) is filled and your program empties it. The CaptureBuffer has methods such as Start, Stop, Read and Write.

The capture buffer captures the signal from a Capture object (the input device), and saves it into an array of bytes with the specified wave format (WaveFormat).

Like the SecondaryBuffer, this can either stop capturing when the buffer is full or can be a streaming buffer which your program has to empty before the data is overwritten. The easiest way is for your program to find out the current position of the write buffer pointer and empty the buffer at the correct point. Alternatively, a Notify event can be set up which fires at the right time.

19.3.5 • The input device

Your PC may have many inputs and outputs that can be used. Your program needs to know which one it is using. It also needs to know the wave format, i.e. the sampling rate, number of channels and number of bits per sample. Later we will see how to set up the correct formats and choose an input device.

19.4 • Playing sounds

Before using the DirectX libraries, remember that we saw in Chapters 10 and 18 how to use the Windows Media Player and how to play sounds using the API calls 'Beep' and 'PlaySound'.

You can also use the **Media.SoundPlayer** for WAV files, as follows:

```
System.Media.SoundPlayer wavPlayer = new System.Media.SoundPlayer();
wavPlayer.SoundLocation = @"C:\windows\media\tada.wav";
wavPlayer.Play();
```

You can instantiate a soundPlayer with a stream: new SoundPlayer(Stream);

These are much simpler to use than the following examples and may be good enough for your needs.

There are five steps involved in using DirectX to play sounds:

1. Create the output device to be used to play the sound,
2. Set the cooperative level,
3. Create the buffers and their description,
4. Fill the buffer(s),
5. Play the sound (and repeat 4 if necessary until done)

In this first example we will play a WAV file.

Start a new project and save it. Right click the project's name in Solution Explorer, select Properties and **change the target .NET framework to version 3.5**, see Figure 19-1. This has to be done, because the latest versions of DirectX only support C++. You will get warnings if you do it later on. You can also select .NET framework 3.5 from the drop-down box when you select the Windows Form Application, see Figure 19-1.

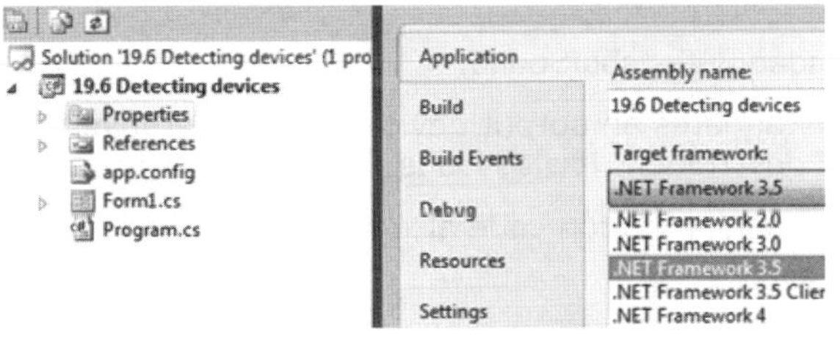

Figure 19-1 Re-targeting the .NET framework

You must also target for x86 machines. Select x86 from the drop-down box in the Build section, see Figure 19-2 on page 268.

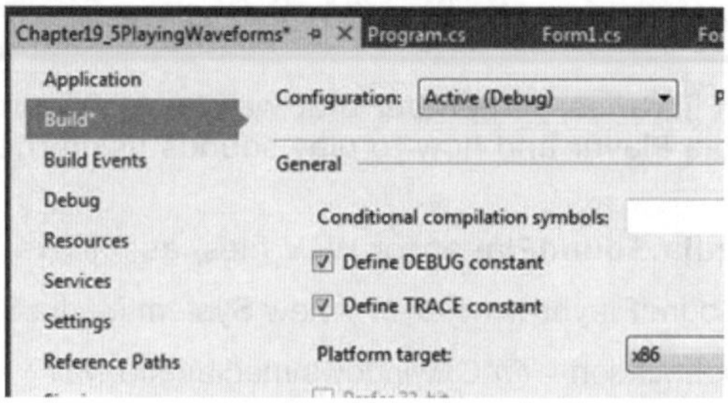

Figure 19-2 Targeting for x86

Add the Microsoft.DirectX.DirectSound driver DLL to the program's References, see Figure 19-3. You will have to browse for them. My drivers were in the folder: Windows/ Microsoft.NET/DirectX for Managed Code/1.0.2902.0.

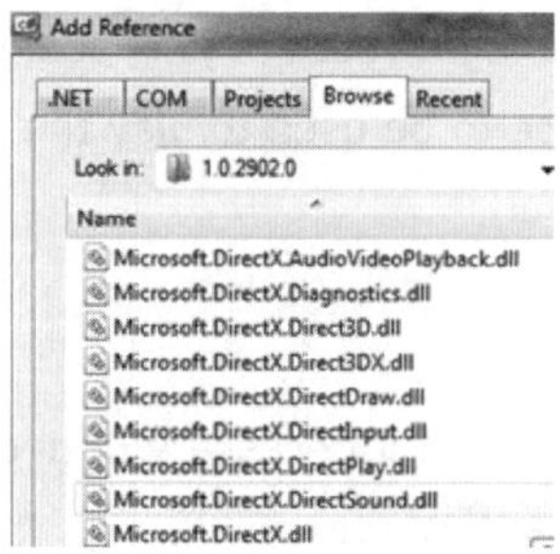

Figure 19-3 Adding DirectX references

Add the using statement: using Microsoft.DirectX.DirectSound;

Before public Form1( ), add the declarations for the output device and secondary buffer:

```
private Device outputDevice;
private SecondaryBuffer sbufSound;
```

The following code instantiates an output device, the cooperative level and the SecondaryBuffer and description. It also loads the sound file to be played.

Add the following sound initialization code after InitializeComponent();

```
// instantiate a new Device
outputDevice = new Device();
// Set the Cooperative level – to normal – nothing clever in this program
outputDevice.SetCooperativeLevel(this, CooperativeLevel.Normal);
// instantiate a new Bufferdescription
BufferDescription bfrDesc = new BufferDescription();
// load the sound into the secondary buffer
sbufSound = new SecondaryBuffer
      (@"C:\windows\media\tada.wav", bfrDesc, outputDevice);
```

The BufferDescription contains the properties and methods of the secondary buffer we create. Ensure the tada.wav exists in the folder or find another suitable wav file.

Add a button and the following code for its click event:

```
sbufSound.Play(0, BufferPlayFlags.Default);
```

Compile the code. You may have to remove the using statement: using System.Threading. Tasks; Do this for both Program.cs and Form1.cs. Remember you can remove unused Namespaces by right-clicking the code area and selecting Organize Usings > Remove Unused Usings.

You may also get a warning about the Microsoft.CSharp reference. To remove this, expand the references in the Solution Explorer and right-click Microsoft.CSharp to remove it.

If you get the error 'LoaderLock was detected", go to Debug > Exceptions > Managed Debugging Assistants and uncheck LoaderLock, see Figure 19-4.

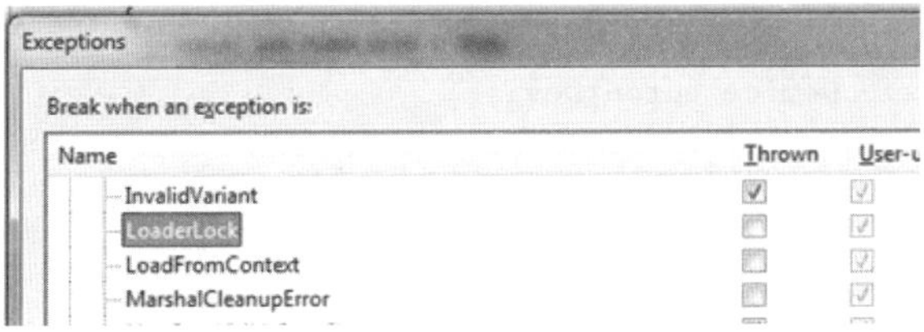

Figure 19-4 LoaderLock exception

Clicking the button should play your sound.

19.5 • Playing waveforms

In the second example we will generate and play a buffer that contains the data for a sine wave. The values for the sine wave will be calculated and put into the secondary buffer in place of tada.wav using the secondaryBuffer.Write() method.

This time we will need to know what the properties are of wave format we are using. For example: the sampling rate, the number of bits per sample, the number of channels and the coding used for the waveform.

This is the DirectSound WaveFormat structure. The properties are:

AverageBytesPerSecond	The average data-transfer rate in bytes per second. For example, 16-bit stereo at 44.1 kHz has an average data rate of (2 bytes per sample * 2 channels * 44,100 samples per second) is 176,400 bytes per second.
BitsPerSample	The number of bits per sample.
BlockAlign	The minimum atomic unit of data in bytes. The product of Channels and BitsPerSample divided by 8.
Channels	The number of channels used.
FormatTag	The waveform-audio format type. (PCM = raw data)
SamplesPerSecond	The sample rate, in samples per second (hertz).

The user interface is the same as the previous example (a button on a form). Remember to **compile for x86** and **.NET version 3.5** as before. The complete code is:

```
using System;
using System.Windows.Forms;
using Microsoft.DirectX.DirectSound;
// Compile / re-target for .NET v3.5 - Build for x86
// Allow Loader Lock exceptions:
//     Debug > Exceptions > Managed Debugging Assistants and uncheck
LoaderLock
namespace Chapter19_5PlayingWaveforms
{
    public partial class Form1 : Form
    {
        private Device outputDevice;

        public Form1()
        {
            InitializeComponent();
            //// instantiate a new Device
            outputDevice = new Device();
            //// Can also use Cooperative level - Normal
            //// SetCooperativeLevel args are owner and level
            outputDevice.SetCooperativeLevel(this, CooperativeLevel.
Priority);
        }
        private void button1_Click(object sender, System.EventArgs e)
        {
            int sampleRate = 44100;
            int duration = 2;      // seconds
            const double FREQ = 554;     // C# ! (A(4)=440)
            WaveFormat format = new WaveFormat();
            // set up WaveFormat properties
            format.BitsPerSample = 8;
            format.Channels = 1;
            format.BlockAlign = 1;     // Channels * BitsPerSample / 8.
            format.FormatTag = WaveFormatTag.Pcm;
            format.SamplesPerSecond = sampleRate;
            format.AverageBytesPerSecond =
            format.SamplesPerSecond * format.BlockAlign;
            // Now set up buffers
            BufferDescription bfrDesc = new BufferDescription(format);
            bfrDesc.DeferLocation = true; // can assign at playing time
            bfrDesc.BufferBytes = 8 * format.AverageBytesPerSecond;
            // calculate data
            byte[] sineData = new byte[sampleRate * duration];
            for (int i = 0; i < sampleRate * duration; i++)
            {
                sineData[i] = (byte)(128 + (127 * Math.Sin
```

```
(2 * Math.PI * i * FREQ / sampleRate)));
        }
        // set up secondary buffer
        SecondaryBuffer sbfrSound =
        new SecondaryBuffer(bfrDesc, outputDevice);
        // load the sound into the buffer = lock buffer whilst doing it
        sbfrSound.Write(0, sineData, LockFlag.EntireBuffer);
        // and play it (perhaps there should be a delay here, but it works)
            sbfrSound.Play(0, BufferPlayFlags.Default);
        }
    }
}
```

Clicking the button should play your sound. It will play the note C#!

Obviously your program could have some selection boxes for the desired frequency, duration, sample rate, etc.

More information on the DirectSound classes and methods can be found on the Microsoft library at: http://msdn.microsoft.com/en-us/library/bb318665(VS.85).aspx

19.6 • Detecting input devices

Before we start to perform any capturing, we need to find out which input devices are available. These are held in a CaptureDevicesCollection – a collection of DeviceInformation structures that contains the properties for each input device. The devices are easily found with a couple of lines of code.

In a new project perform the usual steps to set up the correct environment (x86 and .NET 3.5). Add the reference to DirectSound and if necessary remove the reference to Microsoft.CSharp. Uncheck LoaderLock (Debug > Exceptions > Managed Debugging Assistants)

At the top of the code add the statement: 'using Microsoft.DirectX.DirectSound;'.

We'll let the program find the devices when the form loads and display them in a comboBox. Add a comboBox to the form and call it 'cmbCaptureDevices'. Add the following code for the form load event:

```
private void Form1_Load(object sender, EventArgs e)
{
    CaptureDevicesCollection myDevices = new CaptureDevicesCollection();
    // Display in combobox
    foreach (DeviceInformation Devinfo in myDevices)
        cmbCaptureDevices.Items.Add(Devinfo.Description);
}
```

Your output should be similar to Figure 19-5 on page 272:

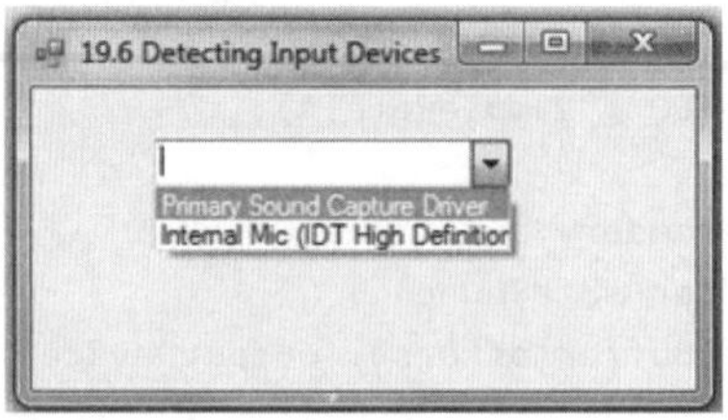

Figure 19-5 Capture devices

Now the name of your device is known, your program could select a suitable input or the input device could be seleted from the comboBox by the user.

19.7 • Sound Capture

We can now try using the sound card's input channels to capture the input waveforms.

The procedure is similar to the playing sounds, but instead of defining the format, filling an array and transferring this to the buffer to be played, the format is defined, a capture buffer set up and the data captured. The data is then in an array that can be read and played or analysed if desired. We shall display the data on a graph.

The procedure is as follows:

1. Set up the capture format: the sample rate, the number of bits per sample, the number of channels and the wave format.
2. Calculate the block alignment for the buffer and the average bytes per second.
3. Calculate the capture buffer size and if using events, set up the notify size.
4. Determine the capture device input and create a Capture object and CaptureBuffer (for the required input device and format determined in 1).
5. If echoing the data, create the output device, format and buffers as we did in the previous section. Two buffers may be required – one to play from whilst the other is loaded from the capture buffer. This should really use threads.
6. Start capturing and read the capture buffer pointer postion. Empty the buffer when required. Alternatively, create and run a thread that reads the capture buffer into an array when notified event occurs. Play the sound if required.

We have seen 1), 2), 4) and 5). We have also discussed the role of the capture buffer. This is filled until either the required capture position is read, or if using threads, the notify size is met.

19.8 • Sound capture program

There is one slight problem trying to display graphically any sounds recorded using a Chart – we need .NET v3.5 to run our DirectX code, but Charts need .NET v4.0. In the following example I have drawn the graph on a panel using the Graphics.DrawLine method.

In a new project start a .NET v3.5 and x86 project (or set up the correct environment, see section 19.6 on page 271), change the size of the form to 500 by 500, add a panel - set its size to 450*350 and its borderStyle to fixedSingle and BackColor to white, add two buttons to start and stop the recording (btnStart and btnStop – set their Enable propertry to false) and a combobox to select the input device (cmbDevices).

The Start button will be enabled when the user has selected an input device from the combobox. When clicked it will start and stop the capturing then disable itself. The Stop button will be enabled once the data has been captured. Pressing the Stop button will display the waveform and re-enable the Start button.

The design should be similar to Figure 19-6 on page 275.

Add the reference to DirectSound (in Windows/Microsoft.NET/DirectX for Managed Code - see section 19.4 on page 267). Add the using statement:

```
using Microsoft.DirectX.DirectSound;
```

Before Form1( ) add the declarations:

```
public System.Array read;
public int captureBfrSize;
public CaptureBuffer captureBfr;
public int capturePos, readPos = 0;
CaptureDevicesCollection myDevices = new CaptureDevicesCollection();
```

In the form( ) initialization code add:

```
CheckForIllegalCrossThreadCalls = false;
```

Change the Form Load event to:

```
private void Form1_Load(object sender, EventArgs e)
{
    foreach (DeviceInformation Devinfo in myDevices)
        cmbDevices.Items.Add(Devinfo.Description);
}
```

Change the comboBox SelectedIndexChanged event to enable the Start button:

```
private void cmbDevices_SelectedIndexChanged(object sender, EventArgs e)
{
    btnStart.Enabled = true;
}
```

Add the code to capture the sound when the Start button is clicked:

```
private void btnStart_Click(object sender, EventArgs e)
{
btnStart.Enabled = false;
var format = new WaveFormat
{
    SamplesPerSecond = 48000,    // or 96000 etc
    BitsPerSample = 8,            // or 16
    Channels = 1,           // or 2 for stereo
    FormatTag = WaveFormatTag.Pcm   // raw data
};
// Calculate BlockAlign and AverageBytesPerSecond
format.BlockAlign = (short)(format.Channels * (format.BitsPerSample / 8));
format.AverageBytesPerSecond = format.SamplesPerSecond * format.BlockAlign;
captureBfrSize = (format.SamplesPerSecond * format.BitsPerSample / 8) * 2;
```

```
// enough for 2 seconds - but we'll stop after 1
// Create Capture buffer and CaptureBufferDescriptor
var cap = default(Capture);
// find device selected in comboBox and create Capture object
for (int i = 0; i < myDevices.Count; i++)
{
    if (myDevices[i].Description.ToLower().Contains
         (cmbDevices.SelectedItem.ToString().ToLower()))
    {
        cap = new Capture(myDevices[i].DriverGuid);
        break;
    }
}
var capDesc = new CaptureBufferDescription
{
    Format = format,
    BufferBytes = captureBfrSize
};
captureBfr = new CaptureBuffer(capDesc, cap);
// Start capturing
captureBfr.Start(true);
/************
* loop waiting for capture buffer to be filled
* use GetCurrentPosition.
* see http://msdn.microsoft.com/en-us/library/bb280835.aspx
* *************/
captureBfr.GetCurrentPosition(out capturePos, out readPos);
// stop capture after 1 second
while (capturePos < captureBfrSize / 2)
    captureBfr.GetCurrentPosition(out capturePos, out readPos);
// stop capturing
captureBfr.Stop();
// and copy the buffer
read = captureBfr.Read(0, typeof(byte), LockFlag.None, captureBfrSize / 2);
// free resources
captureBfr.Dispose();
cap.Dispose();
btnStop.Enabled = true; // enable stop button
}
```

Finally add the code for the Stop button:

```
private void btnStop_Click(object sender, EventArgs e)
{
  const int PANELSIZE = 450;
  btnStop.Enabled = false;
  btnStart.Enabled = true;
```

```
        // plot it
        System.Drawing.Graphics grpObject;
        grpObject = this.panel1.CreateGraphics();
        Pen objmyPen = new Pen(System.Drawing.Color.Blue);
        // panel is 450 wide plot first point
        grpObject.DrawLine(objmyPen, 0, (byte)
             (read.GetValue(0)), 0, (byte)read.GetValue(0));
        for (int i = 0; i < PANELSIZE; i++)
        {
           grpObject.DrawLine(objmyPen, i, (byte)read.GetValue(i), i + 1,
             (byte)read.GetValue(i + 1));
        }
    }
```

Run the code. Figure 19-6 shows what I get when I recorded a streaming radio station.

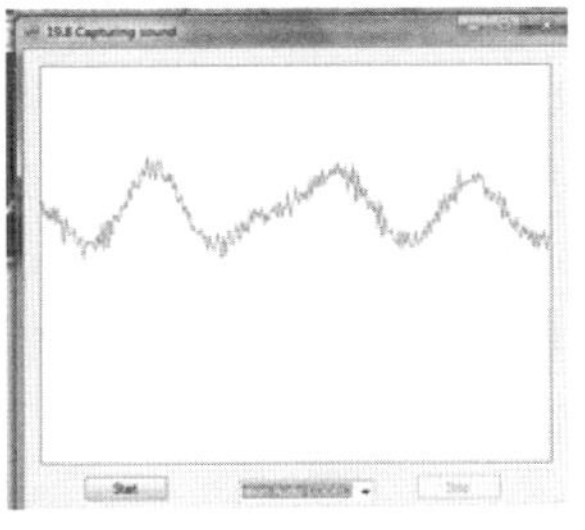

Figure 19-6 Sound capture display

19.9 • Video Capture

Video capture is easy and can be performed in a few steps with the Direct.Capture library as we shall see. Detailed video work (e.g. video mixing) is beyond the purpose of the book.

The DirectX.Capture Class Library which captures video and audio to AVI files was written by Code Project (www.codeproject.com). Information and the libraries can be found at their web site: http://www.codeproject.com/Articles/3566/DirectX-Capture-Class-Library where more information is provided on how it works.

Some of the Capture Class features include:

- Listing the audio and video hardware devices
- Audio and video settings
- Support for audio and video codecs
- Video preview capability and
- Support for TV tuners

At its simplest all that has to be done is select a video source, choose your settings and file name and location and start the capture.

The DirectX.Capture Class is based on Microsoft DirectShow (DShowNET), and you have to include this dll in your references. You might also like to read about this and also Media Foundation. They are multimedia frameworks and APIs that perform operations on media files and streams. They are supplied with the Windows SDK. However the libraries are targeted at C++ and Component Object Model (COM) objects and there are no plans for a managed API or C# support.

For further information, see Introduction to DirectShow at:

https://msdn.microsoft.com/en-us/library/dd390351(v=vs.85).aspx

19.9.1 • Video Capture Devices

Let's start by finding out our audio and video devices as we did in section 19.6 on page 271.

Start a new project (it can be .NET v4.0 and Any CPU) and save it. Download the DirectX. Capture driver and save it in the obj folder. Add DirectX.Capture.dll to the solution's references.

Add a combo box to the form and give it the name cmbDevices.

Add `using DirectX.Capture;` to the 'usings' statements.

Add the statement: `private Filters filters = new Filters();`

Now change the form load code so that the complete code is as follows:

```
using System;
using System.Windows.Forms;
using DirectX.Capture;
namespace Chapter19_9VideoDevices
{
    public partial class Form1 : Form
    {
        public Form1()
        {
            InitializeComponent();
        }
        private Filters filters = new Filters();

        private void Form1_Load(object sender, EventArgs e)
        {
            foreach (Filter fs in filters.VideoInputDevices)
            {
                cmbDevices.Items.Add(fs.Name);
            }
            foreach (Filter fs in filters.AudioInputDevices)
            {
                cmbDevices.Items.Add(fs.Name);
            }
        }
    }
}
```

Save and run the code. My output was as shown in Figure 19-7.

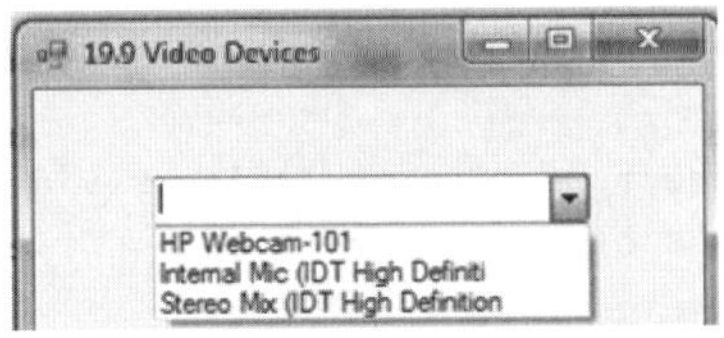

Figure 19-7 Audio and Video devices

You can see that a **Filter** class is used. It contains a list of the audio and video devices and their names as well as many other properties. A Filter performs operations on a multimedia stream, e.g. read a file; capture video; decode stream formats and pass data to the sound or graphics card.

Later we will use filters.VideoInputDevices[0] to refer to the video device we want to use (and similarly filters.AudioInputDevices[0] or [1]).

Now we know the devices we can use to perform our capture, we can try a simple capture.

19.9.2 • Video Capture Program

Start a new project. Copy DirectX.Capture.dll and DShowNET.dll into your program's folder and add them to the references. Add them to the using statements.

Add the private statement: `private Filters filters = new Filters();`

Add a button to the form and change its click code to the following:

```
private void btnCapture_Click(object sender, EventArgs e)
{
  Capture capture = new Capture(filters.VideoInputDevices[0],
    filters.AudioInputDevices[1]);
  capture.FrameRate = 30; // NTSC
  capture.FrameSize = new Size(640, 480); // 640x480
  capture.Filename = "CapturedVideo.avi";
  capture.Start();
  System.Threading.Thread.Sleep(1000); // Pauses 1 second
  capture.Stop();
  capture.Dispose();
}
```

19.9.3 • Video Capture Preview

Now that we know how to capture video, we can also preview and display it on our form.

This is even easier.

Start a new project as before, save the DirectX.Capture files in obj folder, add usings, etc. This time add a panel as well as the button. The panel will be our preview pane; make its size 160*120. I've used the default name: panel1

Add the Filters code: `private Filters filters = new Filters();`

Change the button code to the following:

```
private void btnPreview_Click(object sender, EventArgs e)
{
  Capture capture = new Capture(filters.VideoInputDevices[0],
      filters.AudioInputDevices[0]);
  capture.FrameRate = 30; // NTSC
  capture.FrameSize = new Size(160, 120);
  capture.PreviewWindow = panel1;
}
```

That's it! You may have to change the index of your devices. The code should run and display the video preview when the button is clicked.

Incidentally, I used 'any CPU' and .NET v4 for these programs.

If you wish to take this further (e.g. stream your video), or have any problems, please refer to the code project web site.

19.10 • Streaming Video

You can use .NET version 4 and Microsoft Expression Encoder to stream your video. Expression Encoder is yet another download found in the Microsoft Download Centre. We will not cover that here, but an article 'How to use a web cam in C# with .NET Framework 4.0 and Microsoft Expression Encoder 4' is available at the Code Project web site: *http://bit.ly/1QI9E1S*.

19.11 • Self Assessment exercises

1. Change the code in section 19.5 so that the user can choose the frequency, duration, sample rate, etc.
2. Try different sampling rates and plot these.
3. The sampling rate should be at least twice the highest freqency of the signal. Observe what happens when the sampling rate is near (or less than) that rate.
4. Change the sample code so that the display is permanently updated.
5. Change the sample code so that the graph displays time along the x-axis.
6. Find out how to use threads and events to control Direct Input.
7. Look at the example of capturing and playing sounds at the same time at:

   http://khason.net/blog/capturing-and-streaming-sound-by-using-directsound-with-c
8. Study the DirectX Audio examples in the SDK.
9. Study WPF and take a look at further Code Project examples, or the web site:

   http://khason.net/blog/webcam-control-with-wpf-or-how-to-create-high-framerate-player-with-directshow-by-using-interopbitmap-in-wpf-application/
10. Study the capture.cs code that is included when you add the reference to DirectX.Capture.dll
11. There are more DirextX samples at: *http://bit.ly/1QkQ3d8*
12.

19.12 • Summary

This has been a whirlwind introduction to the DirectX libraries and only touched on a couple of them. The basics of using the DirectX classes (buffers, etc.) and setting up the I/O devices have been covered. The DirectSound library has been used to play a .WAV file and also a software generated waveform. Finally the DirectInput library has been used to detect the input devices and capture and graphically display a sound input.

Video capture and steaming using the DirectX.Capture Class Library has been covered. We have also seen the problems of running DirectX and C# under VS2015 and seen how to work-around this.

Chapter 20 • Smartphone apps for Android

20.1 • Introduction

In the final chapters we shall investigate programming for Android devices in C# using Xamarin (https://xamarin.com/). Xamarin apps can be targeted for Android, iOS, Windows and Mac. The code is written in C# using Visual Studio or Xamarin Studio, and downloaded to an emulator that runs on your PC, where the app can be tested before deploying and further testing on a phone or tablet.

Xamarin works by bundling a fully functional implementation of the .NET runtime called Mono, with your app.

If you want to publish your app you'll need a Developer Licence. This is a one-off cost of $25.

You can of course develop smartphone apps for Windows Mobile. If you are interested in that, please see the Windows Mobile Developer Center at: https://msdn.microsoft.com/en-us/windowsmobile/default.

20.2 • Obtaining the Xamarin software

Xamarin for Visual Studio is included in Visual Studio 2015. It is also supported on Visual Studio 2010 and later, in which case the software is available from Xamarin.com. Scroll down to the Xamarin Platform section of the home page and click the download button. There are a few different versions, but for now choose the free version. The version that supports Visual Studio is time-limited, but you can still use Xamarin Studio after that.

For more details on installing, should you need it, see Appendix B on page 305.

The Xamarin web site has a very comprehensive guide on installation at:

http://developer.xamarin.com/guides/android/getting_started/installation/windows/

Once it's installed you can take a look at the Android exercise 'Hello, Android > Part 1: Quick Start' but for a more gentle introduction, we'll start with a simple 'Hello World' Application.

20.3 • Your First Android Application

Development can be undertaken using Xamarin's own IDE (Xamarin Studio) or using Visual Studio. We will use Visual Studio here.

1. Start a new project (File > New Project) but this time, under **Visual C#**, select **Android** and a **Blank App (Android)**. Give the solution a name and save it in a suitable folder, see Figure 20-1.

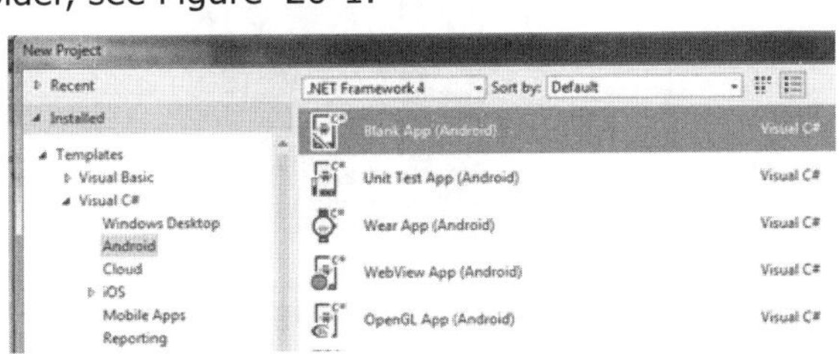

Figure 20-1 A New Android App

If you can't see the Android option, check that Xamarin has installed correctly.

As might be expected the familiar Visual Studio development environment appears, but with different usings and code. Click **MainActivity.cs** to see the code, see Figure 20-2.

Figure 20-2 Android code

2. We now need the layout for our screen. This is the Android Designer and is opened using Resources > Layout in the Solution Explorer. Double-click **Main.axml**, see Figure 20-3.

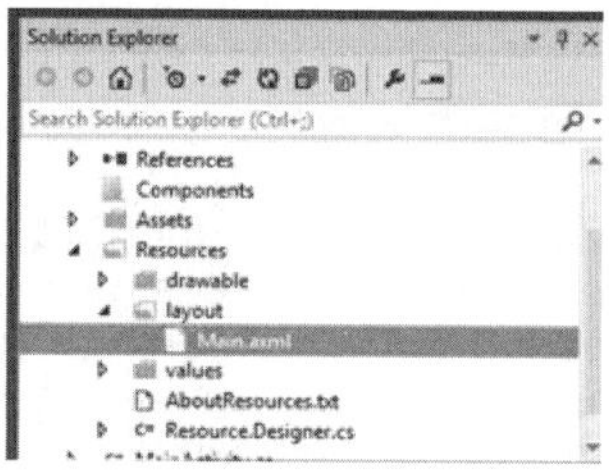

Figure 20-3 Selecting Android Designer

Depending on how you obtained the Xamarin software, you may have to log-in and **Begin a Trial.** The trial is time-limited, so after that you will have to purchase one of the options, or use Xamarin Studio for your development.

The design screen is loaded. This has Design and a Source tabs, rather like the Form.cs and Form.cs[design] we've seen before, see Figure 20-4.

Notice that a button has been placed for you and also that we have a Toolbox with Android related controls.

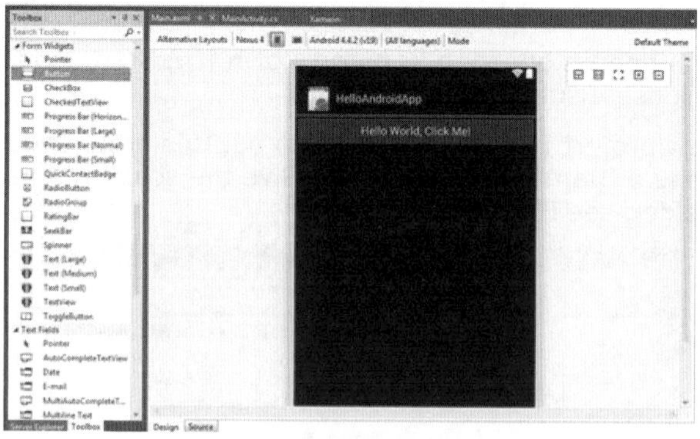

Figure 20-4 The Design screen

This is similar to the WPF design we have seen. AXML stands for **Android XML.** The design layout is held in an XML file seen in the Source tab. As you place controls on the screen, they are added to the AXML file. XML files are obvious enough, but if you don't know XML, see the self assessment exercises for a link and tutorial.

Main.xml looks like this:

```
<?xml version="1.0" encoding="utf-8"?>
<LinearLayout xmlns:android="http://schemas.android.com/apk/res/android"
    android:orientation="vertical"
    android:layout_width="fill_parent"
    android:layout_height="fill_parent">
    <Button
        android:id="@+id/MyButton"
        android:layout_width="fill_parent"
        android:layout_height="wrap_content"
        android:text="@string/Hello" />
</LinearLayout>
```

LinearLayout describes how the items on the screen are placed. There are several layouts that can be used and these can be seen in the ToolBox Layout section. We will not cover layout here, see the Self Assessment exercises for more.

The **<Button />** tag describes the Button. Its **id** is 'MyButton'; the **layout_width** and **layout_height** describe how it's displayed; and its **text** is "Hello".

We will see later how our program accesses this information.

The controls in the ToolBox are different from what we are used to, and we will not describe them all here. That would take another book. To find out what controls are available and their descriptions, see:

http://developer.xamarin.com/guides/android/user_interface/

Let's compile and run the application on the emulator before looking at the code.

3. We will look at the IDE and compile and run the application before we look at the code.

   Before trying our program on a target device (smartphone, tablet or watch!), we will run our code on the PC using an emulator. This can pretend to be a range of devices. If you select **Alternate Layouts** from the Main.axml design screen, you will see (in my case) that the default is Nexus 4, see Figure 20-5. Clicking this shows the range of devices that can run your app. Try some of these out and see how the display changes to suit. You can also change the screen display from portrait to landscape and zoom in on the screen.

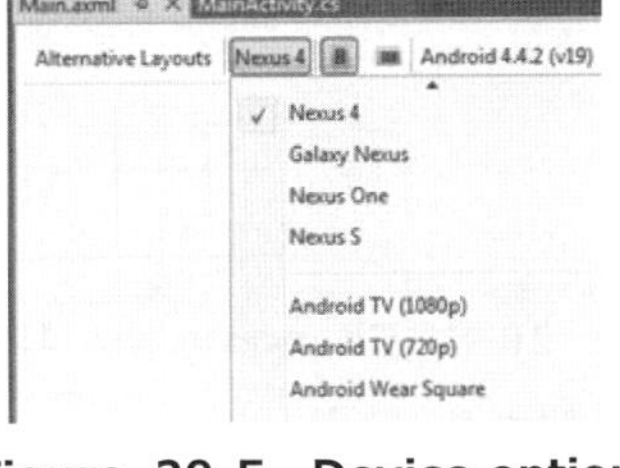

Figure 20-5 Device options

Take a look at some of the button properties. Display the main.axml design screen and click the 'Hello World, Click Me!' button.

Note the ID is **@+id/MyButton** and the text property is **@string/Hello**, but that isn't what's displayed. Remember, the @ symbol means a pointer to a string. In this case the string can be seen if the ellipsis box [...] is clicked. The displayed text is held in Resources, see Figure 20-6.

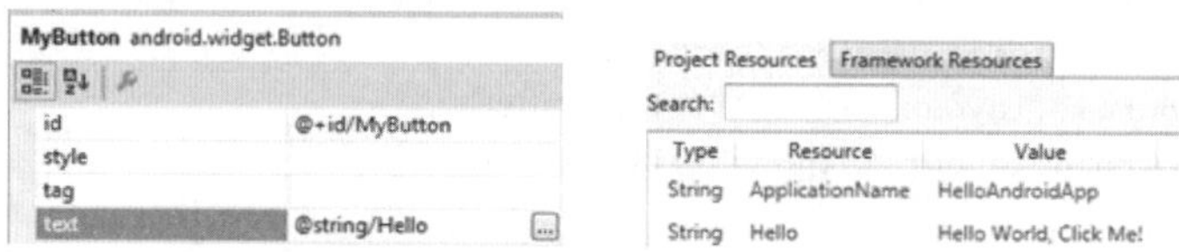

Figure 20-6 Button properties

You can change the text by double-clicking the button.

Note also that there are no events related to the button. We'll come back to this later.

4. Compile and Emulate the program

   We don't have a Start button to compile the code - we have a MonoForAndroid_API_10 button instead. Click this. You may get an 'Incompatible API Level' error message, see Figure 20-7.

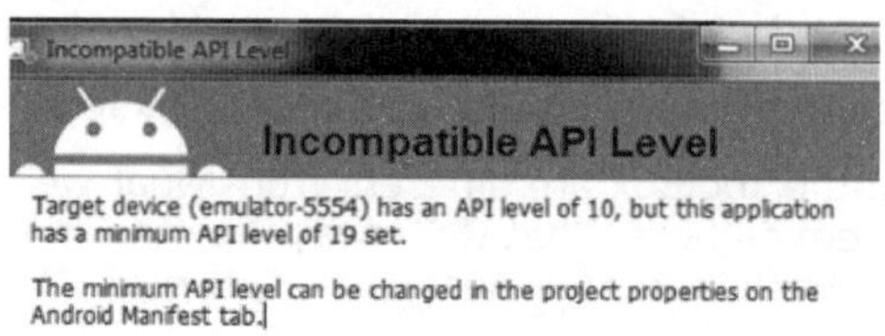

Figure 20-7 Incompatible API Level

Even so, you will see a phone emulator appear which you can operate just like your phone. You can run the calculator, clock, alarms etc.

The program must be compiled under the correct API version. To do this, double-click **Properties** in the Solution Explorer to display the Application configurations.

Make sure the Application tab is set and from the drop-down menu for 'Compile using Android version' select API level 10, see Figure 20-8.

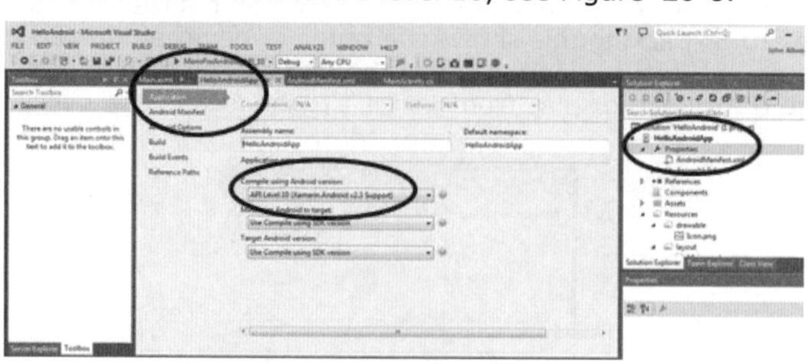

Figure 20-8 Changing the API Level

You may have to reload your solution.

Whilst you have the properties window displayed, note the **AndroidMainifest** tab. It's here that we tell Android which permissions our application needs e.g. Internet access, Location Hardware, Flashlight, Brick?!, Camera, Phone etc.)

You can now run your program. Click '**Mono for Android API 10**' in the toolbar.

You will have to wait a while for the emulator to load. Don't start clicking away when you see A N D R O I D on the screen, but wait for the emulator screen appears and Ready to appear in the Visual Studio window, see Figure 20-9.

Figure 20-9 Emulator Ready

Slide the Lock symbol to the right to turn the device on and the app should appear. Clicking the button displays a message showing how many times it has been clicked, see Figure 20-10.

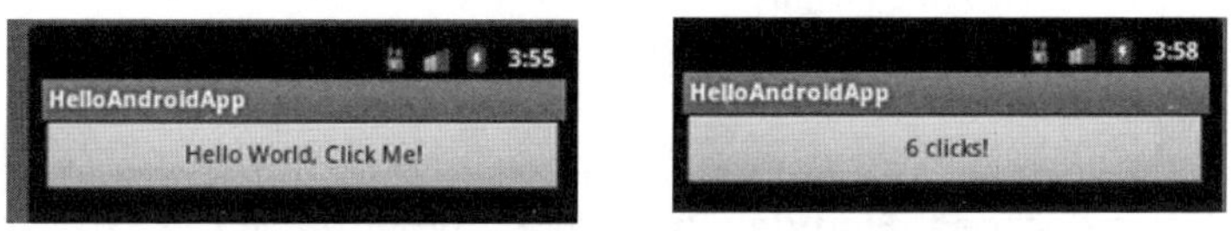

Figure 20-10 Hello World Application

You can click the 'back' button to display the main screen and select other apps from that.

5. Code description

The code is in Main.Activity.cs :

```
[Activity(Label = "Chapter20_3HelloAndroid", MainLauncher = true,
Icon = "@drawable/icon")]
public class MainActivity : Activity
    {
        int count = 1;
        protected override void OnCreate(Bundle bundle)
        {
            base.OnCreate(bundle);
            // Set our view from the "main" layout resource
            SetContentView(Resource.Layout.Main);
            // Get our button from the layout resource,
            // and attach an event to it
            Button button = FindViewById<Button>(Resource.Id.MyButton);
            button.Click += delegate
```

```
    { button.Text = string.Format("{0} clicks!", count++); };
            }
        }
```

A few brief words of explanation. An **Activity** provides a screen with which users can interact (like our Windows Forms). The Activity class creates the window, where the User Interface is placed. In this case the class is called **MainActivity**, but it could be called anything.

The code in square brackets is known as the ActivityAttribute and it registers the Activity with Android telling it about our application. It tells it which Activity to start with (MainLauncher = true), the text at the top of the screen (Label), and the location of the app's icon to display. For more details on Activity, see the Self Assessment Exercises.

SetContentView puts the controls on the screen depending on the code in Main.xaml, which contains information on the display layout and the button as we have seen:

```
<?xml version="1.0" encoding="utf-8"?>
<LinearLayout xmlns:android="http://schemas.android.com/apk/res/android"
    android:orientation="vertical"
    android:layout_width="fill_parent"
    android:layout_height="fill_parent">
    <Button
        android:id="@+id/MyButton"
        android:layout_width="fill_parent"
        android:layout_height="wrap_content"
        android:text="@string/Hello" />
</LinearLayout>
```

Remember, AXML stands for **Android XML** (eXtensible Markup Language) which is where the button control is declared. **FindViewById** finds 'MyButton' in the axml code which describes its layout and text. This command line declares the controls we are using to our program.

Whenever we place an item on the design surface (screen), the axml source code is written for us, but we could also write the axml code instead.

The code to respond to the button click is added using a **delegate** (we've seen these before). This is how object's events are added, just as they were with our C# code, but we didn't have to write the code then. It also contains the code to increment and display the number of clicks:

```
{button.Text = string.Format("{0} clicks!", count++); };
```

Of course it could call a method to do much more.

If you were wondering, a **Bundle** is a class generally used for passing data between various Activities.

Android applications don't have a line of code that the OS calls to start the application. An application starts when Android creates one of its classes, when the complete application is loaded into the memory. You will see classes being written all the time. It makes it overly complicated for simple applications, but very useful for detailed apps.

If you haven't done so, now might be a good time to look at the Xamarin example 'Hello, Android' (see Self Assessment exercises) and read the second part 'Deep Dive'.

20.4 • Recap

Before we continue, let's just review and explain some of what we have seen.

AndroidMainifest.xaml. The Manifest holds information about your application, such as its name, required permissions, Activities etc. You can edit these by clicking **properties** in the Solution Explorer.

Resources. We have seen this before. It's a good place to keep non-code related items such as images, icons, constants.

Layout. This is the User Interface. The layout is kept in the XML based axml files.

Activity. This is the class code that sets up the User Interface. When your App is used, its Activity goes through different stages, e.g. Create, Pause and Resume. We have written OnCreate code and later will see some Pause and Resume code.

20.5 • Show Message application

Let's write an application that simply shows a message. This might be useful in debugging (but there are better ways). We will find out how to add controls and events for them. This will be like the MessageBox.Show() we have seen.

We'll do the design a bit quicker this time.

- Start a new project File > New Project > Visual C# > Android Blank App (Android)
- Choose a name and folder, click OK.
- Open the Android designer (Solution Explorer > Resources > Layout)

This will give us our screen with the button we have just seen.

Add another button that will display a message when clicked.

Drag a button from the Toolbox's Form Widgets onto the form.

Click the Source tab in the bottom left hand corner to see the Main.axml code and note the code that has been added.

In the Properties, change the text on the button to something suitable (Show Message!).

Remember the name for this button is found in its properties **id**, and (unless you changed it) is **@+id/button1**. In our code we it will be called **button1**.

Also remember that no events have been added for this button. If you want something to happen when you click it, you will have to add the event and code for yourself.

We will display a message using the Android **AlertDialog** class. The AlertDialog can display a message and up to three buttons. The **setMessage()** method displays a string, and buttons are added using the **SetNeutralButton()**, **SetNegativeButton()** and **SetPositiveButton()** methods.

Display the **MainActivity.cs** window. Add the following method (if you don't know where, put it before protected override void OnCreate(Bundle bundle)).

```
public void ShowMessage()
{
    var myDialog = new AlertDialog.Builder(this);
    myDialog.SetMessage("Do you like pizza?");
    myDialog.SetNeutralButton("Maybe", delegate { });
```

```
        myDialog.SetNegativeButton("No thanks", delegate { });
        myDialog.SetPositiveButton("Yes!!!", delegate { });
        // Show the alert dialog to the user and wait for response.
        myDialog.Show();
    }
```

Now change the MainActivity OnCreate code to add the button click code as follows:

```
    protected override void OnCreate(Bundle bundle)
    {
        base.OnCreate(bundle);
        // Set our view from the "main" layout resource
        SetContentView(Resource.Layout.Main);
        // Get our button from the layout resource,
        Button button = FindViewById<Button>(Resource.Id.MyButton);
        // and attach an event to it
        button.Click += delegate {
               button.Text = string.Format("{0} clicks!", count++); };
        // Get our new button from layout resource
        Button button1 = FindViewById<Button>(Resource.Id.button1);
        // add a Click event
        button1.Click += delegate { ShowMessage(); };
    }
```

We have simply declared our new button and added a Click event that calls the ShowMessage method.

Compile and run the code, remember to change the 'Compile using Android version' to API level 10. You should get the display as seen in Figure 20-11. The message box appears with the message and you can click any button to close it.

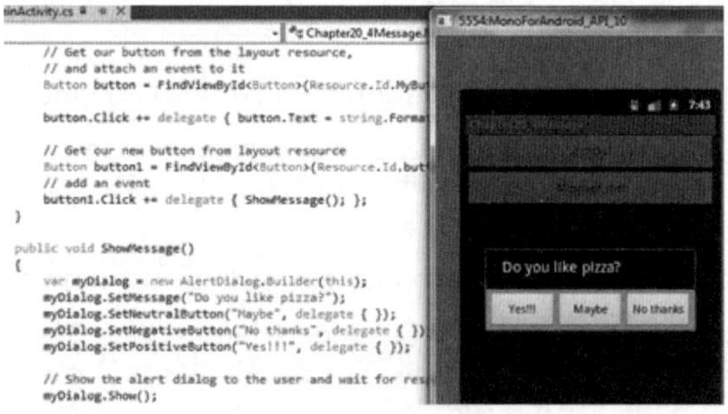

Figure 20-11 Application running

20.6 • Deploying your application

Now we need to download and check out our program on our device.

Before you can debug your App, the device must be setup for deployment and connected to your PC.

The steps are as follows:

1. Enable debugging on your device
2. Install the USB drivers
3. Connect the device to your computer
4. Download and debug your App

1. **Enable debugging**

The procedure depends on the device and version of Android you have. You can find this in Settings > About (I have V4.1.1 on my tablet and V4.1.2 on my phone)

a. Android V4.0 to 4.1

Choose: Settings > Developer Options > USB debugging and tick the Debug mode when USB connected.

b. Android V4.2 and higher.

By default the Develop Options is hidden; to display it, choose Settings > About phone and click Build number seven (7) times.

You can now choose Settings > System to display the developer settings.

Turn Developer Options on before being allowed to enable USB debugging.

2. **Install the USB drivers**

Make sure you have the latest USB drivers for your device. You might like to refer to the Xamarin instructions 'Installing the USB drivers' at:

developer.xamarin.com/guides/android/getting_started/installation/set_up_device_for_development/

USB drivers for specific devices are available via the following link:

http://developer.android.com/tools/extras/oem-usb.html#Drivers

3. **Connect your device**

Connect the device to your PC with a USB cable - your PC should recognise it.

You can also link your devices via Wi-Fi. For more on this refer to the link in the previous section.

4. **Download and run the app**

Start Visual Studio and load your project. This time you should see an extra run option – your device should also be available. In my case you can see my Smartphone: Samsung GT-I8190N, see Figure 20-12.

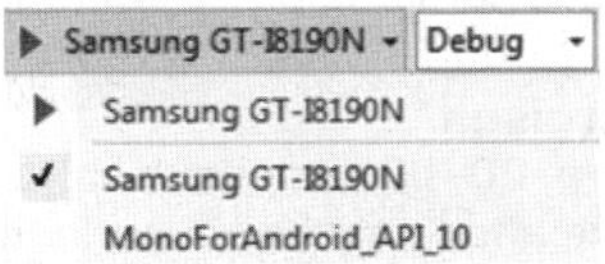

Figure 20-12 Debugging option

To run your program, just select your device. You will be warned that the build is only valid for 24 hours. It will be downloaded to your device and executed.

If you want to set a breakpoint you can do so, just as we've done before, see Figure 20-13 on page 290.

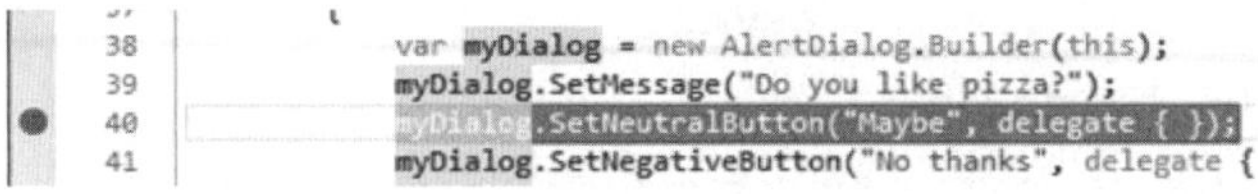

Figure 20-13 Debugging the Application

If you have set any breakpoints the program will run and break at that point, just like a normal debugging session.

Once the program has been run on your device, you will find that you can run the app without it being attached to the PC. It is available via the Apps list.

Detach your device from the PC, find your app in the list and run it just as normal. The default icon is used, but you can change that – see the Xamarin example.

We should mention the Android Debug Log. The log is displayed with View > Other Windows > Android Device Logging. Click the device icon to choose the device you want and refresh to refresh the log.

Writing to the log is through the Android.Util.Log and you can display information, warning or error messages using the code:

```
Log.Info (myString, "Information:");
Log.Warn (myString, "This is a warning");
Log.Error (myString, "Error!");
```

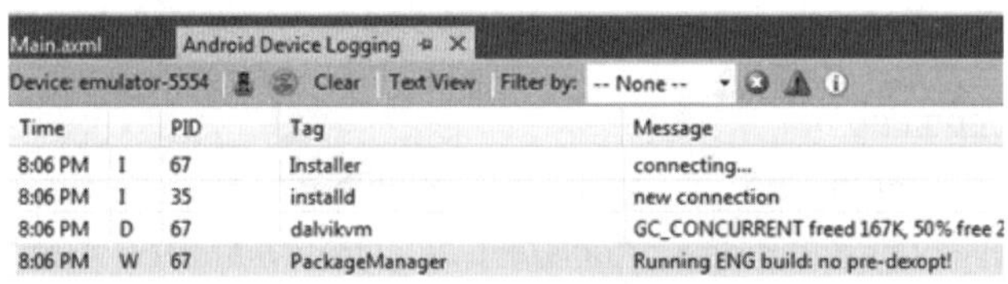

Figure 20-14 The Android Debug Log

For more information, see the Android Debug Log section on the Xamarin web site.

5. **Testing and publishing**

   If you wonder how you can test your app on all the possible devices, Xamarin can help you. See http://xamarin.com/test-cloud for more details.

   Finally you might want to get App Store approval and publish your app. Again the Xamarin web site has some helpful advice: http://bit.ly/1GZ91y6

20.7 • Self Assessment Exercises

1. If you didn't do so, take a look at the Xamarin installation information at: http://developer.xamarin.com/guides/android/getting_started/installation/windows
2. Watch the introductory video at: https://jallwork.tinytake.com/sf/MTM4NjI0Xzg3NTE5NQ
3. Watch the AlertDialog class video at: https://jallwork.tinytake.com/sf/MTM4NjkyXzg3NTU1NA

4. If you didn't do so earlier, follow the Xamarin application

   'Hello, Android > Part 1: Quick Start' at

   http://developer.xamarin.com/guides/android/getting_started/.

   Their program translates an alphanumeric phone number entered into a numeric phone number and then calls that number.

5. Look at the Xamarin DeepDive example at: *http://bit.ly/1Mt4nsV*

6. Look at the Xamarin guides and tutorials at the link e-mailed to you by Xamarin:

   http://developer.xamarin.com/guides/android/getting_started/hello,android/hello,android_quickstart/

7. Find out more about Activity at:

   http://developer.android.com/reference/android/app/Activity.html

8. Find out more about layouts at:

   http://developer.android.com/guide/topics/ui/declaring-layout.html

   In particular look at the section on Common Layouts

9. More information on Android is available at: *http://developer.android.com/guide/index.html*

10. Write your own apps!

20.8 • Summary

In this chapter we have introduced Xamarin which enables us to write C# programs for Android devices. We have seen how to obtain the software, looked at the Xamarin IDE, have seen the design screen and the associated files. We compiled the default application and have seen the emulator running that app and other standard phone apps.

We have discussed the layout and axml file and main activity code and its operation (OnCreate). We have seen how to add controls to the screen, declare them in our code and add events to them. We also wrote a simple app to provide output to the screen.

Chapter 21 • Example GPS location application

21.1 • Introduction

In this chapter we will see how to use one of the Smartphone's features – the GPS receiver. We will also use Location Services to find out our address.

We will write a program uses the GPS receiver to find out our location. From that information we will use Location Services to find our address and calculate how far we are from London (actually Trafalgar Square).

21.2 • GPS example

In this example we will:

1. Set up the Manifest to use the GPS device and Internet to access Location Services.
2. Add the Location interface (ILocationListener) to our code and write the methods to support this.
3. Write our code.
4. Deploy the program to find out our address and the distance to Trafalgar Square, London (at 51.50909 -0.13115).

21.2.1 • Procedure

Start a new project. (File > New > Project), and select Visual C# > Android > Blank App

Give it a suitable name (DistanceToLondon)

Display the Main.axml design screen (Resources > Layout > Main.axml) and delete the Hello World button.

Layout

Drag a TextView to the screen and move the blue round circle to increase its height. Change its id from @+id/textView1 to @+id/addressText.

Do the same for two more TextView controls (Form Widgets). Drag the blue circle down the increase their height. Change their id to @+id/gpsLocationText and @+id/distanceText.

Note: dragging the blue squares changes the margin around the items verses the padding inside. For more information on layout, see the **W3schools.com** web site:

http://www.w3schools.com/css/default.asp , where there is also information on XML if you need it.

Change the TextView **text** properties to 'Address', 'Gps Location' and 'Distance' respectively.

You Main.axml source should be similar to the following:

```
<?xml version="1.0" encoding="utf-8"?>
<LinearLayout xmlns:android="http://schemas.android.com/apk/res/android"
    android:orientation="vertical"
    android:layout_width="fill_parent"
    android:layout_height="fill_parent">
```

```
    <TextView
        android:text="Address"
        android:layout_width="match_parent"
        android:layout_height="59.6dp"
        android:id="@+id/addressText" />
    <TextView
        android:text="GPS location"
        android:layout_width="match_parent"
        android:layout_height="69.2dp"
        android:id="@+id/gpsLocationText" />
    <TextView
        android:text="Distance"
        android:layout_width="match_parent"
        android:layout_height="69.2dp"
        android:id="@+id/distanceText"
        android:layout_marginBottom="25.2dp" />
</LinearLayout>
```

21.2.2 • Permissions

As our program will use a resource (wi-fi, mobile phone location or GPS) to find our location and the Internet to find our address, we need to add those to the Manifest.

You can find a list of all the Permissions and what they do at: *http://developer.android.com/reference/android/Manifest.permission.html*

Open the Android Manifest in your program's properties. (Double click properties in the Solution Explorer) and select INTERNET, ACCESS_COARSE_LOCATION and ACCESS_FINE_LOCATION, see Figure 21-1.

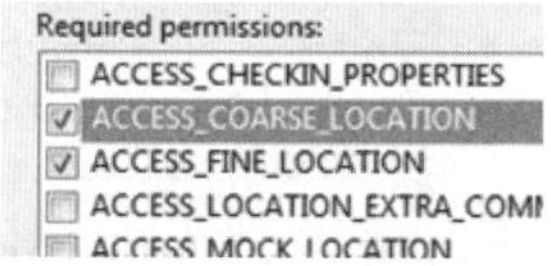

Figure 21-1 Permissions

ACCESS_FINE_LOCATION is needed for GPS services and strictly speaking as this is selected, you don't need to select ACCESS_COARSE_LOCATION.

Whilst you've got the properties window open, select 'Compile using Android version: API Level 10'.

21.2.3 • The GPS Code

Display the MainActivity.cs code.

Remove '`int count = 1;`' and the references to the original button code.

Check that you have the following Android 'usings':

```
using Android.App;
using Android.Widget;
using Android.OS;
using Android.Locations;
using Android.Util;
```

Now add the declaration for the TextView controls and the variables for the location:

```
TextView addressText;
TextView locationText;
TextView distanceText;
Location currentLocation;
LocationManager locationManager;
string locationProvider;
```

The LocationManager class provides access to the location services, which allow applications to read the device's location. This isn't instantiated directly, but accessed using **GetSystemService** as we will see.

As we have seen, our MainActivity class has methods such as OnCreate(), OnPause() and OnResume(). When our application is paused we want to remove any location updates, updating them when our application is resumed. We will add the code for this.

We will also write our main code in the OnCreate method.

To use the location services, we have to extend our MainActivity to include these services. To do this **change the class code** to the following:

```
public class MainActivity : Activity, ILocationListener
```

The 'I' in ILocationListener means it's an interface. Interfaces only contain the method declarations - we have to write the methods. The main one is **OnLocationChanged()** – the code that runs when the location changes. We will also have to add any code for **OnStatusChanged( )**, **OnProviderDisabled( )** and **OnProviderEnabled( ),** which are called when the status of the provider changes, is turned off, or turned on, respectively. In this example they are empty, but they still have to be there.

Change the OnCreate method to the following:

```
protected override void OnCreate(Bundle bundle)
{
    base.OnCreate(bundle);

    // Set our view from the "main" layout resource
    SetContentView(Resource.Layout.Main);
    addressText = FindViewById<TextView>(Resource.Id.addressText);
    locationText = FindViewById<TextView>(Resource.Id.gpsLocationText);
    distanceText = FindViewById<TextView>(Resource.Id.distanceText);
    // initialise the location manager
    locationManager = (LocationManager)GetSystemService(LocationService);

    // define its Criteria
    Criteria criteriaForLocationService = new Criteria
    {
```

```
            // Approximate accuracy constant, Accuracy.Coarse = 2
            // Medium Power requirement, Power.Medium = 2
            Accuracy = Accuracy.Coarse,
            PowerRequirement = Power.Medium
        };
        // find a location provider (GPS, wi-fi, etc.)
        IList<string> acceptableLocationProviders =
  (locationManager.GetProviders(criteriaForLocationService, true);
        // if we have any, use the first one
        if (acceptableLocationProviders.Any())
            locationProvider = acceptableLocationProviders.First();
        else
            locationProvider = String.Empty;
    } // end OnCreate
```

Add the OnPause and OnResume code:

```
    protected override void OnResume()
    {
        base.OnResume();
        locationManager.RequestLocationUpdates(locationProvider, 0, 0, this);
    }         // end OnResume
    protected override void OnPause()
    {
        base.OnPause();
        locationManager.RemoveUpdates(this);
    }         // end OnPause
```

Now add the methods required for the ILocationListener interface. The latitude and longitude is returned when the location is changed.

A geocoder is used to transform a latitude and longitude into an address (or vice versa). See the Self Assessment exercises for more details.

```
    public void OnLocationChanged(Location location)
    {
        try
        {
            currentLocation = location;
            // It could have changed from a valid to a null location!
            if (currentLocation == null)
                 locationText.Text = "Location not found";
            else
            {
                // Display latitude and longitude
                locationText.Text = String.Format("{0},{1}",
                        currentLocation.Latitude, currentLocation.Longitude);

                // Get the address from the Internet
```

```
                Android.Locations.Geocoder geocoder = new Geocoder(this);
                // Pass lat and long and max number of results
                // GetFromLocation Returns an array of addresses (5)
                IList<Address> addressList =
                        geocoder.GetFromLocation(currentLocation.Latitude,
                        currentLocation.Longitude,5) ;
                // Get first address, or default if not found
                Address address = addressList.FirstOrDefault();
                // Found location - don't need address to calc distance
                // Trafalgar Square is at: 51.50 -0.13
                double lat1 = currentLocation.Latitude;  // shorten
                double theta = currentLocation.Longitude - (-0.13);
                double distance = Math.Sin(Math.PI / 180.0 * (lat1)) *
                      Math.Sin(Math.PI / 180.0 * (51.50)) +
                      Math.Cos(Math.PI / 180.0 * (lat1)) *
                      Math.Cos(Math.PI / 180.0 * (51.50)) *
                      Math.Cos(Math.PI / 180.0 * (theta));
                 distance = Math.Acos(distance);
                 distance = distance / Math.PI * 180.0;
                 distance = distance * 60 * 1.15;
                 distanceText.Text = "Distance: " +
                 distance.ToString() + " miles";

                // display address
                if (address != null)
                {
                    StringBuilder deviceAddress = new StringBuilder();
                    for (int i =0; i<address.MaxAddressLineIndex; i++)
                    {
deviceAddress.Append(address.GetAddressLine(i)).AppendLine(",");
                    }
                    addressText.Text = deviceAddress.ToString();
                } // end if
                else  addressText.Text = "address not found";
            }
        }
        catch
        {
            addressText.Text  = "address not found";
        } // end catch
    } // end onLocationChanged
 public void OnStatusChanged(string provider, Availability status, Bundle extras)
    { }
    public void OnProviderDisabled(string provider) { }
    public void OnProviderEnabled(string provider)  { }
```

This all goes in the `protected override void OnCreate(Bundle bundle) code`. The complete code is available via the Elektor's web site.

If you want to test if the device has a GPS, see:

http://stackoverflow.com/questions/6664355/how-can-i-check-whether-the-phone-has-gps-device-or-not

21.2.4 • Emulate, deploy and run

Emulating the GPS location changed is difficult. Compile and run the program on your device. The program finds my latitude and longitude, my address and tells me that I'm 157.79 miles from London.

If you want to emulate the program you could add a button to call the LocationChanged code. An example is shown at the Xamarin web site: *http://bit.ly/1bj9XBT*

21.3 • SMS messaging

Sending an SMS message is easy. It can be done in a few steps. We'll send a message when the button on the default project is clicked.

Start a new project. (File > New > Project), and select Visual C# > Android > Blank App

Give it a suitable name (SendSMS)

Change the Application properties to compile for API level 10, and add SEND_SMS to the required permissions in the Manifest.

Display the MainActivity.cs code and at the top, add `using` Android.Telephony;

Change the button Click event code to:

```
button.Click += delegate
{
    SmsManager.Default.SendTextMessage("01234567890", null,
        "Hello from Xamarin app", null, null);
};
```

(Add the phone number you want instead of 01234567890)

You can also send a message using an **Intent**. An **Intent** is often used to launch an external application with the intent to do something, e.g. make a phone call, open a web page, map an address or in this case, send a message. There are usually two parts to the intent: 1. The intent itself (make a phone call) and 2. The associated data (phone number).

When you use an Intent permissions are not required. The following code can be used to send an email with (an ActionSendTo) intent. It uses **PutExtra()** which is passed the body and the text.

If you want to try this change the button click event code to:

```
button.Click += delegate { SendIntentSMS(); };
```

And add this method:

```
public void SendIntentSMS()
{
    Intent intent = new Intent(Intent.ActionSendto);
```

```
        intent.PutExtra("sms_body", "message Body");
        intent.SetData(Android.Net.Uri.Parse("smsto: 0123456789"));
        StartActivity(intent);
    }
```

The app that is normally used to send messages is used to send your message.

21.4 • Sending an e-mail

E-mails can also be sent using an **Intent**. As above, the procedure is to create the intent, use **PutExtra()** to add the recipients, mail subject, and message test, then set the mime type to "**message/rfc822**" which causes the mail application to launch, and start the activity. Here's the code:

```
    public void SendEmail()
    {
        var email = new Intent(Intent.ActionSend);
        email.PutExtra(Intent.ExtraEmail,
            new string[] { "yourname1@yahoo.com", "yourname@gmail.com" });
        email.PutExtra(Intent.ExtraCc, new string[] { "CCname@gmail.com" });
        email.PutExtra(Intent.ExtraSubject, "Email subject");
        email.PutExtra(Intent.ExtraText, "Message from email app");
        email.SetType("message/rfc822");
        StartActivity(email);
    }
```

And change the button click event to call the method:

```
        button.Click += delegate {SendEmail(); };
```

You don't have to set any permission and you can leave the API level if running on your device.

If you don't know **rfc** stands for 'Request For Comments'. Search for rfc822 for the ARPA Internet Text Messages document.

21.5 • Self Assessment Exercises

1. Take a look at the supporting video at: *http://youtu.be/81NHVdRIJFc*
2. Read more about Location Services at the Android Developer's web site:
   http://bit.ly/1z1WF8n
3. Read more about Location Listener at:
   http://developer.android.com/reference/android/location/LocationListener.html
4. If you need to find out more about XML or CSS, look at *www.w3schools.com*
5. Read about: Criteria, IList, geocoder object and address at:

   Criteria: *http://developer.android.com/reference/android/location/Criteria.html*

   IList, List<T>: *https://msdn.microsoft.com/en-us/library/vstudio/6sh2ey19(v=vs.90).aspx*

Geocoder: *http://developer.android.com/reference/android/location/Geocoder.html*

Address: *http://developer.android.com/reference/android/location/Address.html*

6. Find out more about Android permissions.

21.6 • Summary

In this chapter we have developed a GPS location app. We saw how to set up permissions using the Manifest, write the code using the ILocation interface and its methods, access the device GPS and emulate, deploy and run the app.

We also saw how to send an SMS message and an email.

Chapter 22 • Conclusion

The idea behind this book was to enable you to understand the .NET environment and programming in C#, for both PC and Android devices.

In doing so it has covered a lot of ground; from the software aspects of the .NET framework and libraries; new features of VS2015; WinForms and WPF design; the C# programming language; object oriented programming; file handling; threading and internet communication, through to database handling and drawing charts. It covered Dynamic Link Libraries and Windows API, to using DirectX to record sound and video. It finished with chapters on writing C# programs for Android devices, ending with a GPS, text messaging and email examples.

In updating the book, I have had to remove chapters in the previous book on hardware interfacing and USB design. For readers that would like those, I hope to make them available free via Elektor's web site, although they won't have been updated.

I hope that the book has provided enough to get you going, that the examples have been clear and that it has spurred you on to with your own designs.

Of course there is still a lot more you can learn, from further Windows Presentation Foundation (WPF) designs; more detailed Object Oriented Programming such as polymorphism and delegates; advanced relational databases and more detailed searches with LINQ; to cloud computing and further Android apps.

I hope that this book has given you the background and confidence to discover these for yourself. I wish you all the best in your designs.

Appendix A • Obtaining the Visual Studio software

At the time of writing VS 2013 is free and VS2015RC is time-limited, but a free version of VS2015 should be available later in 2015.

For background study, a series of short videos covering topics on ASP.NET 5, the Visual Studio 2015, cross-platform (Android) development and more are available at:

http://channel9.msdn.com/Series/ConnectOn-Demand/

Before downloading the software you might like to look at the Virtual Academy's video #1 (introduction) and #2 (Installing Visual Studio Express 2013) at:

http://www.microsoftvirtualacademy.com/training-courses/c-fundamentals-for-absolute-beginners

The free Visual Studio 2015 Community is found at:

http://www.visualstudio.com/en-us/products/free-developer-offers-vs

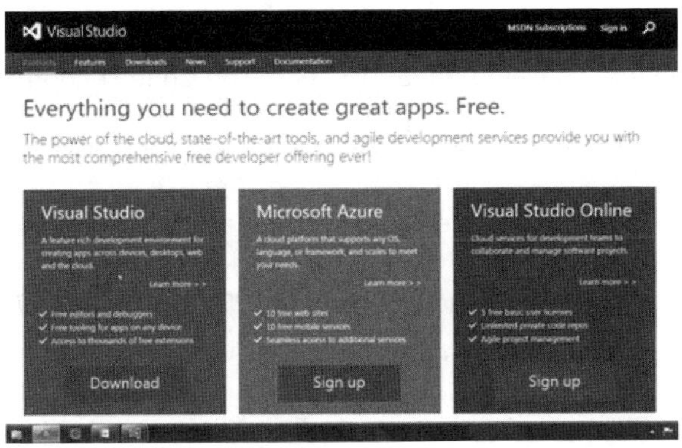

Click the purple Visual Studio area to downloads vs_community.exe and then run it to install VS. It takes quite a long time

When it has completed, restart your computer.

I deselected all but SQL Server Data tools in the options but you don't need that if you aren't going to use databases. (Hold your mouse over the options for more information, but they are mostly for web based apps).

If you want a team to work on a project, or use the cloud, you can set up a Microsoft account with a visualstudio.com web address. You can then start a project using that cloud access, start an account trial or open in Visual Studio 2015.

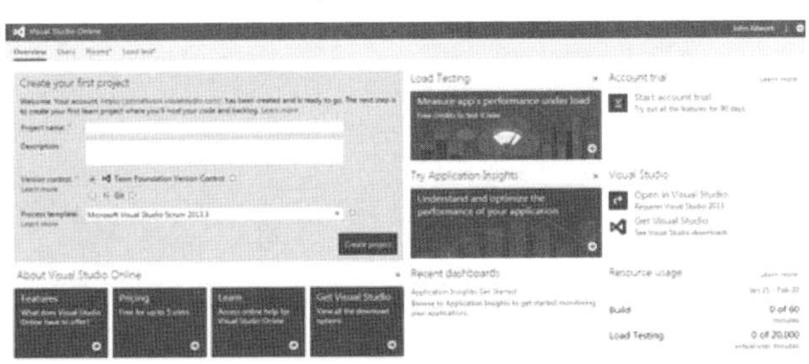

At this stage it may be a good idea to install any updates, including the latest version of the .NET framework.

You will be sent an email confirming your choices and links to 'More information', 'Get started guide' and forums.

The 'Get started guide' covers it all, it can be found at:

http://www.visualstudio.com/get-started/overview-of-get-started-tasks-vs

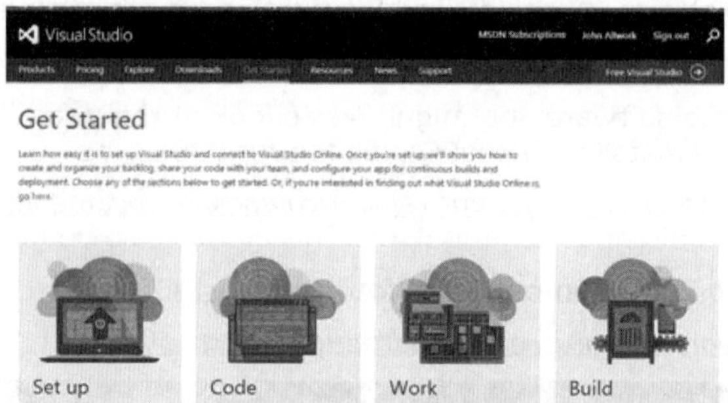

The Set up section covers what you have just read, the Code section shows how to create your first app with a team and using version control (not what we really want at this stage) and the Work and Build section shows how to track a project's work and build and test your apps.

The Microsoft forums are a good place to go for help and if you get stuck there's help at the Visual Studio forums:

https://social.msdn.microsoft.com/Forums/vstudio/en-US/home?forum=TFService

Some videos available under the Q&A section at the 'Create your app' section of the Get Started page:

http://www.visualstudio.com/get-started/create-your-app-vs

If you've set it up you can get to your account any time by going to:

https://youraccount.visualstudio.com

Appendix B • Installing the Xamarin Software

B.1 • Obtaining the Xamarin Software

Xamarin for Visual Studio is included with Visual Studio 2015. It is also supported on Visual Studio 2010 and later, in which case the software is available from Xamarin.com. Scroll down to the Xamarin Platform section of the home page and click the download button. There are a few different versions, but for now choose the free version. The installation asks for some details, and the installer is downloaded. Let the installer run, answer the questions and agreed to the license terms.

The download takes about 2M bytes but other software is needed: Java JDK, Android SDK, GTK, Xamarin studio and Xamarin itself. This all takes some time, see Figure B-1.

Whilst this is happening you could take a look at the installation at the Xamarin site:

http://developer.xamarin.com/guides/android/getting_started/installation/windows/

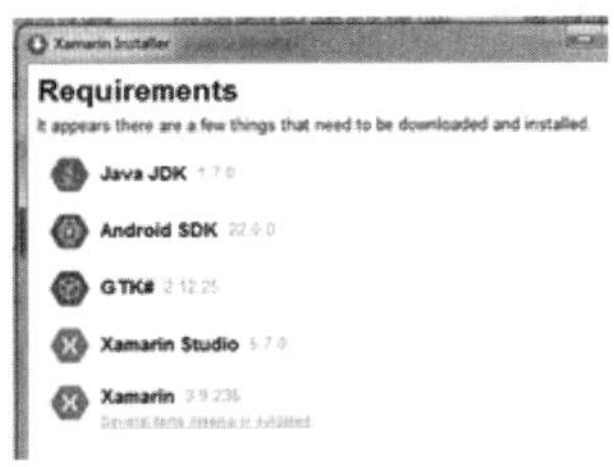

Figure B-1 Xamarin installation files

If any errors occur, e.g. version of Java JDK, correct them.

B.2 • Configure the Installation

Now we need to tell our IDE where to find the files we have installed. Visual Studio has a configuration option where we specify the Android file locations. In Visual Studio, go to Tools > Options > Xamarin > Android Settings, see Figure B-2.

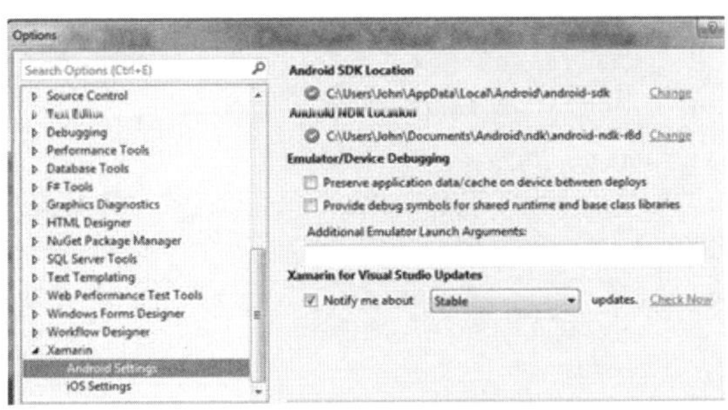

Figure B-2 Visual Studio Xamarin settings

Now you can carry on with the book, or you can take a look at the Android web site 'Hello, Android > Part 1: Quick Start' (see the Self Assessment exercises), but I think this is quite detailed. We start with a simple 'Hello World' Application, read further at 20.2 on page 281.

Note. If you are using Visual Studio 2015, the first time you choose a Xamarinproject you get the following screen. You can read more, download a pre-built template, or just click

Resources > Layout > Main.axml to see the design layout and source windows.

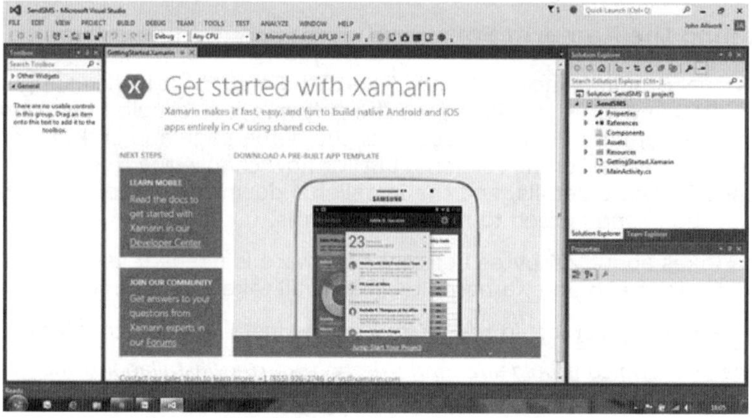

Figure B-3 VS2012 Xamarin start screen

Appendix C • Summary of C# Commands

<table>
<tr><th>Command</th><th>Syntax</th><th>Example</th></tr>
<tr><td>Comments</td><td>// This is a comment
/* use slash-star for multi-line comments */</td><td></td></tr>
<tr><td>Data Types</td><td>Integer - byte, short, int, long, sbyte
Real - float, double.
Characters - char.
String – string
Boolean - bool - TRUE or FALSE.
Object - object</td><td>// e.g.
int bold = 0 ; // declare & initialise bold
char keyBoardChar = '!';</td></tr>
<tr><td>Naming convention</td><td>variablesStartWithASmallLetter
ClassesStartWithACapitalLetter</td><td></td></tr>
<tr><td>Assignment</td><td><variable> = <expression> ;</td><td>// use '=' and ';' - for example:
three = one + two ;</td></tr>
<tr><td>Compound statements</td><td>// contained in curly brackets:</td><td>{
statements
}</td></tr>
<tr><td>if - (else if) - (else) statement</td><td>if (expression) {
statement(s)
} else if (expression) {
statement(s)
} // further else..if ( ) { }
else {
statement(s)
}</td><td>// Example:
if (X>0) {
MessageBox.Show("More than zero");
} else if (X<0) {
MessageBox.Show ("Less than zero");
}
else {
MessageBox.Show ("X is zero");
}</td></tr>
<tr><td>Switch / case statement</td><td>switch <expression> {
case 1 : <statement 1>; break ;
case n : <statement n> ; break ;
default : <statement> ; break;</td><td>// Switch example (N is int or char) :
switch (N) {
case 2: MessageBox.Show ("N is 2");
break; // must have break
case 7: // no break is OK here
case 9 : MessageBox.Show ("N is 7 or 9");
break;
default : MessageBox.Show (" Not 2, 7 or 9");
break;</td></tr>
<tr><td>while statement</td><td>while <bool expression> {
<statement(s)>
}</td><td>// Example - read a char
int count=0;
while (count != 10) {
count++;
MessageBox.Show ("Count = " + count);
}</td></tr>
<tr><td>do while statement</td><td>do { statements
} while (<expression>);</td><td>// Example
do {
count++;
MessageBox.Show ("Count = " + count);
} while (count<10);</td></tr>
<tr><td>for statement</td><td>for (<start > ; <end > ; <increment expr.>
{
statements
}</td><td>// Example:
for (L = 1 ; L <= 100 ; L++) {
array[L]=0;
}</td></tr>
<tr><td>Array declaration</td><td>int[ ] arrayOfInts = new int[10]; // 0 to 9
arrayOfInts[9] = i;</td><td></td></tr>
<tr><td>Relational and Conditional Operators</td><td>>, >=, <, <=, ==, !=, &&, ||,
!, &, |</td><td></td></tr>
</table>

Command	Syntax	Example

Typecasting	// change type using type in brackets:
	dbli = fltj; // OK to convert float to double
	fltj = dbli; // errors - requires explicit cast:
	fltj = (float)dbl;	

Index

Symbols

A

B

C

T

U

V

W

X